Housing Perspectives

Individuals and Families

Housing Perspectives

Individuals and Families

Second Edition

Carol S. Wedin
Iowa State University
Ames, Iowa

L. Gertrude Nygren
Michigan State University
East Lansing, Michigan

 Burgess Publishing Company
Minneapolis, Minnesota

Consulting Editor to the Publisher
Norma H. Compton
Purdue University
West Lafayette, Indiana

Copyright© 1979, 1976 by Burgess Publishing Company
Printed in United States of America
Library of Congress Card Number 79-83677
ISBN 0-8087-2387-1

0 9 8 7 6 5 4 3 2

Preface

The articles in this book cover the many factors related to individual and family housing. We have included articles which are directed to two main objectives that we consider important. First, we present the artifact housing as a product of a large, evolving social-technical process. Second, we examine approaches to housing problems which satisfy both (a) evolving social and personal needs and (b) values of individuals and families.

As we become aware of the influence of our daily environment upon human growth and behavior, there is an increasing need for sound decisions based on the best information available. Since the power of individuals and families is limited in a complex society, it is imperative that we have an informed citizenry willing and able to participate in the public, decision-making process. Our publication indicates where these decisions lie, with emphasis on both personal welfare as well as the welfare of others.

The word *perspective* means a way of looking at things and the intent of this collection of articles is to present a variety of ways to view housing from the vantage point of the consumer-user. Therefore, we selected articles and invited leading authorities to prepare readings to highlight the foreseeable advantages and disadvantages of available options. The articles bring forth both short- and long-term considerations dealing with human well-being and environmental preservation.

Readings are presented in six parts. The first three parts deal with housing in a macro sense; the last three parts focus on individual and family criteria on the micro level, as a basis for making decisions on housing. Our definition of micro is the individual dwelling unit and the immediate neighborhood; macro extends beyond this from the community to the nation.

Part One.   The effects of housing on human beings and a brief description of the forces which influence house forms.

Part Two.   The technology of housing with emphasis on aspects of construction, finance, and the role of governments.

Part Three.   The environmental setting and basic human-need relationships.

81- 0097

Part Four.   The importance of housing to the health and welfare of the individual and support of the family.

Part Five.   An overview of legal and financial considerations in selecting housing.

Part Six.   An analysis of tenure form and structural types.

Acknowledgments

Writing and assembling a book of readings is achieved only through cooperative efforts of many contributing authors and practicing professionals. We are grateful to the authors and to editors and publishers of journals who have assisted us.

Every attempt has been made to give credit throughout this book to authors, photographers, architects, and publishers who have contributed. Where journal editors asked that we also request permission from author(s), such permission was obtained. If any material is not credited properly it is non-intentional on our part.

Spring 1979

C.W.
G.N.

Contents

Part One
Introduction to Housing   1

1. Our Buildings Shape Us, *by René Dubos* **3**

2. A Historical Perspective of Major Forms in American Housing, *by Carol S. Wedin* **17**

Part Two
Macro Forces Affecting Housing   29

3. Industrialization in Housing, *by Paul Muessig* **31**

4. Energy in Housing: Consumption and Conservation, *by Carol S. Wedin* **47**

5. Land for Housing, *by Raleigh Barlowe* **56**

6. Housing Costs: What Can Be Done?, *by Nathaniel H. Rogg* **78**

7. Government Housing Programs: A Brief Review, *by Mary H. Yearns* **83**

8. Codes and Controls, *by Carol S. Wedin* **93**

Part Three
Environmental Settings   99

9. Social Change in Rural Communities, *by Ronald C. Powers* **101**

10. The City as Teacher and Learner, *by Kenneth E. Boulding* **107**

11. The Dilemmas of Neighborhood Revitalization, *by John R. Mullin* **117**

12. Segregation in Housing: Its Costs to Life Chances and Some Solutions, *by Duncan Case* **126**

13. Neighbourhoods and Human Needs, *by Margaret Mead* **138**

Part Four
Individual and Familie   143

14.   Housing and Health, *by Paul V. Lemkau, M.D.*   **145**

15.   The House as Symbol, *by Clare Cooper*   **170**

16.   Planning for Ourselves, *by L. Gertrude Nygren*   **179**

17.   Floor Plan Evaluation, *by Carol S. Wedin*   **184**

Part Five
Legal and Financial   197

18.   How to Read a Lease, *Consumers Union of United States, Inc.*   **199**

19.   Some Legal Aspects of House Buying, *by Neil E. Harl*   **208**

20.   Financing the Home, *Small Homes Council-Building Research Council, University of Illinois*   **220**

21.   Home Warranties, *by Carol S. Wedin*   **236**

Part Six
Consumer Housing Decisions   243

22.   Housing Alternatives, *by William J. Angell*   **245**

Summary—
The Challenge in Housing   279

Glossary   285

Index   287

Housing Perspectives

Individuals and Families

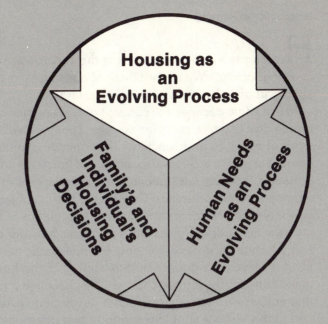

Housing as
an
Evolving Process

Family's and
Individual's
Housing
Decisions

Human Needs
as an
Evolving Process

Part One
Introduction
to Housing

1. Our Buildings Shape Us, by René Dubos

2. A Historical Perspective of Major Forms in American Housing, by Carol S. Wedin

Housing is a social artifact. It is the outgrowth of values and goals of an evolving society.* We cannot think of housing as an isolated entity or structure —it is part of a physical and social environment.

In just a few decades the concept of housing has changed drastically from a simple dwelling to a complex system. Today's dwellings are linked into a network of activities and functions that operate simultaneously, and they must operate in balance. Several examples of functions linked to housing are: transportation, schools and recreation, suppliers of goods and services, and employment opportunities. Complexity in this subject has been brought about by social-technical forces and higher expectations of the citizenry.

In the first article, René Dubos discusses how our buildings shape our social and psychological development. As individuals and as citizens we therefore need to develop a greater understanding of the housing system if we are to make consciously derived change. The challenge is to make housing decisions that enhance the quality of life in a developing, evolving world. In consideration of this task we should respond to two questions: How much do we know about the effects of housing technology on human life? What are the biological and psychological limits of man's adaptability to his built environment?

Part One continues with an examination of the social-technical changes occurring in the housing process as well as the redefinitions of human needs and wants. Just as housing is an evolving process, so are human needs undergoing constant change. Our standards of housing, our life style, and our values have evolved over centuries. The second article, "A Historical Perspective of Major Forms in American Housing," will assist the reader to view American housing as an evolving process.

Human beings differ in their preferences and they have different needs. Our housing environment should allow for these differences and at the same time enrich the lives of all citizens.

*Note that different authors use the terms "cultural" and "social" interchangeably.

1. Our Buildings Shape Us

by Rene Dubos

Many persons are becoming weary and frazzled by the rat race of constant change. Adults are exhausted by the struggle and teenagers do not find it worthwhile. As they watch the maddening complexity of life, and the frantic efforts to invent new technologies for solving the problems that technology itself has created, their cry goes up, "Stop the world—I want to get off." They want to go back to Arcadia in the hope of recapturing the simplicity and purity of original life. But Arcadia has never existed except in our dreams. Furthermore, we could not re-enter Arcadia even if it did exist, encumbered as we are by the biological and social memories of civilized life.

When Captain James Cook, Louis Antoine de Bougainville, and their successors achieved their first contacts with the Polynesian world in the eighteenth century, they thought they had finally discovered primitive life uncontaminated by the artificialities of civilization. Little surprise that sailors, fed on salt beef and hard biscuit, living on the edge of scurvy, and sexually starved, should have thought themselves in paradise on reaching the green and balmy South Seas shores and accepting the amorous welcome of the Polynesian women. They failed to notice the shortcomings and tragedies of Polynesian life because their judgment had been warped by the romantic philosophy of naturalism then prevailing in the intellectual circles of Europe. The magic of their contemporary Jean Jacques Rousseau's message in particular had prepared them to believe that the noble happy savage lived in undisturbed nature and never experienced any problems.

In reality, any form of organized social life (and all human life is socialized) has its own brand of restrictions, conflicts, and frustrations, added to the problems that each individual person experiences in meeting day-to-day requirements. To live is to struggle. A successful life is not one without ordeals, failures, and tragedies, but one during which the person has made an adequate number of effective responses to the constant challenges of his physical and social environment.

Today, as in the time of Cook and Bougainville, most of us at some time yearn to escape to some Friendly Isle and recapture the quality of primitive life. But this we cannot do, partly because the human adventure has implied from the beginning an

"Our Buildings Shape Us" is reprinted by permission of Charles Scribner's Sons from *So Human an Animal* by René Dubos. Copyright © 1968 René Dubos.

René Dubos, professor emeritus at The Rockefeller University in New York City, is a microbiologist and experimental pathologist who over twenty years ago was the first to demonstrate the feasibility of obtaining germ fighting drugs from microbes. For his scientific contributions, Dr. Dubos has received many awards; most recently he won the Pulitzer Prize for *So Human an Animal*. He is well known as an author and lecturer as well as a scientific investigator.

irreversible dependence on the social and technological management of nature, and more importantly because the past is incorporated in the present.

One of the most eloquent warnings that we cannot go back to Arcadia came from the English writer D. H. Lawrence (1885-1930), who also thought for a while that he could overthrow his complicated past and adopt the unspoiled way of life among the friendly people of the South Seas. "There they are, these South Sea Islanders, beautiful big men with their golden limbs and their laughing, graceful laziness. . . . They are like children, they are generous: but they are more than this. They are far off, and in their eyes is an early darkness of the soft, uncreate past. . . . There is his woman, with her knotted hair and her dark, inchoate, slightly sardonic eyes. . . . She has soft warm flesh, like warm mud. Nearer the reptile, the Saurian age. . . .

"Far be it from me to assume any 'white' superiority. It seems to me, that in living so far, through all our bitter centuries of civilization, we have still been living onwards, forwards. . . . The past, the Golden Age of the past—what a nostalgia we all feel for it. Yet we don't want it when we get it. Try the South Seas." [1]

Just as we are earthbound forever by our physiological dependence on the earth's atmosphere, so we are bound to our own times because the needs we have developed through 10,000 years of civilization can no longer find satisfaction in the "darkness of the soft, uncreate past."

While the explorers of space and of ocean depths are struggling to duplicate the terrestrial environment in their capsules, physiologists, psychologists, architects, and city planners are anxiously trying to formulate an environment optimum for man on earth. Most demographers and sociologists believe that, barring a world catastrophe, the great majority of people all over the world will soon live in urban agglomerations that will eventually extend over hundreds of miles. Here is the picture for the United States as seen by one of the American leaders in the field of planning and development: ". . . half a century from now the population of the United States will exceed 500 million people. If this proves true, we will have 500 to 1,000 metropolitan areas as now defined. The largest of these, the East Coast New York region, will contain perhaps 50 million people and will be part of a larger region exceeding 100 million people. There may be several other metropolitan areas with 25 million population. Presumably 85 to 95 percent of the population will be urban." [2]

In the past the basic population lived in the country or in small towns. Because of the enormous increase in agricultural productivity, people now move away from the country even while the total population is becoming larger. Urbanism is the way of life for an overwhelming majority of people, including not only the residents of the compact city, but also the suburbanites and the exurbanites. For all of them, urbanism implies that practically all individual and social activities are influenced by technology. Scientists must therefore concern themselves with the immediate and long-range effects of technology on human life.

The myth has grown that because man has an infinite capacity to adapt to changing environments, he can endlessly and safely transform his life and indeed himself by technology. In reality, there are biological and psychological limits to man's adaptability, and these should determine the frontiers of technological change.

Another myth states that, by proper study, it should be possible to define an environment having characteristics optimum for human life. This is impossible because men differ in their tastes and aspirations and therefore have different environmental

1. D. H. Lawrence, *Studies in Classic American Literature* (New York: Thomas Seltzer, 1923), 201, 202, 203, 206.

2. William L. C. Wheaton, "Form and Structure of the Metropolitan Area," in William R. Ewald, Jr. (ed.), *Environment for Man* (Bloomington, Ind.: Indiana University Press, 1967), 157-184.

needs. To realize the multifarious biological and spiritual potentialities of mankind requires an immense diversity of environments. The real problem therefore is to learn how environmental forces can be best managed to foster the various manifestations of happiness and creativity in mankind. Technology should have as its most important goal the creation of environments in which the widest range of human potentialities can unfold.

Knowledge of environmental effects is most precise and extensive with regard to the needs and responses of vigorous young men functioning under extreme and unusual conditions. For obvious reasons, much physiological and psychological research relevant to these problems has been sponsored by the armed forces, the space agencies, and the civil-defense program. This kind of research deals especially with operational situations in which it is essential to know the thresholds and limits of physical and psychical performance and endurance. The problems of ordinary life, however, are very different from those studied by specialized agencies. They are more complex, and especially less well defined, because normal human populations are extremely heterogeneous and rarely live under extreme environmental situations. In ordinary life, furthermore, the criteria of health, well-being, comfort, productivity and happiness do not lend themselves readily to scientific statements because they are highly subjective and socially conditioned.

A few very broad generalizations can serve as a theoretical basis for discussing the effects of the environment on human life. Ideally, all aspects of the environment should form an integrated ecological system in which the welfare of any part of the system is dependent upon the welfare of all the others. In the light of ecological theory, man is part of the total environment and therefore cannot achieve and maintain physical and mental health if conditions are not suitable for environmental health. For this reason, it is ecologically and indeed logically impossible to define an optimum environment if one has only man in mind.

Another generalization, popularized by Toynbee, is that the type of environment most conducive to human development is one sufficiently changeable to pose constant challenges but not so severe as to prevent successful responses.[3] The temperate regions seem to be most satisfactory from this point of view; in fact, the Yale University geographer Ellsworth Huntington thought that the Connecticut area in which Yale University is located provides an ideal environment for the flowering of civilization.[4] Wherever life is without challenge and too comfortable, as supposedly in the Polynesian islands, the best that can be hoped for is an arrested or static civilization rather than one that is innovating and on-going.

The challenge-and-response theory teaches that the environment should provide the proper intensity and variety of stimulation. In addition, there are a few environmental imperatives that derive from the unchangeable aspects of man's nature. Best understood among these imperatives are the determinants of health and disease so extensively studied by the biomedical sciences. Even this aspect of the environmental problem is less well defined than used to be thought, however, because the patterns of disease change rapidly and unpredictably with the conditions of life. Positive and absolute health has proved so far to be a constantly receding mirage.[5]

The interrelationships between human beings are naturally among the most important of the factors to be considered by planners, but little is known concerning real human needs in this regard. Many anthropologists and sociologists have taken a

3. Arnold Toynbee, *A Study of History* (New York: Oxford University Press, 1964).
4. Ellsworth Huntington, *Civilization and Climate* (New Haven: Yale University Press, 1924).
5. René Dubos, *Mirage of Health* (New York: Harper, 1959) and *Man Adapting* (New Haven: Yale University Press, 1965), Chapters 7 and 9.

Urban sprawl can result in a loss of group identity and produce boredom and loneliness. (United States Department of Agriculture)

gloomy view of the effects that the modern conditions of life have on human relationships; they see in the present scene little chance to satisfy the essential need for the intimate kind of contact with a very few persons that can occur only within a small primary group. "In the old society, man was linked to man; in the new agglomeration— it cannot be called a society—he is alone. . . . All the evidence of psychiatry shows that membership in a group sustains a man, enables him to maintain his equilibrium under the ordinary shocks of life, and helps him to bring up children who will in turn be happy and resilient. . . . The cycle is vicious; loss of group membership in one generation may make men less capable of group membership in the next. The civilization that, by its very process of growth, shatters small group life will leave men and women lonely and unhappy."[6]

Some urban planners advocate social and architectural arrangements which provide each individual person with three or four intimate contacts at every stage of his existence. But the great mobility of our populations, the high levels of crowding, and the increased complexity of social life make such intimate associations almost impossible for the larger percentage of the public. From all points of view, population pressure probably constitutes the most important single handicap to creating urban environments with proper biological qualities. There is no immediate danger that the

6. Quoted by Alexander in Ewald, *op. cit.,* 64.

United States will experience shortages of food or even a decrease in the economic standard of living as a result of population pressure. Nevertheless we suffer from overpopulation because human life is affected by determinants that transcend technology and economics.

The greatest dangers of overpopulation come paradoxically from the fact that human beings can make adjustments to almost anything. Congested environments, even though polluted, ugly, and heartless, are compatible with economic growth and with political power. Similarly, social indifference, aggressive behavior, or the rat race of overcompetitive societies will not necessarily destroy mankind. Crowding, however, can damage the physical and spiritual qualities of human life through many mechanisms, such as the narrowing of horizons as classes and ethnic groups become more segregated, with the attendant heightening of racial conflicts; the restrictions on personal freedom caused by the constantly increasing need for central controls; the deterioration in professional and social services; the destruction of beaches, parks, and other recreational facilities; the spreading of urban and suburban blight; the traffic jams, water shortages, and all forms of environmental pollution.

High-density buildings can produce an increased complexity of social life that makes intimate group identity almost impossible. (Photo by Carol Wedin)

We do not recognize danger in crowding as long as we can produce enough food for physical growth and enough goods for economic growth. We do not sense the evil because we regard ourselves, and other men, as things rather than as fellow human beings. The availability of food, natural resources, and power required for the operation of the body machine and of the industrial establishment is not the only factor to be considered in determining optimum population size. Just as important for maintaining the quality of *human* life is an environment in which it is possible to satisfy the longings for quiet, privacy, independence, initiative, and open space. These are not frills or luxuries; they constitute real biological necessities. They will be in short supply long before there are critical shortages of energy and materials to keep the human machine going and industry expanding.

In theory, all human beings have the same essential needs, but in practice actual needs are socially conditioned and therefore differ profoundly from one human group to another. Even food requirements cannot be defined without regard to the social context. The value of an article of food is not determined only by its content in protein, carbohydrate, fat, vitamins, minerals, and other chemical components. A particular food has in addition symbolic values which make it either essential or unacceptable, depending upon the past experiences of the consumer. [7] These symbolic aspects of nutrition are of importance not only among primitive people. Americans are even more reluctant to eat horse meat than Frenchmen are to eat cornbread.

7. René Dubos, *Man Adapting, op. cit.,* Chapter 3.

Reston, Virginia is designed to offer a physical and social environment that enhances daily human life. (United States Department of Agriculture; photo by Jack Schneider)

The kinds of technical equipment needed also vary with time and from place to place. The ancient Mayas created an extraordinarily sophisticated culture and marvelous monuments of imposing size without using the wheel as a means of transportation, although, as some of their toys show, they knew the wheel and its possible applications. Similarly, the wheel was not used by the tribes of Central Africa until modern times, even though representations of it in Neolithic paintings have been discovered. In Central America and Africa other forms of transportation were more practical until the white man had cut wide roads through the equatorial forest. Human need is not a fixed quality. As stated by Gordon Childe:

"No doubt the efficiency of an automobile to satisfy the need for transport under specific conditions can be determined with mathematical accuracy. But is man's need for transport a fixed quantity in any real sense? Did a reindeer hunter in 30,000 B.C., or an Ancient Egyptian in 3000, or an Ancient Briton in 30, really need or want to travel a couple of hundred miles at 60 m.p.h.?

"To a Magdalenian society in the last Ice Age a harpoon of antler was just as efficient as a steam trawler is today. With the former, tiny groups could get all the fish they needed. . . ." [8]

Similarly, needs that appear vital today may become trivial in another generation, not because man's biological nature will change, but because the social environment will not be the same. For example, the individual motor car may progressively disappear if, as is probable, driving loses its appeal and if, as we may hope, people have more uses for their leisure time within walking distance of their houses. The individual, detached house may also become obsolete once home ownership loses its symbolic meaning of economic and social independence by reason of more generalized prosperity and financial security. A new generation may learn again to prefer the excitement of the compact city to the bourgeois comfort of the suburb and thus bring to an end the lawnmower era.

Henry David Thoreau spent a year in a hut that he built for himself near Walden Pond to demonstrate that the essential needs of man are small. But he had taken along a number of scholarly books, and plenty of paper to write his diary. His biological needs were small indeed, but he had wants that he shared with his Concord circle.

The phrase "essential need" is therefore meaningless, because in practice people need what they want. Needs are determined less by the biological requirements of *Homo sapiens* than by the social environment in which a person lives and especially that in which he has been brought up. The members of a given social group generally come to desire, and consequently develop a need for whatever is necessary for acceptance in the group. The good life is identified with the satisfaction of these needs, whatever their biological relevance.

Wants become needs not only for individual persons, but also for whole societies. Monuments dedicated to the Virgin Mary and the saints were apparently a need for thirteenth-century Europe, which devoted an enormous percentage of its human and economic resources to the creation of churches and monasteries that appear to us extravagant in relation to the other aspects of medieval life. In our times, the Great Society seems particularly concerned with creating a middle-class, materialistic civilization with a veneer of uplifting platitudes. This concern also creates special needs, including frozen fruit juice for breakfast, a different dress for every day at the office, a playroom in the cellar, and a huge lampshade in front of the picture window.

The environment men create through their wants becomes a mirror that reflects their civilization; more importantly it also constitutes a book in which is written the for-

8. V. Gordon Childe, *Social Evolution* (New York: Meridian Books, 1963), 21.

mula of life that they communicate to others and transmit to succeeding generations. The characteristics of the environment are therefore of importance not only because they affect the comfort and quality of present-day life, but even more because they condition the development of young people and thereby of society.

The view that man can shape the future through decisions concerning his environment was picturesquely expressed by Winston Churchill in 1943 while discussing the architecture best suited for the Chambers of the House of Commons. The old building, which was uncomfortable and impractical, had been bombed out of existence during the Second World War. This provided an opportunity for replacing it by a more efficient one, having greater comfort and equipped with better means of communication. Yet Mr. Churchill urged that the Chambers should be rebuilt exactly as they were before. In a spirited speech, he argued that the style of parliamentary debates in England had been conditioned by the physical characteristics of the old House, and that changing its architecture would inevitably affect the manner of debates and, as a result, the structure of English democracy. Mr. Churchill summarized the concept of interplay between man and the total environment in a dramatic sentence that has validity for all aspects of the relation between human life and the environment: "We shape our buildings, and afterwards our buildings shape us." [9]

While the total environment certainly affects the way men feel and behave, more importantly it conditions the kind of persons their descendants will become, because all environmental factors have their most profound and lasting effects when they impinge on the young organism during the early stages of development.

Mr. Churchill was promoting a conservative policy—the maintenance of traditional parliamentary practices—when he developed his argument that our buildings shape us. Most educational and social systems also try to force the young into traditional patterns through environmental manipulations, and despite appearances they largely succeed. Americans, Englishmen, Frenchmen, Germans, Italians, or Spaniards acquire their national characteristics because they are shaped during early life by their buildings, educational systems and ways of life. But such shaping need not be only for the preservation of the past. It can be oriented toward the future.

The Israeli *kibbutz* has demonstrated that a systematic program of child-rearing in collectives can, in a single generation, give to children a healthy and vigorous personality entirely different from that of their parents. [10] The success of this social experiment does not establish the desirability of the results that it achieved, but it does show that the environment can be used to alter persons and institutions as well as to preserve the *status quo*.

Any manager of television or of any other publicity program directed to the young must be tormented, if he has any social conscience, at the thought that he is conditioning the tastes, opinions, and reaction patterns of his audience lastingly and perhaps irreversibly. Would that there were a Winston Churchill of the publicity profession capable of conveying to his colleagues the biological law that: We shape our programs, and then afterwards our programs shape us and our children!

Educators have long known that all aspects of the environment affect the unfolding of human potentialities and the character of their manifestations. Political leaders have also used this knowledge to manipulate public opinion and especially to shape the minds of the young. A broader and more hopeful aspect of the same problem is the possibility of creating conditions that will enable individual human beings to discover

9. Winston Churchill, *Onwards to Victory: War Speeches by the Right Honorable Winston Churchill,* Charles Eade (ed.) (Boston: Little Brown, 1944), 316-318.
10. Peter Neubauer (ed.), *Children in Collectives--Child-rearing Aims and Practices in the Kibbutz* (Springfield, Ill.: Charles C Thomas, 1965).

what they are capable of becoming and to enjoy the freedom of making their lives what they want them to be.

There certainly exist in the human genetic pool rich potentialities that have not yet been fully expressed and that would permit mankind to continue evolving socially if conditions were favorable for their development. The diversity of civilizations originates from the multifarious responses that human groups have made in the past and continue making to environmental stimuli. This versatility of response, in turn, is a consequence of the wide range of potentialities exhibited by human beings. Since most of these potentialities remain untapped, each one of us actually becomes only one of the many persons he could have been.

Human potentialities, whether physical or mental, are expressed only to the extent that circumstances are favorable to their manifestation. The total environment thus plays a large role in the unfolding of man's nature and in the development of the individual personality.

In practice, the latent potentialities of human beings have a better chance to come to light when environment provides a variety of stimulating experiences, especially for the young. As more persons find the opportunity to express a larger percentage of their biological endowment under diversified conditions, society becomes richer and civilizations continue to unfold. If surroundings and ways of life are highly stereotyped, the only components of man's nature that flourish are those adapted to the narrow range of prevailing conditions.

In theory, the urban environment provides a wide range of options. The present trends of urban life are usually assumed to represent what people want, but in reality the trends are determined by the available choice. While people need what they want, what they want is largely determined by the choices readily available to them. It has been said that children growing up in some of the most prosperous American suburbs may suffer from being deprived of experiences. In contrast, the Lower East Side of New York City in the 1900s, despite its squalor and confusion, provided one of the richest human environments that ever existed. Children there were constantly exposed in the street to an immense variety of stimuli from immigrants of many cultures; many of these children became leaders in all fields of American life. [11]

In any case there is no doubt about the sterilizing influences of many modern housing developments, which, although sanitary and efficient, are inimical to the full expression of human potentialities. Many of these developments are planned as if their only function was to provide disposable cubicles for dispensable people.

In *The Myth of the Machine,* Lewis Mumford states that "if man had originally inhabited a world as blankly uniform as a 'high-rise' housing development, as featureless as a parking lot, as destitute of life as an automated factory, it is doubtful that he would have had a sufficiently varied experience to retain images, mold language, or acquire ideas." [12] In this statement, Mumford had in mind the emergence of man's attributes during evolutionary times. He would probably be willing to apply the same concepts to modern life. Irrespective of their genetic constitution, young people raised in a featureless environment and limited to a narrow range of living experiences are likely to suffer from a kind of deprivation that will cripple them intellectually and emotionally.

Man has been highly successful as a biological species because he is adaptable. He can hunt or farm, be a meat-eater or a vegetarian, live in the mountains or by the seashore, be a loner or a team-member, function in a democratic or totalitarian state.

11. Allon Schoener (ed.), *The Lower East Side: Portal to American Life* (New York: The Jewish Museum, 1966).

12. Lewis Mumford, *The Myth of the Machine* (New York: Harcourt, 1967), 76.

Family housing in a major midwest city results in a sterile atmosphere that limits the full potential of an individual's development. (Photo by Carol Wedin)

Urban renewal in some cities has created environments that support the growth and development of individuals. (United States Department of Agriculture; photo by Murray Lemmon)

History shows, on the other hand, that societies which were efficient because they were highly specialized rapidly collapsed when conditions changed. A highly specialized society, like a narrow specialist, is rarely adaptable.

Cultural homogenization and social regimentation resulting from the creeping monotony of overorganized and overtechnicized life, of standardized patterns of education, mass communication, and entertainment, will make it progressively more difficult to exploit fully the biological richness of our species and may handicap the further development of civilization. We must shun uniformity of surroundings as much as absolute conformity in behavior and tastes. We must strive instead to create as many diversified environments as possible. Richness and diversity of physical and social environments constitute an essential criteria of functionalism, whether in the planning of cities, the design of dwellings, or the management of individual life.

Diversity may result in some loss of efficiency. It will certainly increase the variety of challenges, but the more important goal is to provide the many kinds of soil that will permit the germination of the seeds now dormant in man's nature. Man innovates and thus fully expresses his humanness by responding creatively, even though often painfully, to stimuli and challenges. Societies and social groups that have removed themselves into pleasure gardens where all was designed for safety and comfort have achieved little else and have died in their snug world.

Many animal species other than man create buildings and institutions that complement the biological attributes of their bodies and serve as a focus of organization for their life. The beehive, the decorated nest of the Australian bower bird, the dam and house of the beaver are but a few examples illustrating that animals can organize inert materials to create new environments which are the equivalent of the institutions men create out of nature. The artificial environments created by animals often have aesthetic quality because they are built with great economy of means, are designed to fit their purpose exactly, and enhance the relation of the animal to the rest of nature. Many of the institutions created by pre-industrial people have much the same characteristics and qualities. The medieval village, the Italian hill town, the seventeenth-century New England village illustrate that human institutions can also make use of inert materials and topographical characteristics to establish harmonious relationships between man and nature. [13]

All great forms of human architecture incorporate an attitude toward life. This is true of the home, the garden, the temple, the village, and the metropolis. To be successful aesthetically and practically, buildings and other artifacts must reflect the spirit of the institutions from which they originate. Whenever societies have formulated worthwhile thoughts or attitudes, artists have been forthcoming to give them a vivid and appropriate physical form. The Parthenon, Chartres Cathedral, the Renaissance cities symbolize whole civilizations. In our times the great bridges symbolize man's desire to span the gaps that separate him from other men. Brooklyn Bridge was immediately acclaimed thoughout the world, and still constitutes, to my taste, one of the marvels of the modern era. It demonstrated that steel and concrete could serve for the creation of meaningful beauty; through it, technology in the service of a purpose became a joy and inspiration for painters and poets.

Architectural form at its best has always been an expression of the ideals and underlying social philosophy of human institutions; it constitutes an organic structural expression of social need. The German art critic Wolfgang Braunfels recently illustrated this thesis with a number of telling examples: The simple farmhouse represents the family maintaining itself by working on the land. The Carolingian Benedictine monastery incorporates the rule of Saint Benedict, according to which the monks not only worked, ate, and prayed together but also walked in slow-moving processions to the different functions of the day. The city-state of Siena in the thirteenth and early fourteenth century, rich in economic wealth and art, governed by a democratic assembly and citizens' committees, tried at every stage of its development to make the city a mirror of the entire cosmos and of life itself. The Palazzo Farnese, built by Pope Paul III for his sons and nephews in the heart of sixteenth-century Rome, symbolized the greatness of the family and served as a proper setting for the famous Farnese collection of art. The Palais de Versailles was built and designed not only for the personal aggrandizement of the Roi-Soleil, Louis XIV, but also to symbolize his unique position in the state. [14]

13. Lewis Mumford, *Sticks and Stones* (New York: Dover Publications, 1924).

14. Wolfgang Brannfels, "Institutions and Their Corresponding Ideals," in *The Quality of Man's Environment* (Washington, DC: Smithsonian Institution Press, 1968).

Two of these building types, the farmhouse and the monastery, evolved slowly from crude and humble beginnings in the course of several generations. In contrast, the Palazzo Farnese and the Palais de Versailles emerged fully developed, functionally and artistically, from the minds of men with powerful visions. Both these methods of growth operated in Siena, which illustrates at every period of its history a complex interplay between natural environment, social institutions, and the views men form of themselves and of the world. Great architecture and great planning never develop in an intellectual or spiritual vacuum. Plans and buildings express the spirit of the social institutions from which they arise, and then they influence the further development of society.

Several modern factories achieve genuine functional beauty because they express in their design the objectives of great precision, maximum output, and minimum cost, which are the ideals of modern technology. Many great bridges and a few highways are among the most notable achievements of our times, not so much because of the technological skills their construction required, but because they have the larger significance of expressing the compelling desire of modern man to explore and expand his personal world.

Unfortunately, most apartment and office buildings have nothing to communicate beyond efficiency and conspicuous wealth, hence their architectural triviality. As to our cities, no planning will save them from meaningless disorder leading to biological decay, unless man learns once more to use cities not only for the sake of business, but also for creating and experiencing in them the spirit of civilization. [15] We have inherited countless great monuments from the past. The automobile seems to be our most likely bequest to future generations; they will have to retrieve it from junkyards. The automobile is the symbol of our times and represents our flight from the responsibility of developing creative associations with our environment for the sake of the future.

Our dismal failure to develop really desirable cities, offices, and dwellings is not due to deficient engineering or bad workmanship but to the fact that technological skill cannot create anything worthwhile if it does not serve a worthwhile purpose. Our institutions are not really designed to help in developing the good life, but rather to make human beings more productive and more efficient tools of industry and commerce. Yet it is obvious that productivity and efficiency have no value in themselves; they have merit only as means to ends. In fact, excessive concern with productivity and efficiency interferes with the pursuit of significance.

Civilizations are like living organisms; they evolve according to an inner logic that integrates their historical determinants, their natural resources, and their acquired skills. It is also true, however, that most civilizations have suffered and many have died when this logic generated undesirable trends from which they could not or did not try to escape.

The logic of medieval thought led into scholastic verbiage; Gothic architecture toppled when it tried to outdo itself in the high towers of Beauvais; the scholarly learning of the nineteenth century is now degenerating into dehumanizing specialization. Scientific technology is presently taking modern civilization on a course that will be suicidal if it is not reversed in time. What, for example, will be the ultimate consequence for the United States of the fact that three centuries of homesteading, coupled with a national tradition of compulsive nomadism, has imposed on the overwhelming majority of urban dwellers the desire to occupy a one-family house, to drive to work in a private automobile, and to identify leisure time with essentially aimless movement?

---

15. Philip Johnson, "Why We Want Our Cities Ugly," in *The Quality of Man's Environment, op. cit.*

The aspiration to own a single-family detached house may become less meaningful if home ownership loses the symbolic meaning of economic and social independence. (United States Department of Agriculture; photo by Murray Lemmon)

Such compulsions call to mind certain biological trends that have brought about the extinction of countless animal species.

It is a truism that technological advances do not determine what is desirable but only what is feasible at a given time. We shall not improve the quality of life and of the environment merely by developing greater technological skills. In fact, as stated by Norbert Wiener, nothing will make the automated factory work automatically for human good, unless we have determined worthwhile ends in advance and have constructed the factory to achieve these ends.[16] In principle, nobody wants nastiness or ugliness, and everybody is for improvement of life and of our surroundings. In fact, however, our communities want to possess things and to engage in activities that are incompatible with civilized ways of life and pleasant surroundings.

Many times in the past, civilizations have lost the will or the ability to change after they have set on a certain course. Such civilizations soon exhaust the spiritual content and creativeness that characterized their initial phase. They usually retain for a while a certain kind of vigor based on orthodox classicism but soon degenerate into triviality before foundering in the sea of irrelevance.

If it is true, as it appears to be, that our environment and way of life profoundly affect our attitudes and those of following generations, nothing could be more distressing for our immediate and distant future than the decadence and ugliness of our great urban areas, the breakdown in public means of transportation, the overwhelming accent on

16. Norbert Wiener, *The Human Use of Human Beings: Cybernetics and Society* (Garden City, N.Y.: Doubleday, 1950).

materialistic and selfish comfort, the absence of personal and social discipline, the sacrifice of quality to quantity in production as well as in education. The lack of creative response to these threats is particularly discouraging because all thinking persons are aware of the situation and are anxious to do something to correct it. But common action cannot be mustered because it demands a common faith that does not exist. It is because we need a common faith that the search for significance is the most important task of our times.

Discussion Questions

1. Discuss the characteristics of an environment most likely to enhance the quality of life.

2. Dubos discusses effects of overpopulation. How does it affect the individual, the family?

3. How does the environment augment or stagnate human potentialities?

4. Is cultural homogenization beneficial or detrimental to development of civilization?

5. Dubos suggests that "the individual, detached house may also become obsolete." What are the conditions that could lead to this change in housing desires?

6. What does the following statement made by Sir Winston Churchill mean? "We shape our buildings, and afterwards our buildings shape us." Do you agree with Churchill's statement? Give reasons to support your answers.

2. A Historical Perspective of Major Forms in American Housing

by Carol S. Wedin

To build and own one's own home has traditionally been a deep desire for most Americans. Among the various reasons that brought the first settlers to the North American continent, the hope of having their own home was surely a major motivation.

When the first settlers arrived in Jamestown in 1607 and in Plymouth Harbor in 1620 their immediate need for shelter was met by digging holes in the hillsides and covering the holes with lean-to roofs of tree branches and animal hides, or by building huts of twigs and clay similar to the Indian dwellings. Of course, none of these crude earliest dwellings remain today; we have only written references to them. In the New England region the first settlers were besieged with harsh winter weather, marauding Indians, and constant sickness, which made the building of permanent dwellings very difficult. Of Jamestown, a decade after the first settlers had arrived, an Englishman reported in his journal "ther Howses are generally the worst yet that ever I sawe, ye meanest Cottages in England beinge every waye equal (if not superior) with ye most of the bests." [1]

Half-Timber Medieval

The first permanent houses built in Jamestown were of half-timber medieval structure. This was the type of house common in England among the humble rural people who comprised most of the settlers. In the New World they constructed houses as they had in their native land. The typical house contained one room with a loft, as shown in Figure 1. The spaces between the exposed timber framework were filled with a wattle plastered with daub. The settlers soon discovered that the winter winds and snows along the eastern shores of North America were too severe for the half-timber medieval construction. Wood clapboards were adopted on the exteriors of the houses. The steep thatched roof typically used in England dried out in the drier weather of the New World, constituting a fire hazard not present in damp, foggy England. Therefore, wood shingles were used to replace thatch. The early colonists modified the building practices they were familiar with in order to meet new needs with the materials available. Wood was plentiful and, because labor was scarce, water-powered sawmills were developed by 1646.

---

1. Marshall B. Davidson. *History of Notable American Houses* (New York: American Heritage Publishing Co., 1971), p. 10.

Figure 1. Half-Timber Medieval

Log Cabin

Probably the earliest log cabins in America were those introduced around 1640 by Swedish immigrants in Delaware. These first, log-constructed houses were small one-room cabins with low doors and a fireplace, usually of stone or clay, constructed in a corner. Windows consisted of a hole with a moveable-board fastener, since glass had to be imported and was thus very expensive.

In the eighteenth century, German settlers in Pennsylvania introduced their form of log cabins, and soon this practical building type began to appear in Virginia and North Carolina. In the late 1700's, when the western expansion began, the log cabin was a type of construction known and ready to be used. The log cabin could be built with only the aid of an axe, a supply of timber, and average skill. It did not require the joiners' and carpenters' skills that were unavailable on the frontier. Therefore, as the migrating families moved westward, the log cabin, illustrated in Figure 2, became the typical pioneer dwelling. "It was young America's answer to the mobile families' gravest problem—a safe and durable haven that an ordinary family man could build with a few tools, minimum skills, and little money." [2]

Both the small, one-room, clapboard house with a loft and the log cabin, sometimes with a loft also, were widely used from the seventeenth through the nineteenth centuries. As the families prospered, additional rooms were added to their houses. By the late 1700's glass was being manufactured in the colonies and small lead-glass panes were replacing the oiled paper that had been used to cover the windows.

Cape Cod Colonial

The single-room house with the chimney on one side was frequently enlarged by building a duplicate room on the other side of the chimney. The story-and-a-half house with the central chimney and the steep gable roof became known as the Cape Cod style. The Cape Cod Colonial, shown in Figure 3, has been one of the most copied and modified designs in our country.

2. C.A. Weslager, *The Log Cabin in America* (New Brunswick, N.J.: Rutgers University Press, 1969), p. 6.

Two other seventeenth-century houses that have influenced house forms into the twentieth century are the Saltbox Colonial and Dutch Colonial.

These colonial houses, along with the Cape Cod style, have some common characteristics. The styles are unpretentious in design. They usually had narrow wood siding, a central chimney, and a rectangular plan with small-pane windows. Most houses were not painted before the beginning of the nineteenth century.

Saltbox Colonial

The Saltbox Colonial, shown in Figure 4, developed as the families enlarged their houses with a lean-to addition in the rear. The shape of the house resembled the shape of the boxes used to store salt; therefore, the houses became known as the "Saltbox."

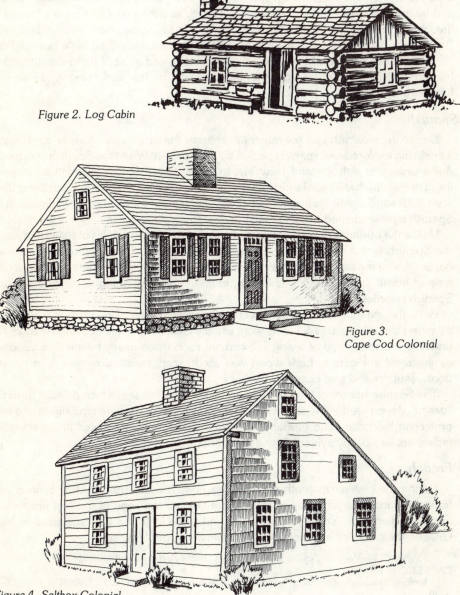

Figure 2. Log Cabin

Figure 3.
Cape Cod Colonial

Figure 4. Saltbox Colonial

Dutch Colonial

The gambrel roof is the characteristic feature of one form of the Dutch Colonial house. The flat gambrel roof with curving eaves which swept out over a porch is illustrated in Figure 5. Many of the Dutch homes built by the first Dutch settlers in the Hudson Valley were of stone construction and had simple, steep gable roofs. The gambrel with upturning eaves was a development on native American soil by settlers of Dutch, Flemish, and possibly French origin. The form is, in truth, American.

Although many of the first houses were built of wood it should be noted that brick was being made in Virginia in 1611 and in the New England colonies soon after. Brick had been used for centuries in much of Europe. Settlers from Europe were familiar with the process of brickmaking; therefore, many desired to build with brick as soon as their means permitted. Abundant clay deposits were found near the Delaware shores and by the end of the seventeenth century, partly as a means of limiting the hazard of fire, much of the construction in the cities of Philadelphia, New Amsterdam, and Boston was of brick. In 1687, the city of Philadelphia was described as "a beautiful city . . . which contains a number of houses all inhabited; and most of them stately, and of brick, generally three stories high, after the mode in London, and as many (as) several families in each." [3]

Spanish

During the sixteenth and seventeenth centuries the southern regions of our country were being explored and sparsely settled by the Spanish. When the Spanish conquistadores arrived in Arizona and New Mexico, they found Indian populations already living in cities in dwellings of practical, mud-wall construction. The design utilizing thick walls with small openings for windows was appropriate for the hot, arid climate. The Spanish readily adapted to using this structural form.

Unlike the northern Europeans who attempted to copy the styles of their homeland, the Spanish in the southwest used the cheap, unskilled Indian labor to build their houses. Using the materials that were available and Indian labor "there resulted a new type of house, half-Spanish, half-Indian, entirely unlike anything developed in other Spanish colonies." [4]

Both the exterior and interiors were of simple design. The interior walls were plastered and whitewashed. Floors were usually tiled. In New Mexico and Arizona, the primitive Indian method of laying flat, earthen roofs upon heavy beams was adopted, as illustrated in Figure 6. Little wood was used except for window and door frames, doors, shutters, and roof beams.

The Spanish houses of Florida had a more "tropical" design which differed from the "desert" design used in the southwest. The houses in Florida were typically stucco with projecting balconies. The Hispanic influence of wrought-iron gates and decorative grille work was clearly evident during that period.

French

During the late seventeenth century, the French established trading centers and forts along the Mississippi River valley. New Orleans was one of the first permanent French settlements. Although the French influence in house design started in New Orleans, the influence is evident in cities along the upper Mississippi.

3. Herbert C. Wise and H. Ferdinand Beidleman, *Colonial Architecture* (Philadelphia: J. P. Lippincott Co., 1913), p. 16.

4. Retford Newcomb, *The Spanish House for America* (Philadelphia: J. P. Lippincott Co., 1927), p. 20.

The first houses were typically constructed on log piers to elevate the first floor of the house above potential flooding waters. Along the southern Mississippi where brick was more readily available, the houses were constructed on brick piers. Other characteristic features of the French house were balconies that often extended around two or three sides of the house, along with decorative ironwork on balconies and porches. An illustration of a New Orleans French house is shown in Figure 7. French homes in the south were frequently of lighter-colored brick than the brick used for houses where the

Figure 5. Dutch Colonial

Figure 6. Spanish House

Figure 7. French House

English influence predominated. The stucco houses were often pastel in color. In the southern houses the kitchens were usually in a separate building connected by a gallery. This was true of not only French houses, but Spanish and English as well. The kitchen was located in a separate building for several reasons: it was a precaution against fires, it kept the heat resulting from food preparation out of the main house, and it separated the slaves or servants from the family living quarters.

Georgian Colonial

As the colonists along the Atlantic seaboard prospered from trade and farming, their homes became larger and more stately. By the end of the seventeenth century, trading between the colonies and England was well established. The land and climate of the southern colonies were ideal for growing tobacco, rice, and indigo. The agricultural products were in great demand in England. Ships would leave the east coast loaded with various agricultural products and return with the latest clothing, books, and manufactured goods from England.

The architectural style currently fashionable in England was copied in detail by the prosperous colonists. Books that included architectural plans and detailed drawings, along with English craftsmen, were brought to the colonies. This style became known as "Georgian," named after the several King Georges of the royal Hanover family.

Georgian architecture was influenced by Italian Renaissance with an emphasis on symmetry. The plans were rectangular to nearly square in shape with the central feature being the door framed in classical moldings, pediment, and carved detail. Unlike the earlier casement windows with the diamond-shaped panes, the windows of the Georgian style were composed of small, square panes with sash construction. The windows were arranged symmetrically as shown in Figure 8.

The Georgian style differed in exterior construction materials, depending on the location along the Atlantic seaboard. The houses in the south were of red brick construction whereas the houses in Philadelphia frequently were made of stone. Houses in the northern colonies were constructed of wood.

The formality expressed in the Georgian architectural design influenced a change in lifestyle, ". . . it involved new concepts of living in which comfort, convenience, and privacy played a leading role."[5] Separate rooms were provided for dining, entertaining, sleeping, and cooking. The fireplaces were usually symmetrically placed at each side of the house rather than in the center, as had been the prevailing style in seventeenth-century New England homes. The centrally located front door opened to a wide hall that extended to the rear of the house where another door was located. The wide extended hall served as additional living space and usually had an elaborate staircase ascending to the second floor. A simple stairway in the rear of the house was used by the servants.

In the major cities where lots were narrow the Georgian influence was expressed in the row houses, which shared common walls and had similar facades, with individuality in door and window detail.

Although the Georgian style is symbolic of eighteenth-century architecture, it was only the wealthier colonists that could afford the Georgian mansions or row houses. The story-and-a-half cottage was still the prevailing house form in both the northern and southern states. The log cabin was being used extensively by settlers moving further west. One-room cabins with dirt floors and meager furnishings were commonplace for slave families. It was not unusual to have several slave families sharing a cabin.

5. Marshall B. Davidson, *The American Heritage History of Notable American Houses* (New York: American Heritage Publishing Co., 1971), p. 62.

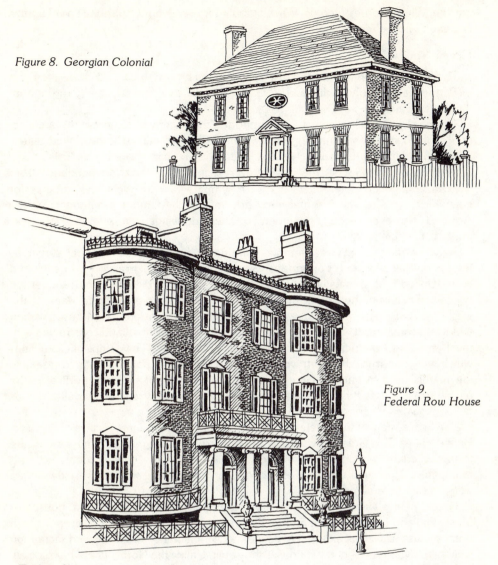

Figure 8. *Georgian Colonial*

Figure 9.
Federal Row House

Federal

After the Revolutionary War, architecture was influenced by the excavations at Pompeii and Herculaneum. The classical spirit was evident in both public and residential architecture. "The new classicism was a national idiom, freely and easily enough used by men who saw in ancient Greece and Rome the models of their new republic." [6]

The Federal period brought new standards of convenience and privacy. Specialized rooms that assured greater privacy, such as dressing rooms, butler's pantries, closets, libraries, and studies, were added. The Roman temple form influenced residential design. Oval- and octagonal-shaped rooms replaced some of the traditional rectangular rooms. Curved exterior projections were frequently used on the Federal mansions as well as the Federal row houses in the cities as illustrated in Figure 9. The Greek and Roman columns, pediments, and classical decorations were used on both the interiors and exteriors. Three houses built during this period that are now national monuments

6. *Ibid.*, p. 121.

are the White House; George Washington's House, Mount Vernon; and Thomas Jefferson's home, Monticello.

Greek Revival

The first Greek Revival structure to be built in the New World in 1798 was the Bank of Pennsylvania in Philadelphia. The Greek Revival style spread rapidly throughout the United States.

There were several reasons which supported the eagerness to accept this architectural style. First, it was a time of growing concern for democracy in the United States. Americans identified their own civic and political virtues with those of classical Greece. At that time (the 1820's), the Greeks were fighting for their independence from Turkish domination. The Americans were sympathetic with the Greek struggle for independence. Also, the first measured drawings of the famous monuments on the Acropolis had been recently documented. These drawings were published in books printed in England.

Although the original Greek temples were never designed for living, they served as inspiration that allowed for enormous variation in personal expression. As developed in the United States, the style was modified to use native materials and to meet the needs and values of the American people. The style rapidly spread from Maine to the western outposts and south to the Gulf of Mexico. City mansions, farmhouses, institutional and commercial buildings, and state capitals were designed and constructed with the forms and ornaments of ancient Greek architecture. The templelike buildings which were constructed of both wood and brick were often painted white to resemble the marble used in ancient Greece. "A simple addition of a Greek portico to the pitched-roof houses that dotted the American landscape was generally all that was needed to imbue the structure with new meaning." [7]

The high society of the nineteenth century flourished in the major cities of northern United States. The Greek Revival row houses provided a dignified framework for the formal entertainment and predominate life style of the day. Drawing rooms with 14-foot high ceilings, large expanses of windows, and broad wall surfaces were decorated with Grecian ornamentation.

Greek Revival architecture was most exemplified in the plantation houses in Mississippi and Louisiana. Cotton had become an important agricultural crop for both domestic use as well as export. Owners of cotton plantations had enjoyed increasing wealth; this was reflected in the houses they built. Unlike the North, where high society was centered in the major cities, in the South the leading social life was centered around the plantations and the commercial centers where cotton was exported. Southern mansions had large porticos flanked with Grecian columns, illustrated in Figure 10. These houses were typical of the wealthy people in the 1830's.

The Greek Revival style, sometimes incorrectly referred to as Southern Colonial (we were no longer colonies of England), was fitting for the hot, humid climate of the southern states. The large, shaded porticos protected the interior rooms from the penetrating rays of the sun, and the spacious, high-ceiling rooms provided for some relief from the sweltering summer weather.

Victorian

The term Victorian refers to the period of Queen Victoria's reign. Most English-speaking countries were undergoing rapid change in technological advancement and aesthetic appreciation. It was an eclectic period where the designs of various historical

7. *Ibid.*, p. 179.

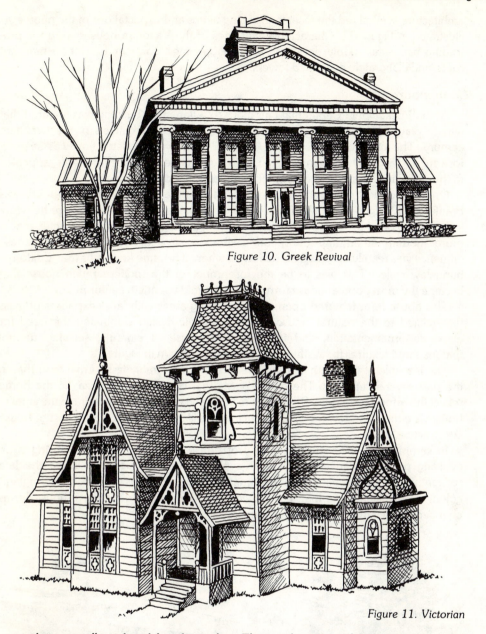

Figure 10. Greek Revival

Figure 11. Victorian

periods were collected and fused together. The result was an elaborate, ornamented design in both architecture and furnishings.

The Industrial Revolution brought about great changes in life style which were reflected in the houses people constructed. This was a period where man felt the need to symbolize his control over materials and nature. The invention of elevators, electricity, telephones, and central heating caused rapid change in residential design. The newly invented jig-saw made it possible to mass produce ornamentation that had previously been hand-crafted. As a result, the carved ornaments and elaborate moldings frequently displayed poor workmanship.

This was also a time of growing wealth in America. The early industrialists were anxious to display their new-found wealth and the ostentatious display of architectural embellishments conspicuously signaled their prominent place in society. Victorian architecture symbolized the incessantly rising needs and expectations of the people, as illustrated in Figure 11. Characteristic features of the Victorian houses were the protruding bay areas, oddly designed window openings, columned porches, mansard roofs, and elaborately decorated towers.

Contemporary

At the Philadelphia Centennial Fair in 1876 a Japanese building was featured that was to play a leading role in influencing the American architects of the twentieth century. The one-story structure of "honest" woodwork construction was straightforward in design. This organic design, with no ornamental embellishments, appealed to those looking for an escape from the ostentatious Victorian style.

One of the most influential architects of the early and mid-twentieth century was Frank Lloyd Wright. After Wright had studied Japanese art and architecture he wrote in his autobiography that the Japanese buildings have an organic character that is more modern "than any European civilization alive or dead." [8] The Japanese influence was readily accepted in California, where it became known as the "California bungalow style." This was to be the forerunner of the modern ranch house that became the most popular house form during the mid-twentieth century.

This house form featured open, spacious living areas with large expanses of glass that related to the natural landscape. The organic design eliminated the need for elaborate ornamentation, and focused on the use of carefully selected natural materials and textures for aesthetic enrichment, as shown in Figure 12.

The life style of twentieth-century America is considerably less formal than that in the past several centuries. The open spaces that combine living areas in the home reflect this informal life style. Other factors that have occurred to encourage the smaller houses are the trend toward smaller, nuclear families plus the increased cost of house construction.

In summary, as we view the history of house forms we see that housing is an evolving process to meet the likewise-evolving needs of people. During the late sixteenth and early-seventeenth centuries the house forms in the New England colonies were little more than basic shelter. As our society developed, house forms changed to meet the demands of a changing life style.

8. *Ibid.*, p. 306.

Figure 12. Contemporary

By the mid-seventeenth century farms were established, cities were forming, and commerce between the colonies and Europe was beginning. More permanent and elaborate housing forms evolved. During the eighteenth and nineteenth centuries increasing wealth was enjoyed by some of the people and this was reflected in the larger, more formal houses they constructed. It was also a time of western expansion where pioneers erected less permanent structures such as log cabins and sod houses as they settled the western frontier.

The Industrial Revolution brought about drastic changes in family living patterns. The house form changed to accommodate the difference in life style. The post-Industrial Revolutionary house has been referred to as "a machine for living." House forms will continue to evolve as new materials and construction techniques are developed and as our human needs change.

References

Beyer, Glenn H. *Housing and Society*. New York: Macmillan Company, 1965.

Ballinger, Richard M., and Herman York, *The Illustrated Guide to the Houses of America*, New York: Hawthorn Books, Inc., 1971.

Davidson, Marshall B. *History of Notable American Houses*. New York: American Heritage Publishing Co., 1971.

Newcomb, Retford. *The Spanish House for America*. Philadelphia: J. P. Lippincott Co., 1927.

Pratt, Richard. *A Treasury of Early American Homes*. New York: McGraw-Hill Book Company, 1949.

Reynolds, Helen Wilkinson. *Dutch Houses in the Hudson Valley Before 1776*. New York: Dover Publications, 1965.

Weslager, C. A. *The Log Cabin in America*. New Brunswick: Rutgers University Press, 1969.

Wise, Herbert C., and H. Ferdinand Beidleman. *Colonial Architecture*. Philadelphia: J. P. Lippincott Co., 1913.

Discussion Questions

1. Discuss how native materials influenced house design.

2. Why was log construction the dominant construction technique used by the settlers at the time of the expansion into the Midwest?

3. What country has made the greatest influence in American housing? What were the reasons for this influence?

4. In the south, kitchens were commonly located in separate buildings during the eighteenth and nineteenth centuries. What was the reasoning for locating the kitchen away from the main house?

5. What effects did the Industrial Revolution have on house form?

6. Discuss the reasons why the people in the United States eagerly accepted the Greek Revival style. How did this style meet the needs and aspiration of the society?

7. What is the meaning of the term "eclectic"? How was this used in residential design in our country?

8. The term "organic design" is referred to when discussing contemporary architecture. Discuss the meaning of this term in relation to residential design.

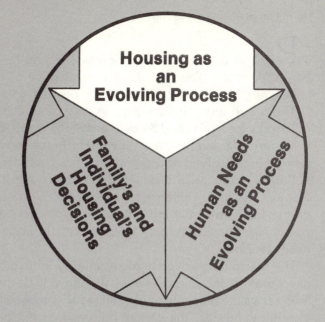

Housing as
an
Evolving Process

Family's and
Individual's
Housing
Decisions

Human Needs
as an
Evolving Process

Part Two
Macro Forces
Affecting
Housing

3. Industrialization in Housing, by Paul Muessig

4. Energy in Housing: Consumption and Conservation, by Carol S. Wedin

5. Land for Housing, by Raleigh Barlowe

6. Housing Costs: What Can Be Done?, by Nathaniel H. Rogg

7. Government Housing Programs: A Brief Review, by Mary H. Yearns

8. Codes and Controls, by Carol S. Wedin

Part Two deals with macro forces affecting housing decisions. Since we live in an evolving society we will never solve all of our housing problems; rather, our aim is to reduce them, especially where they are most severe.

The macro forces (technology, energy, land, economics, and government) will produce conflicts and dislocations at the micro level as social attitudes and values are adjusted to accept different forms of housing. Why have Americans resisted industrialized housing when it has been accepted for several decades in Europe? How will individuals and families adjust to the energy constraints that will inevitably influence house design? Will land use regulations impinge on the freedom of the individual? How do the macro forces affect housing costs? Has the government been successful in implementing programs for needy families?

The macro forces of technology, energy, land, economics, and government directly affect the micro level of the individual's housing environment. Part Two assists the reader in appreciating the complexity of forces that must work together to produce the desired housing for our citizens. Article 3, "Industrialization in Housing," traces the history of the various industrialized housing systems and examines the input of industrialized housing in the present home-building industry.

Articles 4 and 5 address the major concerns of energy and land use. The constraints on both energy and land use are discussed with an emphasis on the urgent need for cooperation between individuals, industry, and government. These articles further indicate some family conflicts and emotional adjustments which are likely to emerge as we comply with restrictions on dwelling size and environmental densities.

Inflation and the rising cost of housing are examined in Article 6. Eight major components of the problem of housing cost are discussed in detail. Some solutions to each of the components are offered.

The last two articles in Part Two explain the role of government as a regulatory institution. There is discussion of the division of regulatory powers at the federal, state, county, and municipal levels.

Since most major housing decisions are made at the macro level, the individual seeking rational change has less impact acting alone than with a group. An organized approach often must be undertaken to support any desired change. One example of how organized citizens can produce change in a community is by applied pressure on the use of revenue sharing funds. A community which is allocated revenue sharing funds may desperately need housing for the elderly; however, the community may direct the funds to some other usage if pressure is not applied by concerned local citizens.

These articles will assist the individual in becoming more aware of the decision-making forces at the macro level. An informed individual can act as a catalyst in preparing others to assume their responsibilities in the public policy decision-making sector.

3. Industrialization in Housing

by Paul Muessig

For more years than I like to contemplate, it has seemed to me that the means of providing homes in Modern America and elsewhere have been strangely out of date. [1]

Albert Farwell Bemis, 1936

Housing is the one industry that did not receive new life as a result of the Industrial Revolution. Any investigation into the home-building process will not only prove the timelessness of Bemis' statement, but will also uncover a unique and constantly evolving industry. When compared to any other segment of business or social undertaking, the home-building process results in more varied forms and quality. In addition, the process is influenced greatly by market changes and distribution methods. And, service industries impinging upon the home-building process are virtually countless.

Why Industrialization?

Technology

Technology used in the housing industry varies from the simple to the complex. Basically, technology in the industry is successful because it is responsible for efficient gathering and usage of energies. Because of the increasing economic importance of both time and natural resources, we can reason that there is also an increasing need for more emphasis on appropriate technology. Where technology is applicable and commensurate with other human needs in housing (e.g., aesthetic, self-esteem, mental and physical health), the housing industry must enhance use of mechanization and standardization. It must respond to surrounding circumstances. Appropriate, higher technologies in housing could help alleviate the costs, variations in quality, and the rising demand for housing. Both consumer and supplier would benefit.

The term "industrialization," referring primarily to factory construction in part or total, is one that will be used throughout this article. Industrialization is a term dependent on magnitude when used to describe housing or housing products. We live in an industrialized environment. Without industrialization, there would be no modern architecture as we know it. The steel and glass skyscrapers have been made possible by the industrialization of building products. Industrialization, or factory production, is seen, without exception, everywhere in this country. There are, however, vast differences in the degree to which it occurs. For example, the 2 x 4 wood stud used for

Paul Muessig, an architect, is Assistant Director to Technical Services, National Association of Home Builders. This article was prepared especially for this book.

1. Forest Wilson (ed.), *A Crack in the Rear-View Mirror* (New York: Van Nostrand Reinhold Company, 1973), p. 11.

framing a house, which is finished or produced in the factory and shipped to the site and installed, is an industrialized product. By comparison, the mobile and modular homes, which are constructed and finished in the factory and shipped to the site and installed, are also industrialized products.

Although the evolution of industrialized housing has been slow, there are remarkable inroads being made in it. In recognition of the recent developments in housing technology and in hope of spurring on its progress, George Romney, past secretary of the Department of Housing and Urban Development, stated that "we are now just in the first stage of the industrial age in housing production," and predicted that "before the seventies are over, industrialized housing will dominate the market." Romney, as others, recognized the need to adopt higher technologies which lend themselves to the production of dwelling units in an organized and standardized fashion without sacrificing variety. The amount of variety need not be minimized by the language of the aesthetics related to technology. Because of increased usage of repetitive, predictable components, we can have aesthetics that are both predictable and rational.

Aesthetics and Technology

Machines lend themselves to the creation of a beauty which is being ignored in industrialized housing. Unfortunately, the concept of industrialized housing has all too frequently brought forth images of mass-produced repetition in housing. A repetition of monotonous forms often creates equally monotonous spaces lacking creativity and denying individuality.

The lack of an aesthetic awareness in industrialized housing has influenced product acceptance. Dr. Kate Rogers, professor of design at the University of Missouri, defines the term aesthetic as the direct expression of a society.

> Whatever aesthetic we have is formed in the matrix of our society . . . . We are a complex, varying, difficult, deadly, exciting society; we are shaken by vital life and dragging decay, with the extremes unresolved in our minds and the established methods unsuited to the now-known problems.[2]

To insure that beauty is part of an industrialized home, the requirements and restrictions of the machine process producing the product, or sub-products, should be viewed as factors which must enter into any calculation or design. Mass production of housing should allow for variations in size, style, and color that can be used in a variety of interchangeable ways. The standardization of materials increases the compatibility among products. Thus, the possibility for variety is endless due to the combinations and permutations within a given framework.

The acquisition of this new aesthetic is dependent upon a willingness to accept the "machine aesthetic." The success of mass-produced housing presupposes a new attitude toward proportion and predictability within the environment. Due to the generally poor public opinion toward industrialized housing and the only slight cost edge it may presently have, there is currently no great market demand for it.

A question that should be examined is why have we persisted in trying to produce conventional looking homes with nonconventional methods? Why do we fabricate steel or plastic to resemble wood? Why do we design a modular home to resemble a Cape Cod cottage? Dr. Paul Lemkau, professor of mental health at Johns Hopkins University, believes many people value the sense of security and continuity symbolized

---

2. Kate Ellen Rogers, "What is Our Measurement in Housing — Aesthetics," in *Proceedings of Fifth Annual Meeting, American Association of Housing Educators* (Lincoln, Nebraska, 1970), p. 15.

by traditional materials and styles. Dr. Lemkau suggests that planners and developers might deliberately attempt, in some obvious public place, to satisfy the demand for architecture symbolizing an imagined high point in history.* Actually, this may be what colonial architecture represents. Having satisfied this demand, the planners and developers have thus freed themselves for technological advancements.

Historical Perspective

Pre-World War I

The concept of industrialization in building is not new. Egyptian pyramids are supposed to have been built of carved stone blocks which were quarried miles away, floated to the area, and then rolled to the building site. As work progressed, a ramp was utilized to place the stones at the proper height. Log cabin construction, which reportedly was brought to America in the late 1630s by the Swedish, is also a lesser form of industrialization. Trees are felled, stripped, finished and notched, taken to the site, and then put in place. At the lower level today, the 2 x 4 wall stud represents an industrialized product quite similar to the pioneer's log.

It is believed that 1625 marks the year when the first panelized home was used, having been transported from England, disassembled and reused by fishing fleets. Another classic example of industrialized housing resulted from an effort to develop more humane treatment for sick and wounded soldiers in Europe during the mid-1880s. Ducker's Portable Barracks were shipped on flatbed wagons and assembled in the field. In this instance, industrialization helped to provide the necessary shelter when time and quality were very important. Both of these examples of early industrialized housing utilized panel wall systems that had post-and-beam roofing supports with all parts easily collapsible and easily shipped. As a result, the site work required only simple tools and fasteners which could be handled by unskilled laborers.

Because of a housing demand created by the gold rush in 1849, the Civil War, and other factors, there was a separate rate for shipping packaged homes on the railways in America as early as the 1870s. In fact, the late 1800s and early 1900s saw the advent of the idea of buying packaged homes from catalogs. In its spring general catalog of 1908, Sears, Roebuck and Co. featured its first packaged house. The house, along with assembling directions, was shipped by rail to the closest point near erection. This frontier housing again had requirements for quick and quality construction completed by unskilled laborers.

The 1920s and 1930s

The years immediately surrounding World War I were extremely significant to the industrialization of housing and the advent of space age technology. The beginning of the war witnessed soldiers riding in on horses with sabres in hand, and the end of the war saw pilots flying in the air and dropping bombs. The speed with which technical advancement took place was never before accomplished in the history of the human race. The catalyst for the development of this specialized technology was the need for more and better products, and this technology was achieved through an understanding of materials, production, economics, and the willingness to accept a product which was based on a new aesthetic resulting from the constraints imposed by the machine.

During World War I the need was created to accept a machine aesthetic in art,

* Paul V. Lemkau, M.D., is the author of Article 14 in this book, "Housing and Health."

$1,400.00 Builds This Modern Eight=Room House
OUR FREE BUILDING PLANS, SPECIFICATIONS AND BILL OF MATERIALS MAKE THIS LOW COST POSSIBLE.
OUR WAY OF GIVING THESE PLANS FREE IS EXPLAINED ON PAGE 2.

MODERN HOME No. 24

The arrangement of this house is as follows:

FIRST FLOOR.

Parlor, 14 feet by 13 feet.
Living Room, 13 feet 6 inches by 14 feet.
Bedroom, 10 feet 6 inches by 12 feet.
Kitchen and Dining Room, 15 feet 6 inches by 14 feet 6 inches.
Pantry.
Closet.
Porch, 11 feet by 8 feet.
Rear Porch, 8 feet by 7 feet.

SECOND FLOOR.

Bedroom, 14 feet by 13 feet.
Bedroom, 13 feet 6 inches by 11 feet 6 inches.
Bedroom, 7 feet by 8 feet 6 inches.
Bathroom.
Large Hall.
Length of building, 38 feet; width of building, 29 feet.

How to get a complete set of blue prints, specifications and bill of materials for this house free, explained on page 2.

A packaged house featured in the Sears, Roebuck & Co. catalog in the spring of 1908. (Courtesy of Sears, Roebuck & Co.)

furniture design, architecture, and nearly every other form of consumer product design. Changes in art and furniture design were extremely noticeable during the period when art nouveau was popular, and this period was immediately followed by a drastic change to the art deco movement. The art nouveau movement, which began in the 1890s, was comprised of sinuous forms and lines that flowed and swirled. It reflected the beauty of unlimiting curves found in nature — beauty which could only be imitated by the hand of a craftsperson. Art deco, which began in the 1920s, was the complete reversal of art nouveau. This movement was represented by lines and forms which were straight and calculated, reproducible, predictable, and of consistent quality. Deco was represented by characteristics not found in nature. The deco movement was responsible for the 1930s movement which echoed the popular desires of a futurist era. Examples which symbolized these desires were futuristic products at the 1938 World's Fair, novels written during this period, and appliances of this age. Thus, the time period surrounding World War I was extremely significant to all forms of industry, a great portion of art, and modern architecture. But housing technology was not influenced as greatly.

The European experience following World War I was markedly different from the American experience. Because of the need for quick reconstruction, industrialization became a welcomed and essential necessity in order for the homeless to be sheltered. This industrialization also typified reconstruction again after World War II when housing forms were quickly designed and constructed of necessity both in Europe and Japan. In Japan particularly, the production of industrialized, high density housing developed.

The European housing systems were not acceptable in the United States since single-family home ownership was of primary concern to those demanding housing. This attitude in housing is still prevalent due to the American dream of owning real estate. Today there are almost three times as many single family as multifamily units built in America.

Since America has not recently experienced a war on home ground, it has seen no need to create immediate housing, except in emergencies caused by natural disaster. Also, unlike Europe or the Orient, America has not come to grips with a land crisis and is therefore not restrained by population and its distribution. The people of the United States have continually sought single-family homes. This has been and remains the "American dream," and anything that diminishes this dream is resisted.

The 1940s

During the 1940s, World War II contributed to many changes. This time of change was most obvious in housing. The end of the war gave the United States a demand for housing never before experienced. Yankee ingenuity developed acceptable answers to this demand. Besides spawning experts in the practice of production management in home construction, this period also gave rise to a few absolute innovators. Examples worthy of recognition were Walter Gropius and Konrad Wachsman who developed the "General Panel System" and Carl Strandlund and Carl Koch who designed the "Lustron Homes" system. Both systems were developed in the late 1940s.

General Panel System. The General Panel System philosophically stripped itself of all those things which would have impeded it from becoming a fully industrialized product with an industrialized beauty. Gropius and Wachsman believed, as did many of their contemporaries, in the beauty expressed by the connections of building parts. The "joint" was not to be a thing of shame. They believed that building joints should be visible to all, and through that visibility, inform the user or participant of the inner workings, strengths, and weaknesses of the building. The underlying idea behind this sort of aesthetic suggested that people would understand how the building goes together by witnessing the joint, and as a result, they would learn and accept the beauty inherent to its form. The building was stripped of ornament to allow the full expression of function. In retrospect, the system can be viewed as progressive for the time, and it was appreciated by only a few professionals in the design field.

Lustron Homes System. The Lustron Homes system represented one of the more successful attempts at producing a truly industrialized home. The first prototype of the Lustron Home was a 1,025-square-foot house produced from steel in 1947. The Lustron production plant was a converted plane factory which had the ability to produce almost 100 houses daily through the use of a conveyor belt assembly system which moved at 20 feet per minute.

The 12½-ton house consisted of 300 parts as compared to a similar-sized, wood frame house which might have as many as 30,000 site-assembled parts. Assembly time efficiency also surpassed any form of conventionally built home. Lustron Homes required 280 hours of factory work and 350 hours of site assembly, a total of 630 hours as opposed to 1,600 hours to assemble a comparable conventional home.

The Lustron Home was made from mat-finished, enameled-steel panels over a steel frame. Utilizing a tremendous number of assembly techniques borrowed from the automotive industry, the Lustron Home was one of the most innovative homes ever engineered and constructed.

Despite the success which the Lustron system had as an innovative piece of engineering, its marketing and financing problems resembled those of the General Panel System. The market accepted the Lustron Home, presumably because of its low maintenance and constant new look resulting from the use of enameled steel. Using mass production methods, however, Lustron produced many of its own components which lacked flexibility for other builders and were therefore difficult to market outside of their use in the production home. For example, producing its own bathtub units was no problem for Lustron, but to make this a sound economic venture, Lustron had to produce 120,000 bathtub units per year — 40,000 to be used in its homes and 80,000 to be sold to an outside market. The outside market did not exist for an off-sized tub.

Financing was (and is today) a major problem for any factory-produced house. In the case of a Lustron home, a $9,000 to $11,000 investment, the dealer was required to pay $6,000 before the house left the factory. Lustron's success was severely lessened when many lenders either refused to make a mortgage commitment, or, having made a commitment, insisted on payment in stages according to the financial practices required by conventional construction. The result was an impossible cash flow problem. If mortgage lenders had been more understanding of the money flow necessary to make the financing system work, Lustron might still be selling today.

Despite all the problems encountered by the Lustron Home, there remained a strong market. When conventional speculative homes would not sell, the Lustron Home generally sold. However, the goal of attaining 1% of the housing market was never realized, and, because of continuing problems and poor timing of financing relief measures, Lustron Homes ceased production in 1950.

Techbuilt Housing System. The Techbuilt Housing System was developed in the 1950s by Carl Koch who had been the principal designer involved in the Lustron Home. After the demise of Lustron, Koch was able to take advantage of his earlier experiences. He realized a better system would be directed toward the money institutions and their conventional methods of financing. Koch went a step further to evaluate the Lustron system itself, and reasoned that to blame the money system would only feed the fire of the opponents to industrialization. These opponents already had pointed out that a high degree of industrialization in housing would never become reality.

Koch's investigation found that the fault with Lustron was the kind of system used. Lustron was a closed system. This specific closed system demanded all special components, which were produced in one central location and which together created a product that could not be modified to suit individual preferences. The Lustron system, or any closed system, cannot properly respond to the endless and complicated demands put on the housing industry.

With the seasonal cycles, the disparity in market attitudes, and the cost of finance and transportation, Koch found that the only system which would work is an open system. Unlike the Lustron House, Techbuilt was a kit of parts that could be added to and subtracted from in order to produce nearly any design. The Techbuilt open system could respond to local building codes, individual family demands, and the seasonal ups and downs of the market.

Koch not only developed the system, but he also knew how to merchandise the product. The system was sold through dealers. The dealers were equipped with a planning package. The dealer and the buyer together designed and budgeted the home within Techbuilt guidelines. This approach allowed the buyer to know exactly what the house would cost if it was designed within the system, and it also provided a base house upon which the buyer could add nonstandard parts to make a more customized house. Both the buyers and the dealers were equally pleased because of the controls within and outside the system.

Mobile Homes. One form of industrialized housing which has been very successful in this country, unlike anywhere else, is the mobile home. The forecast is that the number of mobile home shipments for 1978 will equal 300,000 which, when included as part of all housing starts, may equal as much as 10 to 15%.

Mobile homes drastically undercut the price of single-family homes. Other factors that have increased their popularity are easily obtained financing, quickness of acquisition, inclusion of furniture and appliances, ease of maintenance, and benefits on property tax.

The largest number of consumers for mobile homes are young couples purchasing their first homes. Also, retired couples desiring lower shelter cost and less maintenance have chosen the mobile home as a form of housing. In addition, mobile homes are frequently purchased as second homes and as vacation homes.

After 1950

One dimension of industrialization that has been most successful in the United States is the production of components. Today, the percentage of on-site labor in the home-building industry is significantly lower than in the past. Home building now utilizes prefabricated roof trusses instead of conventional rafters, preconstructed kitchen cabinets, door and window assemblies, stair units, bathroom units, plumbing units, wood foundation systems, as well as wall and overall support systems. During the last thirty years, the innovations which permit a greater use of components have been numerous and have permitted the stick-built approach to house building to prevail.

The past three decades have seen the emergence of the federal government as a strong influence in the United States, as well as the slow evolution of industrialized housing. In the late 1960s, the President's Committee on Urban Housing announced that between the years 1968 and 1979 the United States would need to produce 26,000,000 housing units. Given a projected total for 1978, the United States will have produced a total of 18,900,000 units in that ten-year period. In addition to the urgency for housing, rising costs are also a problem. Realizing the likelihood that conventional construction would be unable to produce in such number (the highest production year was in 1972 when 2,378,000 housing units were built), the Department of Housing and Urban Development (HUD) announced and implemented "Operation Breakthrough" in the summer of 1969. The objective behind this program was to stimulate interest in the development of more effective production methods to enable the United States to accomplish the projected goal of 2,600,000 housing units per year.

Six hundred proposals were received by HUD in response to its request. In February, 1970, twenty-two winners were named as participants in Operation Breakthrough. Most winners developed systems to answer the need for single-family, low-rise and row housing, which responded to the demand found in the American housing market. The twenty-two winners shared in contracts totaling $62,700,000 to produce 2,796 housing units at various sites throughout the country.

Due to the nature of the housing product which demands a continuity within the construction process, each of the program participants was chosen based on the quality of the building system, management techniques, finance methods, progressive thinking, and the possibility of adaptation to differing site conditions.

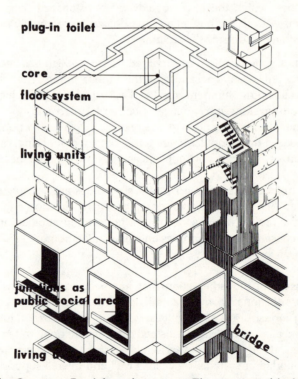

A proposal for the Operation Breakthrough program. This concept of high-rise, multifamily housing can grow in response to increasing needs and the community's desire. (Department of Housing and Urban Development)

Among the twenty-two winners selected, many of the firms, such as Levitt, Boise Cascade, and National Homes, had been previously involved with industrialized processes, and, on their own, were well along in the development of these processes. This may have been one of the pitfalls of Operation Breakthrough: money was used to pay for further development of existing systems, which did not need funding for re-search and prototype production costs. This resulted in a dearth of innovative thinking in some of the product designs.

A negative result of Operation Breakthrough was that it promised a housing market which did not exist. This reinforced the skepticism of financial lenders as to the market demand for industrialized housing.

Operation Breakthrough was founded on a philosophical premise which will some-day be unquestionable: the machine as giver of form and expediter of energies. There were, and remain, many advantages for utilizing industrialization in housing and all were the goals of Operation Breakthrough.

The objective behind Operation Breakthrough was to supersede or eliminate the problems which have continually plagued the industrialization of housing. The program attempted to prove that this type of housing could be produced in such a way as to make it acceptable in the American market, and by doing so, dissipate the other shortcomings.

Influence of Architectural Philosophies

Both far past and recent tribulations of industrialized housing stem to some degree from philosophical movements. Some basic themes behind many of the developments in industrialized housing are subjects of concern to this day. The developments result from the influences of different times, different philosophies, and priorities.

Adolf Loos has succinctly stated that "A country's culture can be assessed by the extent to which its lavatory walls are smeared." [3]

To quote Loos further,

> The evolution of culture is synonomous with the removal of ornament from utilitarian objects . . . . Weep not! See therein lies the greatness of our age, that is incapable of producing a new ornament. We have outgrown ornament, we have fought our way through to freedom from ornament. [4]

Adolf Loos joined many of his contemporaries in the philosophy that we must acknowledge certain constraints. Besides the obvious argument that simplicity is dictated by economics, many people at the turn of the century were, and remain, convinced that a new understanding of building would be generated if the frills were stripped, leaving only the necessary structure and finish. There began at this time in the development of architecture a movement toward a beauty of necessity which is, in fact, a beauty of simplicity.

Major movements in architecture have responded to the continual problems created by the constraints of lack of craftspeople and ever rising prices. Relative to the argument that ornament is crime, the Bauhaus School of Architectural Thought was established by Walter Gropius in 1918. The Bauhaus philosophy was that "form follows function." Formalism as it was known in terms of symmetry was replaced by balance, harmony, rhythm, and other equally esoteric terms. And the ornament of

3. Adolf Loos, "Ornament and Crime," in Ulrich Conrads (ed.), *Programs and Manifestoes on Twentieth Century Architecture* (Cambridge, Mass: M.I.T. Press, 1970), p. 19.
4. *Ibid.,* p. 20.

building was stripped to allow the full expression of function. Ornament then became a matter of how fenestration and the key elements of building were placed, and they, in turn, became indicative of aesthetics and quality. Details were "machined," a term which is still used to describe something which is complete and accurate. The age of the Bauhaus called for new reasons for creating the forms of architecture and housing at a time when it was thought the only road to take was economy and variety through mass production.

A result of the Bauhaus and other movements in architecture was that the supposed truisms of expression were too progressive and misunderstood by all but a few contemporaries. Because of this, many things were imitated without being understood. Gropius was not describing a style, he was describing an approach to arrive at a proper solution.

The Bauhaus movement and others did not place enough emphasis on the personal and psychological needs of the individual. Its obsession with a building's function distracted from those things which allow people to function.

Another highly significant figure of this period was Charles Jeanneret who is better known as Le Corbusier, or Corbu. According to Corbu, the house was a "machine for living." In this description, he not only shows the influence of machine but also that it should not overshadow living. Living is foremost and should be supported by machine, not hindered.

Room-sized reinforced concrete modules are the building blocks in this high-rise apartment building. (Department of Housing and Urban Development)

Interestingly enough, Corbu's approach to designing livability had little to do with the "look" of housing, but rather, the proportions of the size of forms as well as the "fit" of the units. In order to be constantly reminded of the human scale, or humanism, which Corbu believed to be sufficient enough to produce an acceptable or livable housing product, he based all physical configurations on human preferences for certain proportions, sizes, and spaces.

Corbu was one of the few masters of architecture who first addressed housing and who secondly was instrumental in the development of industrialized methods. He was one of the first to identify the open system approach to industrialized housing. Corbu's approach, however, did not address the openness (open system versus closed system) of the building parts as much as the openness of the parts of the building. His approach to high-rise housing was the development of a framework much like a wine rack in which the bottles (or housing) were placed. This approach to an open system freed the space in the structure so that the home itself could be of any design and construction. Corbu firmly believed in the industrialization of housing. To quote Corbu,

> . . . if we eliminate from our hearts and minds all dead concepts in regard to the house and look at the questions from a critical and objective point of view, we shall arrive at the "House Machine," the mass production house, healthy and beautiful in the same way that the working tools and instruments which accompany our existence are beautiful.[5]

The philosophies just discussed originated during times which demanded new approaches and new ideas. Many of the ideas remain merely ideas. Moreover, there have been many successful attempts to test the philosophies established in those times. The development of "Habitat," a demonstration housing project designed by Moshe Safdie and constructed for the Expo 67 World's Fair in Montreal, Quebec, is such an example.

5. Corbu, "Toward a New Architecture: Guiding Principles," in Ulrich Conrads (ed.), *Programs and Manifestoes on Twentieth Century Architecture* (Cambridge, Mass.: M.I.T. Press, 1970), p. 62.

Habitat designed by Moshe Safdie and constructed for the Expo 67 World's Fair in Montreal, Canada. (Department of Housing and Urban Development)

Habitat is an industrialized housing project which was to take advantage of the economies involved in the repetitive use of several building components. When used in differing arrangements, the repeated building components provide the necessary variety to establish the needed individuality in building parts or apartment units. The design of Habitat is such that it enables one, from a distance, to point and pick out "his or her apartment." A resident of Habitat feels independent while functioning as part of the group, a community sense which is essential in such densities.

Upon viewing Habitat, many realized for the first time that industrialization does not force a sterile environment; people do, with their ill placement. Habitat demonstrates that the relationship among parts is what determines the quality of the community. To demonstrate the types of considerations included in the humanizing of Habitat, consider some of the following criteria as defined by Safdie:

- Every family will require private open space for lounging and gardening.
- This outdoor space should be continuous with the living indoor space.
- The house design must allow the individual to adapt and change the dwelling unit.
- Acoustic separation between units equal to single-family house walls with a six-foot air space should be considered minimal.
- People should have visual privacy in the outdoor space and living and dining space, and should not have another dwelling unit within 100 feet with a conflicting view.
- Different meeting places at different distances from the unit for different age groups should be considered.
- Pedestrian and vehicle paths should never cross.
- Parks and shopping should be within fifteen minutes walking distance.[6]

These criteria suggest that Safdie joined the good points of single-family and multi-family living and suburban and urban living. He has included the necessary aspects of nature and land in his outside areas. The visual and acoustic privacy found in suburban living mix perfectly with urban aspects of community and involvement which result from the proximity of services. Instead of driving, people walk and interact with the community.

The Habitat example is one of a number of successful industrialized housing projects, but it is one of the better examples which illustrate all of the previous philosophies. It is a beautiful piece of environment, combining the needs of the technical and economic world with the human needs of intellect, function and spirit. Safdie's success in Habitat and other projects lies in the fact that he illustrated the machine and its resulting products as beautiful. Furthermore, he shows the unlimited possibilities in giving dignity by allowing people to take part in the affluence which they themselves help to produce.

A Glimpse of the Future

For a number of reasons, there has not been an overflow of success by the industrialized housing industry in the United States. A reason above all else is the fact that Americans thrive on tradition and cling to roots which dictate a certain attitude toward what is built and how it is built. Americans have never been forced to reconstruct our cities. They have never been forced to accept industrialized housing as necessity as has been the case in many European countries where the Second World War greatly influenced the development of industrialized housing. The war destroyed hundreds of years of development which resulted in the need for quick and quality construction.

6. Adapted from John Kettle, ed., *Moshe Safdie Beyond Habitat* (Cambridge, Mass.: M.I.T. Press, 1970), pp. 158-163.

Industrialized housing in Europe and Japan is, for the most part, high density housing constructed of concrete and steel or a combination thereof. By American standards, this form of construction is not entirely acceptable because of the monotony and sameness of it, yet it is successful. Lifestyles in Europe are open to it now, resulting from the experiences people had when it was necessary to rapidly establish a new housing environment. Success was also dependent on the fact that government owned and constructed most of the housing.

The increasing role of automation in housing is, for many, a frightening development which evokes visions of monotonous and sterile environments. Presently however, there are manufactured homes which have all the individuality and attractiveness of any conventionally built home.

Industrialized housing can do as much as conventional construction for both single and multifamily homes. Machines lend themselves to the creation of a beauty which is being ignored. It is a disservice to ourselves to produce conventional looking homes with nonconventional methods. A Machine Beauty, or Machine Aesthetic, may be the grounds for what is needed to help judge good and bad. The result would be an object viewed in a different light because in every consideration of beauty would be the understanding of the machine.

Given a willingness to accept industrialized housing as a satisfactory means to produce housing of both good structure and beauty, we can accept the assertion that predictable, constant quality is accomplished through the use of precision equipment. The equipment is capable of achieving higher tolerances and more accuracy, which in turn translates into less waste and less maintenance. The production process lends itself to more accurate timing between construction stages and considerably lessens the inventory problems of vandalism and theft at the site. Constant production also allows the economics of scale to be utilized.

We see a continuing decline in the number of workers upon whom the construction industry is dependent. Industrialization can help answer this problem because the duties of the in-factory workers are specialized to the point where skilled workers become the supervisors to many lesser skilled workers.

Industrialization also eliminates the problems which weather inevitably has on conventional construction and it eliminates the unforeseeable problems which result in conventional building. With these problems solved, the variations in production costs cease, and the manufacturer is allowed predictable product costs and predictable profits.

When properly designed, the industrialized product can offer consumers one-stop shopping. With the sophistication of modular coordination and an interchangeability of parts, the prospective home buyer can select the ideal home from a "kit of parts."

Historically, industrialized housing has had to overcome two major problems: consumer acceptance and financing problems. The former can easily be resolved through more architectural input and market analyses to determine what trade-offs people are willing to make. However, the second problem demands more sophisticated measures.

The monies invested through Operation Breakthrough sought to alleviate the factory installation, tooling up, and prototype production cost problems, yet they in no way could help the cash flow problems inherent in any system. Machine production requires the financing of great inventories of both semifinished and finished products which, during any kind of market turndown, would ruin a producer. Even with constant production and sales, buyers or their agents (the dealers) are forced to pay great sums of money prior to delivery. If dealers wish to do high volume business, they need the support of mortgage lenders who are willing to lend in stages compatible with the manufactured housing product.

Industrialization requires a sophisticated logistical organization among the factors and numbers of cost, time, materials, people, and equipment. This can only be formulated through a conceptual marriage of design production and a continual demand for the product.

The United States will continue to increase the use of industrialization at a pace which will be dictated by production and distribution capabilities, consumer preferences, labor union and building code restrictions, land prices, and overall inflation, to name a few factors. Since the United States is the largest industrialized country in the world and since it is not being largely housed by either industrialized methods or federally sponsored methods, it is allowed an option of paced progression. The United States is, however, reaching the point where industrialization and its resultant aesthetic will be the doctrine of the day. At such a point, as is often times quoted, architecture will become the physical representation of the times: a translation of the forces of the day into environment.

Definitions

As mentioned earlier, the term "industrialization" is dependent upon magnitude when used to describe housing. Many conventionally built homes utilize industrialized parts such as kitchen cabinets, prehung doors, or prefab stairs. These are all made in the factory and merely put in place on the site. When the entire structure is made in the factory, then the home is fully industrialized. Thus, it is the degree of finish which lends itself to the terms defined in this section, all of which are encompassed by the term "industrialized."

Components include roof trusses, windows, doors, cabinets, bathtubs, shower enclosures, prefinished wall and floor coverings, stairs, heating and air conditioning units, even entire bathrooms and kitchens when built in the factory and then used in the building processes. Strictly speaking, all products in housing are industrialized components. In fact, components themselves are responsible for bringing on-site construction costs down because the use of components has decreased the amount of on-site labor and has reduced waste from faulty on-site work.

Precut, prefab, or prefabricated housing is industrialized to the extent that all materials are cut to the proper length and are of the proper strength. Roof trusses, siding, roofing, kitchen cabinets, doors, stairs, flooring, and finishing materials may all be included in a prefab kit. The parts of a prefab kit are the components. Lumber yards may often have a predesigned or engineered package home which can be bought and constructed by the consumer. This prefab or package home can be made to save money and it is a rational answer to the need for reasonably priced housing.

Panelized housing is the next greater degree of industrialization above prefabs. Panelized homes are shipped as finished walls from the factory. In the case of single family homes, factory finish includes the structural members of the wall, insulation, siding, and windows or doors. After the subflooring is in place, the wall panel sections are joined together and the roof trusses placed, followed by the roof sheathing and roofing materials.

Modular housing is simply a completed structure which is made of several modules. One module may be the size of a room or the size of an entire apartment. Modules are made of wood for low-rise units, while concrete is often used for high-rise structures. Most modules have a completed exterior finish, as well as carpeting, plumbing, electric wiring, windows, doors, cabinets, appliances, and interior finishing.

Sectional housing is a modular which is comprised of two, factory-finished modules joined together on the site and fastened to a permanent foundation. Sectional homes are often one level, although there are some two-level models. The typical sectional home is the one-level ranch with gable roof. The home is divided in half at the gable ridge and each half is produced separately at the factory. When the two modules are joined together on a foundation, the house is complete.

Closed and open systems are terms which are often used when discussing components, panels, and the like. A closed system is similar to a car which uses only one brand of parts where even nuts and bolts must be specially ordered. This car is based on a closed system of parts compatible with no other. The open system implies an interchangeability of parts because it is workable along many product lines, and it also offers a compatibility of parts. The open system has the advantage of spreading progress along a broad base, thereby lending itself to endless variety of form. The open system is, in effect, made up of several common closed systems. However, it is the closed system which must first work before it can become a part of an existing open system. Keep in mind the use of the word system. This rational approach is often referred to as "systems building" which is synonomous with the term "industrialized building."

References

American Association of Housing Educators. *Proceedings of Fifth Annual Meeting.* Lincoln, Nebraska, 1970.

Conrads, Ulrich (ed.). *Programs and Manifestoes on Twentieth Century Architecture.* Cambridge, Mass.: M.I.T. Press, 1970.

Cutler, Laurence Stephan, and Sherrie Stephens, *Handbook of Housing Systems for Designers and Developers.* New York: Van Nostrand Reinhold Company, 1974.

Dahinden, Justus. *Urban Structures for the Future.* New York: Praeger Publishers, 1972.

Davis, Sam (ed.). *The Form of Housing.* New York: Van Nostrand Reinhold Company, 1977.

Kettle, John (ed.). *Moshe Safdie Beyond Habitat.* Cambridge, Mass.: M.I.T. Press, 1970.

Wilson, Forrest (ed.). *A Crack in the Rear-View Mirror.* New York: Van Nostrand Reinhold Company, 1973.

Discussion Questions

1. Define the term "industrialization" as it is used in this article.

2. What factors are considered when referring to "machine aesthetics"?

3. Discuss the basic differences in the design of art nouveau and art deco. How did these art movements influence architecture?

4. What is an underlying reason why the high-density housing developed in Japan and Europe following World War II has not been accepted in the United States?

5. Briefly describe the General Panel System and the Lustron Homes that were developed in the 1940s. Why were neither of these innovations successful?

6. A form of industrialized housing that has been successful in the United States is the mobile home. List reasons for the popularity of mobile homes.

7. How did the philosophies of Gropius, "form follows function," and LeCorbusier, "a machine for living," differ in their approach to architecture?

8. List ways in which the architect Safdie attempted to humanize industrialized housing in his apartment complex "Habitat."

9. Discuss the factors which have hindered the advancement of industrialized housing in the United States. Discuss benefits that can be anticipated with greater advances in industrialized housing.

10. Define these terms: components, prefabricated housing, panelized housing, modular housing, sectional housing, and closed and open systems.

4. Energy in Housing: Consumption and Conservation

by Carol S. Wedin

The remaining two decades of the twentieth century offer each of us an opportunity to shift energy usage in housing away from unbridled consumption to prudent conservation. We must, as individuals and as a society, come to grips with this inevitable change in our living. Residential dwellings use nearly 20% of the total energy consumed in the United States. As the cost of energy continues to rise sharply, we can expect that within the decade the utility bills of a single-family house may well equal or be higher than the mortgage payment. The Farmer's Home Administration (FmHA) reported that the greatest percentage of all families defaulting on monthly mortgage payments in 1977 did so as a direct result of rising utility costs.

The Consumption Pattern

A breakdown of the energy consumption pattern in the United States (Figure 1) shows that residential dwellings use 19.2% of total energy consumed. In actuality, housing further influences the amount of energy consumed by the other sectors of our economy. For example, residence location greatly affects energy and costs in transportation (Figure 1). Also, the type and amount of furnishings used within the residence have a direct effect on energy consumed in both the industrial and commercial sectors.

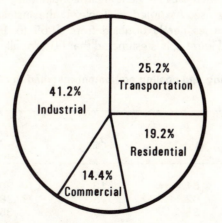

Figure 1. A breakdown of energy usage in the United States, 1973. (Source: Association of Home Appliance Manufacturers, 1973, p. 3. Quoted in Iowa State University Cooperative Extension Service FE-H-132, April, 1977.)

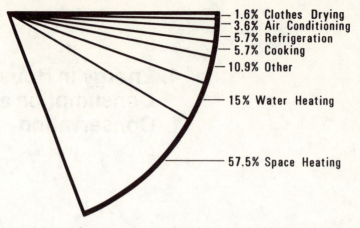

Figure 2. A breakdown of energy usage within the residential sector, United States, 1973. (Source: Association of Home Appliance Manufacturers, 1973, p. 3. Quoted in Iowa State University Cooperative Extension Service FE-H-132, April, 1977.)

By far the greatest energy usage in the residential sector is for space heating (Figure 2). Nearly 60% of all energy used in a typical house is for the heating (57.5%) and cooling (3.6%) of the interior space. The source of energy for heating and cooling in the residential sector has changed considerably in the last fifteen years. In 1965, gas fuel was used for heating in 64% of our homes. The decline in the supply of natural gas, however, has drastically reduced this source of energy. As noted in Table 1, the percentage of new single-family houses that installed gas in 1975 dropped to 35%. The oil embargo in 1973 and the resulting high cost for fuel oil has also caused a drop in the percentage of this source of energy for residential heating (Table 1). The reduction in percentage of new single-family houses installing oil has not been as large as for natural gas.

The reduction in the supplies of natural gas and oil has forced an increase in the use of electricity as the source of space heating in new houses. It is predicted that electricity will be the major source of energy for residential space heating in the future. In addition, increases in central-air conditioning have caused further increases in electricity use. As noted in Table 1, the installation of central-air conditioning in new houses nearly doubled from 1965 to 1975. Extrapolating from data in Table 1 and Figure 2, it is estimated that 60% of all new single family houses

Table 1. Space heating and cooling equipment installed in new single-family housing (percent)

Year	Gas	Oil	Electric	Central air conditioning
1965	64	13	20	25
1970	62	8	28	34
1975*	35	9	55	48

*Extrapolated from 1974 data.

Source: J.E. Snell, P.R. Achenbach, and S.R. Petersen, "Energy Conservation in New Housing Design" in **Science** 192 (June, 1976): 1305-1311. Copyright 1976 by the American Association for the Advancement of Science.

had central-air conditioning in 1978. This would account for nearly 6% of the total energy consumption in a typical new house. [1]

The remaining 40% of energy consumed in a typical house (Figure 2) relates directly to the activities of the occupants for food preparation, personal hygiene, laundry care, lighting, and so forth. Since World II there has been a significant proliferation in types and numbers of home appliances on the market. These attractive, labor-saving appliances are generally viewed as plus factors to our standard of living. In the 1960s, these convenience appliances were in part responsible for increasing our energy usage at an annual rate of 4 to 6%. Because energy was plentiful and inexpensive, increased energy usage was of little concern. The focus appeared to be on our standard of living which was partially measured by the Gross National Product (GNP). We lived in an era of increased production and increased consumption. Now, not only is there a need for an emphasis on designing more energy-efficient appliances, but also there is a need to focus on attitudinal changes.

As noted in Figure 2, the heating of water accounts for the second greatest energy usage (15.1%) in most homes. The conventional water heater is an example of an appliance poorly designed for energy efficiency. In most homes there are peak periods in the day when hot water (130° to 150° F) is required, yet the water is retained at a set temperature twenty four hours a day. Even when occupants are away for long periods, hot water is maintained.

In contrast to the inefficient design of our present water heaters, the old-fashioned wood-burning cookstove was functionally and efficiently designed. In our era of consumption, the cookstove has been replaced by five separate energy-consuming appliances: surface burners, oven, water heater, furnace, and humidifier. In the future, the design of appliances should emphasize multiple functions, e.g., heating — cooling system.

Life-Span Costs Versus Initial Costs

The housing market has been preoccupied with initial cost as opposed to life-span costs (initial cost plus the operational costs over the useful life of the building). This has been prompted by a number of factors. First, most purchasers are young families with expectations of rising incomes. Because energy has been relatively inexpensive, they have not anticipated that rising utility costs would be a financial burden. Second, our nation is a mobile society with the average homeowner moving every 7½ years. Life-span costs have not been a major concern for people who move frequently. In *The Builders,* Mayer discusses the difference in housing attitudes between the French and Americans. He quotes Pierre Schaefer, secretary-general of the French National Federation of Promoters-Builders as saying, "In France the home is the patrimony: it is what a man will leave to his children; it is immortal. In America, a man's home is a consumer good; he uses it like other consumer goods and buys a new one when he is tired of this one." [2] A third factor which has led to a concern for initial profit relates to the competitive nature of the home-building industry. Features incorporated into new houses are usually based on comfort considerations or on reducing the initial cost of heating and cooling equipment rather than on reducing long-term operational costs. With the exception of central-air conditioning, it is well known in the home-building industry that the features and appliances with visual appeal to the consumer

1. Personal communication. Paul W. Barcus, College of Enginering, Iowa State University, 1978.
2. Martin Mayer, *The Builders: Houses, People, Neighborhoods, Governments, Money* (New York: W.W. Norton and Company, Inc., 1978), p. 5.

increase house sales. "The way a house looks when a buyer walks in is usually what sells it," says Ann Brehm, a real estate broker in Scarsdale, New York. "Most people go by the surface."[3]

An Emerging Public Awareness for Conservation

In 1974 and 1975 there was a decline in total energy consumption as a result of the Organization of Petroleum Exporting Countries' (OPEC) price increase, appeals for conservation, and the recession. The public initially reacted to the energy shortage with a zeal towards conservation. A return to increased consumption during 1977 and 1978, however, indicates a period of complacency about energy. Many believe that there really is no energy problem, or, if there is, they rest their hopes in solving the problem through tighter industry regulations and through more research and development.

Public awareness of energy extravagances in housing should be sustained. The educational process requires time, and thus there is an urgent need for information on conservation now so that the effects may benefit us all before severe problems develop. Therefore, education must be an essential component of our nation's conservation policy. Energy policies that emphasize increased supply underplay the importance of conservation.

It has been demonstrated that energy consumption in almost any building can be reduced at least 20% if more careful operational practices are employed and a consciousness of energy conservation is maintained. In housing, the occupants have a direct control over the amount of energy consumed. Educating household members on techniques of energy conservation can have immediate cost benefits.

There are numerous commonsense procedures that are relatively inexpensive methods of conserving energy. These include: installing stripping around doors, applying caulking in cracks, securing tight-fitting storm doors and storm windows, and cleaning furnace filters. Many people are surprised to learn that a typical detached house will exchange the entire volume of its heated or cooled air with outside air on the average of once an hour. Even in the houses now being built with energy conservation techniques and materials, approximately half of the air is exchanged with outside air every hour. The general public has been supplied with numerous checklists and instruction manuals from utility companies, appliance manufacturers, state Cooperative Extension Services, and others on how to conserve energy in their houses. Therefore, as more efficient innovations are developed, we must be certain that the public learns of them.

We presently are adding approximately 2,000,000 housing units to our housing stock each year. For these new units, energy-conserving technology is available in production and use. A major concern, however, is the retrofitting of the 70,000,000 existing units.

In some situations, existing housing can be retrofitted to conserve energy usage. In many cases, however, the initial dollar outlay prohibits action on the part of the owner. The cost is too great for many consumers to make the necessary improvements. Tax incentives and subsidized loans will help to motivate people to make energy-conserving home improvements. In addition, there are many older homes where it is impractical to retrofit with enough insulation to meet optimal insulation levels. Cost-benefit factors must be considered. This obviously leads to concern for rapidly accelerating obsolescence in significant numbers of existing housing units. Additional

3. William B. Mead, "Home Improvements for Love or Money," *Money Magazine* (January, 1973).

research and information is needed to assist the consumer in making decisions regarding long-term benefits from retrofitting.

It is estimated that with our existing technology and knowledge, potential savings in energy usage in the range of 50 to 80% could be effected in new housing. The constraints in implementing available technology are economic, political, and attitudinal.

Examples of these complex and overlapping constraints are the macroeconomics, governmental regulations, and consumer acceptance in the interacting composite of residential-structure types and land-use patterns. The general public should be informed about the importance placed on buildings and land use in long-range solutions because ultimately the approaches adopted will be based on political more than technical decisions. Devices used at the local level that directly influence residential dwellings are subdivision controls and zoning regulations. At the regional and national levels, other regulatory measures indirectly influence housing. National, regional, and local land-use patterns are prime determinants of energy demand.

Consumption Influenced by Structural Types

There are great differences in energy consumption based on the four basic structural types: single-family, detached houses; single-family, attached houses (townhouses); mobile homes; and mid- and high-rise apartments. With the exception of the mobile home, the greatest amount of energy is used in single-family, detached houses. The most energy efficient design has a minimum outside area exposed. Therefore, the townhouse design, where two walls are shared with the attached dwellings, is an energy-conserving design. The heating and cooling expenditures are approximately halved with a two-story, inside townhouse as compared to a single-family, detached unit with the same floor area. Further reductions are found in mid- and high-rise residential complexes where there are less exterior areas. In spite of the concern for energy conservation, the single-family detached house design is the overwhelming preference. The Federal Energy Administration (FEA) estimates that in 1990, 70% of all new housing will still be single-family detached units or mobile homes, 25% will be low-density and low-rise units, and only 5% will be high-rise apartments.

In 1977, mobile homes comprised around 12% of all new residential units. Most mobile homes use aluminum which requires considerable energy to produce. Also, the life-span energy consumption in mobile homes is high due to the design of the dwelling. The rectangular design of mobile homes is associated with greater heat loss in winter than for units with a square-floor plan. Anticipated impacts of energy conservation on new home designs are well summarized in Table 2.

The total energy conservation which can be realized in high-density cluster communities has been cited in a recent study.[4] The study predicts a 44% energy saving. The study defined a high-density cluster community as one having 40% of the housing in high-rise apartments, 30% in walk-up apartments, 20% in townhouses, and 10% in clustered, single-family houses. A high-density community has approximately 4.6 dwellings per acre in comparison to the typical, suburban-grid pattern which includes about 2.2 dwellings per acre. Thus, the clustering of living patterns can be helpful in reducing energy consumption in housing.

Energy Alternatives and Housing Technology

Emphasis on alternative sources of energy which can be used in housing is currently receiving much attention. One of the technological constraints for most of the energy-

4. *Ibid.*

Table 2. Anticipated impacts of energy conservation on new housing design

Housing type

Smaller, higher density, fewer detached houses
Increased shift to townhouse and low-rise from single-family detached
Diminished relative attractiveness of mobile homes in life-cycle cost terms
Improved designs with lower unit demands will help keep fossil fuel economically competitive in many areas for years to come

Architectural features

Thicker wall (cavity and sandwich) and roof construction for more insulation
Fewer picture windows, more double- and triple-glazed windows, some specially coated glass
More functional windows — designed as passive solar collectors
Tighter, better sealed joints, higher performance sealants, better workmanship
Better control of moisture to protect insulation
Attention to shape, orientation, landscaping in design
Control of air movement between floors — fewer open stairwells and split-level designs
Insulated foundation walls in cold climates
Greater thermal resistance for more expensive fuels, such as electric heating
Better thermal comfort and greater acoustical privacy

Mechanical systems

Smaller, more efficient HVAC* equipment, better load matching
Customized ventilation to provide outdoor air when and where needed
Widespread use of heat pumps in moderate climates — integrated heat pump and solar heating
Solar space heating in selected climates where gas and oil are in short supply
More zoning and multipoint control systems in larger residences
Electrical load management control options for hot water and appliances
Solar water heating in the south

Institutional

Life-cycle cost-based performance standards (voluntary or mandatory) for new housing design
Labeling of houses, equipment, and appliances for energy use, cost, and performance
Householders knowledgeable of how to operate homes efficiently

*High voltage alternating current
Source: J.E. Snell, P.R. Achenbach, and S. R. Petersen, "Energy Conservation in New Housing Design" in *Science* 192: 1305-1311, 1976.

producing alternatives is that of storage. Whether the energy source is geothermal, solar, nuclear or other, there is the basic problem of storing the energy until needed.

Solar energy can constitute a significant savings in some regions. Figure 3 illustrates regions in the United States according to the year-round pattern of sun conditions. Obviously, this basic factor has been associated with an interregional shift of population to the West and South since the mid-1950s. The predicted, continuing migration of population to the sunbelt region will have a direct influence on energy consumption for heating. We can anticipate, however, a growing desire for air conditioning in the sunbelt region. Alternative systems to central-air conditioning could use less energy. Greater importance must be given to orientation, landscaping, and design of dwellings, as well as to improved technology and materials that maintain comfort levels within the interiors.

Energy based on solar alternatives may be economical in some sections of the country, while other sources may serve better elsewhere. At the present time, solar energy processes for heating and cooling are costly because of high initial investments.

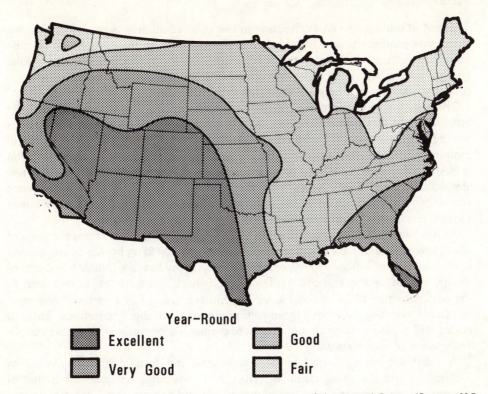

Year-Round

☒ Excellent ☒ Good

☒ Very Good ☐ Fair

Figure 3. Year-round sun conditions in contiguous states of the United States. (Source: U.S. Weather Bureau.)

A solar electric experimental house located at Iowa State University. The solar collector panels are placed vertically on the south wall. Proper placement and selection of trees near the dwelling reduce heat gain in the summer and provide valuable heat gain in the winter. (Photo: Iowa State University Photo Service)

The cost of retrofitting existing housing to use solar equipment is usually prohibitive. With mass production and improved technology, however, the cost should become more competitive. A change in tax policy would also induce increased usage of solar energy systems. Currently, solar energy systems are accompanied by an increase in property valuation, and thus real estate taxes, in most states.

The great variation in climatic condition is a major reason why energy standards for building codes, government regulations, and other legislated or imposed restrictions are difficult to design. The Minimum Property Standards of the Department of Housing and Urban Development (HUD) and the Federal Housing Administration (FHA) were revised in 1976 to provide for greater conservation of energy. The new standards divided the country into four climatic regions to allow for varying construction methods. Even within these separate regions there are still variations in climatic conditions that impose constraints on government regulations.

As has been previously mentioned in this article, the constraints facing the issue of alternative source use are many faceted. For example, building houses below ground level (exterior not exposed to extremes in weather) could save significant amounts of energy in both heating and cooling. Designers have coined the term "terratecture" to define architecture below ground level. Experiments using this approach have been attempted, but they have been faced with numerous obstacles. For instance, building codes and zoning restrictions require specific amounts of window area and specific materials to be used in housing.

A constraint more elusive to deal with than the furthering development of technology and the modification of policy and government regulations is that of acceptance and attitudinal changes of individuals and society. There are many cases where low-cost, energy-conserving housing have been developed but not accepted because it does not fulfill the public's expectations of what a "house should look like." In Article 14 of this book, Dr. Paul Lemkau emphasizes in "Housing and Health," the urgent need for additional research on the effects of housing on people. For example, how would it affect the mental health of people to live underground?

As energy becomes in short supply and very costly, simplistic solutions of themselves will not solve the problem. A popular trend in the United States is for an individualistic approach to create self-sustaining or low-energy consumption environments, such as constructing a wood-burning, heated-log cabin or a small, methane-gas habitat where the animal waste is converted to energy. These approaches may serve to create public awareness and fulfill a psychological need for some individuals, which can both be meaningful endeavors. It should be cautioned, however, that long-range solutions will require the combined efforts of individuals, industry, and governments.

References

Duffie, John A., and William A. Beckman. "Solar Heating and Cooling." *Science* 191 (1976): 143-149.

"Energy Research House." Iowa State University Research Foundation Publication, 12 pp., 1978.

Hogan, M. Janice. "Changing Our Energy Behavior." *Journal of Home Economics* 70 (1978): 18-21.

Keplinger, Duane E. "HUD Standards and National Fuel Conservation Program." *HUD Challenge VII* (1976): 14-15.

Mayer, Martin. *The Builders: Houses, People, Neighborhoods, Government, Money.* New York: W. W. Norton and Company, Inc., 1978.

Mead, William B. "Home Improvements for Love or Money." *Money Magazine* (January, 1973).

Russ, Nancy M., and Molly Longstreth. "Strategies for Energy Conservation." *Journal of Home Economics* 70 (1978): 40-43.

Snell, J.E., P.R. Achenbach, and S.R. Petersen. "Energy Conservation in New Housing Design." *Science* 192 (1976): 1305-1311.

"Solar Energy: Unsung Potential for Wind and Biomass." *Science* 200 (1978): 636.

"Tips for the Home." Iowa State University Cooperative Extension Service Pm 805, 4 pp., 1977.

Turner, Robert C."Complacency: The Real Problem of the Energy Crisis." *The MGIC Newsletter.* Mortgage Guaranty Insurance Corporation: 4 pp., April, 1977.

Discussion Questions

1. How much of the total energy consumed in the United States is for residential dwellings? How does housing further influence the amount of energy consumed in other sectors of our economy?

2. For space heating, what sources of energy are being used less today than ten years ago? Explain why this has occurred.

3. Explain why the housing market in the past has been influenced more by initial cost than by life-span costs.

4. What is meant by the phrase "retrofitting existing housing"? Give examples of how this is done. Give an example of when retrofitting may be impractical.

5. Discuss the constraints in implementing advanced technology in new housing.

6. Of the various structural types of housing, what form is considered to be the most inefficient and what form the most efficient user of energy?

7. Discuss reasons why there cannot be simplistic solutions to energy regulations in housing.

5. Land for Housing

by Raleigh Barlowe

Land and housing are intricately interrelated. Housing represents one of the most important and most essential of the many alternative uses of land. Land in turn is needed to provide spatial orientation and support for housing. Except for those few people who live on boats, human beings normally reside in dwellings attached to land. This attachment makes residential structures a legal part of the concepts of real estate and land resources. In an economic sense, it also ties the supply and demand for housing to the fixed physical location of land.

As emphasis is focused on the interrelationship between land and housing and most particularly on the availability of land for housing, it is logical that consideration be given to several questions. Important among these are the issues of (1) how much demand is there for housing sites, (2) can adequate areas be supplied for this purpose, (3) what is happening to housing land costs, (4) what types of problems are associated with the development of land areas for housing, and (5) what types of public programs can be used to alleviate these problems. These issues are discussed in this article.

Demand for Housing

Attempts to quantify the market demand for housing usually involve a two-step process. Past and present market demand can be expressed in terms of the number of residential units people have been and are willing and able to buy. Future demand is described in terms of estimated housing requirements. These requirements normally involve the number of housing units which analysts feel a population should have if certain assumed standards of adequacy are to be met. The experience of the past three decades shows that the American public has seldom demonstrated the needed willingness or ability to buy or rent all of the housing that many earlier estimates of adequate housing requirements have suggested they should have. Even with this weakness, however, data on expected housing requirements, such as that presented in Table 1, provide the best guide we have for predicting our emerging housing needs.

Table 1 shows that the nation had 24.55 million residential units, 24.4 million of them occupied, in 1920 when the total population was 106.0 million and there were 24.4 million households. By 1970 the number of residential units had increased to 68.6 million, 63.4 million of them occupied, while total population and household numbers had increased to 203.2 and 63.4 million, respectively. As these figures show, the number of occupied residential units is closely related to household numbers.

Raleigh Barlowe is Professor of Resource Development, Michigan State University. This article was prepared specially for this book.

Table 1. Trends in total population, household numbers, residential construction, and average annual housing demand for the United States, 1920-1970, with projections to 2000

Year	Population numbers	Number of households	Number of residential units	Number of occupied units	Decade	Average annual demand for new housing units	New Additions to stock of housing	Replacements of conventional and mobile home units
1920	106.0 mil	24.4	24,552	24,352	1920-30	803.4	795.6	7.8
1930	123.2	29.9	32,495	29,905	1930-40	365.1	473.3	-108.2
1940	132.2	34.9	37,325	34,855	1940-50	809.0	881.2	-72.2
1950	151.3	43.5	46,137	42,969	1950-60	1,522.4	1,255.0	267.4
1960	179.3	52.8	58,468	52,955	1960-70	1,648.7	1,057.4	591.3
1970	203.2	63.4	68,627	63,417	1970-80	2,460.0	1,820.0	640.0
1980	222.2	79.4	83,000	73,000	1980-90	2,560.0	1,620.0	940.0
1990	243.5	94.3	96,900	84,300	1990-2000	2,360.0	1,270.0	1,090.0
2000	260.4		115,600	99,400				

Sources: Population and household numbers, 1920-1970, from *U.S. Census*; projections for 1980-2000 from Series II projections reported in U.S. Bureau of the Census Current Population Reports, Series P-25, No. 607 (1975) and No. 704 (1977). Number of residential units and occupied units, 1920-1970, from *U.S. Census of Housing*; projections for 1980-2000 from Hans H. Landsberg, Leonard L. Fischman, and Joseph L. Fisher, *Resources in America's Future* (Johns Hopkins Press, 1963), p. 621. Data on average annual demand for housing and additions to the nation's housing stock from U.S. Forest Service, *RPA: The Nation's Renewable Resources — An Assessment*, 1975, p. 214.

These numbers increased at a considerably faster rate than total population in the half century between 1920 and 1970 as the size of the average household dropped from 4.3 to 2.9 persons.

Household numbers are primarily dependent upon the number of families — married couples, couples with children, or single parents with children — found in a society. They also are affected by levels of income. When incomes are low because of reduced wages or unemployment, families frequently double up; combinations of two or more separate families or families and unattached individuals live together. This situation results in reduced market demand for residential units and can lead to both high residential densities and undesirable living conditions.

Rising real incomes have done much to revolutionize the market demand for housing in the United States since World War II. Calculated in constant 1972 dollar terms, average disposable incomes per capita rose from $1,887 in 1929 and $1,351 in 1933 to $2,386 in 1950, $2,700 in 1960, $3,620 in 1970, and $4,007 in 1975. Numerous competing demands have emerged to claim segments of these higher incomes. In regard to housing, these higher incomes have played a major role in favoring the formation of new households, the undoubling of families, and in making it feasible for unattached individuals to secure and maintain houses or apartments of their own. Higher household incomes have caused many families to seek larger or better housing facilities. They have provided a strong stimulus for suburbanization. They also explain the fact that thousands of families now own vacation or second homes in addition to their primary housing units.

Several million new housing units must be provided during the next two decades for the millions of young people born between 1955 and 1970 who will soon be forming family and household units of their own. The U.S. Forest Service estimated in its Resources Program Assessment (RPA) for 1975 that an average of 2.46 million new housing units would be needed each year during the 1970s and 2.56 million each year during the 1980s to meet these emerging needs.[1] Of these projected new units, 1.82 million annually during the 1970s and 1.62 million annually during the 1980s will be net additions to the total housing stock. The balance will be needed to replace existing conventional or mobile home housing.

Questions can logically be raised as to whether builders will supply these projected numbers of new housing units and whether there will be sufficient market demand to absorb this volume of new construction. The data on new housing construction during the 1968-77 decade summarized in Table 2 show that construction exceeded the 2 million mark in only four years (1971, 1972, 1973, and 1977). An average of 2.09 million units annually were built during the ten-year period, far less than the 2.46 million annually that are assumed to be needed during the 1970s. Moreover, it is widely recognized that there was considerable excess production during the 1971-73 construction boom. Many houses, apartments, and condominiums constructed during this period remained unsold or unoccupied for a considerable time.

Market demand obviously calls for more than the physical existence of families needing housing. Family and household incomes are important, but the significance of the purchasing power of prospective buyers and tenants must always be considered in light of the cost of the housing product and the cost of other products and services that compete for portions of the consumer's dollar. The failure of people to buy or rent the volume of housing that analysts feel they need cannot always be taken as an indication that additional housing is unwanted. Often it indicates that the cost of the new housing

1. U.S. Forest Service, *RPA: The Nation's Renewable Resources — An Assessment, 1975*, p. 214.

appears high, that prospective consumers have other high priority competing uses for their incomes, or both.

The tendency of most families to accept former luxuries such as automobiles, college educations, vacation travel, restaurant meals, participation in club and recreational activities, television and other new modes of home entertainment, and various hobby pursuits as essential elements in their levels of living has undoubtedly reduced the portions of family incomes that go for housing. Willingness to buy or rent is affected in many instances by the extent to which housing prices have either increased or decreased relative to consumer incomes.

Table 2. Residential construction in the United States, 1968-77

Year	Total units	New units started Single-family	Multiple-family	New mobile units shipped
		(000 omitted)		
1968	1,864	900	646	318.0
1969	1,913	811	689	412.7
1970	1,870	815	654	401.2
1971	2,580	1,152	931	496.6
1972	2,955	1,311	1,068	575.9
1973	2,625	1,133	925	566.9
1974	1,682	889	464	329.2
1975	1,384	896	275	212.5
1976	1,797	1,167	380	249.6
1977	2,263	1,452	534	276.8
Total	20,933	10,526	6,566	3,839.4

Sources: Data for 1968-1976 from U.S. Department of Housing and Urban Development, *1976 HUD Statistical Yearbook,* pp. 278 and 283. Data for 1977 from HUD, *Housing and Urban Development Trends,* December 1977.

American workers have benefited from the increasing ability to purchase housing throughout most of the last four decades. This is highlighted by the comparison of trends in residential construction costs and the average weekly wages of production workers in manufacturing employment which are reported in Table 3. This comparison shows that purchase of a house with a value of $6,000 in 1940 would have required 240.4 weeks of gross wages for the average worker in 1940, 219.0 weeks in 1950, 184.8 weeks in 1960, and a low of 170.4 weeks in 1965. Housing construction costs rose at a more rapid rate than manufacturing wages after the mid-1960s with the result that it would have taken the gross wages of 193.4 weeks to buy the house in 1977.

Another view of the relationship between rising housing prices and consumer incomes is presented in Table 4. The median sales prices for new single-family homes reported by the Department of Housing and Urban Development rose by 170% from $18,000 in 1963 to $48,600 in 1977. With the consumers price index almost doubling from 91.7 to 181.5 (1967 = 100) during this period, median sales prices increased 36.4% when calculated in 1967 constant dollars. Meanwhile, average family incomes and average weekly wages also increased. When the median income reported for male heads of families is compared with average new house prices, it may be noted that it took 2.7 years of median family-head income to buy the median new house in

Table 3. Comparison of trends in residential construction costs and average wages of production workers in manufacturing to indicate relative cost of new housing in terms of weeks of wages needed to pay for new units, United States, 1940-1977

Year	Boeckh index of residential construction costs (1967 = 100)	Reproduction cost of a $6,000 house built in 1940	Average gross wages of production workers in manufacturing	Weeks of average wages to buy house
1940	29.6	$ 6,000	$ 24.96	240.4
1950	63.0	12,770	58.32	219.0
1955	72.5	14,696	75.70	194.1
1960	81.8	16,581	89.72	184.8
1965	90.4	18,324	107.53	170.4
1970	122.4	24,810	133.73	185.5
1975	183.5	27,195	189.50	196.3
1976	198.6	40,256	207.60	193.9
1977	216.5	43,885	226.89	193.4

Sources: Data on Boeckh indices of residential construction costs and average weekly earnings of production workers in manufacturing for 1940-1977 from U.S. Department of Commerce, *Historical Statistics of the United States Colonial Times to 1970*, N-121 and D-804; 1975 and 1976 from U.S. Department of Commerce, *Statistical Abstract of the United States 1977*, pp. 773 and 412; 1977 from U.S. Department of Commerce, *Survey of Current Business*, vol. 58, no. 4, April 1978.

every year from 1963 through 1968. Higher family incomes lowered this ratio to a 2.2 level in 1970, but rising housing costs have since caused it to rise to a 2.75 level.

Average income data cloak the fact that some families have benefited from the high inflation rate of the 1970s while others have lost ground. Table 4 shows that even with rising wage levels, average production workers in manufacturing have found themselves in a worsening position in recent years. In 1970, they could have purchased the median new house for 175 weeks of average gross wages. By 1975 and 1977, 205.8 and 214.2 weeks of gross wages were needed for this purpose.

Additional evidence concerning the adverse impact of rapidly rising housing costs on some segments of the public is provided by the U.S. Department of Commerce's report on distribution of families by money income. [2] Analysis of these data suggests that around 55% of the nation's families could have bought the median new house for 2.5 (or less) times their money income in 1970 while only 39% could have done so in 1976. [3]

Numerous families have been priced out of the housing market by the rapidly increasing prices of recent years. The earlier trend which permitted consumers to buy more and better housing for less real income has been reversed for much of the population. One cannot say for certain whether this trend will continue or will again be reversed. Overall, however, factors such as the expected increase in household numbers and general expectations of continued inflation — a factor that can justify larger commitments of current buyer incomes for housing — can be expected to lead to a continuing strong demand for new residential construction. This new housing will be

2. U.S. Department of Commerce, *Statistical Abstract of the United States, 1977*, p. 440.

3. Two-and-one-half times the family's annual income has been accepted for many years as a general rule-of-thumb measure of the maximum amount an average family should be willing to pay in buying a house.

Table 4. Trends in the median sales prices and constant dollar cost of new single-family houses from 1963 through 1977 with comparisons showing the relationships of these price trends to median incomes for male heads of families and average worker incomes in manufacturing

Year	Median sales price for new single-family houses	Price of new homes in constant 1967 dollars	Median incomes of male heads of families	Ratios of housing prices to incomes	Average weekly earnings of production workers in manufacturing	Weeks of gross average wages to buy median house
1963	$18,000	$19,629	$ 6,561	2.74	$ 99.63	180.6
1964	18,900	20,344	6,883	2.75	102.97	183.5
1965	20,000	21,164	7,310	2.73	107.53	186.0
1966	21,400	22,016	7,910	2.71	112.34	190.5
1967	22,700	22,700	8,358	2.72	114.90	197.6
1968	24,700	23,704	9,096	2.72	122.51	201.6
1969	25,600	23,315	9,965	2.57	129.51	197.7
1970	23,400	20,120	10,480	2.23	133.73	175.0
1971	25,200	20,775	10,930	2.31	142.40	177.5
1972	27,600	22,027	11,859	2.33	154.70	178.4
1973	32,500	24,417	12,965	2.51	165.70	196.1
1974	35,900	24,306	13,863	2.59	176.40	203.5
1975	39,300	24,380	14,816	2.65	189.50	205.8
1976	44,200	25,924	16,095	2.75	207.60	212.9
1977	48,600	26,777			226.89	214.2

Sources: Median sales prices for new single-family houses from U.S. Department of Housing and Urban Development, *1976 HUD Statistical Yearbook and Housing and Urban Development Trends,* December 1977. Median incomes of male heads of families and average weekly earnings of production workers in manufacturing for 1963-1970 from U.S. Department of Commerce, *Historical Statistics of the United States Colonial Times to 1970,* G-180 and D-804; 1971-1976 from *Statistical Abstract of the United States,* 1977, pp. 443 and 412; and 1977 data on average weekly earnings of production workers from *Survey of Current Business,* vol. 58, no. 4, April 1978.

needed both to provide additions to the nation's housing stock and to provide replacements for deteriorating and outmoded existing stock.

Supplies of Land for Housing

Numerous complexities affect the availability of land for housing. Society places a high priority on housing as a land use, and one can logically argue that plenty of land is or should be available for this use. Yet the fact that most people prefer to live close to their places of employment provides a powerful location constraint on housing site choices. Housing land supply decisions are further complicated by the growing distaste many urban workers have for living at sites within the inner core of cities. Most of the demand for urban and suburban housing comes in a doughnut-shaped band around urban centers and prompts the observation that we have a dearth of highly desirable housing sites in the midst of a potentially plentiful supply of land.

Altogether, the United States has a total land area of 2,264,000 acres. Of this total, 1,317, 000 acres, or 58.2%, were in private ownership in 1974 while 1,088,000 acres (48.1%) were included in farms. Urban areas accounted for only 34.7 million acres or

1.54% of the total land area.   Residential units and their surrounding yards and grounds take up only 40 to 50% of the area of the typical city.[4] The total area nationwide that is used for housing purposes can accordingly be estimated as around 15,000,000 acres.

There is little doubt that large additional areas can be shifted into residential subdivisions if lands are needed for this purpose. Provision of new areas for housing is usually accepted as socially desirable. But problems arise when questions are raised concerning which lands should be developed for residential and other urban-oriented uses. Should choice of the sites to be developed be left to speculators and developers or should they be designated in advance on area land use plans? Should they be located, as most new housing developments now are, around existing cities and along roads and streets that provide ready access to these cities? Or should they be channeled into new towns or into special residential development areas where the land may provide excellent sites for housing but is not needed for other socially valued uses?

Figure 1 illustrates several present-day problems associated with the provision of new housing developments. Prior to the development of the automobile and the associated attention that has been given to building all-weather roads, the spatial expansion of cities was hampered by distance constraints. Large numbers of workers walked to their places of employment. High residential densities were accepted in preference to the long walks associated with housing locations at the city's edge. Urban growth entailed the incremental adding of a few blocks around the city's perimeter.

4. Raleigh Barlowe, *Land Resource Economics* (Englewood Cliffs, N.J.: Prentice-Hall, Inc., 3rd ed., 1978), p. 46.

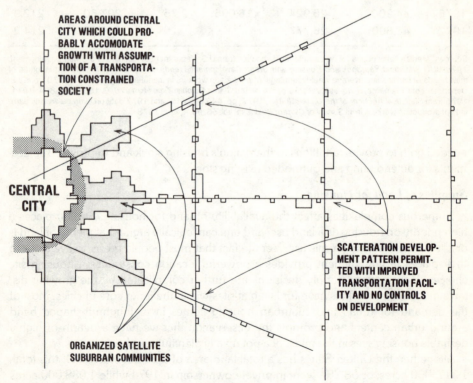

Figure 1. Spatial Expansion of cities.

With the advent of improved transportation facilities, and most particularly with wide-scale ownership of the family car and the opportunities it offers for maximum personal mobility, urban areas experienced a completely new set of expansion pressures. Workers could live in the suburbs or even far out in the country and commute to work easier and faster than their parents had walked much shorter distances to work. Downtown business districts that had once thrived because of their location at the business and transportation hubs of cities found themselves by-passed and boycotted by drivers who avoided heavy traffic and shortages of parking areas. Businesses and industries started to move out to shopping malls and industrial parks that offered more and less expensive space and that were near suburban residents who provided markets and supplies of potential workers.

Little by little, most downtown areas lost much of their earlier attractiveness. Office buildings and buses might remain filled during the day, but the once-vibrant downtown shopping and nighttime entertainment districts became deserted, fearsome canyons after dark. Crime and fear of crime became a persistent threat. Upper- and lower-middle-class residents joined in the flight to suburbia, and the older residential developments they left behind became homes for the poor and disadvantaged. Wide expanses of once intensively used properties experienced blight and decay, and many properties were simply abandoned by their owners, later to be torn down at public expense as hazardous to public health and safety.

Increased individual and family mobility and the outward flow of urban residents to the newer, more spacious, and supposedly safer suburbs and to sites in the open country also have serious impacts on land use in the areas surrounding cities. Whether privately owned land is used for housing, farming, forestry or some other use is usually determined by its relative ability to provide a net economic return to land (land rent) which can be capitalized into property value.[5] The use that can produce the most land rent under given circumstances is the highest and best commercial use of the site. With the suburbanization trend, housing ordinarily represents a higher and better commercial use of the land around cities than farming or forestry. As a result, land developers seldom encounter difficulties in offering prices that will induce the shifting of land from open space uses to housing. This is not bad when the land is really needed for housing. But the combination of speculator activity in acquiring often widely scattered tracts for expected future developments and rural owners' awareness of the ripening of their lands for urban-oriented uses have had an overall adverse impact on rural land uses within the lengthening shadows of growing cities.

Part of this adverse impact stems from the fact that we as yet have little public planning and few procedures for guiding the shifting and development of rural lands for urban uses. Developers, speculators, and purchasers of individual home sites have been free to select those areas that most attract them. Developers have obvious reasons for seeking sites that are easy to develop, readily accessible to markets and places of employment, and that are already supplied with utilities and public services. It is not accidental that these requirements frequently match the characteristics of prime agricultural areas. Farmers were initially attracted to these areas because of their production potential. Highways and other transportation facilities were provided because

---

5. Land rent can involve actual monetary income, as when products are produced and sold, or the imputed returns associated with owner satisfactions. The commercial or marketplace concept of highest and best use can be contrasted with a parallel concept of social highest and best use which emphasizes the social benefits associated with different land uses. Land use practices around our cities provide an excellent example of the frequent divergence of these two standards for evaluating land use situations. For more detailed discussions of the concepts of highest and best use and land rent, cf. *ibid.*, chapters 1 and 6.

these were populated areas with products to sell. Schools, electric power, telephone, and other public utilities were supplied because the local residents needed and could afford them.

Residential developments could be located in many instances on rougher and less fertile rural lands at a lower long-run cost to society. These areas can often provide picturesque and aesthetically attractive sites for housing. But developers have a strong economic incentive in using lands that are level, cleared of forest growth, and drained. They know that buyers want utilities and public services, and they usually find it less expensive to choose locations along established roads than to provide the roads and improvements that would be needed if they were to open up less accessible areas of lower agricultural potential.

While many developers and buyers deliberately select locations near the central cities, many others buy rural acreage in open country areas far beyond the current tide of land development (Figure 1). With these purchases and the developments that follow, they open up large areas for scattered types of suburban development. Their actions alert local tax assessors to the fact that large areas of rural land holdings have potentials for higher and better use-values for urban-oriented uses even though only small portions of these areas may have immediate markets for these uses. Insofar as these purchases result in new housing, they also bring new people into once rural communities and thus create increasing demand for schools, water and sewer service, added police protection, and a host of other urban-type services that the rural residents normally do without.

Suburbanization and scatteration also have their impacts on the attitudes of rural landowners. Some are captivated by the expected ripening of their lands for a higher use. They visualize the capital gains they hope to realize when the expanding suburbs reach their lands. With these expectations, they stop managing their holdings as if they expected to keep them permanently in agriculture. Their management goal becomes that of securing the maximum returns possible from the land with minimum outlays for maintenance of improvements and rebuilding of productive capacity during the years they expect to operate before selling their lands. These operators may bemoan their rising taxes and the inconvenience associated with new demands for services. But in many respects they welcome the rising costs of suburbanization because of their associated opportunities for realizing substantial capital gains from the sale of lands.

Not all rural owners fit in this classification. Many are farmers or owners of forest lands who have a genuine long-run interest in retaining their land in its current use. They recognize that much larger areas are affected by scatteration than can reasonably be expected to move to urban-oriented uses. These operators are adversely affected as they see their communities blighted for continued agricultural or forestry use by the invasion of scattered developments and by the decision of numerous owners to abandon their earlier long-term, current use management programs. They are victimized by the higher assessed values which tax assessors ascribe to their lands and by the higher tax rates needed to provide new public services for a larger population. If they do not sell their lands and move to other areas, they find themselves facing taxation and environmental and other regulations that discourage rather than encourage the continued use of their land for agricultural and other open space purposes.

Questions can be raised about the amount of land needed to provide sites for new housing in the future. The acreage required will depend in large measure on the areas associated with individual housing units. More people can obviously be housed on an acre used for a multi-storied apartment house than on lots used for single-family housing. Future additions to the nation's housing stock will probably include all of the types of housing reported in Table 2. Estimates based on single-family housing can be used, however, to provide a general measure of the new land supplies that may be needed.

The Forest Service's RPA estimates (see Table 1) indicate that annual averages of 1.8 million new housing units should be provided as additions to the nation's housing stock during the 1970s and 1.6 million annually during the 1980s. If all of these units are to involve single-family housing and if they are built on lots that average around 80 feet by 136 feet (four lots per acre), the nation will need 450,000 new acres each year for housing purposes during the balance of the 1970s and 400,000 acres each year during the 1980s. With lots that average around 100 feet by 145 feet or 90 feet by 161 feet (three lots per acre), the annual need for new residential building sites will rise to 600,000 and 533,333 acres, respectively. Insofar as the nation's housing needs are met with condominiums, multifamily apartments, duplexes, and mobile homes, considerably smaller areas may suffice. Supplemental areas will be needed, of course, to provide sites for shopping centers, industries, streets, parks and other residence-associated uses. Overall, however, the nation's need during the next several years for new urban lands to support residential and residential-associated uses should not greatly exceed the average of around 520,000 acres a year that shifted to the urban use classification between 1959 and 1974.[6] Additional areas of up to half this total acreage may be needed to provide sites for nonurban housing developments.

Sufficient land can be made available to supply the nation's housing site needs for many years to come. Indeed, one could argue that more than enough land has probably already been acquired by developers and speculators to provide all of the residential sites the nation will need during this century. Whether or not these are the right lands for development is another matter. Some of the areas that owners would like to develop for housing may fail to ripen to this use for the simple reason that the anticipated demand may not materialize. Many other holdings involve areas that should be retained in their current open space uses for social-priority reasons while settlement is directed elsewhere.

Most Americans seem to have a love for the single-family house located in the midst of a lot that allows space for a lawn, plantings, and play areas. This attitude is deeply rooted in our cultural attitudes about housing. It must be recognized, however, that this attitude supports a luxurious and often inefficient use of land. Cities such as Singapore have demonstrated that dense, urban populations can be housed in multi-storied apartments in a park-like environment. Architects and designers have demonstrated the possibilities for using clustering techniques to minimize wasteful and inefficient uses of space, to reduce the cost of securing access to utilities, and yet to provide every housing unit with improved views and access to an open space environment. Clustering also offers challenging opportunities for savings of heat now lost through outside walls and for better utilization of the by-product heat now generated with numerous industrial operations.

Another important issue centers in the choice of methods by which supplies of land for housing should be allocated among potential users. For generations, we have

6. The total urban land area for the United States is reported as 27.2 million acres in 1959 and 34.9 million acres in 1974. (Cf. Hugh Wooten, Karl Gertel, and William Pendleton, *Major Uses of Land and Water in the United States: Summary for 1959,* U.S. Department of Agriculture, Agricultural Economics Report 13, 1962, p. 10; and H. Thomas Frey, *Major Uses of Land in the United States: Preliminary Estimates for 1974,* U.S. Department of Agriculture, Economic Research Service NRE Working Paper No. 34, p. 11.) The 7.7 million acres that shifted to urban uses during this fifteen-year period encompasses much, and probably most, of the new lands used for housing developments. It should be recognized, however, that substantial areas not classified as urban have been and are being developed for residential purposes.

assumed that land areas offered for sale should be allocated through normal market processes. The first buyer to offer the seller's price receives the land; or on some occasions, buyers might bid up the price and the land goes to the highest bidder. Some have argued that this system is inherently unfair because it favors those with economic means. But what alternative systems for allocating supplies of land would be any better? Should all consumers have equal rights and the allocation of housing sites be determined by the casting of lots? Should the allocation be handled by public agencies that by accident or design may favor some groups as compared with others? Should point formulas be used that base allocation on predetermined factors such as age, income, size of family, or place of employment? Solutions of this nature can simplify the problem some people have in acquiring housing while they should greatly complicate the housing problems faced by others.

Cost of Land for Housing

One of the most critical issues in current housing policy centers is the high cost of residential sites. Some argue that the prices being asked for building lots are exorbitant and that ways should be found to bring them down. Others counter this view with the assertion that land prices are low now compared with what they will be in the future and that the prudent investor should buy land now because "the good Lord doesn't make it any more."

Unlike the situation with farm real estate market prices and with building construction costs, no federal agency reports statistics on the sales prices for residential building sites. The best data available on housing land cost trends come from the occasional observations and reports of builders and from the data the Federal Housing Administration (FHA) reports on the appraised value of the building sites covered by its insured-loans on new and existing single-family houses.

Builders' associations and writers on home-buying problems occasionally report data on residential land costs. These figures in recent years have almost always indicated that land acquisition costs are rising and that they are often 10 or 15% above the costs of the previous year. Formal confirmation of these trends is supplied by the appraised values the Federal Housing Administration has reported since 1950 for the residential properties on which it has approved FHA-insured mortgage loans. As Table 5 indicates, the average appraised values of the building lots for new single-family

Table 5. Average appraised values of residential lots covered by new FHA-insured mortgages, 1950-1976

Year	New houses	Existing houses
1950	$1,035	$1,150
1955	1,626	1,707
1960	2,470	2,356
1965	3,427	3,219
1970	4,952	3,973
1973	5,341	3,982
1974	5,482	4,519
1975	6,382	5,468
1976	6,954	5,632

Source: U.S. Department of Housing and Urban Renewal, *1976 HUD Statistical Yearbook,* p. 110.

houses increased from $1,035 in 1950 to $2,470 in 1960, $4,952 in 1970, and $6,954 in 1976. Meanwhile, the average appraised values of the building sites associated with existing houses increased from $1,150 in 1950 to $2,356 in 1960, $3,973 in 1970, and $5,632 in 1976.

Overall, the appraised market value of the average single-family building site increased between five and six times during the 1950-76 period. This increase for FHA-insured mortgage properties is probably typical of the price trend for all residential lots. Most of the increase represents an upward trend in the cost of each square foot or square yard of residential land. Some of the rising cost per building lot, however, resulted from a trend toward larger lots and lots with sufficient frontage to accommodate the new contemporary ranch-type houses. Some also may have resulted from the fact that most building lots are more developed — are more apt to have improvements such as sidewalks, curbs, paved streets, and sewer connections — than earlier.

Another indication of the rising significance of residential land costs is provided by the increasing ratio of site values to the overall values of residential properties. Throughout the 1930s, land costs typically represented 5 or 6% of the total cost of supplying a new single-family house. FHA figures for the years since 1950 show that land costs accounted for 12% of the total cost of new houses in 1950, 16.6% in 1960, 21% in 1970, and 19.2% in 1976. (See Table 6.) With existing houses, the appraised value of the building sites rose from 12.4% of the total in 1950 to 17.7% in 1960, 21.5% in 1970, and 20.1% in 1976.

Table 6. Average ratios of site values to total appraised values for FHA-insured single-family houses, United States, 1950-1976

Year	New houses	Existing houses
1950	12.0%	12.4%
1955	13.4	14.2
1960	16.6	17.7
1965	19.9	20.9
1970	21.0	21.5
1973	21.2	21.4
1974	18.4	20.4
1975	18.8	19.9
1976	19.2	20.1

Source: U.S. Department of Housing and Urban Development, 1976 *HUD Statistical Yearbook,* p. 110.

As the comparison of the upward trend in the consumer price index, the Boeckh index of residential construction costs, the national index of farm real estate values, and the FHA-appraised values of single-family residential sites reported in Table 7 indicates, the cost of residential sites rose faster than any of the other indices during the 1950-1976 period. The percentage rate of increase for residential sites was lower than for the other indices during the heavy inflation years of the early 1970s; but the increase from year to year was still very sizable.

Table 7 supports the frequently expressed view that it is the high costs associated with land and mortgage credit rather than building expenses that explain the high cost

Table 7. Comparison of rates of increase since 1950 in consumer price index, Boeckh index of residential construction costs, farm real estate values, and value of FHA single-family home sites, United States, 1950-77

Year	Consumer price index	Boeckh index of residential construction costs	Farm real estate values	New single-family home sites
1950	100	100	100	100
1955	111	115	133	157
1960	123	130	167	239
1965	131	143	200	333
1970	161	194	272	481
1973	185	253	349	516
1975	223	291	498	617
1976	236	314	567	672
1977	251	342	659	
Rate of increase from 1970 to 1976				
	46.6%	61.9%	108%	39.7%

Sources: Rates of increase calculated from basic data on the consumer price index and the Boeckh index of residential construction costs reported by the U.S. Department of Commerce *Statistical Abstract of the United States* for the various years; the index of farm real estate values reported by the U.S. Department of Agriculture in reports on *Farm Real Estate Market Developments;* and the FHA-appraised values of single-family home sites reported in the *HUD Statistical Yearbooks.*

of new housing today. Labor and material costs have risen at a significantly faster rate since 1950 and, along with the added cost of borrowed capital, they account for much of the rise in total house production costs in recent years.

Why has the cost of developed housing sites increased so much? Several factors contribute to the higher costs. Developers must pay much higher prices for raw land than they once did. Their out-of-pocket payments for land surveys, provision of utilities, and the like have increased. Considerably more time and expense is required to meet the formal requirements now associated with securing necessary public approval and permits for developments. Higher interest rates plus delays in the land development process also have resulted in increased project waiting costs.

The index of farm real estate market values provides a general indication of what has happened to raw land acquisition costs since 1950. This index increased 2.7 times between 1950 and 1970 and 7.2 times between 1950 and early 1978. Farmland prices more than doubled between 1970 and 1976. Much of the upward surge in farmland values is attributed to a spilling over of urban demands on rural lands, and this spillover had far more impact on areas located near urban markets than in more rural areas.

House and Home reports these development costs for an eighty-eight-lot residential subdivision laid out near Ft. Lauderdale, Florida in 1966:

FHA-appraised value of land $146,461
Land surveys 4,400
Grading of site 9,900
Paving of streets 19,200
Sidewalks 13,000

Provision of water mains...	24,966
Sewers...	40,526
Sewer hookups	4,400
Storm drainage...	5,500
Landscaping..	4,020
Job overhead...	3,768
Contractor and engineer fees plus bond premium	16,600
Carrying charges	9,084
Taxes..	3,000
Insurance..	50
FHA application fee	339
FHA commitment fee...	678
Financing costs..	4,520
Title and legal fees	7,350
Organization cost	1,000

Total development cost $325,282 [7]

The operator's site and subdivision development costs in this case came to $325,282 or an average of $3,696 a lot. If he limited his allowance for profits to a simple 20% of his development costs, he could have supplied housing sites to prospective builders at a minimum price of $4,435 a lot. When allowances are made for sales commissions, possible accumulations of taxes and interest charges while waiting for sales, and possible higher profits, the operator might reasonably have asked average prices in the $5,000 to $7,000 range for his lots.

Developers are sometimes criticized for their profit margins. These criticisms are seemingly based on the assumption that they do little or nothing for the economic return they receive. Examination of the developer's role, however, shows that the developer provides a necessary service in the conversion of raw land to land sites that are ready for the construction of modern houses. Few urban home builders would be content to build, and no urban society could permit them to build, houses on completely undeveloped sites. By acquiring raw land, laying out subdivisions according to public standards, and providing the necessary infrastructure for urban living, developers take a raw product and make it desirable and usable for a new use. In this process, they have little to sell except their time, experience, imagination, and ability to manage and coordinate. They usually operate with borrowed money and take significant economic risks. For these services, they earn and deserve a fair profit.

Many of the costs encountered by developers are fairly routine. But with the growth of public interest in environmental protection, in the provision of park and recreational areas, and in the maintenance of high development standards, developers have often found that they are playing a new ball game. Higher cost outlays are necessary for the provision of added facilities and higher waiting costs are associated with the added time and effort required for getting additional public permits. The impact of these added costs on land costs is illustrated by the examples of two nearly identical houses located in Columbus, Ohio, and Toronto, Ontario which were reported in *House and Home*. [8] Both houses had approximately 1,400 square feet of living space, but the Columbus house sold for $40,000 while the Toronto house sold for $65,000. The comparative land costs of the two houses follow:

7. *House and Home*, vol. 31, May 1967, p. 5.
8. *House and Home*, vol. 40, September 1976, p. 24.

	Columbus house	Toronto house
Raw land for residential site	$1,000	$ 2,000
Land development cost	5,000	9,000
Municipal and regional levies for roads, sewers, recreation facilities, etc.	-----	1,600
Interest and tax-carrying charges	-----	2,200
Developer's profit	1,500	7,500
Sale price to builder	$7,500	$22,500

With this example, it may be noted that development of the Toronto lot involved larger outlays for site development than the lot in Columbus. The Toronto developer also was required to make significant payments for public roads, sewers, and recreational facilities. Two other major differences involve the Toronto developer's higher waiting costs and larger claim for developer profits. The process of waiting additional weeks or months for needed permits and official approvals often means that a developer must pay considerable added interest on borrowed capital plus property taxes he might not otherwise have been required to pay. Similarly, if compliance with public regulations make it necessary for the developer to commit 100 days for the completion of a project that normally would have taken only 20 days, he will feel that he is entitled to a larger compensation (more developer profits) than might otherwise be the case. Development requirements that call for additional outlays for improvements and that require various public permits and authorizations can result in better housing sites and better communities. But they also can lead to materially higher residential land development costs and to higher site costs for builders and consumers.

Some Land Problems Associated With Housing

Several pertinent land use problems arise with the provision of building sites for housing. Some of the more important of these can be grouped areawise under three headings: (1) suburbanization and the flight to the suburbs, (2) scatteration of urban settlements in the open country, and (3) maintenance of the central cities.

Suburbanization

Suburbanization, the movement of large numbers of people from central cities to locations in communities adjacent to and surrounding these cities, was an important phenomenon in the 1920s. It has become a land use development of sizable significance since World War II. From a land use point of view, its major impact has involved the shifting of large areas of once rural lands to urban uses. Other important issues, however, have arisen concerning efficiencies of land use, the roles played by public policy in fostering suburbanization, and the effects of this movement on the central cities.

Suburbanization as it has developed in the United States can be viewed largely as an outgrowth of the widespread acceptance of automobile ownership and the growth of urban mass transit systems. Increased individual and family mobility has made it possible for people to move out of cities and still commute to inner city jobs. Transportation and power developments have furthered this process by making it possible for industries to overcome the "tyranny of site" constraints that once required their locations near waterwheels, navigation ports, or railroad terminals. As industries have moved out to larger and less expensive sites, workers have had added incentives for moving to the suburbs; and commercial establishments have followed to fill the shopping and service needs of the suburban populations.

In an earlier age, transportation constraints had a powerful effect in discouraging the rapid outward expansion of cities. City boundaries divided urban areas from surrounding rural hinterland areas. A need for being within walking distance encouraged high density residential developments and intensive uses of downtown business sites. Properties were frequently remodeled and redeveloped to meet new needs. The adage "use it up, wear it out, make it do" was generally followed as urban residents tried to make efficient use of urban buildings.

With added mobility and affluence, large numbers of people have turned their backs on this early attitude. Suburbanization, given the change in circumstances, was probably a logical process. Yet it has often involved a wasteful use of valuable resources. It has been wasteful in the sense that many suburbs are poorly planned and have usurped the use of lands that might better have been utilized for other purposes. As a process, suburbanization also has been wasteful because it has been fed and fostered by public policies and programs and at the same time has tended to undermine the large investments society already has in its central cities.

Residential subdivisions and new suburbs typically have been laid out as though they were the last areas to be needed for this use. Dependence on the mother city usually has been assumed. Careful advanced land use planning has been lacking; and planning concerning the place of new communities in the metropolitan complex has usually been considered only as an afterthought. Areas that probably should have been saved for agricultural and open space uses have often been covered with houses

Areas that probably should be saved for agriculture and open space uses have often been covered with houses and other urban developments. (United States Department of Agriculture)

and other urban developments. Open spaces were plentiful in the country just beyond the suburbs when they were laid out, and minimal efforts were exerted to save these areas until the most eligible sites were covered with new suburbs. By then, the cost of acquiring land for parks and public open space had risen and communities had to be content with selections from among the few remaining sites still available for public acquisition and use.

Another wasteful aspect of suburbanization relates to the seemingly endless nature of the process. People move to suburbs to escape the environment of cities. They are now leaving the older suburbs to enjoy the environment of newer suburbs. It is human for people to want that which is new, sparkling, and growing. Our willingness to foresake the old and seek the new in housing, however, has major long-run implications. It suggests that over time many established urban areas will decline, probably be cleared of their developments, and perhaps gradually be returned to open space uses while more and more new areas are taken each year for housing and urban uses. Such a process may provide opportunities for architects, builders, and workers. But it suggests an overall wasteful use of land and building materials.

Much of the suburbanization of the past three decades would not have taken place without large indirect public subsidies. The organization of new cities and suburban communities has been favored in most states by legislation and public programs relative to municipal incorporation, grants for schools, local public services, and tax sharing.

Suburban communities have benefited from expressway and street building programs that facilitate speedy access to urban employment and business centers. They have benefited from the extension of water mains and sewers from the central cities or large public subsidies that help them provide their own systems. They have benefited from a pricing structure for public utilities and infrastructure that has allowed them to secure valuable services by paying only the marginal costs associated with adding new increments to existing systems. Instead of paying the full cost of services, as would be the case if the suburb or the new house owner had to pay for extending a water or sewer main all the way to a central city plant, they have often paid only for their immediate connections to existing mains.

Suburban home owners have benefited from federal and state income tax regulations that allow deductions from taxable income of payments made for mortgage interest and property taxes.[9] Our tax system favors owners over tenants by ignoring the rental value of the use an owner receives from his or her home investment while it taxes tenants on the full interest income they receive from their savings and investments. Most suburban home owners benefit from housing credit policies that look with more favor on the granting of long-term, residential, real estate loans in suburban communities than in the older sections of central cities. Property values in suburbs also are

---

9. Federal income taxation regulations also have had a marked impact on investments in rental housing. Investors can charge off their payments for property taxes and interest on mortgages as operating costs. Allowances for depreciation can also be treated as deductions from current income. Several analysts feel that these deductions, along with the prospects for capital gains with increasing property values, now provide the principal incentive for investments in rental properties. If an investor assumes that he or she must allow an amount equal to 3% of the value of a residential property for annual payments of property taxes, 2% for repairs and maintenance, 2% for depreciation, and 5% for return on the investment, he or she will need a total annual return in the form of rents equal to 12% of the market value of the property. This calls for monthly rents equal to one or more percent of the property's value. Residential rental values in most areas in the United States were considerably below this level in 1978. Removal of the special income tax incentives investors now enjoy from investments in rental properties could very well require an offsetting increase of 30 to 50% in property rental rates.

protected to a considerable extent by zoning ordinances, subdivision regulations, and by fire, electrical, plumbing, and other municipal codes.

A third aspect of suburban waste concerns the negative impact of suburban developments on their mother cities. The new bedroom suburb is normally dependent upon the central city for jobs and services. It may seek political independence for self-government, taxation, or other reasons; but it could not exist without the employment opportunities of the central city. More often than not, it starts off depending upon the central city for a wide variety of commercial and professional services. It also looks to the central city for recreational, educational, and cultural services in the form of municipally provided civic centers, parks, zoos, playgrounds and sports facilities, colleges, high schools, trade schools, concert series, dramatic societies, and so on.

As suburban communities expand and mature, they usually take on the function of providing more of their own jobs and services. They still lean on the central cities, however, for their influx of residents, industries, and commercial establishments; and they are often reluctant to bear much responsibility for revitalizing older cities. Like ungrateful children who are heavily dependent on their parents at first and eventually become self-supporting, they often argue that the mother city's infirmities are not their concern and that welfare assistance should come from the state.

Scatteration

Scatteration can be viewed as an extension of suburbanization. It involves the single families and occasional subdivisions that move out beyond built-up suburban areas to establish homes in the country. Less expensive land, opportunities to own several acres rather than a small building lot, and desire to be away from the city and close to nature are major goals with these types of developments. Insofar as these locations require commuting over long distances to work, they often involve wastage of energy resources. More important, however, their activities can have a blighting effect on local areas in that they ruin the agricultural character of rural areas, prompt many owners to view their land more as potential subdivision sites than as farm- or forestland, give tax assessors a valid reason for increasing local assessed valuations, and create demands for urban-type public services that might otherwise not be needed.

As described earlier, the location of scattered housing developments in the rural zone that surrounds the central cities and their built-up satellite suburbs can be viewed as the entering wedge that changes the character of rural communities. A case could be made for these developments if the areas affected were really needed for housing and urban developments. Yet in practice, only small portions of the affected areas will be needed for urban developments in the foreseeable future. The inevitable result is instability in land use and inefficient and wasteful use of much of the land affected.

Continued scatteration is strongly favored by automobile ownership, the construction of all-weather roads, and the desire of many urban workers to live in the country. It could be discouraged by energy conservation measures, such as gasoline rationing, that would give workers strong incentives to live closer to their places of employment. Communities in our society do not have the legal right to build fences around their borders and prohibit the movement of people into their areas. Strong arguments may nevertheless be advanced for policies that will permit controlled and staged growth and that will permit the official protection of large areas of rural lands in their current open space uses. The location of scattered residential developments in rural areas is not necessarily bad; but positive policies are needed to prevent their presence from operating as a cancer on our land use fabric.

Problems of the Central Cities

Unlike certain rural areas where steps are needed to discourage housing developments, the central cities need policies that will stimulate revitalization and redevelopment of existing developments. Numerous central cities are suffering from the flight of their more substantial citizens to the suburbs, from a loss of leadership and tax base, and from the outward movement of industries and commercial establishments. Revitalization is needed because society has a tremendous investment in its cities and because large urban populations can be stranded if means are not found to maintain the economic and social integrity of cities as places to work and live.

In many respects the basic problem of many central cities has been that of advancing age. Families, workers, and investors have been attracted by the opportunities associated with the development of new areas. As they have moved to the suburbs, existing investments in housing and other types of property have trickled down to other uses and users. Little by little many central cities have become the homes of those poor and disadvantaged people who have not been able to join in the flight to the suburbs. Redevelopment and revitalization through infusions of new capital investments and influxes of new businesses have been needed. Sometimes this has happened, but as often as not, these revitalization efforts have involved a redesigning of office buildings and commercial facilities used during office hours without prompting any noticeable return of upper- or middle-income workers to the inner cities.

From a land use point of view, the gradual decline of the central cities is closely related to their failure to maintain their competitive attractiveness relative to their suburbs. The land redevelopment process has not operated fast or efficiently enough to counter the lure of new developments in the suburbs. A strong reason for this is found in the natural reluctance of residential and property owners to accept the rapid depreciation of their investments that would be necessary if they were to be replaced

Revitalization of the central cities is needed to maintain the economic and social integrity of cities as places to work and live. (Department of Housing and Urban Development)

more often with newer properties. This situation has been further complicated by public policies that have often worked against, rather than for, the long-run interests of cities.

Numerous examples can be cited of public actions and programs which have been counterproductive in the impacts they have had on housing and land use conditions in central cities. Most central cities have gone out of their way to provide and share public services and infrastructure such as water and sewer facilities that have been of great value to their suburban satellites. City officials have argued for the extension of expressways into cities with the hope that they would bring in additional customers and business. Unfortunately the roads have run in two directions and have also provided avenues by which workers and their families could leave the cities. Urban credit agencies have emphasized security in their lending practices with the result that they have favored loans on suburban housing while they have sometimes redlined older housing areas within the cities. Slow-moving urban renewal programs have created commercial deserts and encouraged the migration of businesses to outlying shopping centers when the intent was to revitalize downtown commercial districts. Similar programs in residential areas have disrupted or destroyed older neighborhoods without supplying adequate housing for displaced families. Busing and desegregation programs, while noble in their objectives, also have undermined the cohesiveness of established neighborhoods and in so doing have accelerated the flight of middle-class families to the suburbs.

Requirements for various public permits and municipal insistence on owner- and landlord-adherence to particular standards have complicated and frequently discouraged private redevelopment operations. Tax-concession arrangements, such as New York City's practice of freezing preimprovement tax assessed valuations and granting sizeable property tax abatements for several years for the rehabilitation of certain classes of rental housing, can facilitate desired housing improvements. [10] Unless similar concessions are available with new developments, however, these arrangements can cause owners to remodel old structures when community interests could best be served through the complete redevelopment of properties. Rent controls have been used to protect tenant interests over the short run but have had an adverse longer-run impact in discouraging additional needed investments in residential rental properties.

Tenant protection legislation and public provision of legal services for tenants, while needed in many instances, have made it possible for hard-pressed and unscrupulous tenants to avoid the payment of housing rent for months at a time. As one South Bronx landlord has observed, it is possible for landlords to own and manage low- and moderate-rental cost apartments "profitably even with a vacancy rate of 5%, provided rent collections are continuous and assured." [11] But when tenants cannot be evicted until after months of adjudication during and after which they refuse to pay rent, landlords may find that abandonment is the only logical answer to their continuing negative cash flows.

Programs for the Future

What types of land programs are needed to facilitate the provisions of reasonably priced housing at those sites where it is needed in our society? How one answers this

10. James Heilbrun, *Real Estate Taxes and Urban Housing* (New York: Columbia University Press, 1966), pp. 112-113.

11. "A South Bronx Landlord Says Poverty Is Not to Blame for Blight," *New York Times*, October 14, 1977, p. B3.

question depends somewhat upon one's point of view. In terms of physical ability, there is little doubt that the United States can supply all of the land that will be needed for housing for years to come. But is this land where it is most needed and what overall costs to society are associated with its use?

Continuation of the current practice of supplying new residential sites around the outskirts of population centers will lead to a further outward surge of suburbs and scattered settlements in rural areas. It can result in wasteful and inefficient use of rural lands around the cities, areas which in many cases should be kept in their present agricultural and open space uses. It can also contribute to further siphoning off of the economic life and vitality of the central cities and the older suburbs. Severe energy constraints and programs emphasizing the revitalization of the cities, in turn, have a potential for turning the suburbanization movement around and regenerating the strength of the inner cities.

If one starts with the assumption that the central cities are worth saving, it would appear that strong positive programs should be pushed for conserving and upgrading property values and the quality of the living environment in existing urban neighborhoods. Neighborhood conservation calls for measures that will reverse the blighting process and pump new life and vitality into individual neighborhoods. It calls for the development of neighborhood pride, for group determination to maintain neighborhood quality, for the continuing repair and improvement of individual properties, and for acceptance of neighborhood renewal as a continuing process.

Unfortunately, many urban neighborhoods are filled with even-aged structures — buildings that blossomed with their highest social values at the same time and later began to look old and tended to become disfunctional at the same time. This uniform age cycle must be broken if neighborhoods are to enjoy a healthy perpetual life. Individual properties must be repaired, remodeled, and redeveloped on a regular basis. But the process for the neighborhood as a whole should be gradual and piecemeal so that neighborhood cohesiveness can be maintained and overall environmental and property values can remain constant or tend to rise.

Individual developments normally have a predictable economic and social life during which they appear as attractive investments for the simple reason that they have a potential for yielding economic and social benefits in excess of annual operating costs. Remodeling and redeveloping activities should be scheduled before the prospect of negative economic or social returns brings any downgrading of the servicing or use of the property. Urban renewal projects that involve several blocks or significant portions of whole neighborhoods should be viewed as a type of radical surgery to be applied only under critical circumstances when and where it is necessary to clear the land and start over with the urban development process.

Incentives for the types of modernizing and redevelopment envisioned here have often been lacking in central cities. Programs are needed to increase the attractiveness of urban life, to provide preferred credit for housing renewal, to strengthen rather than weaken the cohesiveness of urban neighborhoods, and to provide economic incentives for property rehabilitation or redevelopment. Along with these programs, new attitudes are needed concerning urban property investments. Annual depreciation should be accepted as a fact of life, and investors should expect to either remodel or totally redevelop properties on a regular basis once they approach the ends of their normal economic lives.

In the redevelopment of housing areas in cities, serious consideration should be given to the possible use of new planning techniques that can lead to better housing and neighborhood conditions. Cluster-housing developments and planned-unit developments (PUDs) might well be sponsored as means for bringing housing units closer together to enjoy the benefits of compact developments while at the same time providing landscaped grounds and extensive open space. Consideration might also be given to the development of new towns both within and outside of central cities where emphasis can be given to the provision of a socially and psychologically attractive living environment within which people will enjoy a sense of belonging.

Additional planning emphasis also should be given to the provisions of those residential sites that will be located outside of presently built-up subdivisions. Thought should be given to the designation of agricultural and open space areas that will be protected in their current uses. Housing developments, where possible, should be directed to sites that can, with the provision of adequate infrastructure, provide a desirable environment for residential living but which do not represent prime areas for agricultural, recreational, mining, or other needed uses. Major emphasis in planning should be given to ways and means for providing highly desirable neighborhood environments. Arrangements should be made to preserve adequate open space; and thought should be given to use of techniques such as graded zoning, cluster developments, PUDs, and the like that may result in better communities. [12]

As we move towards the future, it appears that governments acting as the agents of society should play a stronger role in directing the future development of housing and community developments. This will limit some of the free agency now exercised by private developers. But it will mean that new developments will be subjected to careful planning and that they will be located where the elected representatives of the public feel that they can best serve the interests of the total community.

12. Consideration might also be given to adoption of a concept of land banking under which municipalities can buy large tracts of land around their environs for controlled future development. This practice has been used with success by some European cities but has not been seriously considered by American cities.

Discussion Questions

1. How can we account for the increase in households at a considerably faster rate than the increase in population between the years of 1920 and 1970?

2. Explain how inflation can be a factor that causes a stronger demand for new housing.

3. If houses and their immediate lots occupy only .05% of the United States' total land, how can land scarcity and land cost be a major constraint?

4. Explain why the cost of developed housing sites has increased so greatly in the past twenty years.

5. What specific development in the United States has been largely responsible for suburban growth?

6. Give several examples of how public actions and programs aimed at improving housing conditions in central cities have in actuality proved to be counterproductive.

7. Describe several ways that the government could facilitate needed housing at a reasonable cost to the citizens.

6. Housing Costs: What Can Be Done?

by Nathaniel H. Rogg

To analyze the rising cost of housing, it is necessary to look at the components of the problem. These are (1) land; (2) processing and regulatory actions; (3) financing; (4) labor; (5) the production cycle, seasonality, and shortfall of production versus demand; (6) taxation and federal policy; (7) building technology and (8) materials.

Running through the cost spiral is *inflation* which hits home building harder than any other industry. The reasons are simple: inflation affects attitudes toward a major expenditure; inflation enters into interest rates; inflation enters into wage negotiations; inflation increases the cost of land and land development; inflation increases the cost of materials; in short, inflation cuts home building way back from what is needed.

Land

Land costs in twenty years have gone up almost 500% and now amount to 25% of sales price. The problem is one of scarcity, misguided land use policy and greatly increased development costs. It touches on unwillingness of settled communities to welcome newcomers, and also treads on environmental issues. We need better land use approach by local governments and federal standard setting, not intervention. The federal role should be a leadership role in (a) identifying problems and in urging localities to avoid exclusionary processes, i.e., large lot zoning, down zoning, etc., which by limiting the land supply raise costs; (b) examining all environmental and processing requirements and discarding overlapping ones which the federal government adds to local procedures. For example, in the Coastal Zoning Act, in the Interstate Land Sales Act, and in the Water Pollution and Clean Air Act, excessive requirements make up a helter-skelter federal land use policy administered by a dozen federal agencies, although theoretically there are strictures against this.

Excessive local developmental costs result from both large lot zoning and technological over-requirements. The size and composition of subdivision streets or sewer connection costs add to land costs. In one Virginia suburb, for example, sewer and water connection charges have gone up from $275 in 1970 to $1625 in 1975.

Time as a cost factor is frequently ignored. Archaic processing in local as well as in federal programs, adds thousands of dollars to cost.

Any action with respect to land use will arouse feelings. Some of the forces at work include: (a) local communities that do not want any more housing; (b) some

Reprinted by permission from *MGIC Newsletter*, Published by Mortgage Guaranty Insurance Corporation, Milwaukee, Wisconsin.

Nathaniel H. Rogg is Housing Consultant and Former Executive Vice President, National Association of Home Builders.

environmental groups who feel that any change permitting more intensive land use defiles our natural heritage; (c) speculators in land who feel they should be permitted unlimited opportunities for profit-making; and (d) various special interests with a concern for a bigger role for their specialities, such as cement and asphalt companies and labor unions that would like to see higher developmental standards because it means more work for their membership, and groups that want to keep out lower income families.

Regulatory Problems

There is no way to quantify the cost of unnecessary regulation but it has grown alarmingly. Studies are under way in a number of areas by the National Association of Home Builders, the General Accounting Office, the Urban Land Institute, Rutgers University, and the Builders Research Advisory Board (BRAB). NAHB is studying the "cost of delay" including carrying costs, property taxes, inflation impact, changes in the market and the labor supply.

We should focus attention on the problem by: (a) a national conference on the cost of regulation; (b) federal funding of studies to identify cost components and their necessity; (c) devising suggested guidelines for regulations on local, state, and federal level from such studies and utilizing varying types of incentives and deterrents to promote them; and (d) a review of all federal regulations which affect land use and removal of those where cost exceeds benefit.

Cost and Availability of Financing

Except for construction financing and land development costs, interest rates may not seem to be part of costs. Nevertheless, they are a vital determinant of the ability of the consumer to afford a house and the economics of rental housing. Since 1965 interest rates have risen 55%. On a thirty-year $30,000 mortgage this means that monthly mortgage payments have risen from $177 to $241 or more than $23,000 additional payment over the life of the mortgage. These figures suggest the significance of the interest rate factor to the average consumer and the need for considering it as a part of the housing cost picture.

Explanations for high rates are as diverse as the explainers. Causes can be found in many areas, including inflation, federal reserve monetary policy, Treasury debt management policy, and the state of the economy.

Treasury debt management policy affects the availability of funds for home building in terms of the denomination of short-term treasury securities. When these are available in amounts as small as $1,000, it causes disintermediation among thrift institutions. Decisions by the Treasury with respect to the maturities of its securities also affect interest rates, both construction and mortgage.

Some of the policies that might reduce the cost and improve the availability of financing over time include: (a) easier money policy; (b) selective credit controls, if tighter money policy is necessary; (c) alternative mortgage instruments; (d) a Development Bank to make loans to consumers and builders when traditional sources fail; (e) the federal government as a financier of last resort. This last concept appears to be gaining more acceptance, particularly in housing for moderate and low income families. It can take many forms. One is the 235 interest rate subsidy; others are the Brock-Ashley proposal, Brooke-Cranston, and NAHB's front-end subsidy proposal. All add up to subsidy for the spread between so-called "affordable" interest rates and market rate.

Wages

Hourly construction wages are probably higher than in any other industry, reflecting both uncertainty of employment and seasonality. They also reflect the tangled complex of unions in building, with some fifteen to twenty separate unions.

Direct labor costs in construction account for only about one-fifth of the sales price. In themselves they are not the major factor in rising housing costs. The wage pattern is chaotic because of the craft union approach with a crazy-quilt of different wages in the same city for work seemingly of comparable skills. Unions are extremely protective of both their jurisdictional turfs and wage patterns.

Nevertheless, there is also an awareness by progressive union leaders that something needs to be done to increase employment and that high wage costs are a deterrent to more jobs.

A start toward a more rational wage approach was made in 1970 with an executive order setting up a Construction Industry Stabilization Committee under John Dunlop. An effort was made to provide authorization for this approach in Title II of the vetoed Situs Picketing Act. This would have provided voluntary wage boards, and have given national unions a say in local contracts. It was a favorite of Secretary Dunlop and seemed to be accepted by labor leaders and builders. Other recommendations for wage action include:

1. Modifying Davis-Bacon — This act requires prevailing wages on government projects. There is reason to believe that it boosts project costs by 10 to 15%. At least this was the conclusion of the General Accounting Office. Removal of Davis-Bacon per se would encounter vigorous opposition from organized labor. Placing it on a more rational basis so that wages actually are those prevailing might encounter less opposition.
2. Review and Removal of Restrictive Labor Practices — This would require appropriate studies to review the reasons for restrictive practices and a vigorous effort to get agreement both from organized labor and management about the need for removing them.
3. Do away with costly seasonality and uncertainty of employment by providing *guaranteed employment* for a period of time. Minimize labor opposition to holding the line on hourly wages. This cannot be tackled as a wage issue alone but only as part of an overall approach toward more stability in the housing industry.

Stabilizing Housing Production

Nobody has been able to quantify the cost of uneven housing cycles. Yet they are substantial, not only in terms of efficiency, but in hourly wages, in the loss of jobs, in the inability of building companies to do any long-range planning, and in the need to retain labor lost during the downswings.

One approach, involving some interference with the market, would be to adopt consistent policies toward housing, setting both a lower limit and an upper limit governed by needs and resources available. It has been suggested that setting a minimum limit of 1,800,000 units a year would be useful. Necessary actions to support this level can readily be identified.

Another consequence of the cycle is that the shortfall in production is in itself inflationary. Lack of an adequate supply of housing is a contributor to higher housing prices because of the lack of choices available to the consumer.

Taxes and Tax Policy

Tax reformers have argued that providing tax benefits through real estate investment is a shotgun approach. They claim a better way would be to subsidize directly rather than to give all investors the same shelter. The argument is appealing, except that at no time has there been a concurrent effort to make up for loss of investment attractiveness which occurs when tax benefits are removed. There is a growing awareness that the tax element is important in making housing investments attractive and holding rentals and prices down.

There are several issues in the area of taxation that affect housing costs including:

1. Tax deductibility of mortgage interest (variously estimated at from $4 to $6 billion) which is frequently described as the largest subsidy available in housing. This, *if a subsidy,* goes basically to middle American families and may well be the only tax "loophole" for the average family. Its removal would greatly dampen home sales.
2. Mortgage tax credit for financial institutions. This proposal was advanced by the Hunt Commission. It is considered a device to entice more investment into mortgages. It is also considered an alternative to the current bad debt reserve of savings and loans.
3. Conditioning continued tax exemption for pension funds upon investment of assets in mortgages. Pension funds, a fast growing source of investment money, actually have become less attracted to residential mortgages. Some years ago 4% of all pension funds were invested in residential mortgages. Today the figure is closer to 2%.
4. Tax deductibility or tax credit for a portion of interest earned on savings accounts. It is believed this would induce an additional flow of funds to mortgage lending institutions. Treasury figures suggest that a $750 deductibility would cost the Treasury's tax collections about $1.5 billion annually.

Building Technologies

There is a myth that improved technology will provide a magic solution to housing costs problems. This has excited people since the days of the Wyatt Veterans emergency housing program in 1946 and the Romney Breakthrough operation in 1969.

The theory holds producing houses in factories would make up for all the other inefficiencies. The Kaiser Commission Report (The President's Committee on Urban Housing, 1968) answers this issue. Less than half of a house's sales price is in "hard" items to which a new technology could be applied, and only half of this half is in the shell and structure — the rest being appliances and mechanicals.

Building houses has been changing for many years, but in an evolutionary rather than revolutionary way. In 1930 half the sales price was in on-site labor costs. Today, it is about 20%. The change has been gradual but steady, from building with pieces, to building with parts, to building with components. The pace of change may well accelerate in years to come, particularly if additional savings can be obtained by buying more finished parts, if not the whole house, at the factory, and if on-site labor costs keep rising.

Factors that have discouraged technology advances include: (1) the instability of the market; (2) problems of organized labor on the issues of factory built components; (3) lack of uniformity in building codes and development standards; (4) failure to demonstrate that efficiencies of off-site production are superior to what a builder could do with a sizeable on-site operation and with what amounts to a "factory in the field."

What is needed is both further research with government encouragement and an effort by government at all levels to see that improved technology is adopted.

Materials

The issues here again relate to the cyclical instability of the market and the consequent unwillingness of manufacturers to invest in new plants. Complicating the materials price issue is the wide swing in pricing of lumber — the most important material used.

Lumber products people stoutly maintain that lumber prices reflect the free market. Be that as it may, since 1975 plywood prices are up almost 50% and structural lumber up 40%. In dollar terms, this could mean an additional $2,000 plus on each unit. While there is lack of agreement on pricing, there is considerably more agreement on forestry policies. All projections of lumber usage and supply indicate that the supply will be inadequate for the nation's housing needs unless we adopt a different forest policy approach. This means not only more intensive use of national forests on a commercial basis but also a national willingness to invest in good forest practices, access roads and the like.

Discussion Questions

1. Why does inflation have a greater impact on the home-building industry than on other industries?

2. Identify the components considered to be basic problems in the rising cost of housing. Explain how each of these components influences the cost of housing.

3. The author of the article has offered some solutions for each of the components considered to be root causes of rising housing costs. Discuss one possible solution for each of the eight components.

7. Government Housing Programs: A Brief Review

by Mary H. Yearns

An examination of government housing legislation over the past forty years reveals a bewildering array of programs. Many approaches — often with conflicting purposes — have been tried and the results have not always been successful. Every level of government has been involved in efforts to influence the production and consumption of housing. At the local level, building and health codes and zoning and subdivision regulations have set standards for housing quality. At the state level, the passage of enabling legislation to capitalize on available federal monies for housing assistance programs and the creation of Housing Finance Agencies (HFAs) have extended better housing possibilities to many low- and moderate-income families. And at the federal level, as will be discussed in greater detail in this article, the government has directly and indirectly influenced the availability of decent housing through mortgage insurance, subsidy payments, tax policies, and numerous other activities. The most consistent theme to emerge from all of these housing efforts has been governmental actions to facilitate and encourage home ownership. The introduction of the amortized, long-term mortgage and the development of tax incentives for home ownership, especially, have been important steps in the advancement of the owner-occupied, single-family, free-standing home as the "American dream."

1930s: Response to the Great Depression

The federal government's first major thrust into the housing field came in response to the collapse of the mortgage-finance system during the Great Depression. Half of all home mortgages fell into default and foreclosures neared one thousand per day in late 1931 and in 1932. Prior to this time, private lenders typically charged large down payments of up to 50% with short-term repayment periods of seven to ten years, which made it difficult for even middle-income families to become home owners. Furthermore, the periodic payments usually covered only the interest while the full principal was not due until the final, huge payment (so large it was often called a "balloon" payment). When large numbers of buyers lost their jobs and were unable to meet the interest or final payments on their homes, the government saw the need to step in with legislation to devise a new mortgage-finance system and to lay the foundations for a national policy to strengthen home ownership.

The Federal Home Loan Bank Act of 1932 created the Federal Home Loan Bank Board (FHLBB), a central banking system for home-loan banks, similar to the Federal

Mary H. Yearns is Extension Specialist in Family Environment (Housing), Iowa State University. This article was prepared specially for this book.

Reserve System for commercial banks. This assured a flow of money to thrift institutions even in times of tight money. In 1933, the Home Owners Loan Corporation (HOLC) was established to aid hard-pressed lending institutions by purchasing mortgages that were about to be foreclosed. And in 1934, the National Housing Act provided legislation to stimulate construction and employment and to further support the ailing mortgage market. The Federal Savings and Loan Insurance Corporation (FSLIC) was devised to protect the savings of small investors and thus encourage them to deposit savings in lending institutions which would in turn loan the money to families who wanted to buy homes. This act also created the Federal Housing Administration (FHA) to provide a system of government insurance for residential mortgages on a long-term, amortized basis. With this protection, lenders were willing to liberalize mortgage terms, thus making it possible for many additional families to purchase their own homes.   Since 1935, more than ten million new and used homes have been insured under the FHA Section 203 program. It has been one of the most successful housing programs to date and is still in operation. Figure 1 illustrates that mortgages insured by FHA currently account for less than 10% of private housing starts, compared with 23% of private starts between 1935 and 1939 and 45% of the starts in the 1940 to 1944 time period. A brief flurry of renewed FHA activity occurred in 1970 with the introduction of several new subsidy programs. But with the advent of private mortgage insurance companies, the FHA's role has declined. These private companies increased mortgage insurance activity from 3% of single-family starts in 1970 to 20% in 1976.

The National Housing Act also established a secondary mortgage purchase facility which in 1938 became the Federal National Mortgage Association (FNMA, known as "Fannie Mae"). Its primary purpose was to provide a mechanism for the sale of FHA and Veteran's Administration (VA) underwritten loans (also known as government issue or GI loans).

Another depression-related piece of housing legislation was the United States Housing Act of 1937. This act authorized the construction of federally financed public housing, primarily as a method of relieving unemployment, but it was also the first

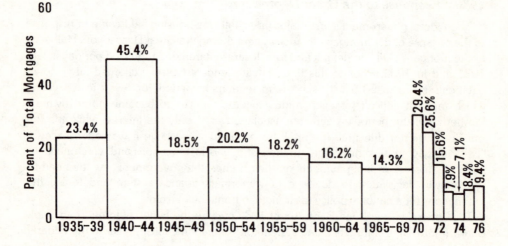

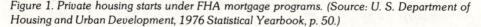

Figure 1. Private housing starts under FHA mortgage programs. (Source: U. S. Department of Housing and Urban Development, 1976 Statistical Yearbook, p. 50.)

program to provide a subsidy. The federal contribution to local public housing authorities (PHAs) allowed rents to be reduced so that housing could be made available to very low-income families. Throughout its forty-year history the public housing program has provided more than 1.3 million housing units, 500,000 of these during the past ten years, and currently represents about 1.5% of the nation's total housing stock.

1940s: Aftermath of World War II

Shortages of building materials during the war years seriously curtailed all types of housing activity. Returning veterans were given priority in their search for housing units with a new veterans' mortgage-guarantee program that was administered by the VA. Created in 1944, this program provided long-term, no-down-payment mortgages. The generous terms encouraged many veterans to become home owners. With the exception of the FHA 203 program, all other housing programs are dwarfed by the scale of the VA program. More than nine million home loans have been guaranteed or insured since the beginning of the program.

During 1947 the Housing and Home Finance Agency (HHFA) was created to succeed the National Housing Agency and to consolidate the housing activities of the Home Loan Bank Board, the Federal Housing Administration, the Federal National Mortgage Association, and the Federal Public Housing Authority. Although the new HHFA did help to streamline and coordinate some of the housing activities of these various agencies, it did not enjoy departmental status and thus was not in a position to make dramatic changes in housing policy.

Severe housing shortgages for the lowest-income families were still a serious problem when Congress passed the Housing Act of 1949 with the now famous goal of " . . . a decent home and a suitable living environment for every American family." Although it was stated as national policy, Congress assumed only limited responsibility for achieving it. The federal role was viewed primarily as one of providing assistance and support to the housing efforts of the private sector. While Congress did authorize federal assistance for the construction of 810,000 units of public housing over the ensuing six years, the major emphasis was on establishing a slum-clearance program as a means of encouraging private housing development on the cleared sites.

The 1949 act also recognized the special housing needs of farm families. Because lending institutions had often been reluctant to make home loans in rural areas, the Farmers Home Administration (FmHA) in the Department of Agriculture was authorized to make loans to families for the purchase or rehabilitation of farm homes. Unlike the FHA, which made loans through financial institutions, the FmHA dealt directly with the individual or family who was obtaining the loan. Although the predecessors of FmHA had started in 1935 with various kinds of rural development assistance, it was not until the 1949 act that housing was incorporated as one of its rural development responsibilities. Since that time the FmHA has had a major role in the development of rural housing due to its highly decentralized organizational system of 1,750 county offices.

1950s: Renewal of the Cities

Housing programs of the 1950s were curtailed by budget stringencies imposed by the Korean War. Construction of previously authorized public housing units was cut back in terms of both numbers of units and types of amenities provided. The now infamous (and razed) Pruitt-Igoe project in St. Louis was built during this period. Despite the limitations on public housing, there was intense urban renewal activity that fostered the development of much unassisted construction. Starting with the 1949 act and continuing through the 1950s, 1960s, and early 1970s, slum clearance was gradually expanded to cover larger and larger areas: first, neighborhoods, then sections of cities, and finally entire cities and counties. Unfortunately, the slums were often replaced with high-priced housing or commercial structures which reduced the number of affordable units available to lower-income households.

Legislation during this period attempted to perfect existing programs, rather than to create new innovations. The Housing Act of 1954 added conservation and rehabilitation programs to broaden the slum clearance provisions of the 1949 legislation. The act also required communities to prepare a "workable program" for community improvement before they would be eligible for public housing and urban renewal assistance. Grants were provided to finance the necessary planning.

A direct loan program was a major innovation in the Housing Act of 1959. Section 202 authorized below market interest rate (BMIR) loans to nonprofit sponsors of rental housing for elderly and handicapped persons, thus allowing sponsors to reduce the rental fees they charged to tenants. This was the first recognition of the special housing problems of those with incomes too high to qualify for public housing, yet too low to be able to obtain decent housing on their own.

1960s: Evolution of Subsidies

The urban unrest of the 1960s fostered a variety of housing subsidy programs. The 221(d)(3) provisions of the Housing Act of 1961 extended the sponsorship of BMIR projects to private corporations as well as to nonprofit groups if profits were limited to 6%. Because of increasing costs of federal borrowing, the BMIR program was no longer effective in reducing rental fees. To solve this problem the Housing Act of 1965 set the BMIR at no higher than 3%. Sponsors were then subsidized the difference between interest payments at this rate and those at the higher market level. The act also created the Rent Supplement Program which required a family to pay at least 25% of its income toward rent while the federal government subsidized the difference between this payment and the actual rental value of the unit. Another innovation of the 1965 act was the Section 23 leasing program which enabled local public housing authorities to lease existing housing units and rent them on a subsidized basis to public housing tenants.

Housing history was also made in 1965 with the creation of the Department of Housing and Urban Development (HUD) to succeed HHFA. Cabinet-level status for HUD was an indication of increasing congressional concern for the interrelated problems of inadequate housing and urban decay. Unlike FmHA, HUD was not required to restrict its housing operations to communities of a particular size. However, its dependence on local credit institutions often limited the availability of its programs in smaller communities. Also, its system of widely scattered field offices meant that HUD officials were relatively inaccessible in rural areas, as compared with FmHA personnel.

In 1966 the Demonstration Cities and Metropolitan Development Act established the Model Cities program. This was a comprehensive effort to coordinate a variety of physical, social, and economic programs within a particular urban neighborhood.

The landmark Housing and Urban Development Act of 1968 reaffirmed the national housing goal established in 1949 and also introduced a new technique of subsidizing interest rates. Private lenders were paid to assist sponsors in the development of low- and moderate-income housing. Government subsidies covered the difference between monthly debt expenses at market interest rates and those

Youngsters in the play area of a federally funded Section 236 housing project. (Department of Housing and Urban Development)

which would be required on a mortgage with an interest rate of 1%. The savings were then passed on to the potential home owner or renter. Under the Section 235 home ownership program, a family paid at least 20% of its income toward the monthly mortgage payment, while a tenant using the Section 236 rental program spent a minimum of 25% of his or her income on rent. Rent supplements were tied to some of the Section 236 housing units so that these would be available to households who could not afford to pay basic rents at the subsidized level with 25% of their adjusted incomes. Section 235 home owners paid a lower percentage of monthly income than Section 236 renters due to the additional costs of maintenance and repair associated with home ownership.

Another feature of the 1968 act was the establishment of a ten-year construction goal of 26,000,000 new and rehabilitated housing units, including 6,000,000 subsidized units for low- and moderate-income families. It also directed HUD to prepare an annual report to assess progress toward this goal and to serve as a basis for planning future housing programs. Due to increasing costs of the Viet Nam War and other budgetary constraints, production fell far short of the ten-year expectations. The only years that the goal was reached or exceeded were the years 1971 to 1973.

The Brooke Amendment to the Housing and Urban Development Act of 1969 addressed the problem of tenants who were "too poor" to afford public housing. The act limited rents to no more than 25% of tenant's gross income. This action had the effect of reducing monthly receipts of PHAs and causing severe budget deficits. To solve the problem, Congress authorized payment of additional operating subsidies to bridge the budget gap.

Legislation during the 1960s enabled the FmHA to expand housing activities in rural areas. The 1961 act permitted FmHA to make housing loans to nonfarm rural families in communities up to 2,500 people. It also provided loans for the construction

Carpenters work on the roof of a home financed through the Farmers Home Administration. A completed FHA financed home is shown in the background. (United States Department of Agriculture)

of rental apartments for elderly persons (Section 515) and for farm labor housing (Sections 514/516). In the Housing Act of 1965, the area of potential FmHA borrowers was increased to towns with 5,000 residents; in 1968 the limit was expanded to communities of 10,000 population; and in the Housing and Community Development Act of 1974, FmHA jurisdiction was extended to places of 20,000 persons. With the extension of areas served, FmHA was able to expand its loan activities from 2,000 units annually during the 1950s, to 16,000 units annually in the 1960s, and to 77,000 homes annually during the 1970s. The FmHA's major program is the Section 502 home ownership loan program to help low- and moderate-income families buy, build, or repair housing. Loans are as low as 1% interest with up to thirty-three years to repay. For residents too poor to repay a Section 502 loan, the Section 504 home ownership repair program provides 1% loans or outright grants for eliminating housing conditions that affect the health and/or safety of the family.

1970s: Period of Reassessment

There was a period of tremendous construction activity following the introduction of the Sections 235 and 236 programs. Total housing production increased from 1.9 million units in 1968 to 2.6 million units in 1971 and to a record-breaking 3.0 million units in 1972 (including mobile home production). Subsidized production was at an all-time high, exceeding the total of federal activity for the previous thirty-five years. The federal share soared from 166 thousand units in 1968 to 430 thousand units in 1971 — nearly one-fifth of annual production.

Construction trends turned around sharply in January, 1973, when the Nixon administration abruptly suspended all new activity on government-subsidized units.

Officials of HUD had become concerned over the increasing costs of subsidizing units over the lifetimes of their mortgages — up to forty years in some instances. In addition, abuses and failures in the programs had come to public notice. Old rehabilitated units in central city areas were found to be of low quality and foreclosures and abandonment were common. The moratorium was conceived as a way to evaluate the effectiveness of existing housing programs and also as an opportunity for reassessing housing policies and examining alternative subsidy programs. (It also meant the end of the ten-year construction goal established in 1968). Total annual production (including mobile homes) droppd to 2.6 million units in 1973, further declined to 1.4 million units in 1975, then bounced back to 1.8 million units in 1976. The HUD subsidized portion of these starts fell dramatically from 430 thousand units in 1971 to 41 thousand units in 1976, while FmHA starts maintained betwen 80 and 100 thousand subsidized units annually during the same period.

The Housing and Community Development Act of 1974 revived federal housing activity. Two of its major provisions were the Community Development Block Grant (CDBG) program and the Section 8 program. The CDBG approach replaced the former "categorical" programs, such as Model Cities and urban renewal, with a more flexible funding mechanism. Local governmental units were charged with the responsibility for developing master plans that would identify long-range community development needs and outline a course of action for implementing their plans, thus moving more of the decision-making from the federal to the local level. A mandated part of the CDBG application was a Housing Assistance Plan (HAP), a document that identified how the community intended to meet the housing needs of its lower-income residents. With its required HAP component, the CDBG program served as an incentive to encourage low-income housing activity.

The new Section 8 program was an improved version of the old Section 23 leasing program. Instead of leasing units from landlords for subsequent subleasing to tenants, the PHAs provided eligible families with a "certificate of family participation" which allowed them to select suitable housing from the private rental market. The family would sign a lease with the landlord and the landlord would then sign a contract with the PHA to receive payments. Owners were paid the difference between "fair market rent" and the amount a tenant could afford — between 15 and 25% of gross income. The Section 8 rental program placed more reliance on the private sector and could use newly constructed, substantially rehabilitated, or existing rental housing units. At the end of 1977 a total of 358,000 units were provided under Section 8. Of this total, 328,000 were existing units. Section 8 is now the major HUD program for providing federally assisted rental housing.

The 1974 act also authorized an urban homesteading program that allowed HUD to transfer at no cost its acquired homes to local governments. The homes were then sold for as low as one dollar to selected homesteader families who agreed to make necessary repairs to bring the homes up to local code standards. Participating communities provided loans to the homesteaders for rehabilitating the properties. After repairing and living in the home for three years, families then received title to the property.

The steep decline of housing production, massive unemployment in the home-building industry, and large inventories of unsold houses led to the enactment of the Tax Reduction Act of 1975. To spur lagging sales of new homes, the act authorized a 5% tax rebate — not to exceed $2,000 — to persons purchasing new, unsold homes that had been previously built or were already under construction. Obviously, this program was not of much benefit to low-income families in need of housing assistance.

Further home ownership incentives came when the Housing and Community Development Act of 1977 increased FHA maximum mortgage amounts on single-family homes from $55,000 to $60,000 and raised mobile home loan limits to $16,000 on single-wide units and to $20,000 on double-wide units.

The 1970s also saw an upsurge of interest in housing programs at the state level. By 1978 more than three-fourths of the states had created Housing Finance Agencies (HFAs). The HFAs obtained their financing by issuing tax-exempt bonds, by receiving appropriations from their state legislatures, by using money from federal housing subsidy programs, or from a combination of these sources. The HFAs that depended on federal money from the Section 236 program were hard-hit by the 1973 moratorium. Others that concentrated on indirect financing activities, such as mortgage purchase and loans-to-lenders programs for middle-income families, weathered the period of economic uncertainty relatively well. Currently, HUD is encouraging HFA activity under the Section 8 program through its bulk set-asides of subsidy funds as well as expedited processing procedures.

Evaluation of Results

When evaluating the effectiveness of government housing policies, it is important to recognize that the actual intent of many housing programs has not necessarily been consistent with the stated legislative goals. Housing programs have been conceived as a means of achieving a variety of purposes — creating jobs, stimulating the economy, and clearing the slums — as well as increasing the quantity and quality of available housing. Certainly, providing housing for the poor has never been its sole purpose. In fact, creating prosperity has usually been a more important goal than providing decent housing for low-income families.

Throughout the past forty years of government housing activity, the encouragement, development, and support of home ownership has been a major thrust. Families sought to buy a home because of the generous tax benefits associated with home ownership. But to receive these benefits, a family had to be able to afford a home, thus

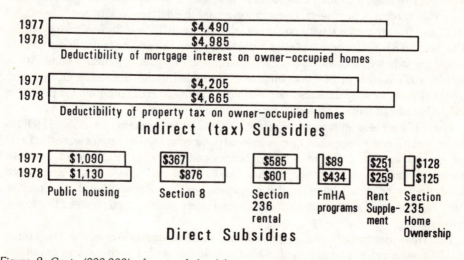

Figure 2. Costs (000,000) of major federal housing subsidies, fiscal years 1977 and 1978 (estimate). (Source: The Budget of the United States Government, Appendix, Fiscal Year 1979, pp. 159 and 478, and Special Analysis of the United States Government, Fiscal Year 1979, p. 158.)

excluding many lower-income families. An examination of federal budget expenditures reveals that the major recipients of government housing subsidies have been middle- and upper-income home owners. Figure 2 illustrates that the indirect subsidies of deductions for mortgage interest and property tax expense on federal income tax returns during fiscal years 1977 and 1978 each exceeded the combined costs of all other major housing subsidy programs. Budget documents released by the Office of Management and Budget indicate that more than half of the tax expenditures for home mortgage interest and property taxes (indirect housing subsidies) benefited taxpayers in the $20,000 to $50,000 income bracket.

If the effectiveness of government housing policy is measured in terms of increasing the numbers of home owners, then it has been successful in helping achieve the highest percentage of home ownership ever known. (Census data indicate that 65% of the housing units in 1975 were owner-occupied, as compared with 44% in 1940.) But if the national objective is measured in terms of the adequacy of housing provided for citizens, a Joint Center Study of MIT and Harvard University concludes that as many as 12.8 million households — some 18% of the nation — suffered some form of serious housing deprivation in 1973. Thus, much remains to be accomplished before we have reached the goal of " . . . a decent home and a suitable living environment for every American family."

References

A Decent Home. Report of the President's Committee on Urban Housing. Washington, D.C.: U.S. Government Printing Office, 1969.

American Institute of Architects. *National Housing Policy: The American Institute of Architects.* Washington, D.C.: The American Institute of Architects, 1976.

Bird, Ronald, and Ronald Kampe. *Twenty-five Years of Housing Progress in Rural America.* Agricultural Economic Report No. 373. Washington, D.C.: Economic Development Division, Economic Research Service, U.S. Department of Agriculture, 1977.

Dolbeare, Cushing N. *Federal Tax Rip-offs: Housing Subsidies for the Rich.* Washington, D.C.: Rural Housing Alliance, 1972.

Downs, Anthony. "The Success and Failures of Federal Housing Policy." *The Public Interest* 34 (1974): 124-145.

Glazer, Nathan. "Housing Problems and Housing Policies." *The Public Interest* 27 (1967): 21-51.

Hartman, Chester. "The Politics of Housing: Introduction." *Society* 9 (1972): 30.

"The Nation's Housing: 1975-1985." Cambridge: Joint Center for Urban Studies of MIT and Harvard University, 1977.

Ryan, Robert. "Low-Income Housing Programs." *HUD Challenge* 9 (1978): 29.

"The Seventh Annual Report on the National Housing Goal, Pursuant to Section 1603 of the Housing and Urban Development Act of 1968." President of the United States Message. Washington, D.C.: U.S. Government Printing Office, 1975.

Stone, Michael E. "The Politics of Housing: Mortgage Bankers." *Society* 9 (1972): 31-37.

U.S. Congress, Congressional Budget Office. *Real Estate Tax Shelter Subsidies and Direct Subsidy Alternatives.* Washington, D.C.: U.S. Government Printing Office, 1977.

U.S. Congress, House of Representatives. *Housing in the Seventies, Report of the Department of Housing and Urban Development.* Committee Print of Hearing Before the Subcommittee on Housing of the Committee on Banking and Currency, House of Representatives, 93rd Congress, 1st Session. Washington, D.C.: U.S. Government Printing Office, 1973.

U.S. Congress, Joint Economic Committee. *Federal Subsidy Programs.* Committee Print of a Staff Study Prepared for the Use of the Subcommittee on Priorities and Economy in Government of the Joint Economic Committee, Congress of the United States 93rd Congress, 2nd Session. Washington, D.C.: U.S. Government Printing Office, 1974.

_____. *Federal Housing Policies.* Committee Print of Hearings Before the Joint

Economic Committee, Congress of the United States, 94th Congress, 2nd Session. Washington, D.C.: U.S. Government Printing Office, 1977.

U.S. Department of Housing and Urban Development. *Housing in the Seventies Working Papers,* Volumes 1 & 2. Washington, D.C.: U.S. Government Printing Office, 1976.

_____. *Consumer's Primer of Housing and Urban Development.* Washington, D.C.: Office of Consumer Affairs and Regulatory Functions, U.S. Department of Housing and Urban Development, 1977a.

_____. *1976 HUD Statistical Yearbook.* Washington, D.C.: U.S. Government Printing Office, 1977b.

U.S. Office of Management and Budget. *The Budget of the United States Government: Fiscal Year 1979.* Washington, D.C.: U.S. Government Printing Office, 1978a.

_____. *The Budget of the United States Government, Appendix: Fiscal Year 1979.* Washington, D.C.: U.S. Government Printing Office, 1978b.

_____. *Special Analyses Budget of the United States Government, Fiscal Year 1979.* Washington, D.C.: U.S. Government Printing Office, 1978c.

Zumpano, Leonard V. "Housing Finance Agencies: Current Appraisal and Future Prospects." *Housing Educators Journal* 4 (1977): 14-20.

Discussion Questions

1. Describe how the different levels of government have been involved in influencing the production and consumption of housing.

2. What is the consistent theme that has emerged from the housing efforts of governmental actions?

3. What conditions led to the creation of the FHA-insured mortgages? How does this mortgage system differ from the typical mortgage system prior to 1934? Define the term "balloon" payment.

4. Explain the reason for the recent decline in FHA-insured mortgages.

5. What is meant by the term "public housing"? When was legislation first passed for public housing in the United States? What income levels of individuals and families are assisted by public housing?

6. What agency is responsible for the VA mortgage-guarantee program?

7. Discuss the major differences between Farmers Home Administration (FmHA) and the Department of Housing and Urban Development (HUD).

8. Must a family live on a farm to apply for a FmHA loan? What is the major reason for FmHA's substantial input in the development of rural housing?

9. In 1969, the Brooke Amendment to the Housing and Urban Development Act of 1965 was passed. What did this amendment authorize?

10. Discuss the major reasons for the numerous housing programs which have been designed.

11. Define the terms "indirect subsidies" and "direct subsidies." Explain what income levels of our citizens receive these subsidy benefits.

8. CODES AND CONTROLS
Building Codes, Housing Codes, Zoning Codes, and Subdivision Controls

by Carol S. Wedin

Building codes, housing codes, zoning codes (often referred to as zoning ordinances), and subdivision controls are protective devices designed to serve specific needs; each is a legal device directly influencing the qualities of housing. People not involved in the housing process are frequently confused as to the purpose and use of these four different codes and controls and think of them only as unnecessary constraints. A brief definition of each code and control follows:

Building Codes

A building code is a series of standards and specifications designed to establish minimum safeguards in the erection and construction of buildings, to protect the human beings who live and work in them from fire and other hazards, and to establish regulations to further protect the health and safety of the public .... [1]

Building codes can exist under the authority of the federal government or under the authority of the state, counties, and local municipalities. Although this is usually the case, there are exceptions depending on state legislation. The lack of uniformity in building codes can result in confusion, delays in construction, and ultimately, an increase in the cost of housing.

There are four model building codes used throughout the country. These codes are known as: the Basic Building Code, the Uniform Building Code, the Southern Standard Building Code, and the National Building Code. Commonly, local municipalities adopt and revise one or more of these model codes for their use.

Complaints directed against our present building codes are numerous. To write, maintain, and revise building codes is a costly and laborious task. The codes must be constantly updated as new materials and construction techniques are developed; therefore, small towns and rural communities cannot afford to hire and retain individuals with the expertise required to maintain building codes specifically applicable to their conditions.

The federal program known as Operation Breakthrough, formulated by the Department of Housing and Urban Development in 1968, encouraged and supported uniformity in state building codes. Within the past several years, twenty-three states have adopted state building codes, and thirty states have adopted building codes for manufactured housing. In June, 1976, a federal mobile home and construction safety

---

1. *Building the American City*, National Commission on Urban Problems to the Congress and to President of the U.S., House Document No. 91-34, 1968, p. 254.

standard was implemented that pre-empted all state and local regulations governing mobile home construction. Industrialized housing will make a greater input into our nation's total housing production as more uniform building codes are adopted.

Housing Codes

A housing code is an application of State police power put into effect by a local ordinance setting the minimum for safety, health and welfare of the occupants of housing. It covers three main areas:

(1) The supplied facilities in the structure, that is, toilet, bath, sink, etc., supplied by the owner.

(2) The level of maintenance, which includes both structural and sanitary maintenance, leaks in the roof, broken banisters, cracks in the walls, etc.

(3) Occupancy, which concerns the size of dwelling units and of rooms of different types, the number of people who can occupy them, and other issues concerned on the whole with the usability and amenity of interior space. [2]

The history of housing codes in the United States dates back to the late 1800's when the city of New York enacted a tenement-house law that was designed to correct unhealthful living conditions in New York City. A number of the major cities adopted housing codes in the early 1900's; however, the majority of today's housing codes are based on criteria used by the city of Baltimore when the city amended the housing code in 1941 to require that:

. . . dwellings be kept clean and free from dirt, filth, rubbish, garbage, and similar matter, and from vermin and rodent infestation, and in good repair and fit for human habitation,

2. *Ibid*, p. 274.

A major difficulty in enforcing housing codes in cities is to find decent housing for all displaced residents. (United States Department of Agriculture)

Many rural areas do not have adequate housing code enforcement. (United States Department of Agriculture; photo by Jack Schneider)

and authorizing the Commissioner of Health in Baltimore City to issue orders compelling the compliance with said provision or to correct the condition, at the expense of the property owner, and charge the property with a lien to the extent of the necessary expense. 3

Most housing codes are operative in our larger cities; however, the majority of substandard housing is found in the rural areas. Within the past few years a concern has been shown for designing housing codes that may be enforced in these rural areas.

If housing codes are to be adequately enforced other steps must be considered. First, we must make available an abundance of quality housing or families evicted from unsafe housing will be faced with even worse conditions than before. Secondly, we must provide funding or grants for the needy owners to rehabilitate the dwelling to meet the minimum housing code requirements. We should also consider that when housing codes are adequately enforced it will preserve and extend the life of the present structures.

In most cities, housing codes are usually enforced only on rental properties. There has been much discussion as to how far the government should go to regulate housing conditions without the danger of imposing on property rights and privacy unduly.

Numerous problems exist because at almost all levels of government there are conflicts in the purpose of housing codes, what are the minimum standards, and how they should be enforced and updated. For example, in the city of Des Moines, Iowa the housing code applies only to rental property unless an owner-occupied property is a

3. *Ibid*, p.274.

source highly detrimental to health or safety to the inhabitants themselves or to the surrounding neighborhood. In many cities, housing codes have only recently been adopted. Hopefully, the new codes will be carefully considered and effectively enforced to gradually augment changes associated with more healthful and safe homes for all our citizens.

Zoning Codes

> Zoning was meant to interweave people's needs for employment, housing, commercial services, and transportation, in a system planned by the residents of a community . . . . [4]

> The practice of zoning—an institution barely 50 years old—is now widespread throughout urban areas of the United States. The basic purpose of zoning, a laudable one, is to minimize land development activities on one parcel (of land) which will detract unreasonably from the value of other parcels . . . . [5]

The history of zoning in the United States began in the late 1800's in our major cities. Cities such as San Francisco and Los Angeles passed ordinances restricting the location of laundries in the 1880's. At about the same time, Washington, D.C. passed a law restricting certain heights of buildings. New York, Chicago, Boston, Philadelphia, and others passed laws which restricted the tenement's lot coverage.

By 1925, zoning was widely spread with 368 municipalities having passed laws. By the end of the next decade, over 1,000 municipalities had enacted zoning ordinances.

Zoning ordinances usually prescribe how each parcel of land in the community may be used. Most ordinances cover at least three major concerns, although it is not uncommon to have additional considerations covered, also. The three most common restrictions are:

1. The designation permitting certain activities, usually into three basic categories —dwellings, businesses, and industry. Often these basic categories are further divided into subcategories.
2. The limitation on population density—this is commonly achieved by either setting minimum required size for each lot or limiting the number of families per acre.
3. The limitation on building bulk. This is accomplished by limiting building height, by limiting the proportion of a lot that can be covered by a building, and by requiring that yard areas along lot boundaries have specific sizes.

Although zoning ordinances were designed to assure the orderly growth of an area, too often they have had negative side effects. Examples of negative side effects are discussed as problems resulting from exclusionary zoning in Article 12.

Subdivision Controls

> Subdivision control. . . .is closely related to zoning control in that both are preventive measures intended to avert community blight and deterioration by requiring that new development proceeds in defined ways and according to prescribed standards. Zoning relates to the type of building development which can take place on the land; subdivision control relates to the way in which land is divided and made ready for building development. The two are mutually dependent because the layout of an area is inseparable from the character of the use to be made of the land. [6]

4. *Source* (Chicago: Swallow Press, 1972), p. 172.
5. *A Decent Home,* The Report of the President's Committee on Urban Housing, 1968, p. 140.
6. Jacob H. Beuscher and Robert R. Wright, *Land Use Cases and Materials.* (St. Paul: West Publishing Co., 1969), p. 258.

A land owner must obtain the approval of a governing agency before he can divide a parcel of his land into lots for sale. There are several reasons for this type of control:

1. The community will obviously be affected by a new subdivision. The original layout of a subdivision will influence all future decisions. Problems of traffic congestion, police and fire protection, overly-crowded schools, and inadequate public services can be minimized if consideration is given at the planning stage.

.2 The home buyer and mortgagor are both assured that a sound investment has been effected. Subdivision controls require a survey and plat of the planned area and this documentation then provides the home buyer information on accurate boundary lines to his property. The subdivision layout will show future street development, commercial and recreational areas; thus, providing for the buyer an idea of what the area will be like when it is fully developed. The prospective home buyer may go to the planning division in city or municipalities and request this information.

3. The subdivider (or speculative developer) has greater assurance of financial success. Therefore, the subdivision control law protects the honest subdivider from the fly-by-night operator.

An alternative to subdivision controls is municipal ownership and development which has been used successfully in many European cities. In the United States, however, we have traditionally preferred government supervision of the private developer. As long as the free enterprise system is valued as highly as it is in this society, we must have regulations to safeguard the welfare of the consumer-user.

Conclusion

The adoption and enforcement of government regulations is essential to the orderly growth and development of any community, and for the maintenance and improvement of safe and healthful housing. During the past several years, however, government regulations have been greatly criticized as a significant factor in the rising cost of housing. While most requirements suggest positive improvements in housing and neighborhood conditions, some of these improvements can be viewed as extravagant. Many builders believe the cost of complying with the proliferating government regulations enforced within the past ten years has resulted in a 10 to 15% increase in the total cost of housing.[7] The consumer-user should be aware of the increased cost resulting from additional government regulations. Knowledgeable citizens can have an effect on public policy that insures a safe and healthful housing environment.

References

Beuscher, Jacob H., and Robert R. Wright. *Land Use Cases and Materials.* St. Paul: West Publishing Co., 1969.

Building the American City. National Commission on Urban Problems to the Congress and to the President of the U.S., House Document No. 91-34, 1968, p. 254.

A Decent Home. Report of the President's Committee on Urban Housing. Washington, D.C.: U.S. Government Printing Office, 1969.

"High Price of Government in Housing." *Professional Builder and Apartment Business,* May 1977, pp. 136-143.

Source. Chicago: Swallow Press, 1972.

7. "High Price of Government in Housing," *Professional Builder* (May 1977), p. 137.

Discussion Questions

1. Distinguish between a building code and a housing code. Who has authority over each?

2. What functions do the four model building codes serve? Is there uniformity between states in building codes? How extensively are building codes developed over the various states?

3. What are the advantages and disadvantages of uniformity of codes and controls?

4. How did housing codes develop in the U.S.? What are necessary steps in assuring that housing codes are adequately enforced?

5. Recap the history and the purpose of zoning. What are the most common restrictions?

6. In a "free" country, why is subdivision control necessary?

7. During the past several years, government regulations have been criticized. What is the major reason for the criticism?

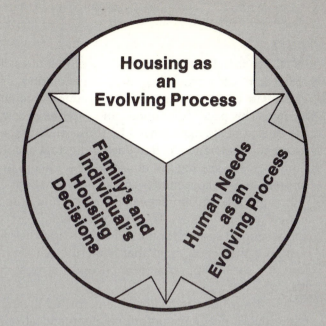

Housing as
an
Evolving Process

Family's and
Individual's
Housing
Decisions

Human Needs
as an
Evolving Process

Part Three
Environmental
Settings

9. Social Change in Rural Communities, by Ronald C. Powers

10. The City as Teacher and Learner, by Kenneth E. Boulding

11. The Dilemmas of Neighborhood Revitalization, by John R. Mullin

12. Segregation in Housing: Its Costs to Life Chances and Some Solutions, by Duncan Case

13. Neighbourhoods and Human Needs, by Margaret Mead

When individuals or families buy or rent a residence they are acquiring far more than just the dwelling; they are acquiring a package of goods and services. Part Three examines the environmental settings where the dwellings are located. This package of goods and services becomes a major determinant of the quality of life experienced by those making the selection. There is a hierarchy of social networks that each individual encounters. Individuals relate to other persons sharing the household ——→ the housing is part of a community ——→ and, communities make up the nation.

It is the relationship between housing and community which is examined closely in Part Three. The "neighborhood" or "community" provides the social support system for the individuals and their families. The social support system is the set of forces that relate the person to the environment. Therefore, the social support system becomes a most important aspect of human life.

Americans have, to a large extent, trusted their elected and hired officials to make public decisions; unfortunately, many of our citizens think themselves incapable of being effective change agents. Community Development Block Grants and other governmental actions now require citizen participation. Social responsibility means weighing the costs and benefits to a total neighborhood, community, or society in general because the effects are transferred to so many in ways that determine the quality of their daily existence. Individuals must, therefore, take into consideration more than the personal advantages to be gained.

Concepts of community change resulting from advances in technology are discussed in Dr. Powers' article in Part Three. As the community has evolved to encompass a greater geographical area, there has also been a shift in population. This shift in population is occurring not only in the "community" but also on a regional level.

Professor Boulding examines the theory of the city from the standpoints of geography and location, organization, a social phenomenon, and a teacher of humankind. He discusses why some cities flourish and others do not. The relationship of the city to housing is so intimate that in a physical sense they are almost the same concept. To maintain the desired quality of urban life we must seek an optimum mix of public and private decisions and public and private property.

Article 11. "The Dilemmas of Neighborhood Revitalization," presents a case study that illustrates the struggles facing many of our urban neighborhoods. The article on segregation in housing discusses how an individual's life chances are related to the housing and neighborhood environment.

Finally, an article by the late Dr. Margaret Mead explains basic physiological needs of all human beings and how the neighborhood must fulfill these needs.

9. Social Change in Rural Communities

by Ronald C. Powers

There are numerous definitions of *community,* but one feature which is included in most definitions is geographical space. Thus traditionally, community has been defined as the "geographic space" within which most of one's social and economic needs are met. These social and economic needs include the need for shelter (housing), jobs, education, safety, and social participation. Though such a definition of community is quite imprecise, it readily brings to mind the turn of the century image of a small town and the surrounding open country. The boundary between one "community" and the next was determined by the point along the dirt road between the two where the wagon tracks from the farm lane turned out in the other direction. The times people ventured outside their home community were few in number, usually to the county seat to conduct legal business or to obtain a good or service not available in the closest town. On special occasions there might be a longer trip to visit relatives, to attend the state fair, or to sell livestock at a central market.

Understanding Community

The viewing of a community as a small "geographic space" is largely a nostalgia trip today and has been ever since the limitation imposed by the speed of the horse was broken, despite the fact that large numbers of communities established in the horse age are still in existence. When the speed of the horse gave way to the speed of the automobile and the power of the tractor, a vast change began in which new technology was the prime mover. There was production technology (machines in agriculture and industry) which allowed more work to be done by fewer people — especially in agriculture. There was the rapid change in transportation technology (cars, trains, and airplanes) which permitted frequent and distant travel and eventually the practice of job commuting which is now a widespread phenomenon. There was the new technology in communications: telegraph, postal service, telephone, radio, television, and the print media. New communication technology permits more rapid acquisition of information by people which in turn affects their decisions. It also permits movement of information to people, rather than movement of people to the information, and it may reduce the need for as much face-to-face interaction. The implications of developments in communication technology for settlement (where people live and work) and human interaction patterns are just beginning to be realized as applications of computer technology explode onto the scene of business, personal, and family life. The use of two-way com-

Ronald C. Powers is Director, North Central Regional Center for Rural Development, Iowa State University. This article was prepared specially for this book.

munication through television, the terminal in the home which permits access to libraries and businesses, and shopping by computer from one's home are just a few examples of such changes already here or certain to come.

A final dimension of technological advance that deserves mention as background information to understanding community and community change is the chemical technology (fertilizer and pesticides) which has influenced agricultural production in particular. Combined with genetic improvements in crops and livestock, this chemical technology and the earlier breakthroughs in machine technology led to the population change in rural areas. In 1910 there were 32,000,000 people living on farms, about 1/3 of the total U.S. population; in 1974 this farm population had been reduced to 9,300,000, less than 5% of the total U.S. population.

Dynamics of Population Change

The large migration of people from the farms to towns and cities impacted the many small towns and villages that were the "centers" of rural communities. From about 1920 until the very recent past, there was a steady stream of population movement from the farms and from the small towns to the urban areas. It has been said that farmers sold their wheat and corn and gave away their children because so many left after completing their high school education. In many rural states the vast majority of the towns under 2,500 and the surrounding countryside declined in population from 1920 until 1970. The visible signs were there for all to see: vacant farmsteads, boarded-up and run-down buildings, and consolidated schools with strange-sounding or hyphenated names as residents clung to old community identities.

The pattern of one town and the surrounding area being a community (a place where most of one's needs were met) gave way to an exploded territory where a community became a central city of 15,000 or more with smaller towns arranged around the larger one and still smaller places around each of the others. The size of such communities approximated an area of one hour's commuting time from the "edge" to the central city. In the midwestern United States, this was equal to about eight average counties or 10,000 square miles.

This "new" area now approximates the space within which most of one's social and economic needs can be met. The change in the territory within which we *interact* to meet our needs has exploded, but the area with which most still *identify* remains much smaller and often focuses on the town or place we go to school. Stated in a different way: the technology of the last five decades has resulted in a separation of our community of identification from our community of interaction. The effect of this change for most small towns has been a steadily declining population since 1920.

Since 1970 there has been a turn-about of sorts for some smaller towns. Towns and counties in nonmetropolitan areas (places of less than 50,000) which were declining in population are now increasing. Center cities of large metropolitan areas are growing slowly or even declining. But the population turn-about is occurring in those areas where jobs are available and those which are desirable for retirement and recreation. Small towns which are too far away from an area of economic viability to permit job commuting on a long-term basis are not growing unless there is a sufficient economic base. In short, those towns and places with a population of less than 1,000 which do not fall into one of the categories just cited are continuing to lose population, or, at best, to stabilize. It is well to realize that there are many places with a population of less than 1,000 in the country (approximately 8,400). About half continue to have population declines. Of the 13,292 towns and cities under 50,000 in 1970, 44% lost pop-

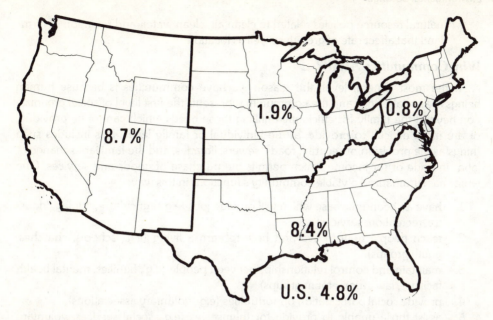

Figure 1. Percentage increase in population from 1970-1975, United States. (Source: Current Population Reports, Series P-25, No. 615., U.S. Bureau of the Census.)

ulation between 1960 and 1970. The population shift in the United States is toward the South and West. (See Figure 1.)

Given the dynamics of population change, it is important to be sensitive to the idea that communities are social, economic, and political phenomena formed in "brick and mortar" images. Such long-life physical structures may create a sense of permanency at a point in time that becomes incompatible with the *rate* and *direction* of social and technological change. When this occurs we eventually see vacant business places, houses, and abandoned school buildings. If long-term changes result in new economic reasons for a community, such as becoming a retirement or recreation center or a bedroom-commuting town, the earlier physical structures may provide the base for historical preservation, renewed business, and restoration of older homes.

Even in the context of the many crosscurrents of social and economic change, it has been possible to generally predict the directions of population change in the United States. It also has been possible to project the general changes in composition (i.e., age, size of families, etc.) of the population. There has been much less success in predicting the future of *specific* communities. At the level of a particular town or city there are too many unknowns. Leadership capacity, specific resources, external decisions in the private or public sector, and the changes occurring in nearby communities are just a few of the unknowns which make it difficult to predict which towns will grow and which will decline.

Major events affecting the entire nation can also affect the capacity to predict trends in population numbers and composition as well as migration patterns. Among those of recent note which have caused revisions in earlier predictions are:

1. decreases in the birth rate;
2. increased longevity;
3. rapidly escalating energy costs; and

4. natural resource policies related to clean air, clean water, and retention of farm-land that affect rate of growth as well as location.

Why Communities At All?

At the most general level, the reason we have communities is because human beings are social beings and the community represents the first level of social organization beyond the family for efficiently fulfilling those needs which cannot be provided, or are more difficult to provide, at the individual or family level. This includes such things as the provision of security, roads, sewers, libraries, and the familiar exchange of labor in trade or for income which permits the purchase of goods and services. One writer has summarized a viable community's functions in this way:

1. have an economic base which will provide jobs (e.g., agriculture, mining, industry, recreation, services).
2. teach people how to live and how to earn a living (e.g., schools, churches, youth groups).
3. maintain and control relationships between people (e.g., families, mental health facilities, law enforcement groups).
4. provide social participation opportunities (e.g., voluntary associations).
5. assist those unable to provide for themselves (e.g., social services, voluntary health groups, service clubs).*

A viable community requires a major commitment of resources to support the daily activities of people going about the business of satisfying individual needs for food, clothing, shelter, and such social needs as belonging, recognition, and self-esteem. In economics this underlying support base is called "infrastructure" and refers to streets, sewers, other utilities, schools, transportation, and other governmental services. The inability of a community to pay for these services can cause decline because people move away and thus exacerbate the problem for those who remain. The provision of such services (e.g., rural water systems today or rural electricity in the early 1940s) by the government through grants and loans can bring people to a community and sometimes lead to severe pressure on other services such as schools. The expansion of a sewer system which permits a housing boom in a small town near a large city almost always leads to the need to expand the school system, improve streets, and recreation facilities. It is this web of cause-and-effect relationships which makes decisions by families, businesses, and local governments difficult. A change in federal policy related to water quality, sewage treatment, housing loans, road funds, industrial development, land use, energy, and health-facilities standards can have major impact on the location of jobs and the required infrastructure in communities.

The Future of Rural Communities

Insofar as rural development is concerned, there has not been a strong policy in the United States. The policies related to community development have traditionally been weighted in favor of urban and metropolitan areas. In view of the recent facts indicating the growth of nonmetropolitan areas it may be that more assistance will be provided to rural communities to make them better places to live. Such a policy cannot be committed to making every small community a modern-day version of meeting most of one's social and economic needs in the small, geographic space surrounding each town. Technology did cause an explosion, and the widespread population changes

*Adapted from Roland Warren, *Community in America* (Rand McNally: Chicago, 1963), pp. 167-208.

that have occurred, like popcorn, cannot be put back in the kernel. So some towns established to serve the railroad, the stagecoach, and the horse-and-buggy days will not experience a revival because there is no economic base to support such a change.

Housing and Community

The concept of community can be tied to housing in several ways. People's need for shelter has been translated into housing. Housing as a physical structure represents a mix of resources: materials, labor, capital, and land. Housing also generates a demand for sewer services, water, electricity, gas, streets, parks, and schools. These are all parts of the community infrastructure. These require tax dollars, usually a combination of fees, property tax, and federal revenues. To the extent that local property tax is involved, this has a direct impact on home owners.

Housing is also a relatively immovable structure; it has a long life; and it requires servicing (plumbers, electricians, etc.) on site. If the community has declined to the point that such skills and services are not present, it increases the cost to the home owner. Housing may "outlive" a community if the economic base disappears (as when a mine closes or the only industry leaves). When this occurs, there may be substantial losses in property values. The lack of housing may also keep a community from growing, or from obtaining the "new industry" which would provide the base for growth.

Conclusions

Individual decisions about housing can affect communities by increasing the demand for new public services, by increasing the capacity of the community to attract new business and more residents, and by increasing the tax base. Individual decisions can also lead to the opposite situation. Community decisions regarding the type and amount of new jobs to be created can affect housing. Industries that pay high wages and have a high proportion of professionals will generate a different demand for housing than those with lower wages and less-skilled labor. To the extent that larger families are associated with lower income levels, the type of industry will also affect the type of housing demand in a community.

Discussion Questions

1. Define the term "community" as it is referred to traditionally.

2. How has the concept of community been changed by modern technology?

3. Discuss the difference between our community of interaction and our community of identification.

4. Since 1970 there has been a population turnabout for some smaller towns. What factors account for this change in some small towns but not in all small towns?

5. Identify major events affecting the entire nation that also influence population composition and population migration.

6. List the functions of a viable community and discuss how these functions provide for human needs.

7. Define the term "infrastructure" as it refers to the functions of a community.

8. Why will governmental policies that relate to small rural communities not be as strong as policies affecting urban and metropolitan areas?

9. Discuss the relationship between housing and community, including both the individual decisions and the community decisions.

10. The City as Teacher and Learner

by Kenneth E. Boulding

It is one of the paradoxes of our day that the more the agricultural population declined and the urban population rose, the more research, inquiry, and support went into agriculture and the less into cities. One has only to contrast the state of agricultural economics which boasts large departments, well-supported faculties, and research stations with the almost rudimentary state of urban economics in spite of some hardy and courageous pioneers. In part, this probably can be accounted for by the grand old phenomenon of lag. The business of preparing to solve the problems of the last generation has always been a pretty extensive one. The problem of cities, however, is already the problem of the last generation, and the lag here goes back practically to our great-grandparents.

A Theory of the City?

Suppose, for instance, that one wanted to offer a course or even to write a textbook on the "theory of the city." Where would it be put? We find plenty of teaching and formal textbooks on the "theory of the firm." We find an occasional course in a political science department on municipal government. But where around a university will one find anything which looks at the city as a whole as a social organism, as a cultural pattern, and as an entity in itself? There may be something of this nature in the department of city planning; this will mostly be dominated by engineers and architects, and the social sciences will have very small pickings. Up to a point we may blame social scientists themselves for this state of affairs. They tend to stay in conventional patterns, and for some reason the study of the city has not become conventional.

It is an interesting speculation, therefore, in which I have been indulging somewhat irresponsibly: to think what one would put in a course on the theory of the city if it were treated from a broad interdisciplinary point of view. What are the kinds of questions which one would want such a theory to illuminate? Could we expect it to come up with any testable propositions which might be disproved or confirmed? How would it fit into a general theory of the structure of society in time and space? I am not sure that I can give a very satisfactory answer to any of these questions. All I can do at this stage of my reflections is to throw out a few hints and suggestions.

Kenneth E. Boulding is Distinguished Professor of Economics at the University of Colorado at Boulder and President of the American Association for the Advancement of Science (AAAS). This article was revised specially for this book.

Geography and Theory of Location

One would start, I think, with geography and the theory of location. In spite of the recent emergence of regional science as a discipline in its own right, there are still many puzzling aspects of the spatial structure of human activity. One would certainly take a look at the economic theory of location, Adolph Weber, and of course Lösch, whose perception of how a market might structure activities in space in a complex honeycomb is a profound theoretical insight. Lösch's theory is, however, a little hard to test because of the presence of what might almost be called spatial noise. As the laws of motion operate only in a vacuum and explain very little about the detailed behavior of snowflakes and leaves, so Lösch's structure would develop only on a homogeneous plane and is greatly distorted by the accidents of actual topography. Still, it is a good place to start, and it gives us some clue as to why activity concentrates in cities and in towns and is not diffused uniformly over the countryside. One thing a theory of the city has to explain is why the city exists at all, which perhaps is better stated as why its size is not zero or why population is not uniformly diffused.

Once we have established that there will be concentrations of population and that the density of population will not be uniform over the face of the earth but will exhibit very marked divergencies between areas of very high density and areas of low density, we run into some puzzling questions about the nature of these organized distributions. What I have sometimes called Zipf's Law — that the population of the nth-ranking community multiplied by n is roughly equal to the population of the first community — not only has a certain amount of empirical evidence to support it but even its exceptions seem susceptible of some interpretation. Zipf's own efforts at explanation are very far from satisfactory.[1] And even attempts to develop stochastic models which will give distributions of this kind by Herbert Simon, for instance, do not seem very convincing somehow.[2] We have here a rather uneasy situation where the empirical regularities of organized distributions can hardly be denied, but where no simple theory, at least, has been developed to account for them.

Organization of the City

Once we have established the necessity for aggregations of different sizes, the next thing to look at is the way these aggregations are organized. Here we run into some very tricky problems indeed. All cities are characterized by some kind of central organization. The central organization may be a fairly small part of the total activity, but it would be hard to find any aggregation of people where it did not exist. It is hard for us, at any rate, to conceive of a city without a municipality and a bureaucracy, though we perhaps get something close to this in the favellas and barrios of Latin American and the shantytowns of Asia which cluster around the organized cities and participate very little in their organization. Nevertheless, it is significant that even these clusters are on the edges or in the interstices of organized cities, and it would be very difficult indeed to find any aggregation of people, even of fairly small size, that did not throw up something in the way of organization.

Now, of course, we get a hen-and-egg question: which comes first, the aggregation or the organization? Did aggregation inevitably produce organization? Can the lack of organization prevent aggregation? Do we have in organizational skill and competence an independent variable which affects the growth and size distribution of cities, or are

1. George Kingsley Zipf, *Human Behavior and the Principle of Least Effort* (Cambridge, Mass: Addison-Wesley Press, 1949).
2. Herbert A. Simon, *Models of Man* (New York: John Wiley & Sons, 1957), p. 161.

the forces which produce aggregation so strong that the organizational element is quite subordinate to them? I must confess I incline to the view that it is aggregation that created organization, rather than the other way around, except perhaps in the case of political cities like Washington, D.C., or Brasilia. Nevertheless, this is something which should be possible to test in some degree, and a study of cities that attempted to differentiate between those with efficient organizations and those without would be of enormous interest.

The City as a Social Phenomenon

We seem to have no general word to describe what the city is an example of as a social phenomenon. It is not an organization like a firm or even a church or school, which have hierarchies that extend to all the members and which have some kind of control over their membership. General Motors, for instance, has what might be called a membership boundary. It is fairly clear who is employed by it and who is not; it is defined on the whole by the assets which it possesses; and it has relationships with its suppliers, dealers, and customers which are to some extent formalized.

A city, however, such as Detroit, has a geographical rather than a membership boundary. Its membership is defined simply by the people who happen to live within a certain area. It has a hierarchical organization, but the hierarchy and the organization is much smaller than the population of the city itself, and its activity is a mere fraction of the activity which goes on in the city. A city, furthermore, especially in a market-dominated society, has practically no control over the numbers or the kinds of the people who live in it; it simply has to take these as a datum.

The relation of General Motors to its customers, therefore, is very different from the relation of a municipality to its citizens. In the case of a city it is the aggregation which creates the organization. Many of the peculiarities and difficulties of the city arise from this fact, and perhaps also a certain feeling of frustration and dissatisfaction which seems to arise almost universally with municipal government as an institution. The firm seeks out customers and tries to please them with its product. It lives essentially in an exchange environment. The citizens of a municipality come unsought, and the income of the municipal organization comes from taxation, not from sales.

In the case of the firm, equilibrium theory has turned out to be quite useful, even though it has sharp limitations, mainly because the assumption that the firm maximizes something, notably profits, is at least a fair first approximation to its behavior. We may be getting increasingly dissatisfied with equilibrium theory in the case of the firm and demanding some true dynamics; in the case of the city, however, we do not even seem to have any equilibrium theory to start with. We may, perhaps, postulate a certain equilibrium range of taxation, for instance, at the upper extremity of which the outraged citizens either invade the palace or vote out the mayor and aldermen, and at the lower level of which the sheer inadequacy of essential services likewise creates political discontent sufficient to change the policy. The range between the upper and lower limits, though, may be pretty broad, and are very rarely reached.

However, one does see, especially in such matters as voting on bond issues, and now, of course, with the passage of Proposition 13 in California, a certain tendency to pirouette at an upper limit. What this means in terms of modern organization theory is that the municipal organization has a great deal more slack than the ordinary business firm. In this case there is nowhere to go but into dynamics, and we have to take recourse to what I have sometimes called D'Arcy Thompson's Law: that everything is what it is because it got that way. We then see the structure of the organization of the city, the extent of its tax collections, the nature of its taxes, the distribution of its expenditures, the form of its organization, and so on as the result of a long dynamic process. This process may have some random elements in it, although it will also certainly have strong nonrandom elements. In explaining what makes Milwaukee different from Detroit and still more different from Siena, we have to invoke history — the culture of the people who formed the aggregate, the particular decisions that were made, the precedents that were set, the patterns that were established, and so on. Still, there is enough repetitiveness in the pattern so that an ideal type of city history or perhaps a series of ideal types is by no means absurd.

The City as a Teacher of Humankind

This brings me to an idea which is almost becoming a theme song: that the key to any process of social dynamics is the process of human learning, the way in which the experiences of people change their images of the world and the distribution of these images in the population. Knowledge is the only thing which is susceptible to continuous and sustained development. Everything else is subject to fatal laws of conservation or of entropy. The city in its physical manifestation — the streets, the buildings, the transportation system, the firms, the households, the organization, the municipality itself — reflects the images, past and present, which govern human behavior. Its situation is complicated by the deposits of the past. The layout of streets and the architecture of the city are frequently the result of the images and decisions of people long dead. A city is more like a hermit crab which inhabits the cast-off shell of a former living organism than it is like an oyster which secretes its own shell to fit itself as it lives. Still,

The architecture of the city is frequently the result of deposits of the past. (Department of Housing and Urban Development)

each generation makes its impact on the shell, and the shell itself acts as a teacher of the present generation.

Certainly children growing up in a noble and well-planned city, inherited from a great past, will be taught certain tastes and values from the structures around them. In this sense the sheer physical structure of a city may exhibit an extraordinary degree of homeostasis and almost come to dominate the life of the people who inhabit it. A good example of this is Leningrad, which was reconstructed after enormous destruction in the Second World War almost exactly as it had appeared before. Warsaw is perhaps an even more striking example. It is perhaps a little odd at first sight that the socialist countries which think of themselves as progressive are most bound by the chains of the past in this way. Even where the past is rejected, however, the city still stands as a symbol of the permanance of roles, of the transience of people and of the possibility for immortality of social organizations.

The problem of having to reconcile the needs of the present with the deposits of the past is often difficult enough, even in the individual human being. In the case of the city it is often an almost insuperable problem, but the presence of this problem also gives the city a lot of its life. This perhaps is why the artificial cities like Brasilia, Canberra, and, in its early days, Washington, D.C., have an air of deadness and unreality which no amount of elegant planning and architecture can overcome. These are monsters pieced together by the Frankenstein planners and architects, not organic growths deposited generation after generation.

The idea of the city as a teacher of humankind, brightening the eye, quickening the step, enlivening the discourse and spurring the ambitions, and even spilling over into the countryside to rescue it from the cloddishness of rural life, is an ancient theme. One finds it, for instance, in the writings of Adam Smith.[3] Smith's delightful chapters in Book III of *The Wealth of Nations*, headed "Of the Rise and Progress of Cities and Towns after the Fall of the Roman Empire," and chapter 4, "How the Commerce of the Towns Contributed to the Improvement of the Country," should be required reading for all students of urban affairs. It is interesting, and certainly contrary to the stereotype of city violence versus rural peace, that Adam Smith makes the great contribution of the cities the establishment of "order and good government, and along with them the liberty and security of individuals." These, he says, "were established in cities at a time when the occupiers of land in the country were exposed to every sort of violence." Here again we face the question as to whether order and good government emerge as a result of certain population densities or whether the population densities are produced by order and good government, and we probably have to content ourselves with the observation of a vague reciprocal relationship. It is hard to create order and good government over a very scattered population; it may equally be hard to maintain it in areas of extremely high density, where sheer mechanical social friction is high. This suggests that there is some optimum density for the ease of establishing order and good government, one is almost tempted to say, in suburbia.

The Flourishing of the City

This leads to the very interesting historical question as to the conditions under which the city-state will flourish. This is a matter on which a good deal more empirical and statistical work needs to be done. The dilemma of the city, as it is of many forms of social organization, is that the creation of order and good government within it is often associated with the creation of disorder and bad government outside it. The city-state had order and good government of a kind, at any rate, within the walls, but it paid a

3. Adam Smith, The Wealth of Nations. (London: Dent, 1966).

heavy price for this in terms of disorder and war between the states, of which pre-Alexandrine Greece is a good example. There seem to be certain principles of social entropy here which we have not yet clarified.

A good deal of the association of the city with the development of order and good government can be explained by another principle of Adam Smith: that the division of labor depends on the extent of the market. A high density of population in itself increases the market and permits specialization. Order and good government can be regarded as a specialized activity which only a large market permits. As long as the population is of low density, people have to provide for their own protection against violence, just as they have to make their own clothes. In both cases this is very badly done. It is only the specialization that is produced by increased density that permits either good commodities or good government.

It is not fanciful to see this principle of the extent of the market as a special case of a wider principle: that the rate of human learning depends on the amount of human interaction and that the amount of human interaction increases almost certainly in more than linear fashion with population density. Rustics are traditionally clods because they never talk to anybody; their neighbors are too far away or they're confined to a very small circle of acquaintances, all of whom are very much like themselves. In the city, people are exposed to a wide variety of other human beings, and the sheer interaction produces learning. There may again be some kind of optimum density from this point of view, and too great a density may inhibit learning simply because people have to insulate themselves from each other and defend themselves against too great an information input by stereotypes, prejudices, nationalism, and cultural isolation. One should add, of course, that this differentiation in culture and in the rate of learning between the city and the country is characteristic of preindustrial civilization, but is much less characteristic of developed societies. In the United States, for instance, we have very largely eliminated the cultural difference between urban and rural areas. This is, indeed, one of our great achievements. The midwestern farmers have an occupational subculture, but not a rural subculture which is much differentiated from that of their city equivalents. This is, because the whole world in effect has become a city, thanks to the improvements in the means of communication. I have elsewhere referred to "the death of the city," meaning by this, the disappearance of the city of classical civilization which was closely bounded and sharply differentiated in its culture from the countryside around it.[4] What we have in the world today is the development of the world city, and again one hopes that world order and good government will result.

The development of order and good government, however, whether within the classical city or the world city, depends on a learning process within the structure of the city itself. More than anything, it is the virtues and defects of this process which make the difference between mere agglomeration and organization. If a city is to survive and prosper, the rulers of the city themselves must learn. A process of information collection and processing and of testing the existing images of the city must be established through which images which do not conform to the changing realities are rejected and images which do conform are accepted. In the city, as in any other organization, the tyrants bring about their own downfall because their very tyranny cuts them off from unbiased sources of information. Hence, their image of the world gets more and more distorted and unreal, until, finally, they are operating in an almost purely imaginary world.

4. K. E. Boulding, "The Death of the City," in *The Historian and the City,* Oscar Handlin and John Burchard (eds.) (Cambridge, Mass.: M.I.T. Press, 1963), pp. 133-145.

Even without tyranny, however, there are many defects in the information system by which images are tested and changed. These can be quite serious, even in a democratic society. Many city leaders, for instance, who have been floating along under the impression that all was going well have been shocked and surprised by race riots, by scandals, or by angry groups of citizens. Sometimes the failures of leadership cause a city to stagnate and decline. Sometimes crises stimulate to new images and new activities. Sometimes they are too much for the community. It loses its good leadership, if it ever had any, and it starts on the slippery slope towards decline and disintegration.

The City and Housing

The relation of the city to housing is so intimate that in a physical sense they are almost the same concept. A city consists of buildings, access to and from buildings, streets, transportation facilities, sewers, power lines, water pipes, gas pipes, and so on, all of which provide for the inputs to and outputs from buildings in terms of people and things, energy and materials. Parks and gardens could almost be regarded as open-air buildings and are certainly as artificial. The physical structure of cities in regard to housing arises from our intense dislike of the open air, except in very limited times and places. The open air is almost always either too cold or too hot, too wet or too dry for human comfort. It also lacks privacy. Therefore, housing, not only domestic housing which shelters the family but also factories, office buildings, public buildings, theatres, shops, and so on which shelter other kinds of human activity for both work and play, is a result of our need for protection from the inclemency of the out-of-doors. Human beings possess a deep ambivalence toward nonhuman environments and nonhuman artifacts. Mountains and trees and beaches are all right for vacations, even for working in, provided that we have a retreat close at hand in the form of a house or even a tent which protects us from the basic hostility of nature. It is not much fun anywhere in the world to be houseless, even in the most favorable climates.

The problems of the city, therefore, revolve to a very great extent around the necessity for housing under conditions of congestion, that is, dense populations. Congestion raises the value of the land on which housing is placed, which in this case represents not biological fertility but simply area and potentially volume. Consequently, urban buildings tend to get tall, as tall as technology permits and congestion demands. The invention of the steel frame created a major revolution in the appearance and in the access problems of cities and produced the skyscraper, just as the vertebrate skeleton produced the dinosaur. Skyscrapers, however, cause severe problems of access in terms of traffic congestion, the need for public transportation, (usually underground), and the connections of electricity, gas, water, and other important inputs.

Externalities of Housing

Another major problem of urban housing, whether domestic or commercial, is that of externalities. In the countryside one can build a house without much affecting a neighbor's view or amenities. In the city, a building of any kind changes the environment of all surrounding buildings and may change their values. This is the main reason why we get zoning: so that a new building will increase the value of the neighboring area rather than diminish it. Thus, it is desirable to segregate those structures like canneries or oil refineries, which severely diminish the value of a neighborhood, into neighborhoods that have low values to begin with. Zoning arises, of course, because of a defect in the property and market structure. When the market is as thin and exchanges are as infrequent as they are in real estate and where the assessment of the causes of changes in values is very difficult, we cannot rely on property and exchange alone to solve the problem of externalities. If a person builds something or even allows something to go to ruin — there are sins of omission as well as commission here — which depreciates the neighborhood, he or she might be sued or charged with the loss and this would change the behavior. But this is often impracticable and we have to recourse to political decisions enforced by legitimated threat in the shape of police and courts.

Public and Private Enterprise

One of the most difficult problems in urban housing is the proper mix of public and private. Too much, or the wrong kinds, of one or the other will produce a "tragedy of the commons" with its attendant waste and injustice. Given a sufficient sense of community and enough organization to provide the necessary public goods, property and private enterprise can be very effective, as we have seen in the American suburbs. They are aesthetically charming, however weak they may be from the point of view of neighborliness. In urban breakdown, as we see it in South Bronx, private property has collapsed because of the absence of any sense of community or local scale. The famous Pruitt-Igoe public housing in St. Louis, however, also collapsed for lack of public goods and public order as well as poor design. These are classical instances of failure. The "new cities" of Columbia, Maryland and Reston, Virginia are at least a reasonable success.

In the private sector, the role of the price structure and of income distribution is of great importance. Rent control, as it has usually been administered, can not only create great injustices, subsidizing the old timers at the expense of the newcomers, but can also lead to deterioration of property and can create urban decay. Even its justification on the grounds of income distribution can be very dubious. It not only discriminates among tenants, but there are occasions where tenants are richer than landlords and rent control transfers income from poor landlords to richer tenants. It is usually much better to help the poor by direct subsidy than by making the things cheap that we think they buy. This latter approach often ends up subsidizing the rich and distorting the consumption patterns of the poor, often in irrational directions. For the poor, it is much better to live in poor housing and have adequate nutrition and medical care than it is to have good housing and poor nutrition and health.

Finance and Ownership

The economics of urban housing is dominated not only by externalities but also by finance as a result of the long time periods involved. Finance is a device for separating ownership from control, whether this is through rents, mortgages, or other devices. The distribution of ownership of anything, and especially of housing, is a result of a long historic process of purchase and sale, depreciation, restoration, maintenance, and inheritance. We have a strong prejudice in our society in favor of owner occupancy on the quite legitimate grounds that this is where the "magic of property" is most likely to be efficacious. It is the virtue of property that mistaken decisions by the owner are paid for by the owner. In a society where mistaken decisions injure other people but do not injure the maker of the decisions, the chance of bad decisions is much greater. On the other hand, even though the institutions of society may favor owner occupancy — devices like subsidized mortgages, tax relief, and the like — they become very difficult to expand beyond a certain point. This point we have almost certainly reached. Furthermore, the rise in real rates of interest over the last generation have put an increasing burden on young people who wish to acquire their own houses. Underlying both urban blight and suburban charm, there is the invisible ghost of the financial structure and this requires very careful study and understanding.

Education for Better Policies

In this setting one may usefully inquire as to the possible future role of the social sciences in improving the information collection and processing apparatus of the city, with a view to developing more accurate and realistic images of its state and movement in the hope that better knowledge will produce better policies.

Up to now, the learning process by which the city decision-makers have achieved their images has been haphazard and almost of necessity biased in the direction of those problems which are obviously visible and prominent. The city politician and administrator learn their images of what the city is like mainly from their day-to-day experiences. Decisions are made by the method of what Lindblom and Braybrooke call "a disjointed incrementalism," which is an elegant way of saying that the squeaky wheel gets the grease. Over wide ranges of decision-making, this is quite a workable method. The assumption that it is the squeaky wheel that needs the grease is by no means stupid. Nevertheless, processes of this kind have certain built-in filters which result in the neglect of problems which may be real and cumulative and in the long run very important, but which do not obtrude themselves.

The social sciences have now gotten to the point, or at least very close to it, where they could act as an important corrective for this bias in the system. What is needed is a constant monitoring of the state of the social system by formalistic and repetitive procedures, such as those, for instance, which on a national scale produce national income statistics. I have argued that we need this on a world scale, that we need, for instance, a network of social data stations just as we have a network of meterological stations, which will report, record, and process information about the sociosphere just as the meterological stations report information about the atmosphere. If we need this on a world scale, we also need it on the scale of the city.

The provisions of a monitoring system of this kind should be a major challenge to social scientists in the coming generation. There are many problems in connection with it. For instance, there are ethical problems regarding the domain of privacy and the definition of the public domain in the field of knowledge. Knowledge has optimum quantities like anything else, and a great deal of organizational structure is designed to protect the decision-makers against too much knowledge, or at least too much information input, as well as to insure that they get enough information. Here again the methods and procedures of the social sciences may have considerable significance. Insofar as knowledge about social systems in the large can be quantified and indexed, it protects the privacy of the individual and creates images which are significant without being overloaded. It is necessary, however, for social scientists themselves to consider the decision-making implications of the knowledge which they are producing and to raise constantly the question as to what is significant and what is trivial. This task I think we have neglected, and we need to be more self-conscious about the nature of our own knowledge-producing processes as social scientists if we are to play the role, either in the city or in the world, which is unquestionably opening out before us.

References

Handlin, Oscar, and John Burchard eds. *The Historian and the City.* Cambridge, Mass.: M.I.T. Press, 1963.
Simon, Herbert A. *Models of Man.* New York: John Wiley & Sons, 1957.

Smith, Adam. *The Wealth of Nations.* London: Dent, 1964-66.

Zipf, George Kingsley. *Human Behavior and the Principle of Least Effort.* Cambridge, Mass.: Addison-Wesley Press, 1949.

Discussion Questions

1. Discuss the relationship of aggregations of people and municipal organization.

2. What are basic differences between an organization of a city and an organization of a large industry?

3. If interaction with other human beings produces learning, why does too great a density inhibit learning?

4. What has advanced the concept of "world city"?

5. Describe how buildings may increase or decrease the value of a neighboring area.

6. How can problems arise if there is an imbalance between public and private urban housing?

11. The Dilemmas of Neighborhood Revitalization

by John R. Mullin

The revitalization of older urban neighborhoods across the United States is becoming an increasingly complex problem for planners, lenders, and citizens. From the planners' view, there is the need to bring back the middle class to the city while not forcing poor residents from their homes. From the lenders' view, there is the problem of making sound investment decisions in areas where there is high risk or extensive community agitation. From the citizens' standpoint, there is the question of either making a commitment to an older neighborhood or moving elsewhere. All of these issues are interdependent and require participation of planners, lenders, and citizens in order to arrive at the most appropriate decisions. The failure of any one of these three parties to come to agreement with the remaining two will undoubtedly damage the long range prospects of a neighborhood to survive. And yet, the three parties often have different standards, goals, objectives, funding considerations, and priorities. The bringing together of these interests to a common understanding is one of the most challenging tasks that any planner can face. It must be accomplished, however, if improvement is to result.

What then are the requirements of each? In order to illustrate how each operates, a typical hypothetical case study that depicts as evenly as possible the pros and cons of various revitalization decisions as seen from the perspective of the city, the financial groups, and the neighborhood organization has been set up. Naturally, not all of the elements of this case study will be found in each neighborhood. However, there will be enough of them to insure that a large majority will be present.

Components of the Study

The case study will be presented in five parts. Part one is a description of a typical neighborhood in an inner city that is in need of rehabilitation of some sort. It is a savable neighborhood, given standard definitions of what is "savable." The crucial question is: where will the neighborhood go in the future? Will it decay, stabilize, or totally change its character by becoming a "high-rise quarter"? Part two describes how the city interests respond to the internal and external tensions and pressures affecting the neighborhood. Parts three and four, respectively, depict the roles of the neighborhood itself and the financial institutions. Finally, part five is a summary of the case study, a review of the critical factors influencing each party and a listing of crucial factors that greatly influence how an inner-city neighborhood can cope with the future.

John R. Mullin is Assistant Professor of Urban Planning and Landscape Architecture, Michigan State University. This article was prepared specially for this book.

The Neighborhood Described

The city in which our typical neighborhood is located is a heavily industrialized midwestern city with a core population of 150,000 and a Standard Metropolitan Statistical Area (SMSA) population of 250,000. For the past ten years, there has been a decline in job numbers, population, and numbers of retail stores, all at the expense of growth in the suburbs. City officials, merchants, and civic groups have embarked on a strong redevelopment effort focusing upon improvement of its central business district (CBD) and the creation of an adjacent civic center. This effort has already had a payoff. Two major department stores have decided to expand their downtown operations, and at least 30% of the stores now have building renovation permits outstanding.

Our typical neighborhood (ALEXIS) is located immediately to the north of the CBD. It has a population of 2,500 people located in 600 homes. The homes are 90% single-family and 10% duplex. They were built approximately sixty to seventy years ago and are the last intact vestige of Victorians in the city. The homes are large, in relatively good condition, and are built close together on long, narrow lots.

The boundaries of the neighborhood are strong — three, heavily traveled through roads. To the south is the aforementioned CBD. To the west is a 100-year-old manufacturing plant, presently booming with three shifts operating seven days per week. To the east is a former urban renewal area that has been cleared. It now is the construction site for the new civic center which focuses on a long-established courthouse.

Within the neighborhood itself, several changes have occurred over the past five years. Mixed land uses have become increasingly common on the fringe. This is particularly evident on the easterly edge where law offices, bail bondsmen, title search companies, and similar activities have located themselves in the large homes found on Queen Street. Also, in the same five-year period, absentee landlords have increased from 5% to 30% of all properties in the area. These people have purchased the properties as long-term investments; they collectively feel that the area will be rezoned over the next five years to allow high-rise apartments throughout the entire neighborhood. Since they care little for the existing housing on the properties, they have provided only minimum upkeep. Lawns are unkempt, cars are parked all over the property, and many of the properties have become "rent-by-the-week" rooming houses. And yet, those people presently living in their own homes have kept up their properties. There has been substantial personal reinvestment and few code enforcement citations. The neighborhood is made up of 33% professional families, 10% student, 15% senior citizens, 20% rooming house "transients," with the remainder being working-class families. The largest change beyond the rooming-house residents has been the increase in professional families from 15% to 33% (while working-class families were displaced at about the same rate from 40% to 22%). Due to the demographic pluralism of the area, one could not label it as having a strong sense of "community." In fact, there is no common meeting place, park, or school in the neighborhood itself. Furthermore, up to the present there has not been a neighborhood organization.

Over the past two years there has been great developer interest in the area. The city recently approved rezoning requests for two, fifteen-story, high-rise residential towers located within the neighborhood on corner lots at the fringe. The city planners estimate that there is an extreme shortage of apartments in the city and that at least the equivalent of ten more fifteen-story towers could be developed without saturating the market. This figure was based on planned developments in the CBD for several additional government and insurance-oriented office buildings, the civic center complex, and the expanded shopping activity.

Two weeks ago, a developer came to the city planner explaining that he had just purchased several contiguous lots in the center of the neighborhood and that he would like to build a fifteen-story highrise on them. He would like the city to rezone the area so that he can begin building. The issue went to the chairperson of the city planning commission who called a public hearing. In the meantime, the residents realized this could be the death knell of their neighborhood and started to organize. The chairperson of the city planning commission wanted a thorough look at the neighborhood, and asked that representatives of the city planning department, the neighborhood, and the local mortgage lending association be prepared to discuss the crucial elements affecting this neighborhood as seen from their own perspectives.

The City's Interest (The Planner)

The key representative responsible for the city's interest in this situation is the city planner. In a city of this size the planner must be a skilled technician, a political advisor to the chief executive, a policymaker, and a politician. The political aspects of the job are perhaps the most important. In this case study, for example, the city planner will have to convince the mayor to take a nonpolitical, analytical look at the high-rise tower. In most cities of this size with similar demographic trends, new high-rise towers take on an image of symbolizing the "positive forward thrust" of the city under the tutelage of the current mayor. For this reason there is a strong desire on the part of politicians to provide incentives that would stimulate city development. And yet, this reaction, often undertaken without a careful analysis of the potential impact, can have grave consequences in the existing neighborhoods where the new development is proposed. Thus being able to understand the politics of decision-making and to play political games can, at times, be quite crucial.

Once the proposal begins the formal review process, the city planner can then begin to look at the proposal in terms of its impact upon the city. Planning theory would have us believe that the planner would first look at the proposal in terms of the current master plan. The reality is that the planner may use this document if it can be construed as being supportive of his stand. In other words, if the master plan fits the planner's needs, it will be used; if it does not, then it will be ignored.

The goals and objectives of the master plan, however, will not be ignored. There are several reasons for this. First, as more and more planning problems enter the courtroom for final resolution, judges are looking back to the goals and objectives as being the fundamental basis for decision making. Secondly, they provide a general guide for the planner to follow. The planner must control and coordinate changes; yet change is a phenomenon most people hate to accept. Therefore, he has an enormous task. If he has goals and objectives that are workable, then his work is made much easier. Thirdly, given the increased pluralism of local democracy, it is often difficult to obtain a comprehensive perspective of what is good for the city. How often, at a city council meeting could someone ask, "Who speaks for the city"? Each councilor, whether elected at large or by district, has a certain targeted populace to whom he or she owes loyalty. This loyalty is often in conflict with loyalty to the city. (To see this phenomenon at work, watch how city councelors vote on "halfway houses." Vote one, to approve development of the program, will usually pass quickly without dissent. Vote two, on the other hand, to specifically locate the houses, takes months of patient hearings before a watered-down decision.) Because of the unwillingness of councils to focus on the "good of the city," it often falls on the planner to focus on this difficult issue. The master plan's goals and objectives can provide him with some means of politically counteracting the sub-city oriented pressure.

At the same time, the planner looks at the site in question to evaluate both tangible and intangible factors relating to the neighborhood. In terms of the ALEXIS Neighborhood, there are certain standard questions that would be focused upon immediately by the planner. Perhaps the first basic question is "Can the neighborhood handle the third, high-rise tower without changing its single-family character?" The planner's staff would probably reply negatively, due to several factors. First, the tower is located at the exact center point of the neighborhood, thus serving as an obstruction to cohesiveness from both the standpoint of design and personal interrelationships. Secondly, the influx of apartment dwellers (with differing living standards, life-styles, backgrounds, education levels, and income levels), as opposed to home owners, would provide little reinforcement to the area. Apartment dwellers usually do not mix with single-family home owners. Thirdly, traffic flow would be greatly increased. Also, fourthly and fifthly, privacy would be reduced, and a shadow from the high-rise building would be cast on some of the adjacent buildings in at least six months of the year.

Following this quick assessment, the planner would then focus on critical trends in the area. He would note the intrusion of nonresidential uses, the increasing percentage of absentee landlords, the age of the structures, the absence of neighborhood cohesiveness, the external pressures from the CBD and civic center, and the traffic aspects as being indicators that the neighborhood as a single-family residential area is being greatly threatened. On the other hand, he would note the quality and age of the homes. Whether or not Victoriana is considered aesthetically pleasing is not the issue. The issue is that once this area is destroyed, a link with the city's past will have been forever severed. The tree-lined streets, well-kept, single-family homes, and the high number of professional-class residents would cause him not to make an immediate decision based upon trends. He would ask, "What are the positive and negative attributes of the proposal?" On the positive side, it would greatly enhance the CBD by bringing apartment dwellers next to the core, thus stimulating a larger retail market. There is a certain logic in bringing apartment dwellers to the fringe of the CBD. Apartment dwellers are most often at a pre- or post- "children-in-the-nest" stage. In terms of the group, they have a greater degree of personal mobility and can readily partake of what the core has to offer — restaurants, night life, etc. The post-group is desirous of having easy access to the essentials for day-to-day living. For this reason, a location adjacent to the CBD would be considered highly advantageous.

The project would also serve as a stimulus for other high-rise development projects. With the two towers developed on the edges of the neighborhood, the construction of the civic center project, the easy access to the CBD, and a shortage of apartment units, all of the ingredients for large-scale development are present. Furthermore, there is the usual "increase-in-tax-base" argument. If the infrastructure is in place and has excess capacity, if city services will not have to be expanded, and if there is no major negative environmental impact, then this agrument will have merit.

Lastly, there is the fact of the development itself. While the mayor would like to support the project for political enhancement, the citizens often want it for other reasons. In particular, in our northern and eastern cities, there has been a return to a "depression era" attitude. This attitude seems to say "take whatever development that comes our way because it will only come once." This argument is difficult to counter. It is also difficult to turn down a development proposal that requires little from the city in terms of financial commitment and that is to take place in an area that can be labeled as being marginal.

These points must be weighed against the loss to the neighborhood. The high rise would enter into the local marketplace in even greater numbers and the "quality of

This historic scene at "Benton Place" shows the Victorian charm of a St. Louis restoration area. (Department of Housing and Urban Development)

If this area was destroyed, a link of the city's past would have been forever severed. (Department of Housing and Urban Development)

life" of living on quiet, tree-lined streets in large, well-kept Victorian homes would be forever lost. It is difficult to weigh jobs and tax revenues against history, tradition, aesthetics, and quality of life but still the comparison must be made. Perhaps by examining the role of finance, the decision can become clearer.

The Banker's Perspective (The Lender)

The participation of banks and other mortgage lenders in the development process is, quite simply, to make money for their stockholders within the constraints of law, regulation, and sound financial standards. In spite of all of our social legislation, anti-redlining measures, the "community charter" of our banks, and pressures to make banks more responsive to areas needing revitalization, loans will not be granted in marginal areas unless there is evidence that the investment is an "acceptable risk." Local lenders are caught in an internal dilemma. On the one side, there is the need for profit, sound investment, and minimum risk. On the other side, there is the need to meet the financial needs of the community. Extensive study of this dilemma is presently being undertaken by lending institutions, legislatures, and universities in order to determine ways of ameliorating the problem. Federal guaranteed loans for poor neighborhoods, high-risk pooling, and greater lender involvement in the revitalization process are being examined. Positive changes are being made and more can be expected.

Given the ALEXIS Neighborhood, what can be said about the role of the lending institution? There is little doubt that the high rise would be funded. If the developer has a record of success, has adequate equity, is able to demonstrate that a market exists, and, through his feasibility study and pro forma statements, that it is a sound investment, the banks would be more than willing to give him a mortgage. On the other side, what would the response be if the neighborhood organization requested funds to stabilize itself according to its own revitalization program? The lenders would be far less willing. Lenders, like planners, deal first in standard criteria. In older neighborhoods they look for evidence of stability, strong code enforcement, community organizations dedicated to self-help, and evidence of property appreciation. Given the rapid rate of turnover and the lack of community cohesiveness, the ALEXIS Neighborhood's eligibility is, at best, questionable. On the other hand, if the threat of high-rise development is removed, then the market for speculation would be less and a degree of stabilization could be realized. Coupled with this is the fact that the neighborhood is showing signs of becoming organized. Thus, it is not a totally negative investment climate.

It should also be realized that the ALEXIS Neighborhood has certain structural and functional characteristics in it that are considered as contributing to a higher risk by lending institutions. First, any neighborhood that has mixed uses is suspect. In particular, rooming houses, rental property and "intrusionary uses" are higher-risk characteristics. Secondly, the "age" of the structures must be assessed. While vintage homes may be considered as being civic assets by historic preservationists, they may be classified as potential investment liabilities by lenders. Housing that is more than one generation old is often considered as being inferior and as requiring, from the loan applicant, greater than normal justification as to why the loan should be given. Thirdly, to improve the neighborhood along conservation lines, home improvement loans will be required. These loans are usually well under $25,000 and are usually "less-than-profitable" to the lender. Therefore, if alternative investment opportunities to rehabilitation loans are available to the lender, they will be taken. In other words, rehabilitation loans generally have a higher risk and have low priority for bankers. Thus, lenders would be more apt to support the high rise than neighborhood rehabilitation. Should the threats to destabilization be removed, should the city begin to assist home owners, and should the neighborhood become strongly organized, then the opportunities for reinvestment assistance would be less negative. The key determinator in this case seems to be the stability of the neighborhood.

The Neighborhood Interest (Citizens)

Where does the neighborhood stand? There is no doubt that there are great pressures upon it and very little organization to counteract them. What can be done? It appears that a strong organizational effort is crucial. Given the lack of close involvement and the economic pluralism of the area, this would seem to be a difficult task. It must be accomplished, however, if the area is to survive. Only through organizing can the means to counteract the speculation, mixed-use intrusions, and the high rise be accomplished. Also, it will help to overcome the doomsday spirit that is most likely present in the area. There is nothing so disheartening to a single-family neighborhood than to watch a high rise going up and up within its midst.

The type of neighborhood organization is really immaterial. At times cool rationalism succeeds, while, at others, heated confrontation succeeds. What is crucial is that the organization be able to accomplish a tangible task quickly. For this reason, it is crucial that it be multi-issued (not merely "stop the high rise"). Success begets success and maintains property values.

Upon organizing, the neighborhood groups must cultivate political support from its local representatives. This will then give the organization an overt political sanction that will allow it to participate in municipal proceedings. Also, it must obtain the assistance of professional architects, planners, historic preservationists, and lawyers. Lastly, it must be able to generate alternatives to the proposal presently under consideration. This last point is crucial since planning agencies are becoming increasingly immune to the negative response of citizens' groups. There are few instances where the "do-nothing" alternative works.

If the neighborhood is going to survive as a residential neighborhood, it must convince the city officials and the lending community of that fact. There are several options open to it. It can "up-zone" to stop the infiltration of mixed uses. It can "down-zone" to create a harmonious tie-in with the current mixed uses — after all, they are not inherently negative uses. It can advocate the development of a special district zone or become an historic district. All of these are essentially stop-gap or accommodation moves. There are also several positive efforts that could be undertaken. It could use Community Development Block Grants (CDBG) to bring sensitive code enforcement, to bring public improvements, and to provide low-cost loans for the residents. It could even use CDBG funds to give home improvement rebates if this policy was deemed critical to success. The commitment of the city is crucial here.

Thus, upon organizing into an action group and gaining political support, the neighborhood could begin to revive. This support could then be used as leverage to modify the present zoning law in order to provide protection against commercial intrusions and high-rise structures. At the same time, public improvement funds could be provided to the neighborhood as an incentive to stimulate self-help programs. At this point the opportunity for bank loans would greatly expand.

The Synthesis for Action

The views of the city planners, lenders, and citizens then must be synthesized. Will the high rise be approved or will the neighborhood be allowed to prove that it can survive? The argument boils down to two sides. On the one side there are city goals (i.e., maximize tax revenues) and the principles of sound planning practice (i.e., place high rises close to the CBD). On the other, there is the desire for strong neighborhoods, community uniqueness, historicity, and character.

There is no one answer to the problem. In one city the tax argument will prevail, while, in another, the neighborhood organization will be successful in gaining a commitment from the city to support revitalization. The key point is to understand how each of the components of the problem, the players in the development process, and the variables determining possible courses of action are all interdependent. Only then can a participant attempt to find the best possible course of action.

Summary

Several crucial points can be made that will be of assistance to those who will be participating in similar cases:

1. The key structural element in neighborhood revitalization is the existing condition of the housing stock.
2. Lending institutions must be convinced of the soundness of investing in older neighborhoods.
3. Neighborhood revitalization must be analyzed from both an external, city-wide perspective and an internal, local perspective.
4. City policies and neighborhood power are often in conflict.
5. A nonaggressive, nonorganized neighborhood has little chance in revitalizing itself.
6. The crucial players in neighborhood revitalization include the residents, lenders, planners, and politicians.

The dilemmas addressed in this study are not easily untangled. They require hard work, a sense of commitment to the neighborhood, and a thorough knowledge base of the intricacies of the revitalization process. And yet it is not an insurmountable task. Cities are re-reviewing their older neighborhoods and are finding that they are great assets. In fact, President Carter's National Urban Policy has placed an expanded emphasis on reviving older areas. The task is just beginning.

References

Ahlbrandt, Roger S., and Johathan E. Zimmer. "County Emphasizes Neighborhood Preservation." *Practicing Planner* 6 (1976): 22-25.

Alinsky, Saul. *Rules for Radicals: A Practical Primer for Realistic Radicals.* New York: Vintage Books, 1972.

Allensworth, Don T. *The Political Realities of Urban Planning.* New York: Praeger, 1975.

"Boston's 20% Cash Rebate Helps Pay Rehab Costs." *Practicing Planner* (6) (1976): 19-20.

Connor, Desmond. *Citizens Participate.* Oakville, Ontario: Development Press, 1975.

Frieden, Bernard. *The Future of Old Neighborhoods.* Cambridge: The MIT Press, 1963.

Gammage, Grady, Philip N. Jones, and Stephen L. Jones. *Historic Preservation in California: A Legal Handbook.* Stanford: Stanford Environmental Law Society, 1975.

Goetze, Rolf. *Building Neighborhood Confidence: A Humanistic Strategy for Urban Housing.* Cambridge: Ballinger, 1976.

Grissman, Richard. "Mortgage Banker Says Planners Can Encourage Private Lending in Older Neighborhoods." *Practicing Planner* 6 (1976): 26-30.

Hester, Randolph T. *Neighborhood Space: User Needs and Design Responsibility.* Stroudsburg: Dowden, Hutchinson, and Ross, 1975.

Keller, Suzanne. *The Urban Neighborhood.* New York: Random House, 1968.

Marciniak, Edward. *Reviving an Inner City Community*. Washington, D.C.: National Center for Urban Ethnic Affairs, 1977.

McNulty, Robert H., and Stephen A. Kliment. *Neighborhood Conservation*. New York: The Whitney Library of Design, 1976.

Mortgage Bankers' Association of America. *Redlining Solution Requires Unified Approach*. Washington, D.C.: Mortgage Bankers' Association of America, 1977.

National Trust of Historic Preservation. *A Guide to Delineating Edges of Historic Districts*. Washington, D.C.: The National Trust, 1976.

Discussion Questions

1. Discuss the roles that the planners, the lenders, and the citizens each play in the revitalization of a neighborhood.

2. Why do city policies and neighborhood power often conflict?

3. What are the usual effects on a neighborhood that has a high percentage of the housing owned by absentee landlords, rather than owner-occupied housing?

4. What are some of the characteristic differences in high-rise apartment dwellers versus single-family home owners?

5. Discuss the overt changes likely to take place in a neighborhood when a high-rise apartment building is constructed.

6. Why would a neighborhood with mixed-land uses be considered a higher-risk area for lending institutions than a solely residential neighborhood?

7. Some of the information presented about the lender relates directly to Article 12, "Segregation in Housing: Its Costs to Life Chances and Some Solutions." Discuss the relationship between these two articles.

12. Segregation in Housing: Its Costs to Life Chances and Some Solutions

by Duncan Case

America can be described as an unequal society that would like to think of itself as egalitarian. [1]

Herbert Gans

Despite democratic ideals for an egalitarian society, it should come as no surprise that America is stratified into groups of rich and poor. This stratification is reflected in our housing, both in the quality of individual units and in the quality of neighborhoods. Many communities, for example, have an identifiable "society hill" and a "shack town across the tracks." This residential segregation by social class is often taken for granted. Social action is more likely to occur when issues of race are at stake. The 1968 Presidential Commission on Housing found, for example, that nonwhites have to pay more to gain the equivalent housing of whites. [2] Economist John Kain suggests that residential segregation of blacks affects access to good jobs and decent wages. [3] Others point to the effect of residential segregation on education. But the problems faced by nonwhites do not escape whites. Residential segregation is a problem that involves both race and social status. Low-income households, white or black, find access to jobs, education and housing restricted by residential segregation. How residential segregation affects life chances for all low-income groups and the practices which perpetuate it are the subject of this article.

Residential Segregation and Its Effect on Life Chances

Life chances such as access to a decent education, good medical care, and a well-paying job are affected by the availability of resources and opportunities to individuals and their families. Social class is considered a major factor in determining the distribution of these opportunities and resources. Consider the case of educational achievement. If one comes from a higher social class than someone else, one is likely to have more income to buy a better education, the benefit of parents with a higher educational training, and acculturation to values and aspirations which activate achievement. [4] Since residential segregation has been defined to include social class, it too

Duncan Case is Associate Professor of Human Ecology and Design, Michigan State University. This article was prepared specially for this book.

1. Herbert Gans, *More Equality* (New York: Pantheon, 1968), p. xi.
2. U.S. President's Committee on Urban Housing, *A Decent Home* (Washington, D.C.: Government Printing Office, 1968).
3. John F. Kain, "Housing Segregation, Negro Employment, and Metropolitan Decentralization," *Quarterly Journal of Economics* 82:2 (1968), pp. 175-197.
4. Samuel Bowles, "Unequal Education and the Social Division of Labor," *Problems in Political Economy*, ed. David M. Gordon (Lexington, Mass.: D.C. Heath, 1977, 2nd ed.), p. 246.

must affect life chances through the distribution of resources and opportunities. This distribution is spatial and has an effect at two scales: the neighborhood and the metropolitan.

The Neighborhood Scale

The lessening of life chances attributable to segregation at the neighborhood scale is suggested by considering the social benefits claimed for its opposite, the integrated or balanced community. Balanced communities have two principal benefits: (1) higher aspirations among the children of lower-class groups, and (2) greater tolerance of social differences among all groups.[5] Conversely then, it is to be implied from these propositions that residential segregation contributes to (1) limited aspirations among children of lower income groups, and (2) lessened tolerance of social differences among all groups.

The effect of residential segregation on aspirations stems from the assumption that homogeneous environments lock people into present ways of life. Children of working-class parents, for example, are primarily exposed to the life-styles and occupations pursued by their parents and the parents of their peers. This exposure limits the career alternatives to which they see themselves aspiring and the education level which they think will be necessary to achieve those careers. Thus, the sons and daughters of coal miners may mostly aspire to become coal miners, and the sons and daughters of workers in the automobile industry may mostly aspire to jobs on the assembly line. This principle also applies for educational aspiration. Wilson has shown that working-class and middle-class youth from a predominately middle-class neighborhood are more likely to aspire to a college education than working-class and middle-class youth from a predominately working-class neighborhood.[6] The dominant class group in a given residential neighborhood then has an effect on the aspirations of its youth for both education and work opportunities.

Student aspirations are also affected by the attitude and expectations of teachers in the classroom, which in turn are influenced by residential segregation. Experiments have shown that the teacher's expectation of a student's performance influences the support and encouragement the teacher gives to the student to perform well, and this influences the student's sense of self-esteem and motivation. Ryan argues that class and race are often used as determinants of "expected" capabilities to perform regardless of any objective measure of academic potential.[7] Since school systems are often organized on a neighborhood basis, particularly at the elementary school level, a teacher walks into the classroom with a bias of expectation through knowing the reputation or character of a student's neighborhood.

The social isolation of diverse groups characteristic of segregated neighborhoods also lessens social tolerance. Advocates of a balanced community claim that it is only through day-to-day encounters with people from diverse backgrounds that people will learn to tolerate one another. Residential segregation prevents testing myths of prejudice against real-life experience. Lessened social tolerance may lead to confrontation and political conflict. The problems of achieving racial balance in schools through busing reflects this problem. The beliefs and myths perpetuated by residential segregation, even among communities of similar economic status, promote battles in the

5. Herbert Gans, "The Balanced Community: Homogeneity or Heterogeneity in Residential Areas?," in *People and Plans* (New York: Basic Books, 1968), pp. 166-182.

6. Alan B. Wilson, "Class Segregation and Aspirations of Youth," *American Sociological Review* XXIV (1959), pp. 836-845.

7. William Ryan, *Blaming the Victim* (New York: Vintage Books, 1971, 1st ed.), p. 54.

classroom and the courts. The result of conflicts such as these is to limit life opportunities by restricting access to better schools and by diverting energies and resources to quell the conflict rather than to the primary task of education.

According to some sociologists, residential integration may not solve problems of social aspiration and tolerance. They point out that day-to-day contacts in the neighborhood are relatively superficial in comparison to the much stronger social relations of family. Thus, the opinions of one's neighbor are considered to have far less influence than one's parents. The presence of alternative life-styles is less important than the willingness of parents to point out those life-styles as desirable to their children. The same is said to be true for changing beliefs and prejudices. Keller reports several cases in which neighborhood social heterogeneity actually promoted conflict. Resolution of those conflicts often resulted in hostile territorialization of community spaces and facilities: one group claimed the use of particular playgrounds and parks while another controlled the local community organization.[8]

The manner of integration may have a significant effect in mediating outcomes, however. Keller offers that integration can be creatively accomplished by mixing around only one social variable at a time, i.e., race while holding income constant.[9] The resulting moderation of diversity would allow some "like-mindedness" to exist upon which tolerable social relations could be built.

The problem of integrating neighborhoods, however, lies less with the success of achieving workable social relations than with the presumption that balanced communities are the best way to solve social inequality. Gans contends that residential segregation is a symptom rather than the cause of social differences.[10] Residential segregation is the result of unequal distribution of resources, the result of the inability of certain groups to afford better housing in better neighborhoods where better educational opportunities exist. Until these groups have the same necessary economic resources as their more affluent neighbors, good jobs, and a decent income, efforts to create balanced communities are merely cosmetic solutions which do not address the central issue. Policy should instead focus on programs which directly affect education, job training, health care, and the like. This is not to say that residential segregation has nothing to do with the problem; rather, it is to say that the wrong issues and scale of residential integration are under consideration. Gans cites as an example the effect of local taxation and segregated residential areas on financing education. Given that the richer communities have a more viable tax base, they can afford to "build modern schools with all the latest features," while "the low-income suburb is forced to treat even menial education progress as a luxury."[11] This unequal distribution of resources among communities is not a result of residential segregation at the neighborhood or block scale, but rather at the metropolitan scale.

The Metropolitan Scale

Residential segregation at the metropolitan scale does not form a random pattern; many researchers argue that there is a systematic confinement of poorer communities to the center with richer ones surrounding them in the suburbs. Since cities historically tend to grow from the center outwards, this means that the high-income households of the suburbs live in new housing in communities with new facilities, while the low-

8. Suzanne Keller, *The Urban Neighborhood* (New York: Random House, 1968).

9. Suzanne Keller, "Social Class in Physical Planning," *International Social Science Journal,* 18 (1966), pp. 494-512. A study by Gerald Suttles shows similar territorializing of space: *The Social Order of the Slums* (Chicago: University of Chicago Press, 1968).

10. Herbert Gans, *People and Plans* (New York: Basic Books, 1968), p. 177.

11. *Ibid.,* p. 174.

income households of the center live in older, filtered-down housing in communities with old facilities.[12] Urban economists and geographers find that this pattern has consequences for life chances of both rich and poor: while the poor incur the cost of living in center city neighborhoods, the rich gain the benefits of living in better communities. These costs and benefits fall into four categories: (1) jobs and income, (2) housing costs and wealth accumulation, (3) education, and (4) costs of the crisis ghetto.

Jobs and income. Research on the effect of residential segregation on jobs and income has dealt primarily with nonwhite populations. As there is a relationship between race, income, and residential segregation, many of the effects identified here have implications for all low-income groups, white and nonwhite, though in varying degrees.

The effect of residential segregation on employment opportunities for blacks has been principally documented by economist John Kain.[13] His research shows that while blacks have been residentially restricted to central metropolitan areas, jobs have in the meantime decentralized to the suburbs along with high-income white populations. The time and money required by blacks to commute to these decentralized jobs puts them at a competitive disadvantage with the more proximate whites. Center-city blacks also have the disadvantage of lack of information about jobs, information that is usually passed by word of mouth among fellow workers and neighbors. Since most of their neighbors in the center city, like themselves, do not work at these suburban jobs, blacks have limited access to this information. Even if blacks are willing to commute and do obtain information about jobs, Kain suggests that suburban employers will discriminate against blacks for fear of reprisals from their primarily white clientele. Blacks therefore lose job opportunities which presumably pay more and are more meaningful than those found in the center city. In principle then, opening up the suburbs residentially would give blacks these presently lost life chances. Since residential segregation is not merely a matter of race but also income, the benefits of residential integration in the suburbs would also help low-income whites as well.

Housing costs and wealth accumulation. As is the case for jobs and income, research on the effect of housing discrimination on housing costs and wealth accumulation has concerned itself primarily with its effect on nonwhites. The principal finding is that blacks pay more for the equivalent housing of whites.[14] This means that if blacks choose to reside in housing equal to whites (supposing it is made available to them), they must put more of their incomes toward it. As a result blacks then have less disposable income than whites for other life chance enhancing opportunities such as medical care, education, or reliable transportation for commuting to work.

Discrimination in housing also restricts the opportunity for blacks to purchase single-family homes. This is in part because housing of this type is more available in the suburbs than in the city and because realtors are often reluctant to sell houses to blacks. Thus, blacks are limited primarily to renting. As a result they are unable to accumulate "wealth" in the form of the equity represented by an owned house. While whites of an

12. Kain, op. cit, and Anthony Downs, *Opening Up the Suburbs* (New Haven: Yale University Press, 1973).

13. Kain, op. cit., and "Housing Segregation, Black Employment, and Metropolitan Decentralization: A Retrospective View," in *Patterns of Racial Discrimination,* Vol. 1, eds. George von Furstenberg et al. (Lexington, Mass.: Lexington Books, 1974), pp. 5-20.

14. Chester Rapkin, "Price Discrimination Against Negroes in the Rental Housing Market," in *Housing in Urban America,* eds. Jon Pynoos et al. (Chicago: Aldine, 1973).

equal income are able to recapture some of their housing costs through home owner-ship, blacks lose it completely to landlords in the form of rent. [15]

The effect of residential segregation on housing costs is also a problem for whites. Low-income households as a whole have their housing opportunities restricted to what is available in the center city. Both whites and nonwhites are often compelled to rent for lack of any alternatives. When home ownership is possible, low-income, center-city households face costs not incurred in the suburbs: the premium that banks charge for handling older housing in declining neighborhoods. This premium comes in the form of higher down payments and higher interest rates. Thus, both blacks and whites wind up with less disposable income after paying housing costs than if they were to own homes in the suburbs.

Education. Educational costs arise from the disparity in tax base between center-city communities and those in the suburbs. As Gans has pointed out, lower income communities cannot provide the equivalent educational facilities as the suburbs, and thus the children of those forced to reside in city neighborhoods lose the opportunity of a better education, which in turn affects their job chances and income-earning capability.

Costs of the crisis ghetto. Selective exclusion of most poor from the suburban areas means concentration in the center city. According to Anthony Downs, author of *Opening Up the Suburbs,* this precipitates the formation of crisis ghettos, areas where the worst problems of poverty predominate: broken families, crime, juvenile deliquency. [16] For households attempting to hold their own or upgrade themselves, the presence of crisis ghettos frustrates their efforts and forces the expenditure of valuable resources just to ward off immediate threats to survival. Their children, for example, have a difficult time escaping the influence of peer pressure to join the street life. Governments responsible for these areas have to devote significant shares of scarce resources for welfare and crime prevention, rather than on life chance bettering activities such as schools and job development. Meanwhile, high-income communities get the edge over all groups by virtue of having excluded the members of crisis ghettos from their communities as well as their budgets. It is circumstances like these which prompt social critics like Anthony Downs to protest: "Any arrangement that benefits the wealthy and the middle class at the expense of loading large costs onto the very poor is a gross injustice that cries out for correction." [17]

The solutions proposed to solve these problems of residential segregation usually involve some form of "opening up the suburbs." Unlike advocates of a balanced community where integration must be by block or neighborhood, advocates of "opening up the suburbs" find it sufficient just to ensure housing opportunities for low-income households within suburban communities as a whole. This, they argue, will facilitate the desired access to jobs and education previously limited. To achieve integration of suburbs, however, involves knowing how suburbs presently maintain residential segregation and hence what constructive policies may need to be adopted.

Practices Which Augment Residential Segregation

Downs contends that there are two forms of discrimination, "overt" and "institutional." [18] An example of overt discrimination in housing is the refusal of a landlord or

---

15. Mahlon R. Straszheim, "Housing Policy Recommendations," in von Furstenberg et al, op. cit., p. 181.

16. Anthony Downs, *Opening Up the Suburbs* (New Haven: Yale University Press, 1973).

17. *Ibid.,* p. 11.

18. Anthony Downs, "Racism in America and How to Combat It," in *Urban Problems and Prospects* (Chicago: Rand McNally, 1976, 2nd ed.), pp. 41-76.

realtor to rent or sell a dwelling to a nonwhite. Institutional discrimination is less direct; it involves use of criteria such as income or education which disproportionately favor one group over another. Use of zoning to limit the price and types of housing available in a given area is an example of institutional discrimination in housing. Overt discrimination which historically has been a major contributor to residential segregation, is now illegal. Most residential segregation today is a result of the indirect, institutional practices of exclusionary zoning and "red-lining."

Exclusionary Zoning

The most widely acknowledged source of residential segregation at the metropolitan scale is exclusionary zoning. Exclusionary zoning is the abusive use of zoning powers by local municipalities to limit or prevent the development of housing in which low- and moderate-income households can afford to live. Zoning law allows a local community to control (1) the use to which specific pieces of land may be put within its jurisdiction (residential, commercial, industrial, open space); (2) the density or intensity of land use by restricting lot sizes; and (3) structural bulk by stipulating distance between buildings, their heights, and the percentage of the lot which they can cover. It is in the strategic manipulation of these powers that a community can effectively prevent low- and moderate-income housing from being built.

Let's consider some of these manipulations in detail. One method is to set minimum lot sizes and house sizes so high that a developer is forced to construct only expensive homes. Lots of one acre or more and houses of 1,600 square feet, for example, are considered excessive. A study of zoning practice in suburban, northeastern New Jersey indicated that 78% of all land for residential use had been zoned to one acre or more.[19] This tendency to zone for large lots is believed to be characteristic of most major metropolitan areas in the United States. Setting large-lot sizes also has the effect of restricting the overall density and hence the total number of houses which can be built in any one community. This too drives up the price of housing through creating an artificial scarcity of land suitable for housing development.

Another practice of exclusionary zoning is to set aside excessive amounts of land for uses other than housing, i.e., commerce, light industry, or open space. This practice is known as "over-zoning." By "over-zoning" a municipality takes land potentially developable for residential use off the market and in so doing helps to drive up the cost of the remaining land. This only serves to compound the problem of housing cost inflation caused by large-lot zoning.

A closely related practice is to declare land unbuildable for reasons of "environmental protection." While some environmental protection practices, such as restricting development in flood plains, are justified, many are not. Like over-zoning, this removes land from the market, further restricting housing construction that might serve low- and moderate-income households.

A third practice, more overt than the first two, is to restrict the amount of land for multifamily housing (apartments) and mobile homes. Rental housing and mobile homes are among the cheapest forms of housing for those who cannot afford to purchase a single-family house. In the same study cited earlier of suburban, northeastern New Jersey, barely ½ of 1% was zoned for multifamily housing and less than 1/10 of 1% for mobile homes with many communities excluding mobile homes altogether. Without restricting land for multifamily housing, zoning law can also effectively limit their access to low- and moderate-income families by setting a limit on the number of

19. Williams and Norman, "Exclusionary Land-Use Controls: The Case of North-Eastern New Jersey," *Syracuse Law Review* 22: 1971.

bedrooms allowed per apartment to only one or two. This is done on the assumption that low-income families are large and, therefore, would not want to rent a one- or two-bedroom apartment. Instead, these suburban apartments are occupied by middle-class singles, childless couples, or young families, many of whom will ultimately move into single-family houses.

The overall effect of these three practices, and this is not an exhaustive list of all the methods which are used, is to make housing less available to low- and moderate-income households. While the effect is mainly to restrict income groups, the unspoken intention is often to restrict nonwhite populations whose members are disproportionately low-income.

Mortgage Banking Practices: Redlining

A low-income household's problems in obtaining decent housing doesn't end with exclusionary zoning. Its ability to purchase and maintain the older housing which is left to it in the center city is hampered by the mortgage bank lending practice of "redlining."

Redlining is the policy of some banks to declare a whole neighborhood of housing too risky for investment and therefore ineligible for receiving home mortgages. This is done in spite of the knowledge that many residents may be able to afford the necessary payments. What the banks mean by "risk" is that they suspect that land values are declining in the neighborhood and should the home owner "default" in his or her payments, the bank would be unable to recapture the full value of the loan from resale of a house which is now worthless.

The term "redlining" derives from a practice of many years ago whereby bank loan officers outlined in red on a map the areas where loans would not be made. Today such an explicit act is illegal, but banks are able to accomplish the same thing by setting up criteria which achieve the same purpose. One of these criteria is "neighborhood in transition," which includes the factors race change and age of housing. In and of themselves these two factors do not dictate neighborhood decline, but they are often sufficient grounds for the bank to refuse to make a loan. Recently, the U.S. Justice Department has attempted to put an end to this practice through a suit against the American Institute of Real Estate Appraisers, an organization that helps to set these criteria.[20]

Excluded from suburban housing and refused loans on center-city housing, low- and moderate-income households find themselves confronted by a tragic dilemma. The only way that older housing is to be kept from deteriorating and being eliminated from an already restricted supply of housing for these households is for the banks to make the necessary loans for purchase and home improvement. Redlining becomes a self-fulfilling prophecy, however, when the banks refuse to make loans to neighborhoods they expect to decline, for they most assuredly will decline when the banks cut off the necessary loans.

The most morally disdainful aspect of redlining comes from the suspicion that one motivation of the banks to carry out redlining is to enable more lucrative investments in the suburbs. Statistics unearthed by a researcher in San Francisco show that default rates in supposed redlined or high-risk areas of the center city are not so high as to prevent banks from still making a profit; it's just that default rates are even lower in the suburbs and hence the profits to the bank higher.[21] A survey conducted in Chicago

20. Tee Taggart, "Appraisal Practices Need a Thorough Reappraisal," *Planning Magazine* (ASPO: August 1977), pp. 17-18.
21. Tee Taggart, "Red-lining: How the Bankers Starve the Cities to Feed the Suburbs," *Planning Magazine* (ASPO: December 1974), pp. 14-16.

showed that "for every dollar deposited in the inner city zip code areas, as little as 1% (no more than 16%) was invested in the area." [22] Instead these funds were being invested in suburban housing. What is considered immoral in this practice is the ironic fact that the source of funds for these suburban mortgages is the hard-earned savings of inner-city households, monies which they are not allowed to borrow against to purchase or repair their own homes. The inner-city poor wind up subsidizing the suburban homes of the rich.

Solutions to Residential Segregation, Exclusionary Zoning, and Redlining

Conventional solutions to residential segregation tend to lie in attacks on the legality of exclusionary zoning and redlining. It is believed that through a series of successful courtroom battles and revision of the laws which currently make these practices possible, residential segregation will become a thing of the past. With the end of these practices, it is further believed that the costs to life chances currently incurred by low- and moderate-income households will be lessened.

Challenges to exclusionary zoning have initially come in the form of "class-action" suits taken against individually offending municipalities on behalf of collective, client groups. Suburban Action, Inc., a group of socially motivated lawyers working in the New York metropolitan area, has succeeded in enough cases in New Jersey suburbs to prompt the state of New Jersey to revise the law which enables local municipalities to practice zoning. In the same state, one court case, known popularly as the "Mt. Laurel decision," not only invalidated the local zoning ordinance, but also required the community to come up with a plan which would insure sufficient housing for a "balanced community." By "balanced community" the court meant a representative distribution of all income and ethnic groups in the region surrounding Mt. Laurel. [23]

A problem with the court-case approach is its cost in time and money. It is time-consuming because communities must individually be taken to court, a process which could take years; it is costly because the initiators of the suit, low- and moderate-income households, are the ones who must pay the lawyer's fees and yet are least able to do so. This puts an unjust burden on the clients this action is intended to help. Furthermore, the whole process depends on willing lawyers, a type not as plentiful as the task demands.

These objections have led several policy advisors to recommend strategies which will spread costs in a more equitable manner. One method is to establish regional "fair-share housing plans." The objective of this approach is to obtain an agreement from each community in a given region to provide a share of the low- and moderate-income housing proportionate to its own population. This collective agreement would eliminate the fear among individual communities that in opening themselves up to low-income households, they would be flooded with an unfair share of new residents. Examples of this policy are the Dayton Plan and the Twin Cities Metropolitan Council Plan (Minneapolis-St. Paul). [24] Currently, fair-share housing plans are a voluntary solution to residential segregation. A more far-reaching proposal is to make fair-share housing a mandatory condition for receiving revenue sharing or other federal funds. [25] Fair-share housing would then become a national policy.

22. *Ibid.*, p. 15.

23. Ed McCahill, "In Mount Laurel, Issues Are Not Black and White," *Planning Magazine* (ASPO: May 1975), pp. 12-13.

24. McFall, Trudy, "Housing Delivery on a Regional Basis: Minneapolis-St. Paul," *Journal of Housing*, September 1976, pp. 427-430.

25. Straszheim, op. cit., p. 184.

Initial attacks on redlining have also depended on court action, though not exclusively so. The biggest breakthrough has been the passage of the Mortgage Disclosure Act of 1975. Under this act, mortgage-lending institutions (banks) are required to disclose the geographic source of their assets (savings) and the geographic distribution of their loans. This information will enable savings depositors in the inner city to see whether their banks have a commitment to investment in the homes of their friends and neighbors or whether they are subsidizing housing in the suburbs. In at least four cities, enterprising citizens' coalitions have used this type of information to influence banks to stop red-lining practices. They have accomplished this by encouraging members of their coalitions to withdraw what amounts to hundreds of thousands of dollars of saving deposits and to transfer them to banks which agree to increase mortgage loans in their neighborhoods.[26] The limitation of the Mortgage Disclosure Act is that it does not make redlining illegal, leaving the burden of action on individual citizens. A more comprehensive and effective law has yet to be written.

Another attack on red-lining is occurring through the Housing and Community Development Act of 1974. Through regulations currently in effect, the U.S. Department of Housing and Urban Development (HUD) is encouraging communities to use the funds allocated by this act for creating "viable" neighborhoods. This means using the funds to improve the physical structure of declining neighborhoods so that banks will reestablish loans to home owners. Many communities use the money to "leverage" banks into making new home loans by offering the federal funds as a direct subsidy to the banks. Both strategies help to achieve the same objective of ending red-lining.

In spite of the progress being make to prevent exclusionary zoning and redlining, there are those who question whether these actions will bring about the desired effects of residential integration: more jobs, higher wages, and better education. Research by MIT economist Bennett Harrison suggests that the jobs available for nonwhites in the suburbs are likely to be more menial and lower paying than those already available in the city.[27] He finds that employers in the city are less likely to be discriminatory because nonwhites are already a near majority, if not the majority, of the work force. On the other hand, integration of the suburbs could result in reducing nonwhites to a permanent minority, a circumstance which would leave them vulnerable to discrimination. Harrison is not against integration of the suburbs; his fear is that a policy of opening up the suburbs would be used to justify cutting off funds for economic development of our center cities. If there is already tolerance for nonwhite employment in the center city, why abandon the potential that presently exists? He believes that both integrating the suburbs and building the employment base of center city is more desirable.

Harrison's argument raises again the fundamental problem addressed by Gans of pervasive discrimination throughout our society. Residential integration alone will not change the beliefs and economic forces which sustain discrimination; it will not prevent the actions of employers, realtors, and educators which bring about the costs in life chances we have previously identified as a result of residential segregation. Residential segregation is a symptom of discrimination, not its cause. This is not to say that residential segregation doesn't complicate the problem, rather it is to say that strategies of opening up the suburbs and ending redlining must be accomplished by other social

26. Taggart, op. cit., p. 15.
27. Bennett Harrison, "Discrimination in Space: Suburbanization and Black Unemployment in Cities," in von Furstenberg et al., op. cit., pp. 21-54.

Residential integration must be accompanied by other social and economic programs, and policies which address the full range of problems underlying discrimination. (Department of Housing and Urban Development)

and economic programs and policies which address the full range of problems underlying discrimination.

Conclusion

The objective of this article's discussion has been to consider the effect of residential segregation on life chances and the factors which have contributed to its persistence. Residential segregation is found to have consequences at two scales: the neighborhood and the metropolitan. At the neighborhood scale, segregation affects aspirations for better jobs and higher education and lessens social tolerance. Metropolitan segregation, on the other hand, limits access to decent jobs and to better education. It also contributes to increasing housing costs and the expenses of living in crisis ghettoes, both of which deprive low-income households of valuable income. Meanwhile, high-income households escape these costs through exclusionary zoning and have a freedom of residential mobility not available to low-income households. Proposals offered to rectify this situation include "opening up the suburbs," "fair-share housing plans," and putting an end to exclusionary zoning and redlining. While some legislative and legal actions have already contributed to the solution of these problems, broader and more effective policies seem in order. If our primary objective is to enhance life opportunities, these policies must address the root problem of discrimination for which residential segregation is merely one of its many symptoms.

References

Downs, Anthony, *Opening Up the Suburbs.* New Haven: Yale University Press, 1973.

_____ . *Urban Problems and Prospects.* 2nd ed. Chicago: Rand McNally, 1976.

Gans, Herbert. *More Equality.* New York: Pantheon, 1968.

_____ . *People and Plans.* New York: Basic Books, 1968.

Gordon, David M. *Problems in Political Economy.* Lexington, Mass.: D.C. Heath, 1977.

Kain, John F. "Housing Segregation, Negro Employment, and Metropolitan Decentralization." *Quarterly Journal of Economics* 82 (1968): 175-197.

Keller, Suzanne. "Social Class in Physical Planning." *International Social Science Journal* 18: 494-512.

_____ . *The Urban Neighborhood.* New York: Random House, 1968.

McCahill, Ed. "In Mount Laurel, Issues Are Not Black and White." *Planning Magazine* 12-13. (ASPO: May 1975.)

McFall, Trudy. "Housing Delivery on a Regional Basis: Minneapolis-St. Paul." *Journal of Housing,* September 1976, 427-430.

Pynoos, Jon, Robert Schafer, and Chester Hartman (eds.). *Housing Urban America.* Chicago: Aldine, 1973.

Taggart, Tee. "Appraisal Practices Need a Thorough Reappraisal." *Planning Magazine* 17-18. (ASPO: August 1977.)

_____ . "Red-lining: How Bankers Starve the Cities to Feed the Suburbs." *Planning Magazine* 14-16. (ASPO: December 1974.)

U.S. President's Committee on Urban Housing. *A Decent Home.* Washington, D.C.: Government Printing Office, 1968.

Von Furstenberg, George, Bennett Harrison, and Ann R. Horowitz. *Patterns of Racial Discrimination.* Vol. 1. Lexington, Mass.: Lexington Books, 1974.

Williams and Norman. "Exclusionary Land-Use Controls: The Case of North-Eastern New Jersey." *Syracuse Law Review* 22: 1971.

Wilson, Alan B. "Class Segregation and Aspirations of Youth." *American Sociological Review* XIV (1959): 836-845.

Discussion Questions

1. Define the term "life chances." Discuss how residential segregation affects life chances.

2. What are the two principal benefits of a balanced community?

3. Explain why residential segregation is a symptom rather than a cause of discrimination.

4. What are the four major categories of costs and benefits that influence the lives of people living in metropolitan areas? Give examples of each of these four categories.

5. Black families more frequently rent than own their housing. How does this affect their accumulation of wealth?

6. Explain the two forms of discrimination that augment residential segregation.

7. Define the terms "exclusionary zoning" and "redlining" and give examples of each.

8. What institutional practice can be used to restrict the location of mobile homes in metropolitan areas?

9. Residential segregation is found to have consequences at two scales. Identify these two levels and explain their differences.

10. Discuss ways that can help to eliminate residential segregation.

13. Neighbourhoods and Human Needs

by Margaret Mead

Human beings must be brought up among human beings who have learned from other human beings how to live in a particular way. There are very few cultural differences when we discuss basic human needs; that is, the floor below which the human being must not be permitted to fall.

Primarily, the neighbourhood is the place where children are brought up to become members of their own society. Inevitably, within a neighbourhood, children encounter various older adults from whose experience they learn how to adapt themselves to the kind of society into which they are growing. In a static society, older experienced people who have learned nothing new in their lifetime are the greatest asset, for they transmit the entire heritage to the children. But in a society that is changing, grandparents who are continually learning and who have themselves participated in change have the highest potentiality for transmitting a sense of adaptation. The neighbourhood, where children learn to meet basic human needs and to move toward the use of higher human capacities, is where they first encounter adults—parents and grandparents and unrelated adults of these two generations. The older people may not include their own grandparents (for in some parts of the world there is an extraordinary lack of tolerance of one's own relatives), but there will be some members of the grandparental generation who are treated with consideration.

Of course, any neighbourhood that we design, or that we attempt to ameliorate, must meet the basic physiological needs for all human beings—the essential needs that human beings share with animals; the need for food, water, space, sleep, rest, and a minimum of privacy.

Of these, privacy is one of the most variable. These are societies that have no word for privacy, and when the idea is explained to them they think it is horrible. In one society in which I worked—Samoa—a curtain hung between me and other members of the household gave me a certain privacy; but in a house without walls nothing separated me from the rest of the village, from whose eyes, obviously, I did not need the protection of privacy. Nevertheless, some sort of privacy, some small, identifiable spatial territory of one's own—even if it is only a hook on which to hang one's own hat—seems to be a basic human need.

A second basic need is for some continuity in human relationships. It need not be af-

Reprinted by permission from *Ekistics*, Vol. 21, No. 123, February 1966. Published by the Athens Center of Ekistics, Athens, Greece.

The late Margaret Mead was Curator of Ethnology, American Museum of Natural History, and author of numerous books.

fectionate or even kind. One society that I studied—the Mundugumor—reared their children to be effective and happy cannibals, but Mundugumor methods of child rearing would seem very harsh to us. It never occurred to a mother to give her baby the breast when it cried; instead, she put it in a flat scratchy basket, which she hung up high so the baby could see what was going on. Then, when the baby became restless, she scratched the outside of the basket, making a sound like the squeak of chalk on a blackboard, and the baby stopped crying. It was not an affectionate sound, but it was a sound that assured the baby of continuity in its human environment.

The idea that a baby must be brought up by its biological mother and that it will be traumatized by the mother's absence for a week derives from a recognition of this need for continuity. But, in fact, the child who is reared from birth to be accustomed to eight different human beings, all of whom are close, can be given a sense of continuity by any one of them. And where the immediate environment—the shape of its bed and the smell of its room—is part of what is continuous, the child can stand a greater variety of persons close to it.

This means that in planning neighbourhoods for the future, various possibilities are open to us. We can turn the family car into a house, and when the child, together with the cat and the dog and familiar toys, is moved to a strange place the car will still be a familiar home. Or we can bring children up to live in the same place every summer but in a different place each winter. We can do a great many different things, providing we keep in mind the basic need for continuity and familiarity. There is considerable evidence that failure to take this need into account may lead to severe conflict in young children, and so we are faced with the problem of how to move children safely from highly familiar to entirely unfamiliar environments, with nothing to bridge the gap. A familiar and trustworthy environment is necessary for the child to learn that things will be here tomorrow that are here today and that its hand, reaching out, will find what it is seeking for. But we must also recognize that continuity can be provided for in many different ways.

If children are to be ready to live in a changing world, they must also be prepared to deal with strangeness almost from the day of their birth. For those who live in the modern world, it is a disabling experience to grow up knowing only their own relatives. The fewer the relatives, the more disabling an experience it is. And yet, all over the world, as older forms of the extended family are breaking down into small, isolated nuclear family groups, the child is becoming disastrously overdependent on its two parents. Disastrous in the sense that living in large cities is disastrous for those who have not learned to deal with a variety of people and who have not learned to expect that the strange will be interesting and rewarding or to recognize that it must be treated with a certain wariness.

The inclusion of the strange has implications for the size of the basic neighbourhood. That is, the neighbourhood cannot be modeled on the primitive village where everyone knows everyone else and everything is familiar. There are, however, some people who would like to keep everything within a safe, closed environment—keep all the cars out, keep all the strangers out, and turn the neighbourhood into a grass plot where all the children can run. There is no doubt that a neighbourhood must have something that is child-scale, some place where children can walk about. I am inclined to think that if children can walk enough, the question of whether or not adults are walkers is less serious. Adults can tolerate enormous specialization—even many kinds of deprivation—if, as children, their senses have been stimulated. One striking example of this can be seen in the experience of people who have suffered deafness, blindness or paralysis in later life, but who still can draw on earlier experience of hearing, vision and movement. Helen Keller is probably the best example of such a person. She could hear and see up to the time she learned her first word, and this early experience preserved for her a sense of the world that carried her through her later incredible sensory isolation. All this suggests that the better we can build into neighbourhoods ways of humanizing the small child in the fullest sense of the word, the greater tolerance the adult will have for the strangeness and stresses of a world in which some people may be physically highly restricted for long periods as they move into outer space or deep in the sea—experiences for which human beings have had little evolutionary preparation. Certainly, we need areas where young children are safe and where they can move on their own legs (and this, of course, will affect the location of nursery schools and primary schools); but we also need to provide for their living dangerously part of the time, even while they are very young. Strangeness and danger are part of living in an urban environment.

The anonymity of the city is one of its strengths as well as—carried too far—one of its weaknesses. Even the young baby, growing up to live in a city, needs to have windows on the unknown world. The shopping center, in which the child encounters strangers and sees its mother encountering strangers, is one such window. But at the same time, the child needs the grass plot, the protected walk, and the nursery school where everything is close and familiar. Only in this way can the small child achieve the autonomy that is necessary at every stage of development. There must be play places and front yards where children can walk safely without fear of traffic. When children move into a newly built housing estate that is inadequately protected from automobiles, parents may be so frightened that the children—who have no preparation for dealing with traffic—will run under the wheels of the cars, that they give the children no freedom of movement at all. In one tribe I know of, the village was located at some distance from a big river. Then, one year, the river changed its course and ran right through the village. The adults, who had no idea what to do, were terrified of the water and, of course, their children fell into the river. In contrast, another people who had lived on the river for a long time knew how to teach their children—and their children were safe. Today, we have to teach our children not only about rivers, but also about traffic: to realize its dangers and be wary of them and also to know how to take chances safely. So, too, in every neighbourhood, there must be places where older children can move freely away from the familiars with confidence, trust, and toleration of strangers and the strange.

Children also need multisensory stimulation. There are several reasons for this. Because of tremendous individual differences, we do not know whether a particular child will be most dependent on hearing, sight or touch. Moreover, in different contexts, there may be a greater emphasis on the use of the eyes or the use of the ears. The child who, as a small child, has lacked multisensory stimulation will be handicapped in making the necessary transition from one to the other. But, beyond these considerations, there is evidence that multisensory cross-referencing is a very creative source of innovation in thought, and we want to bring up children who have the capacity for innovation in a dynamic world.

Children need an environment in which they can learn fine discrimination—in which they can hear small sounds and learn to differentiate between footsteps, learn to hear slight differences in tones of voice, learn to wake and know what time it is. Some peoples have a greater sensitivity to noise and want to shut more of it out than other peoples do. This is something in which whole cultures can be differentiated one from another. But in all cultures, human beings—in order to be human—must understand the non-human. They must have some understanding of plants and animals, water and sunshine, earth, the stars, the moon and the sun. People who have not appreciated the stars cannot really appreciate satellites; they are confused as to which is which. This need to know about the non-human also affects what is necessary for a good neighbourhood. There must be water, preferably water that moves, for moving water is one of the major experiences through which a child's senses are amplified. There must also be earth—not merely a sandbox. There must be animals, although not necessarily large animals. A child can learn about animals as well from fish in a pond as from buffalo on a prairie, and he can dig in a miniature garden as well as in a great field.

Providing the pattern is complete, the scale can be reduced and the details of the arrangement can be different in different neighbourhoods. The child needs to learn what lives in the water, what lives in the air, what lives on earth, and how human beings are related to these growing, living, singing, fighting and playing creatures. Any environment is crippling if it cuts the child off from such experiences. The child who has grown up in peach country—who has learned to register, as he wakes up, a drop in temperature and knows how this will affect what people will do—has acquired a lifetime familiarity. He can live in a city for forty years, but when he goes back to the peach country and sees the peach blossoms, he can still wake up at two o'clock in the morning and say what the people are going to do. Experience of this kind is never lost.

A principal aim in building a neighbourhood must be to give the child trust, confidence, and the kind of autonomy that can be translated into a strength to bear the strange, the unknown, and the peculiar. So children need some experience of the range of humanity in its different versions. It is nonsense that children do not have racial prejudices. Of course, they do not know which race is "superior," and this is the root of racial prejudice. However, children are sensitive to differences in physique, and a child to whom only dark-skinned people are familiar may get used to seeing white faces but shriek with terror at the sight of a white man in a bathing suit. Equally well, a white child may get used to seeing dark faces but be terrified at the discovery that the middle of someone's back is dark. We need an environment in which the child experiences differences in colour, type and physique, with sufficient range so that no one group is solely associated with unskilled labour or with the exercise of some highly skilled profession. Instead of being presented with stereotypes by age, sex, colour, class, or religion, children must have the opportunity to learn that within each range, some people are loathsome and some are delightful.

I think we must also consider how children can be presented with models of the kinds of thinking that will be required of most educated adults. Though not all children will learn in the same way, in general it is known, for example, that children who have grown up in rooms that conform to ordinary geometric forms later learn geometric thinking with relative ease. Similarly, children can learn about volumes and ratios from blocks long before they learn words to express the ideas they have grasped. And today they need somehow to learn that their own language is only one of many languages. They need to experience the fact that this object—this container for holding liquids—is called "glass" *in English.* This is something that must be learned very early, but it is part of learning that one's own culture is one of many cultures. It is part of acquiring freedom of movement in the modern world.

In building a neighbourhood that meets human needs, we start with the needs of infants. These give us the groundwork on which we can build for contact with other human beings, with the physical environment, with the living world, and with the experiences through which the individual's full humanity can be realized. For every culture, the criteria must be modified. We cannot set our sights too low, but we can aim at any height, for we have as yet scarcely begun to explore human potentialities. How these are developed will depend on the learning experiences we can provide for children through the human habitat in which they live.

Discussion Questions

1. Mead discusses the basic physiological needs for all human beings. What are these needs? Explain what need is most variable and why it differs greatly among cultures.

2. How can "the inclusion of the strange" as an important factor in child-rearing be brought out in various size neighborhoods?

3. Discuss the elements that are important to children in a neighborhood.

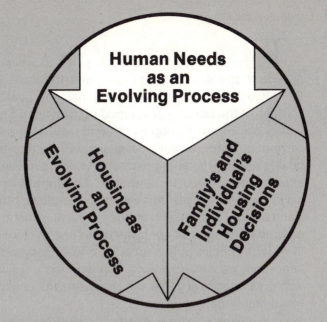

Human Needs
as an
Evolving Process

Housing as
an
Evolving Process

Family's and
Individual's
Housing
Decisions

Part Four
Individual and
Family

14. Housing and Health, by Paul V. Lemkau, M.D.

15. The House as Symbol, by Clare Cooper

16. Planning for Ourselves: Interior Design to Meet Social Needs, by L. Gertrude Nygren

17. Floor Plan Evaluation, by Carol S. Wedin

The first half of this book stressed examining housing from a macro-approach. In the remaining three parts, the focus is on the potential power of the micro forces to effect improvement in the quality of housing.

Much of the housing developed in the United States has been a response to values placed on physical health and technological feasibility, which may be a carry-over from our early religious and pioneer background where physical health, efficiency, and practicality were perceived as essential and lesser attention was given to aesthetics. To emphasize how strongly instilled this belief is, U.S. census surveys still categorize housing as standard or sub-standard on the quality of the physical structure. Also, any government-assisted housing must conform to this image of what is essential to human life in order to obtain public support. While today we recognize other factors as important, we can, obviously, ascertain the physical soundness of a structure with greater accuracy than we can assess the quality of housing which satisfies social-emotional needs.

Dr. Lemkau's extensive article, "Housing and Health," emphasizes that there is no simple relationship between health and the quality of housing in which people live. The micro-environment does not influence all people equally. The attitudes and abilities, whether inherent or environmentally determined, make a difference. Discussed in this article are the factors to be considered in the housing environment. These include: structural factors, external factors, internal features of the dwelling, and the effects of moving.

Professor Cooper suggests in "The House as Symbol" that there is a complex intertwining of the house and the psyche which means that house is a symbol of the self. If there is validity to this concept, does it help to explain why public housing has been relatively unsuccessful in our country?

Part Four further emphasizes the importance of recognizing our individual differences in the article "Planning for Ourselves: Interior Design to Meet Social Needs." Suggested is the concept that the social aspects of human-environment interactions serve as a basis for the design of the interior of human dwellings.

A variety of floor plans are evaluated in Article 17. The floor plans illustrate zoning for activities (living, working, and sleeping), circulation patterns, and room relationships. This article will assist the reader in selecting a convenient, functional, and comfortable residence.

14. Housing and Health

by Paul V. Lemkau, M.D.

There is no simple relationship between health, including mental health, and the kind and quality of housing people live in. It is possible to spin a great deal of poetry around the principle that a housing situation is mentally "healthy" or "unhealthy" depending on how far it gets in the metamorphosis of "house" to "home." This formulation, however, does little more than add a series of ill-defined and unmeasured emotional factors to physical parameters in housing. Estimates of the power of emotional factors in influencing the healthfulness of housing are so rarely based on sound data, or any data at all, that the relationship of them to health is possible only in the most extreme conditions. At the present state of knowledge, the factors in the equation must be few and their etiological relationships simple and direct to allow solid conclusions to be drawn.[36]

It appears that the one area in which health and quality of housing can be unequivocally related is in that of infectious disease. In this case the pathological mechanism, competing biological systems, is clear. The transmission mechanisms are simple, involving direct contact or short distance transmission by an identifiable agent: the success of the mechanism is dependent usually upon the distance the agent must travel and on barriers placed in its path.

Problems appear at once, however, when the cause-and-effect-relationships involved become more complex. There is, moreover, a progression in the piling up of complexities. For example, badly run institutions provided the first evidence of the pathogenic effect of gross lack of stimulation in infants and young children.[7] This was probably because the lack of stimulation was extreme in this situation through a shortage of needed personnel and failure to educate such personnel about an infant's needs. The result of inadequate stimulation was also to be seen in a clearly measurable personality factor, test intelligence. As soon as the studies moved beyond this extreme and relatively simple sequence of events, the issues became confounded. What happens if the lack of stimulation is only half as bad as it is in the most mechanical sort of institution? Does deprivation of emotional and sensory stimulation count as much at four as at one month of age? Are there critical periods of development at which stimulation means more than at other times? Is the factor that makes the difference "maternal care," emotionally laden concern with the child, or is it more intellectual, relatively indepen-

Dr. Lemkau is a Fellow of the American Psychiatric Association and the American Public Health Association. He was formerly Director, New York City Community Health Board, and Consultant to the World Health Organization. Dr. Lemkau is Professor Emeritus, Johns Hopkins University Medical School. This article was prepared specially for this book.

dent of affectional ties? Does it relate to the child's hearing language directed toward it individually or to conversation in the environment generally? And does the sophistication of the language make any difference, and if so, when?

Does it make any difference whether the tone of the communication is angry and depressed or gentle and lifting? And what is the relationship of the mood of the communicator to such things as bottomless wells of dust in cracks in poorly maintained floors, or to a badly functioning toilet the reek of which pervades the apartments which share its use? And are there other results, albeit only to be estimated, which are important? Is it true that deprived infants and children become aggressive, loveless adults who are unable to join in a consensus of feeling and thinking? Do female infants who get only meagre maternal care find themselves incapacitated to furnish adequate maternal care to their infants? For almost every question raised in these paragraphs there is clinical, anecdotal evidence, but thus far it is of such a character that clear, statistically evaluative data has proved impossible to come by.[2, 49]

The baseline for a third level of complexity cannot even be set. Findings cannot be extrapolated from a secure base such as the extreme of a child raised in a consistently inadequate institution. The characteristics of this level of situations are ambiguity and inconsistency. The mother is both loving and rejecting; the father a kindly man except when he is drunk; the house sometimes a home and sometimes a prison for the child; or a place from which he or she is locked out. The level of stimulation varies from the loneliness of isolation to the deafness-producing loudness of popular music blared from an electronic guitar before or after passing through a radio, phonograph, or tape deck. It is generally agreed that intrapersonal emotional conflict is a source of much parental inconsistency. Antithetical goals and values, loves and hates, and struggle within the person for supremacy result in the parents' inconsistent behavior. How much of such conflict arises out of the conflict between what the mother dreams of and what she has in the way of housing?[40]

When the computer arrived, it was predicted that its enormous capacities for correlation might make it possible to answer some of these questions. It has been learned, rather ruefully, that the computer can only handle items, that it cannot weigh them. It cannot answer questions of quality, only of quantity. When one item is more important than another in ways other than its simple recurrence, the computer is of no help; a human must weigh the data. The only "black box" that can do the ultimate weighing and evaluating is the human brain, thus far.

When the influences under study become even more subtle, such as the colors in the home environment, the place of the item in the complex of factors presumably having effects is obviously very small. Any effect it may have on well-being or health will have to be quite large to make it discernible when the measurement devices are inexact estimates.

The net result of all this introductory material is that the complete solution of the problem of relationship between housing and health is not at hand, and that there are a great many intervening methodological problems to be solved before the answers will be available.[10]

As the range of possible etiological complexes extends from the relatively straightforward, one overwhelming-cause type seen in acute infectious diseases to the multifactorial, long-acting type of factor which appears to have its effect by bringing stress to bear upon the individual or group, evidence accumulates that more chronic types of illness may be induced by environmental factors. An example is seen in the generalization that higher rates of hypertension have been found in blacks in the South than in those living in the North.[45] Leighton has indicated that neurotic types of reaction are more prevalent in disorganized communities than in well-organized ones, at least as evidenced in the semirural Nova Scotia towns studied.[38]

Physical, social, health, and political planners cannot wait for all these problems to be solved. It is likely that we will, in housing, build many useless "bonfires in the streets" before we arrive at "taking the handle off the pump," if indeed the problem should ever turn out to be simple enough for such a single-factorial action at all — and this certainly appears unlikely. It seems characteristic of the human race that it believes it can help itself if it tries; that the odds are that action will more often be right than wrong if based on the best knowledge available and on good will. Health and good housing being desirable, we shall strive to improve both and hope that the efforts will prove synergistic. In this major task, the designer, the architect, the physician, the sociologist, and the psychologist will contribute to the planning. The goal of healthful housing demands contributions from many disciplines working together to produce the best possible product within available resources.

The Epidemiology of Behavior Disorders

Definitions of Outcome

Evaluating health status is a notoriously difficult objective. The very words used in describing good health carry highly emotionally toned associations which make operational definition all but impossible. For example, the word "vigor" is still inextricably involved with John F. Kennedy's use of it for many people old enough to have observed his administration. To any who have seen military service at leadership levels, "morale" as a word has been contaminated almost irrevocably. Defining health is usually abandoned in favor of trying to evaluate the extent of ill health or the presence of disease.[34]

Making this step does not ease the situation very much, however, because one immediately runs into the problem of ill health influencing presumed causative factors in retroflexion. Indecision and lassitude associated with depression of mood may lead to neglect of the home so that irritating factors are magnified, increasing the stress on the depressed person as well as on the other members of the household.[8]

Behavior disorders include a vast array of illnesses and patterns of action, some of them quite specific, others quite nonspecific in definition and etiology. For example, it is very easy to see the relationship between quality of housing and the incidence of syphilis and its complication, central nervous system syphilis, which shows psychiatric symptoms.

There are certain illnesses in which a genetic factor is the primary etiologic agent. Some of these, such as phenylketonuria and Trisomy 23, relate to mental retardation; the support of a nonproductive member of the family may force the household into a lower income and, possibly, more stressful environmental situation. Prematurity carries an increased risk of mental retardation and is known to be associated with some types of nutritional stresses as well as with others. Schizophrenia is another example of an illness with a genetic factor in its etiology. The "drift" hypothesis, that those with the disease tend to fall in socioeconomic status, is still a viable one though unproved.

Neurosis, which may be considered etiologically related to psychological and physical stress, is perhaps easier to relate to the frustrations inherent (in the mind of the beholder, at least) in living in an inconvenient, uncleanable, noisy, drab house with too many people in too little space. But in neurosis another difficulty is immediately encountered. The differentiation between the sick and the well appears to depend upon the presence of symptoms and the subjects' reaction to the symptoms so that there emerges no clear separation of the population into two groups, the "sick" and the "not-sick," except by some arbitrary standard.

The same circumstances exist with most of the less incapacitating behavior disorders. Juvenile delinquency is notoriously badly reported everywhere. Many juvenile crimes are never solved so that, at best, statistics are very incomplete. There are, furthermore, many subtle judgments to be made on what shall be counted as delinquent acts. Should cases be included which have not been adjudicated because the parent has made recompense and the charges withdrawn? And should stealing jewelry from the dime store be counted equally with stealing it from a jewelry store? The outcome criteria for delinquency are as difficult to establish as those for neurosis. The same may be said for the patterns of habitual misbehavior and addiction which make up the basic material for the diagnosis of socio- or psychopathy. These difficulties of determining the prevalence of mental illnesses and of behavior deviations must be, and are, the subject of continuous research. The aim is to define them clearly enough so that the relationship between the illnesses and disorders to possible etiological factors, including such composite ones as housing, may be determined. The difficulties do yield to operational definitions rigorously applied and to the appropriate use of controls.

Attitudes and Housing Deficiencies

It is well recognized that the environment does not influence all people equally and that attitudes and abilities, inherent or environmentally determined, make a difference. An American stereotype is that leadership thrives on early adversity; or perhaps in those people who start in "log cabins" and end as great leaders, capacity exists in such abundance that even if some is lost there remains more than most people have. Some families maintain unity, morale, and spirit for long periods of time under what seem to be grindingly severe deprivations, while others lose morale easily and never seem to regain it; some appear never to have had it to lose. People have varying personalities and varying strengths of personality structure. No tool as convenient as the thermometer or noise- or light-meter has appeared for the measurement of such variables. And we know little as yet concerning how these varying factors react on one another. This represents still another variable in the health-housing equation not yet satisfactorily controlled.

Factors to be Considered

Many factors are, or have been assumed to be, related to the mental healthfulness of housing, varying from very general aspects to such specific ones as the quality and quantity of noise to which one is exposed. The latter factors, which at first may appear to be very simple and unifactorial, immediately become complex when authors point out that the noises dependent upon the physiological functions of humans have particular disconcerting effects on the mental healthfulness of housing. Included in noises of this type would be the flushing of toilets and those deriving from the psycho-sexual sphere (e.g., noises associated with sexual intercourse). Noise may also mean danger in some circumstances and, for some, its presence interferes with restorative sleep. An added complexity lies in the fact that people differ widely in sensitivity to noise. The extent to which sound (and the emotional factors which are clustered with it) influences attitudes and opinion was demonstrated in 1977 by the controversies about the supersonic airplane, the Concorde.

Areas which have been examined or discussed in the literature as relating housing to mental health are examined in the paragraphs which follow. No factor may be considered to be the sole one effective in any situation; in every case effects are obviously dependent upon various factors acting together. It is this that makes the methodology of studies so difficult and which has resulted in so few, if indeed, any definitive results. When the input data are largely unquantifiable and the output to be judged involves a differentiation between illness and discomfort, disease and happiness, one does not expect to find clearly quantified results.[44]

Structural Factors

Architecture. There appears to be general agreement that exposure to properly proportioned buildings, tastefully decorated by works of art, is a good thing for a person's peace of mind and satisfaction with life and, by inference, for his or her mental health. The relationships between beauty and ethics and between the good life and art have been accepted since the pharaohs built palaces and monuments and the Greek philosopher-architect built the Acropolis. Many cities have ordinances to the effect that a percentage of the cost of public buildings should go for art works for their decoration, in addition to the fees paid architects for sound basic designs.

There are probably two bases for the notion that beauty and health are associated. Neither has been, or probably can be at the present state of methodology, in any sense accurately quantified and thus they are extremely difficult problems for research. First, there is probably a basic organizational pattern of the central nervous system of a human which allows it to respond to certain proportions and relationships as satisfying and to others as intrusive and aggravating. That these proportions are not exactly the same for all individuals is obvious from various tastes of different people. The radical changes represented by the Tuilleries and the Seagram Building indicate that popular taste and acceptance vary widely over periods of time. Nevertheless there persists the belief that gross architectural design and decoration somehow resonate with the structure of the nervous system.

It is also true that in all societies it has been the well-off who have dictated what aspects of taste will be exhibited in a particular era and who have subsidized architects to create new patterns to submit to the public to determine their satisfaction with them, to test whether the patterns fit the central nervous system's perceptive organization well enough to be accepted. David points out that masses of public housing have an architectural force of their own in the urban landscape:

> The physical buildings, standing alone, generate great power. And properly integrated with a range of supporting services, they can radiate considerable benefit to the surrounding neighborhoods and to the city at large.[15]

Fortunately, the perceptive quality of the nervous system appears to be related in some way to utilitarian or functional factors so that useless decoration and odd construction which do not make for efficient use by people tend to be rejected eventually as tasteless. "Show," to be beautiful and satisfying, usually has to have some usefulness or it is soon abandoned. A recent example is found in the exaggerated fins which were placed on the backs of automobiles a few years ago. The Renaissance broken cornice is another example, though one still sees it occasionally in interiors.

Some authorities are rather suspicious of an ideal architecture that might prove too satisfying and lead to an undisturbed homeostatic state that would discourage change, adventure, and creativity. Kendrick concludes:

> On this basis, then, "optimum conditions" should perhaps now be considered as a set of variable oscillations in the whole range of environmental conditions, and perhaps not even within the comfort range at all times, but rather with conditions changing and

operating in random fashion to provide stimulation and variety in all aspects of physical environment.[37]

People's lives have been ruled by the rhythm of nature for so much of their existence that perhaps they are no longer able to get along without some ugliness in the form of the lightning-struck stump to offset the well-formed elm in architecture as well as in the woods.

The second basis for satisfaction in architecture appears to lie in its symbolic character. This quality finds its most obvious expression in structures which are essentially nonfunctional, such as the Eiffel Tower, the St. Louis Arch, and the Unisphere, which symbolize some particular event in human aspirations — a world's fair or the like. They partake architecturally of the same impulses that lead to the maintenance of historic places and buildings. They are symbolic of a unity of purpose enthralling all. In a sense, such symbols represent the human social drive and make it easier to agree on a purpose which all can share. This symbolic function of buildings is even harder to quantify than that of satisfying proportion. It is recognized as important but its measurement appears to defy present methodology except in such gross terms as "the number of people who come to see."

The factor of relation of proportion to satisfaction of users of buildings is not confined to their exterior and their effect on the landscape. It also involves internal space arrangements. In this aspect, utility is a most important factor. Sommers points out that too often the evaluation of new buildings ceases as soon as the buildings are completed; no one tries to find out how the places work out in practice. He defines some of the parameters to be considered in interior space design:

> We have seen that the spacing of individuals in small groups is not random but follows from the personality and cultural backgrounds of the individuals involved, what they are doing, and the nature of the physical setting. Stated more simply, we can say that spatial arrangements in small groups are functions of personality, task, and environment.[52]

Hall has pointed out that satisfaction with space allowances and the amount of personal space desired per person vary widely in different cultures.[29] Violation of "private space" is shown by restlessness and other evidence of ill-ease in people, reactions obviously having relationships to mental well-being.

External Factors

The setting of the building. In spite of the extremely rapid urbanization taking place in all populations of the world, the still accepted ideal appears to be that people should live close to nature, with green grass for children to play upon and space enough for adults to do a bit of walking on something less jarring to the feet than cement and less artificial than a carpet. The desire to have a plot of ground around one's home appears all but universal for families of child-bearing age. It has led to the enormous suburban development which has been called "urban sprawl" as well as to the attempts to correct it through planned communities.[18, 19]

The ideal of "living close to nature" is not the only one driving people from inner cities to the suburbs. Competitive upward social mobility is seen in many cases to provide impetus for people to follow the economically successful of their groups from the cheapest rent to ownership areas to more prestigious (and more expensive) areas as soon as they have achieved a reasonably stable position in the culture. The pattern of the newest immigrant groups succeeding those who have become established and moved on is a familiar one, particularly in eastern port cities earlier and now in almost all urban areas. The emergence of the elderly as an influential segment of the population appears to be setting a new type of trend for them to return to the central city which offers some relief from transportation difficulties.

Transportation and other problems appear to make it inevitable that the continual removal from the city to the suburbs cannot go on without the development of improved transport systems to keep the areas from "strangling themselves in their own lines of traffic." In Canada the proportion of single-family homes being built has fallen from two-thirds of all housing starts in 1962 to almost one-third in 1967 and the same trend appears elsewhere.[42]

Suburban real estate developments have been severely criticized as reduplicated drabness in housing style, leading to boredom for the wife who is abandoned early in the morning by her husband to a dreary day of child watching and aimless housework and reunited with him in the evening when both are exhausted and irritable. The whole concept was epitomized by Paul Stevenson as we drove by such a subdivision with the derisive epithet, "breeding pens." There have been many allegations that such living produces mental illnesses — depression, neuroses, and alcoholism — though there is little real data to support the statements.[6]

The ideal of more completely planned communities, "new cities" or "new towns," was developed partly in reaction to such criticism. The trend began in Europe and has extended to the United States. The primary difference between the "new cities" and "developments" is their size, which is dependent upon the extent of the capital available for development. The new cities obtain land in large parcels of tens or thousands

In planning the new town of Columbia, Maryland the goal was to create "a garden where people grow." (United States Department of Agriculture — Soil Conservation Service)

of acres which allows planners to design the city with an eye to the terrain, to plan separate but coordinated communities within the area, to arrange for full service, to insure open land, to group schools and other service functions, to control traffic patterns, and to arrange for difficult communities to have some individual functions and characteristics. James Rouse, in describing his aims for Columbia, Maryland, epitomized the idea as "a garden where people grow."[9]

The new city idea is exciting and an enormous challenge for planning. It attempts to do in a brief time what a piecemeal development process might evolve into if given a number of generations.[18] It preserves natural features of the land so that later costly and difficult reclamation for park usage can be avoided. Some, however, are concerned that these brave new worlds may not prove to be the boon expected, mainly because they fear the loss of individual liberty that adherence to plans, however good they may be, inevitably entails. There are also economic factors to be considered. Certainly to be a useful social institution the new city must house a wide range of socioeconomic strata in its population mix. Many of the new cities do not pretend to be able to do this financially. Those who hold it as an aim generally admit that housing of the poorest in the population is a commercial impossibility in new housing; the capital costs are simply too great to be met without large subsidy. So, with all the advantages the new city can offer, it cannot supply a full range of exposure to the real world of people to its inhabitants. To this extent, the new city must restrict the life experiences of its inhabitants. The high rate of inflation in building costs has made this problem much more pressing recently.

In spite of these problems, the new cities concept has led to firming up the goals of city planning generally by demanding research results and thereby improving research techniques. Planning can be on a large enough scale to make tapping a wider range of expertise possible in the planning effort. Unfortunately, research methods for continuous surveillance of the effect of such cities on the life-styles of the people living in them have not developed sufficiently to afford accurate evaluation of their effects. In observing Columbia, Maryland after ten years of development and when it had reached about one-half of its projected population, I was impressed mostly with the success achieved in obtaining the people's interest in their own government. Although the percentage of the population voting for representation of the unofficial local government which controls many recreational and other amenities was low, it was clear that many highly capable leaders had come forward or had been developed under the system. The people had found many ways to discuss and negotiate not only internal town issues but those involving the official government of their county as well. I was particularly impressed by the number and quality of volunteer services donated by residents to their social system.

On the other hand, certain problems have appeared which were not foreseen by the planners.[39] Columbia is encountering more problems of race relations than was expected. It appears that the sanguine assumptions that economic equivalence or near equivalence of the races would avoid racial confrontations were unfounded. Nevertheless, there is apparently sufficient tolerance to make Columbia a more comfortable place to live for interracial couples than elsewhere. A second unforeseen major problem encountered by the community is drug usage. The provision of an adequate life-style for adolescents received much consideration during the planning period, but the resulting design for living was not sufficiently satisfying to the population to offset the spread of drug usage, at least for a period of time. Unfortunately, no data are available to compare the extent of drug usage in Columbia with that in comparable populations. A third circumstance, a high divorce rate, was to some extent expected by the planners, but it has tended to place a rather large number of single-parent house-holds in the community as well as contributing to a relatively high mobility of the population.

Columbia, situated between Baltimore and Washington, was expected to be mostly a "bedroom community" for workers in these two metropolitan areas. After ten years of development, industries in Columbia's industrial parks and retail areas are employing a higher percentage of its wage earners than had been hoped for by the planners.

Damon reports on a housing project in Jamesville, a section of Boston.[14] The area has a population of 15,000 in one square mile. Two sets of apartment buildings were selected for study, one close to a major highway with high noise levels (80-100 decibels during the day time, 74 at midnight) and one "interior sector" with noise levels between 5 and 10 decibels. Four criteria were used for evaluation: (1) rate of arrests; (2) school delinquency; (3) medical clinic visits; and (4) condition of entryways of buildings. The first two and the fourth criteria showed a significantly greater number of problems in the noisy apartment areas. Clinic visits were not significantly different for either physical or behavioral complaints.

High-rise versus low-rise housing. Early in public housing ventures in the United States and abroad the goal was for single-family or multiple-unit dwellings for a relatively small number of families. There were many advantages of such development, primarily the avoidance of the mechanical problems inherent in multi-story buildings and particularly the avoidance of high-cost elevators which invite vandalism. The walk to the ground was easy. The parent could watch children at play in the yard and be able to reach them in a moment should there be trouble or accident. The scheme was much closer to the goals mentioned earlier than the high-rise apartment house. The problem that led to high-rise buildings to supply low-cost housing was the high cost of land. If overcrowded slums were to be replaced by more commodious housing in the same area, the only way to do it was to get the extra square footage by piling more floors on one another.

The high-rise, low-cost housing experiments appear to have few supporters at the present time, or at least few who write in the literature. The explosion in a high-rise in London during the summer of 1968 brought a flood of newspaper publicity, almost all of which condemned the system.

One observation of interest is that people living in "flats" tend to have less social contact with their neighbors than do those living in low-rise dwellings. "The flat in the tower-block is cocooned against noise, deliberately; the front door may open only onto a vestibule shared by two other flats' entrances and its emptiness and milk bottles look onto the gray sliding doorway of a lift."[28] This in contrast to the typical slum street where outdoor living space includes the stoop. Fanning writes in an excellent article on the general subject:

> The most striking contrast between life in flats and that in houses was the lack of com-munication between families living in flats compared with those in houses, and this was probably the principal cause of the isolation and loneliness of the wives in flats. Apart from the discussions in the surgery when this was revealed, it was noticed by the doctors and by the health visitor in the daily round, when one could observe the contrast during domicilliary visits. It was not uncommon to find neighbors visiting and talking when one visited a house, and if a wife was ill in bed, the door would often be opened by a neighbor who had come in to help. This was not nearly so frequent in the flats, where it was more usual to find a wife coping by herself, or whose husband had to stay away from work to help.[22]

People living in high-rise apartments tend to have less social interaction with their neighbors than do those living in low-rise dwellings. (Department of Housing and Urban Development)

Downing furnishes an excellent list of the more or less mechanical problems in high-rise living. He lists noise, waste disposal, laundry, stairways and their cleanliness, elevators and auto parking as recurrent sources of difficulty.[16] A more personal problem is the provision of play space for children and furnishing toilets for their use at ground level. These problems are, apparently, always to be faced in high-rise living.[26, 54] The most frequent suggestions for their alleviation deals in ways to organize tenants into associations so that they can fill their own needs and police themselves collectively and to offer space for communal or cooperative activities such as auditoriums, swimming pools, gymnasiums, hobby areas, and open spaces. Where the elderly are involved, telephone communication (and communicators) are suggested along with a buddy-system so that two or more people accept responsibility for each other. There appears no doubt that if high-rise, low-cost living is to be successful in reaching the same level of healthy living that would be the case in low-rise living, more personal services will be required.

Fanning's report recounts a study contrasting living in flats and houses so far as health is concerned, and reviews the literature. The sample, families of members of the armed forces living in Germany, is an unusual one carrying a special load of problems, but the study was carefully done and has value nevertheless. Respiratory infections showed considerably higher rates for those who lived in flats. Psychoneuroses in women were also higher in this group, though the author admits to deficiencies in the data collection system.[22]

The low-rise, single house in large agglomerates has also been heavily criticized as already noted, mostly on the ground that it tends, because of geographic dispersion, toward one-parent homes with bored wives in command most of the day, plus a depressing sameness of existence. The increased percentage of married women in the work force adds problems of child care to the others listed. Housing faces a dilemma: high-rise with fewer transport and square footage issues but with social isolation only to be offset by more expenditures for tenant services, or low-rise with greater transport problems and, probably, an increasing need for tenant services as time goes on. Perhaps the most important issue is that modern congregate living probably requires as great attention to finding satisfying ways to live as in finding satisfactory dwellings in which to live.

Hare in a study of health of people living in new housing estates in London, concludes that, in addition to the usual finding of more respiratory disease in poorer housing, there is an association between dissatisfaction with housing and the prevalence of poor physical and mental health.[32]

The suburban "industrial parks" which are ringing American cities, are tending to make the high-rise problem even more acute. The "balanced" city, which provided work for those who lived in it, is being destroyed as industries seek the periphery, leaving their workers behind them. Obviously, this issue is complicated by the changed pattern of industrial work, moving toward more white- and fewer blue-collar jobs, and involves the educational system in producing workers able to staff the industries in their new locations.

Arrangement and location. Metropolitan areas have grown mainly by engulfing communities at their peripheries. These old towns usually showed some local character and had some rivalries between them which tended to unite their inhabitants. These distinguishing characteristics are lost in the engulfing process so that the local loyalty, perhaps to a town of a few thousand people, is dissipated in the melange of tens or hundreds of thousands. The population is too large for anyone to experience the feeling of being a member of it. The city covers so large an area that rivalry can be expressed only in statistics or professional athletic teams' scores as compared with those of another faceless metropolis.

Although no research data has been found to support the theory, planners are beginning to consider this issue of the size of the population unit which allows its citizens to develop the feeling of "membership." Attempts are being made to revivify the town consciousness of sections of cities. Health services and many other services are striving to get planning input for the design of services from the consumers of those services, with the size of the consumer group tending to be relatively small in relation to the total size of the city.

The rebuilding of the core areas of many cities has, in a number of instances, increased the attention paid to natural minorities which are often found concentrated in particular sections of cities generations after the family immigrated. City fairs and special celebrations bring the cultural diversity of the city to the foreground and, in the process, build morale and local identification within the larger city. Planners of new cities divide their land to stimulate consciousness of belonging to a locality of 10,000 to 20,000 people while being integrated into citizenship in the city as a whole as well. This reemphasis on local government and on local, metropolitan, state, and national loyalties is seen as a necessary but, for a period, neglected part of a satisfying existence.

Art and its uses. In addition to the recognition that people somehow resonate to proper architectural design, there appears to be growing recognition that art, be it rugged, vandalism-resisting sculpture or mosaic or delicate print or canvas, is a necessary ingredient to people's content. There is also increasing recognition of a need

There appears to be a growing recognition that art is a necessary ingredient to people's content. (Department of Housing and Urban Development)

for people to be creative artistically which will become more important as increasing automation in industry releases a greater amount of time for more leisurely styles of life. Again, no data are at hand to support these beliefs, but they are sufficiently widespread to affect the design of housing and the decoration of grounds about dwellings. High-rise dwellers in England and other European countries have been supplied with garden plots because they appeared to miss this sort of avocation more than others when they moved from single-family row or terrace housing.

Internal Features of the Dwelling

Size. The space needed per individual member of a household has been given a great deal of attention by others and need not be repeated here. That standards cannot be applied equally for all populations but depend upon tradition, building materials, and cultural patterns is obvious though not always taken into consideration when governments build in their dependencies. A good example of the issues involved can be seen in Karunaratne[35] and in Kasl[36].

The frustrations and problems of overcrowding and inadequate housing are thoroughly discussed in Schorr.[51] Woodin gives a few striking case studies indicating the enormous complexities of the interaction of character, illness, and housing and a suggestion as to how some, at least, can be unravelled and reknit so that more successful households result.[56] The combination of factors is extremely difficult to evaluate one by one, and is further complicated by the apparent tendency for difficulties to "nest" together. Unfortunate events and circumstances appear to hit certain families in groups in nonrandom fashion. Downs and Simon noted this tendency as one finding of the National Health Survey in Baltimore. It could be shown that diseases, including psychoneurosis, tended to nest together rather than be evenly distributed throughout the population.[17] Buell and his associates found the same concentration of problems in certain families in a community survey of St. Paul.[8] The source or sources of this tendency is unknown. Conservative critics of attempts to abate slum conditions by providing proper housing argue that the primary deficiency is characterological: that the slum dweller is, somehow, a degenerate person. Others contend that using the bathtub to bathe in, instead of as a coal scuttle, demands learning, which in turn demands leadership and intensive teaching. Still others argue that the primary issue is frequently ill health — physical or mental — which sets off a train of difficulties — medical, social, and financial — which eventually defeats the family so that it no longer has a will to resist its degradation. Most agree that children should not be exposed to the worst of such conditions and that for them, if not for the adults, efforts at untangling the skein of problems should be undertaken.

The "nesting" phenomenon reinforces the earlier conclusions that rehousing in the physical sense cannot be expected to solve all problems. The multiple difficulties of families must be attacked together. Buell and many others have pointed out the frequency with which services are applied seriatim when it is very clear that no single one can have effective impact on the family which needs many services at once.

The crowded household clearly interferes with the life of the individuals included in it. The child in school has no place to study uninterruptedly so that it is very easy for him or her to give up the effort which is not highly valued by people in his or her

A crowded household clearly interferes with the life of the individuals included in it. (United States Department of Agriculture)

environment in any case. The mother has no surcease from her children who are frequently more than she can bear and, probably, more than she should have borne. Sharing in making family decisions is next to impossible where there is not enough space for family consideration. Vacillating autocracy is likely to result, with consequent confusion in the children about desired standards of behavior. Exhaustion from continuing failure to be able to control too many people in too small a space may result in giving up the effort.[48]

Crowding makes for increased infectious disease but there is less direct evidence that it makes for increased mental illnesses. There is no lack of indirect evidence, however. Epidemiological studies of prevalence of mental illnesses of almost all kinds show these diseases occurring more frequently among the poor who are, presumably, living in the most crowded households.[24]

The issue is somewhat clouded by the relatively large number of psychiatrically ill people who live alone.

Room arrangement. The convenience of room arrangement has also not yielded to analysis, so far as is known, as a separate factor determining mental health or disorder. The violation of privacy when some members of the family have to go through the bedrooms of others to get to the bathroom, or when all have to go through the kitchen to reach it, or when the bathroom must be shared by multiple families, is perfectly clear. Neglect of toilets is notorious when use by more than one family is necessary; like the stairways of high-rise dwellings, what is everyone's responsibility appears quickly to become no one's. These issues and more abstract ones are well discussed by Chermayeff and Alexander.[12]

There has been a great deal of discussion on issues of sleeping arrangements as determinants in the psychosexual development of children. Children sleeping in the parents' bedroom are exposed to the "primal scene." This exposure, when they are at a critical age, confuses them as regards parental interrelationships, the sex act being misinterpreted as aggressive, according to some authors. Similarly, mothers sleeping with sons beyond the years of infancy appears to warp personality development through the appearance of distorted mother-child relationships. Brothers and sisters sleeping in the same bed or same room beyond the earliest years is said to lead to harmful sexual stimulation and experimentation. Anecdotal material is presented for the support of each of these ideas, but there is no statistical proof clearly showing a relationship to mental ill health.

The relief of crowding and the proper arrangement is appreciated by tenants as evidenced by statements of those who have moved from inconvenient to more convenient quarters.[55] The relationship of this finding to mental ill health is not clear, but as improved morale is a factor in good mental health, it appears that relief of overcrowding and inconvenience contributes to it.

The kitchen. The fact that more poverty-stricken homes are headed by females only and that the cultural patterns of the poor usually place the father outside of the home for much of his recreation, make the mother's workshop, the kitchen, of importance. In many families, and not only those of lower social economic classes, the kitchen is the living room in a literal sense — most of the living goes on there. The room is frequently both the place where food is prepared and eaten, its table the place where studying is done, and, in very crowded homes, it may also serve as sleeping quarters. It may be the only room warm in winter, cooking heat being used twice. It is the young children's play space, the pots and pans and more dangerous bottles doubling as playthings. The laundry and ironing may be done there. It is an all-purpose room with many opportunities for interfering, competitive activities.

This is the mother's domain. When it is poorly equipped with inconvenient appliances which impose inefficient use of the human body, such as sinks or work surfaces of improper height, the mother takes the brunt of the pain and fatigue. If there is no proper storage for her tools, it is she who bears the irritations, who wastes time hunting things, and who chases the children to recapture some dangerous object purloined as a plaything. It is the mother who has to rewash the material stepped on during the process of its ironing. The kitchen frequently includes an entry door; the tracking in of outside soil may combine with outworn floor covering to produce a formidable cleaning task. The kitchen is an industrial area loaded with things and activities that make the mother's productivity difficult and threaten her disposition from many sides. Her disposition and temperament are most frequently the key to the family's comfort and emotional equilibrium; as the mother goes, so goes the family.

The reduction of the material of this previous paragraph to experimental methods to determine the power of the causes and the relevance of the presumed effects presents methodological problems of very considerable difficulty. It involves the analysis of movements of family members within the outside of the house with consideration of the purposes of the movements, their extent and the values attached to them. Chapin and Hightower in an investigation of the subject, show clearly the magnitude of the problems involved.[11] Some contribution, although on a much less empirical base, appears in the architectural analysis, *Community and Privacy*.[12]

By far the largest and most careful before-and-after model tests of the ideas involved appear to be those employed by Wilner et al which indicated change for the better after rehousing, though the changes were not as large as had been hoped.[55] Mood of the respondents did not change very markedly, though an optimistic outlook upon the world was more prevalent after housing improvement. It is of interest that there was distinctly greater satisfaction with the new environment and an increased feeling of satisfaction with other things. These findings may be interpreted as increased positive mental health of the mother (the respondent), and, by inference, of the family.

Closet space. The issue of space for storage has already been mentioned in connection with the discussion of the kitchen. The problem is the same for the storage of clothing, bedding, etc. Inadequate storage facilities make for difficulty in cleaning, require fatiguing bending and stooping, make for clutter compounded by adventurous and curious toddlers and, in all, contribute to the lowering of the morale and likelihood of intemperate and inconsistent sorts of disciplinary actions on the part of the mother. They risk her eventual defeat into an apathetic, careless state. The measurement of these effects is difficult, and again the studies last quoted appear to contain the best evidence that such factors are facts — that they, in Adolf Meyer's definition of a fact, "make a difference."

Quiet areas. Most authorities believe that people have needs both to be sociable and to withdraw from groups from time to time. Crowded, inadequately heated living space most frequently makes the latter quite impossible. There is no surcease from being sociable, whether one needs it or not. The Baltimore study shows a trend toward husbands spending more time at home after resettlement in improved housing which may, perhaps, be interpreted as less need to find anonymity in a crowd — a separateness not possible in the house. It was also noted that a larger proportion of the resettled families owned record players and television sets; perhaps this may be interpreted as indicating a greater possibility to enjoy a kind of solitude without interruption at home. Again the data are not conclusive, only suggestive, but suggestive in the direction of increased satisfaction of human needs when more adequate housing is available.

Multiple use of space. This topic has also already been discussed in relation to the kitchen which is often a multiple-use room in poor as well as in more adequate housing. But when there is multiple use of space — the bed for sleeping at night, as a chair or sofa by day, the space under it to hide storage boxes, etc. — keeping all the functions orderly becomes a Herculean task.

One specific danger of multiple use of space is increased frequency of accidents. No medicine cabinet means exposure of potentially dangerous drugs to access by children. Chronic plumbing problems means the presence of caustic materials to open drains, and inadequate safe storage spaces mean that these may be accessible to adventurous children. From a longer view, multiple use of space means more litter and greater wear on flooring materials with resultant greater danger of tripping and falling. Again, one ends with a complex of increased need for physical care, of work to keep quarters clean, neat, and orderly with inadequate resources to devote to housekeeping, of further disruption of the household, and of erosion of the morale of the mother and, through her, of the family. It is but a narrow step to carry the deduction a little farther and add greater prevalence of mental illnesses related to poisoning, trauma, and retreat into neurotic defenses or precipitation into depressive states, even though there is only the very general data already mentioned to support the extension.

Bathrooms. The bathroom and problems related to it will be further discussed in relation to noise. So far as is known, the problem of cleanliness of toilets has not been extensively studied but it is, of course, known that public toilets everywhere generate vulgar forms of art and writing.[1, 50] This tendency appears to correlate with the number of people using the toilet. Like the steps of the high rise, multiple responsibility appears to lessen individual responsibility and to lead to defacement, soiling, and neglect. The resultant smells add to the frustrating character of the total living situation.

Although there is no evidence at hand to support the surmise, it is possible that the toilet is more important than other items listed previously in its effects on morale. The activities directly associated with the satisfaction of physiological functioning of an individual could become habitually distorted, leading to psychosomatic or more clearly neurotic types of reaction.

Furnishings. Closets and similar storage spaces are obviously the concern of the architect and demand careful study as to their ratio in size to the rest of the home, to prevailing climate, etc. Older homes, built when closets were pieces of furniture rather than structural elements of the building, present difficulties which appear in programs of housing renovation. The difficulties of too little storage space have already been noted.

Built-in and other furniture. Built-in furniture offers some solutions to multiple use of space, the best known being the folding bed which disappears into the wall or becomes living room furniture. Such usage is economical but creates friction when a room is occupied by two or more persons who have different sleeping, reading, and television-watching habits. When more than a very few people are involved, the transformation of a living room into a bedroom disrupts the group and, frequently, makes privacy almost impossible.

Fixed, built-in furniture provides economy in space usage but also dictates a sameness of one living space to another and thwarts the individual homemaker's creativity. It also tends to freeze room arrangements in a single, unvarying pattern which may be aggravating to the homemaker even when multiple use of space is not a factor. Sommers gives illuminating discussions of this problem, particularly in regard to student housing.[52]

Heating. Although central heating is considered ideal in America, the absence of an open fire is criticized in England. This is clearly related to long traditions that have acquired a sentimental character. The heating of the whole of the dwelling unit is now considered ideal, though in the not distant past a cold bedroom was praised as a health measure. In poor people's homes, heating of a few rooms or only one room is often a necessity. Such heating requires the storage of fuel in small quantities and its burning in the living space itself, which entail many accident hazards. Kerosene poisoning of children and carbon monoxide poisoning (from unvented heaters or from manufactured gas) present risks to the central nervous system with consequent behavior disorder as well. Accidents resulting in burns entail the psychological disorders associated with scarring.

Heat for cooking, as has been mentioned, may also serve to warm a room. Crowding about a hot stove is obviously an accident hazard. Stoves of improper height may invite children to spill hot liquids upon themselves.

Refrigeration. Refrigeration is an important determinant of general health; it is possible that the absence of electrical refrigeration is the primary reason for "summer diarrhea" in developing countries. The size of the refrigerator is also important economically because adequate capacity of the unit and its freezer allows buying food in the most economical amounts rather than only as needed. That the poorly housed have in the past been unable to buy in quantity may have something to do with the establishment of the attitudes of being unable to put off satisfactions, often alleged to be characteristic of lower social classes.

The built-in refrigerator has advantages since it can be designed to fit the space allotted to it. When the machine is bought by the family, it may not fit conveniently; its door may open on the wrong side, and it may otherwise be a source of constant irritation. (The cookstove may present similar difficulties, and, like the refrigerator, is more frequently being considered a part of the house than a piece of furniture.)

Appliances. Housing quality and satisfaction are determined, in part, by appliances which may be, and now commonly are, permanent parts of the structure. The refrigerator and stove have already been discussed separately because of their relation to other aspects of housing and the health issue in considering refrigeration. Washer, dryer, and dishwasher are becoming permanent fixtures of the house also.

Air conditioning is rapidly approaching as important a place as heating, particularly in hot and humid climates. Air conditioning may be of value on two counts: first, for controlling humidity and thereby protecting property from mildew and other forms of deterioration; and, secondly, for controlling discomfort, particularly for people especially sensitive to heat discomfort and those with special health problems. While property destruction is not of concern to this article, it should nevertheless be pointed out that things owned, particularly family heirlooms, easily take on an emotional patina which may precipitate grief reactions if they are lost.

The comfort factor in air conditioning has not been evaluated. The common belief that living in the tropics tends to establish a torpid and unambitious way of life has no real base in results of scientific research, so it would be very difficult to judge whether it would be less severe and "debilitating" were the temperature and humidity of the environment altered by air conditioning. It is obvious, however, that complaints would probably decrease. There is also, so far as is known, no evidence as to whether demand for adaptation to widely differing temperatures, as between working place and home, is a good or bad thing for health or work productivity. There remains a great deal of research to be done in this field though there is no question of the popularity of temperature control in the developed countries.

Sleep, implying proper rest and rebuilding for work to be done, is for many people greatly interfered with by high ambient temperatures, and hot nights, at least in temperate climates in which they are relatively infrequent, appear obviously to interfere with people's productivity. Nothing is really known scientifically about the extent of human adaptability in this area, and it is difficult to come to any firm conclusion relating ambient temperature and emotional disturbances.

Air conditioning obviously can affect architecture in radical ways. It may become more economic to build buildings without windows — witness experiments in the United States in schools — and this raises the question as to whether or not continued contact with "nature" is essential to a person's emotional health or satisfaction in living. Like rapid eye movement (REM) sleep, woolgathering by gazing out a window may be found to be important to emotional economy.

The garbage disposal unit in the kitchen sink is a convenience and aids in reducing rat and fly populations. It is closely related to the great issues of litter and trash disposal and the disposal of organic wastes so that its discussion becomes an integral part in considering the total residential environment as well as the immediate surroundings of each unit. The elimination of decomposing organic matter reduces smells which may be especially potent in relation to physiological and emotional upset. That the issue is important is borne out by the fact that polls show cleanup of litter to have high priority in the minds of inhabitants of slums. The scattered papers and broken glass so obvious to the outsider who visits neglected areas are apparently disturbing to people who live there also.

Color. As already noted for architecture, ambient color clearly has something to do with mood, but the establishment of exact relationship has proved impossible. The language is full of consensual allusions — blue Monday, sees red, rose-colored glasses, etc. Most of the theory regarding the use of color in homes and institutions rests on little more than interpretation of such expressions as evidence of a certain neuro-physiological organization in humans.[53] It is often offset by obvious differences in traditions such as that black is the color for grief in some cultures while white is the symbol in others.

Technological advances have relieved one of the factors that previously made institutions drab and unicolored. Whether the brighter and easily maintained colors now available for use in schools and hospitals make a genuine difference in mood and/or success is extremely difficult to judge. It is certainly true that furnishing a stimulating environment — in color and in content — induces less "hospitalism" in children and has, along with other factors, helped in the disappearance of marasmus. The wider use of stimulating colors in mental hospitals is thought to reduce the social breakdown syndrome, although this is simply one unweighted factor in a congeries of factors thought to be effective.[4]

There is little or no scientific information on the varying effects of color in the home.

It is believed that variety of color is better than monochromatic treatment and that lighter shades are preferable to darker shades because they conserve light and, probably, lighten the mood.

Goromosov has summarized information on the quality and quantity of light necessary for comfortable completion of tasks.[25]

Noise. Instrumentation has led to considerable study of noise factors from the physical as well as the psychological aspects. Noise as a "pollutant" of the environment does not stand alone. For example, the advantages of garbage disposal units and air conditioners must be weighed against the fact that one produces loud noises for a short time, the other a lower level for a longer time. The quality and quantities of noises which produce deafnesses do not occur in homes usually and noises of this level are not discussed here. Farr points out, however, that some home sounds, if long continued, reach levels that could be destructive to hearing.[23]

The level of scientific certitude regarding the importance of sound in the home is well expressed by Farr:

> The trauma of noise may bring to the surface a scarcely submerged tension and result in an emotional outburst, or it may provoke symptomatology manifesting itself as a well-recognized medical syndrome. The control of pathways which lead to these diverse expressions is not known. Perhaps with telemetry now becoming a practical means of study, it may be possible to design adequate, meaningful experiments dealing with this problem.[23]

In spite of such cautious statements, many make sweeping interpretations regarding the pathogenic quality of noise. One such interpretation reads, "However, the term 'noise neurosis' has been used in many quarters and examples have been given in support of it, e.g., the frequency of suicidal attempts, criminality, stomach illness and disturbances of glands in the new but badly insulated noisy buildings."[13] Another such statement reads, "Excessive noise is recognized to be a serious factor in causing nervous strain and in interfering with rest and privacy. Yet nuisances from noise are being increasingly aggravated rather than reduced by present day housing methods and living habits. Reversal of the trend toward a noisy environment can be a significant contribution to health and amenity."[3]

Underlying such statements is evidence relating physiological disturbances to noise. [20,21,25] Such evidence is significant in itself, but it is a considerable step from demonstrable physiological disturbances to a relationship to psychiatric disorder. An intermediate step is the relating of noise to the degree of annoyance to those in the noisy environment. There are a number of factors involved, the main ones being:

1. the level of sound and its quality, including rise and fall characteristics;
2. the meaning of the sound; and
3. the individual variation of sensitivity of hearers.

Sudden loud and high-pitched sounds are more disturbing than low-pitched ones which are constant. This appears to be due in part to the fact that sound is frequently a warning of danger. The "startle reaction" of the soldier too long exposed to artillery fire lasts much longer than his exposure to the sound of the guns. During World War II, patients in general hospitals, far from danger, were observed to react violently to such sounds as an automobile backfire. Obviously, the annoying quality of sounds depends upon the state of the hearer as well as the intensity and the qualities of the sound. This problem is the source of the greatest difficulty in evaluating sound pollution. In the case of the soldier with a startle reaction, the etiology is probably multifactorial, the exposure to recurring frightening sounds being but one factor.

Noise which interferes with the understanding of communication is particularly important in causing annoyance according to a number of studies which also indicate levels and qualities of sound that are effective in interfering with intelligible speech.[5, 31, 46]

Presbycusis appears to decrease the capacity of individuals to segregate noise from meaningful sounds so that older people are more sensitive to auditory distraction than younger, and the hard of hearing are more sensitive than those of normal hearing. The physiology of the decrease in a person's capacity to select sounds from the welter about him or her when hearing acuity is decreased remains a mystery, but the phenomenon is very real and disturbing. It causes withdrawal reactions in some hard-of-hearing persons and often interferes with learning to use a hearing aid. It is often stated that hard-of-hearing people have a tendency to paranoid types of thinking; this may represent a clearer relation between psychopathology and noise than others which have been propounded.

Noises which have meaning are more distracting and annoying than other sounds. This is obvious from everyday reactions seen to screeching tires, howling sirens, or clanging bells. The phenomenon has already been referred to in relation to sounds such as the flushing of a toilet[47], of persons having intercourse[27], and those of kitchen appliances used in food preparation. Clearly the startle reaction is related to a psychological spread of meaning from one specific type of sound with definite warning characteristics until nonspecific ones are reacted to. For example, instrumental music is less distracting than songs with words.

Background sound, as an alternative to silence in dwellings, is desired for two purposes: to raise the level of desirable sounds to where they can be heard and to lower the relative loudness of intermittent sounds. Absolute silence is psychologically upsetting to people experimentally exposed to it; the human nervous system appears to be adjusted to a wealth of random-type noise in the environment and is not disturbed by it, provided the level is not too high and that it has a fixed, unchanging meaning.

Another aspect of the meaning of sound has to do with the inhibition of activities that produce noise which may bother others. Because of this, parents may hesitate to punish children, and the sexual life of marital partners may be interfered with.

Finally, there is the problem of sensitivity to noise. Prestemon found that in housing developments in which there were complaints about noise, the proportion of tenants complaining varied from 20 to about 90%; unfortunately, actual noise level is not indicated.[47] Howell lists these five factors to be considered in evaluating the effect of noise:

1. The specific way in which a person experiences
2. The given situation
3. The specific quality of the sound
4. The present activity of the person
5. The sound level[33]

Of these five factors, only the last two are seen to be independent of the state of the hearer. In such a situation the research problems involved become extremely complex and difficult.

Animal experimentation and some clinical observations of humans show that the central nervous system can be thrown into convulsive discharge by sound. Whether such violent and acute reactions indicate that lesser stimuli precipitate less all-encompassing behavior disorders remains a problem for further research.

Moving and Mental Health

The fact of moving from one house to another is known in some cases to precipitate psychiatric disorders. Although several such cases have been seen in patients, the fact that they occur is apparently not recognized widely by real estate agents.[43] Hall reviews the field thoroughly and concludes that well-adjusted personalities are rarely upset by a move.[30] Those persons who were thrown into symptomatic states were found to have had earlier personality problems, often concerned with difficulties in emancipating from parents.

Summary

The quality of housing is clearly related to the mental health of its inhabitants in that it controls to a considerable extent the intimate environment in which individuals live, particularly during their formative, early years. It exerts its influence in a large number of ways, some of which are subject to relatively exact measurement and some of which remain, to too large an extent, more or less obvious but not measurable. The main factors are:

1. General health is affected. There is no doubt that mental illnesses are symptomatic of many types of somatic pathology[41] and that some of these are related to poor housing. Unfortunately, housing rarely stands alone as the objectionable feature of the environment; it is accompanied by dirt, poverty, poor nutrition, noises, inadequate heat, etc. Poor housing also frequently implies poor neighborhood conditions which are lacking in physical space and equipment. The neighborhood is also frequently lacking in social organization. Nevertheless, the fact that more respiratory illness accompanies poor housing attests that there will be more mental illness since respiratory illnesses are in some cases followed by complications such as meningitis, brain abcesses, and encephalitis which interfere with proper brain function. Other factors contributing in this area are higher rates of premature births and the "nesting" characteristics of diseases. Higher accident rates in poor housing are predictive of a greater rate of brain damage and resulting behavior problems.

2. Social organization is affected. Housing type and location affect the extent to which persons socialize with each other, and the thwarting of people's social needs is generally believed to affect their health. When the structure of housing dictates restricted socialization, the plan for the organization of the housing must offset any isolation induced by structure. Furthermore, the extent of community organization has been shown to be correlated with the extent of psychiatric symptoms in a population. Those responsible for housing, particularly the rehousing of masses of people, must pay particular attention to the community organization of the people moved.

    The fact of moving itself, with the implication of the breaking or loosening of the net of associations and the changed relationship with the extended family, may precipitate psychiatric symptoms, particularly in persons who have previously demonstrated some personality deviation or immaturity.

3. Housing indirectly brings annoyances. Aside from other factors of noise, color, and structural and appliance inconvenience, characteristics of poor housing such as difficulty in cleaning and keeping clean and minor accident hazards

present nagging annoyances. These probably influence mood negatively and may produce feelings of frustration. This frustration, in turn, may lead to exhaustion of the will to resist the apparently insurmountable difficulties. When such factors are relieved, increased morale results over a period of time. The burden of annoyances falls heaviest on the homemaker who is usually in the primary position of maintaining the emotional equilibrium of the household and to most influence the children. Inconvenience and over-crowding interfere with children's accomplishments in education, the prime institution for preparing children to cope with the organizational and technological complications of the age. They also act to drive the father out of the home to seek rest and relaxation away from the crowded house, a relief frequently not available to his wife.

4. Beauty in architecture and decoration is generally believed to contribute to satisfaction with the house.

5. Particular mental health risks may be higher in high-rise structures used for homes. These must be offset by more personal services to tenants.

6. Noise is annoying to a considerable proportion of people. There are indications that it is the cause of physiological and psychological disturbances which may relate to some forms of psychiatric symptoms.

7. Although there are few definitive research results relating any single factor or congeries of factors directly to the constellation of influences comprised in the housing situation, most writers in the field agree that there is a relationship between good housing and good mental health and bad housing and poor mental health.

Literature Cited

1. Agorio, E. "Lavatory Defacement in Elementary Schools." Research paper prepared for Mental Hygiene II, School of Hygiene and Public Health, Johns Hopkins University, 1969.

2. Ainsworth, M.D. *Deprivation of Maternal Care: A Reassessment of Its Effects.* Public Health Paper No. 14. Geneva: World Health Organization, U.N., 1962.

3. American Public Health Association, Committee on the Hygiene of Housing. *Planning the Neighborhood.* Chicago: Public Administration Service, 1948.

4. _____. *Mental Disorders: A Guide to Control Methods.* New York, 1962.

5. Berendt, R.D. *A Guide to Airborne, Impact and Structure-Borne Noise Control in Multi-Family Dwellings.* Washington, D.C.: U. S. Department of Housing and Urban Development, 1967.

6. Bhandari, N.P., and Harold Hill. "A Medico-Social Study of Rehousing." *J. Royal Institute of Public Health* 23 (1960): 187-204.

7. Bowlby, J. *Maternal Care and Mental Health.* Geneva: World Health Organization, U. N., 1952.

8. Buell, B. *Community Planning for Human Services.* New York: Columbia University Press, 1952.

9. "Can These Thinkers Help Put Across a Vast New Town?" *House and Home,* December 1964.

10. Cassel, J. "The Relation of the Urban Environment to Health: Towards a Conceptual Frame and a Research Strategy." In *The Effect of the Man-Made Environment on Health and Behavior.* Washington, D.C.: Department of Health, Education, and Welfare Publication No. (CDC) 77-8318, 1977.

11. Chapin, F.S., and H.C. Hightower. *Household Activity Systems.* Chapel Hill: Center for Urban and Regional Studies, Institute for Research in Social Science, University of North Carolina, 1966.

12. Chermayeff, S., and C. E. Alexander. *Community and Privacy.* Garden City, N.J.: Doubleday and Company, Inc., 1963.

13. Council of Europe, Expert Committee on Public Health. *Noise Abatement: A Public Health Problem.* Strasbourg, 1963.

14. Damon, A. "The Residential Environment, Health and Behavior: Simple Research Opportunities, Strategies, and Some Findings in the Solomon Islands and Boston, Massachusetts." In *The Effect of the Man-Made Environment on Health and Behavior.* Washington, D.C.: Department of Health, Education, and Welfare Publication No. (CDC) 77-8318, 1977.

15. David, P. "New Expectations for Public Housing." *American Journal of Orthopsychiatry* 36 (1966): 673-679.

16. Downing, G.L. "Living in High Flats — Problems of Tenants and Management." *American Sociological Health Journal* 83 (1963): 237-243.

17. Downs, J., and K. Simon. "Characteristics of Psychoneurotic Patients and Their Families as Revealed in a General Mortality Study." *Milbank Memorial Fund Quarterly* 22 (1954): 42-64.

18. Eichler, E.P., and M. Kaplan. *The Community Builders.* Berkeley: University California Press, 1967.

19. Eichler, E.P., and M. Kaplan. *Urban Sprawl and Health.* National Health Council, 1959.

20. Eisenberg, R.E. "Auditory Behavior in the Human Neonate: Functional Properties of Sound and Their Ontogenetic Implications." *Audiology* 3 (1969): 34-35.

21. Eisenberg, R.E. *Auditory Competence in Early Life: The Roots of Communicative Behavior.* Baltimore: University Park Press, 1976.

22. Fanning, D.M. "Families in Flats." *British Medical Journal* 4 (1967): 382-396.

23. Farr, L.E. "Medical Consequences of Environmental Home Noises." *Journal of the American Medical Association* 202 (1967): 99-102.

24. Freedman, A.M., and H.E. Kaplan, eds. *Comprehensive Textbook of Psychiatry.* Baltimore: Williams and Wilkins, 1967. Chapter 5.1, Lemkau, P.V., and G. M. Crocetti. Epidemiology.

25. Goromosov, M.S. "Physiological Basis of Health Standards for Dwellings." In *Acoustic Comfort in the Home.* Geneva: World Health Organization, U.N., Public Health Papers 33, 1968.

26. Gregoire, M. "The Child in the High-rise." *Ekistics* 186 (1971): 331-333.

27. Grootenboer, E.A. "The Relation of Housing to Behavior Disorders." *American Journal of Psychiatry* 119 (1962): 469-472.

28. Gunn, A.D.G. "The Medical-Social Problems of Multi-story Living." *Nursing Times* 64 (1968): 468-469.

29. Hall, E.T. *The Silent Language.* New York: Doubleday and Co., Inc., 1969.

30. Hall, P. "Some Clinical Aspects of Moving House as an Apparent Precipitant of Psychiatric Symptoms." *Journal of Psychosomatic Research* 10 (1966): 59-70.

31. Hardy, H.C. "Some Observations on Man's Noise Environment." In *Sound and Man.* Proceedings of Ind. I.C.A. Congress. Cambridge, Mass., 1956.

32. Hare, E.H. "Do New Housing Estates Endanger Mental Health?" *Nursing Mirror and Midwives Journal* 124 (1967): 8-10.

33. Howell, W. "Personality, Situation, Activity and Sound as Parameters of the Subjective Evaluation of the Annoyance of Noise." In *Acoustic Noise and Its Control.* London I.E.E. Conference Publication No. 26, Institution of Electrical Engineers, 1966.

34. Jahoda, M. *Current Concepts of Positive Mental Health.* New York: Basic Books, 1958.

35. Karunaratne, W.A., and P. Ganewatte. "Community Participation in Housing and Environmental Hygiene in Ceylon." In *Housing Programmes: The Role of Public Health Agencies.* Geneva: World Health Organization, U.N., 1964.

36. Kasl, S.V. "The Effects of the Residential Environment on Health and Behavior: A Review." In *The Effect of the Manmade Environment on Health and Behavior.* Washington, D.C.: Department of Health, Education, and Welfare Publication No. (CDC) 77-8318, 1977.

37. Kendrick, J.D. "Human Factors Affecting Design of Physical Environments in Buildings." *Medical Journal of Australia* 2 (1967): 267-269.

38. Leighton, D.C., J.S. Harding, D.B. Macklin, A.M. Macmillan, and A.H. Leighton. *The Character of Danger: Psychiatric Symptoms in Selected Communities.* New York: Basic Books, 1963. Sterling Vol. 3 of the series.

39. Lemkau, P.V. "Human Factors in a New Town." *Building Research*, January-February, 1966.

40. Lemkau, P.V. *Mental Hygiene in Public Health.* New York: McGraw-Hill Book Co., Inc. 1955.

41. Lemkau, P.V. "Prevention in Psychiatry." *American Journal of Public Health* 55 (1965): 554-560.

42. Lipman, M. "Social Effects of the Housing Environment." Prepared for the Canadian Conference on Housing, October 20-23, 1968.

43. Magness, Josephine. "Emotional Reactions of People Changing Homes: Interviews with Real Estate Agents." Research paper prepared for Mental Hygiene II, School of Hygiene and Public Health, Johns Hopkins University, 1968.

44. Manderscheid, R.W. "A Theory of Spatial Effects." In *Progress in Cybernetics and Systems Research*, vol. 1., R. Trappl and F.R. Pichler (eds.). Washington, D.C.: Hemisphere Publishing Corp., 1975.

45. Neser, W.B., H.A. Tyroler, and J. Cassel. "Stroke Mortality in the Black Population of North Carolina In Relation to Social Factors." Paper presented at the American Health Association meeting on Cardiovascular Epidemiology, New Orleans, March, 1970.

46. "Noise Control in Architecture: More Engineering than Art." *Architectural Record* 142 (1967): 193-204.

47. Prestemon, D.R. "How Much Does Noise Bother Apartment Dwellers?" *Architectural Record* 143 (1968): 155-156.

48. Rogler, Lloyd H., and August Hollingshead. *Trapped: Families and Schizophrenia.* New York: John Wiley & Sons, Inc., 1965.

49. Rutter, M. *Children of Sick Parents: An Environmental and Psychiatric Study.* London: Oxford University Press, 1966.

50. Sachs, D. "A Study of Writings on Walls of Public Bathrooms." Research paper prepared for Mental Hygiene II, School of Hygiene and Public Health, Johns Hopkins University, 1959.

51. Schorr, A.L. *Slums and Social Insecurity.* United States Department of Health, Education, and Welfare, Washington, D.C.: Superintendent of Documents, 1963.

52. Sommers, R. *Personal Space: The Behavioral Basis of Design.* Englewood Cliffs, N.J.: Prentice-Hall, 1969.

53. Stolper, Jane H. "Color-Induced Physiological Response." *Man-Environment Systems* 7 (1977): 101-108.

54. Wekerle, G., and E. Hall. "High-rise Living: Can the Same Design Serve Young and Old?" *Ekistics* 196: March 1972.

55. Wilner, D.M., R.P. Walkley, T.C. Pinkerton, and M. Tayback. *The Housing Environment and Family Life.* Baltimore: Johns Hopkins Press, 1962.

56. Woodin, D. "Better Housing for Better Health." *Nursing Outlook* 10 (1962): 100-102.

57. World Health Organization. *Housing Programmes: The Role of Public Health Agencies.* Public Health Paper 25. Geneva: World Health Organization, U.N., 1964, pp. 146-180.

Discussion Questions

1. The author refers to the difficulty in assuming a cause-and-effect relationship between health and housing because of "a progression in the piling up of complexities." Give your interpretation of this statement.

2. Explain why a given environment does not influence all people equally.

3. Noises dependent upon the physiological functions of man appear to have

special significance. Hypothesize how this may influence the lack of acceptance to multifamily housing.

4. Some authorities believe that an ideal architecture which would lead to an undisturbed homeostatic state should not be encouraged. Explain why such an ideal environment could have detrimental effects.

5. It has become an accepted ideal that people should live close to nature for a healthy housing environment. There are other causes that have contributed to our sprawling urban developments. Discuss the social influences that have contributed to "urban sprawl."

6. Explain the differences between the planning of "developments" and the planning of "new cities."

7. An aim of many "new cities" is to provide for a complete mix of people of various socioeconomic levels. Why is this so difficult to achieve?

8. Discuss the contrasting life-styles of families living in high-rise apartment buildings and families living in low-rise dwellings. List health problems assumed to be associated with high-rise apartment living.

9. Interpret the statement, "Perhaps the most important issue is that modern congregate living probably requires as great attention to finding satisfying ways to live as in finding satisfactory dwellings in which to live."

10. Discuss the relationship between art in our living environment and the trend toward a leisurely life-style.

11. People have needs both to be sociable as well as to withdraw from groups. Suggest how these needs may be either more or less satisfied because of their housing.

12. In recent years there has been a trend towards multiple-use rooms in house design. What are some of the disadvantages of this design? Give specific examples of how this could affect the physical or mental health of the occupants.

13. Relieving annoyances in the housing environment can result in higher morale of the occupants. Give suggestions as to how annoyances may be reduced in relationship to the following factors: storage, color, noise, appliances, and room arrangement.

15. The House as Symbol

by Clare Cooper

Man was a symbol-making animal long before he was a tool-maker. He reached high degrees of specialization in song, dance, ritual, religion and myth before he did in the material aspects of culture. Describing the rich symbolism of Africa, Australian architect Amos Rapoport notes that "Among the Dogon and Bambara of Mali, every object and social event has a symbolic as well as utilitarian function. Houses," continues Rapoport, "household objects and chairs all have this symbolic quality, and the Dogon civilization, otherwise relatively poor, has several thousand symbolic elements. The farm plots and the whole landscape of the Dogon reflect this cosmic order. The villages are laid out in the way the parts of the body lie with respect to each other, while the house of the Dogon, or paramount chief, is a model of the universe at a smaller scale."[1]

How different it is in the so-called civilized world, where recognition of the *symbolism* of what we do, how we live, the environments we plan and the houses we live in has been all but lost. But—it is my contention—our contemporary environment is rich in symbolism, too, though it may take more searching for than among the Dogon and Bambara of Mali.

Defining Self

Although impossible for most of us to define or describe, we are all aware of the existence of something we call "self." It is in the nature of man that he constantly seeks a rational explanation of the inexplicable, and so he struggles with the question, what is self? why here? why now? In trying to clothe this tantalizing and invisible self, to give it concrete substance, man grasps at physical forms or symbols which are close and meaningful to him and which *are* visible and definable. The first and most consciously selected form to represent self is the body, for it appears to be both the outward manifestation and the encloser of self. On a less conscious level, I believe, man also frequently selects the house, that basic protector of his internal environment (beyond skin and clothing) to represent or symbolize what is tantalizingly unrepresentable.

The French philosopher Gaston Bacheland has suggested that just as the house and the non-house are the basic divisions of geographic space, so the self and the non-self represent the basic divisions of psychic space. The house both encloses space (the

Reprinted courtesy *Design & Environment* from *Design & Environment,* Vol. 3, No. 3 (Fall 1972). Copyright © 1974 by Clare Cooper.

Clare Cooper is an Associate Professor at the University of California, Berkeley, where she teaches courses in social and psychological factors in design in the Department of Landscape Architecture and the Department of Architecture.

1. Amos Rapoport, *House Form and Culture* (Englewood Cliffs, N.J.: Prentice Hall Inc., 1969), p. 50.

Most housing preference studies in the U.S. and the English-speaking world show that the average family prefers a house-on-the-ground and has a strong negative reaction to high-rise living. (Photo by Mitchell Payne and Linda Montano)

house interior) and excludes space (everything outside it). The house thus has two very important and different components: its interior and its facade.

The house, therefore, reflects how man sees himself, with both an intimate interior, or self as viewed from within and revealed only to those intimates who are invited inside, and a public exterior or the self that we choose to display to others.

The House and the Psyche

Most of us have had the experience of moving to another house, and of finding the new abode initially strange, unwelcoming, perhaps even hostile. But, with time, we get used to the house and its quirks, and it seems almost as though it gets used to us. We can relax when we return to it, put our feet up, become "ourselves." But why in this particular "box" should we be ourselves more than in any other? Probably because the personal space bubble which we carry around with us and which is an almost tangible extension of our self, expands to embrace the house we have designated as ours. As we become accustomed to, and lay claim to, this little niche in the world, we project something of ourselves onto its physical fabric. The furniture we install, the way we arrange it, the pictures we hang, the plants we buy and tend to, all are expressions of our image of ourselves, all are messages about ourselves that we want to convey back to ourselves, and to the few intimates that we invite into this, our house.

Few have recognized the complex intertwining of the house and the psyche as well as the psychologist Carl Jung, who sometimes dreamt of himself as a house.

Concerning the building of his own house, he wrote, "From the beginning, I felt that the Tower was in some way a place of maturation—a maternal womb or a maternal figure in which I could become what I was, what I am and will be. It gave me a feeling as if I were being reborn in stone. It is thus a concretization of the individuation process. . . . During the building work, of course, I never considered these matters. . . . Only afterwards did I see how all the parts fitted together and that a meaningful form had resulted: a symbol of psychic wholeness."[2]

The contemporary house-buyer is often unconsciously seeking a symbol of self when choosing his environment. In a recent study of how contemporary California suburbanites chose their homes, Carl Werthman concluded that, for example, extro-verted, self-made businessmen will tend to choose somewhat ostentatious, mock-Colonial "display" homes, while people in the helping professions whose goals revolve around personal satisfaction rather than financial success tend to opt for the quieter, inward-looking architect-designed styles conforming to the current standard of "good design."[3] The styles chosen reflect the self-image of the owner and announce to friends and strangers—perhaps again at an unconscious level—the kind of person who lives there.

The house as symbol-of-self is so deeply engrained in the American ethos (albeit unconsciously for many), that this may partly explain the inability of our society to come to grips with "the housing problem"—which is quite within its technological and financial capabilities to solve and which it persistently delegates to a low level in the hierarchy of budgetary values. America is the home of the self-made man, and if the house is seen (even unconsciously) as the symbol of self, then it is small wonder that there is a resistance to subsidized housing or the state providing houses *for* people. The frontier image of the man clearing the land and building a cabin for himself and his family is not far behind us. To a culture inbred with this image, the house/self identity is particularly strong. Little wonder then that, in some barely conscious way, society has decided to penalize those who, through no fault of their own, cannot build, buy or rent their own housing. They are not self-made men.

The Free-Standing House

Studies in England, Australia and the United States have indicated that, when asked to describe their ideal house, people of all incomes and backgrounds will tend to describe a free-standing, square, detached, single-family house and yard. Whether the attachment to this form is the form itself, or the fact that it subsumes *territorial* rights over a small portion of the earth, is difficult to say, but we do know that, almost universally, the image of the high-rise apartment building for family living is rejected. An apartment is not seen as "home," for a home can only be seen as a free-standing house-on-the-ground. According to a recent survey of 748 men and women in 32 metropolitan areas of the U.S., carried out by the Survey Research Center of the University of Michigan, about 85 percent said they preferred living in a single-family house rather than in an apartment. Although 70 percent of the sample were already living in single-family houses, this preference is not necessarily a rationalization of current habits, since two-thirds of those living in multi-family dwellings also said they preferred private houses. [4]

2. Carl Jung, *Memories, Dreams and Reflections* (London: Collins, The Fontana Library Series, 1969), p. 253.

3. Carl Werthman, "The Social Meaning of the Physical Environment" (Ph.D. dissertation, University of California, Berkeley, 1968), pp. 56-58.

4. William Michelson, "Most People Don't Want What Architects Want," in *Transaction,* July/August 1968.

Introverted intellectuals often choose an inward looking dwelling, which may barely resemble the stereotype house. (Photo by Mitchell Payne and Linda Montano)

One could argue that people have been conditioned to want such a dwelling through advertising, model homes salesmanship and the image of the "good life" portrayed on television. To a certain extent this must be true, but these media are in turn only reflecting what seems to be a universal need for a house form in which the self and the family unit can be seen as separate, unique, private and protected.

Is a High-Rise a Home?

The high-rise apartment building is rejected by most Americans as a "home" because it gives one no private territory on the ground, violates the archaic image of what a house is, and, I would suggest, is perceived unconsciously as a threat to one's self-image as a separate and unique personality. The house form in which people are being asked to live is not a symbol-of-self, but a symbol of a stereotyped, anonymous, filing-cabinet of selves. Even though we may make apartments larger and with many of the appurtenances of the suburban house, it still may be a long time before the majority of lower- and middle-income American families will accept this as a valid image of "home."[5] It is too great a threat to their self-image. It is possible that the vandalism inflicted on high-rise housing projects is, in part, an angry reaction of the inhabitants to this blatant violation of self-image.

The mobile, hippie house-on-wheels is another instance of a new housing form

5. The urban rich accept apartments because they generally have a house somewhere else. The elderly seem to adapt well to apartments because they offer privacy with the possibility of many nearby neighbors, minimum upkeep problems, security and communal facilities.

Some members of the counter-culture have chosen to live in vehicles, much to the consternation of city officials. (Photo by Mitchell Payne and Linda Montano)

greatly threatening people's image of what a house *should* be. The van converted to mobile home and the wooden gable-roofed house built on the back of a truck are becoming fairly common sights in Berkeley. It is tempting to speculate that this house form has been adopted by hippies not only because of its cheapness as living accommodation, but also because its mobility and uniqueness of form is a reflection of where many hippies are in psychic terms—concerned with self, with their own uniqueness, with the desirability of inward exploration, with the freedom of being without roots so as to move and swing with whatever happens. Hippies view themselves as different from the average person, and so they have chosen to live in house forms—converted trucks, tree-houses in Canyon, California, geodesic domes and Indian tepees in wilderness communes—which reflect that uniqueness.

In February, 1970, the City of Berkeley passed an ordinance that makes it illegal to live in a converted truck or van. The residents of these new "houses" mobilized and formed the Rolling Homes Association, but it was too late to prevent the ordinance from being passed.[6] When others too openly display the appurtenances—clothes, hair-styles, houses—of a new self-image, it is a threat to the values and images of the majority community. And the image of the self as a house-on-wheels was too much for the Establishment to accept.

Even the edge-of-town mobile home park occupied by the young retireds and transient lower-middle-class is somehow looked down upon by the average American

6. A similar ordinance was passed in San Francisco in March, 1971.

home-owner as violating the true image of "home" and "neighborhood." A person who lives in a house that moves must somehow be as unstable as the structure he inhabits. Much the same view is held by stable house owners in Marin County near San Francisco about the houseboat dwellers in Sausalito. They are "different," "Bohemian," "nonconformists," and their extraordinary choice of dwelling reflects these values. Again the "self" and the "house" are seen as reflections of each other.

The contrasting views that people of different socio-economic classes in the U.S. have of their houses reflects again the house-as-a-symbol-of-self. The more keenly people feel that they are living in a dangerous and hostile world with constant threats to the self, the greater is the likelihood that they will regard their house as a shell, a fortress into which to retreat. Anthropologist Lee Rainwater has shown that this image of the self, and of the house, is true of many low-income blacks (particularly women) in the ghettoes and housing projects of this country. [7]

Fortress or Expression of Self?

With increasing economic and psychic stability (and in some cases, these are linked) a person may no longer regard his house as a fortress-to-be-defended, but as an attractive, individual expression of self-and-family with picture windows so that neighbors can admire the inside. Thus. for many in the middle-income bracket, the house becomes an expression of self, rather than a defender of self. The self-and-environment are seen in a state of mutual regard, rather than in a state of combat.

The fact that the decoration of the house interior often symbolizes the inhabitants' feelings about self has long been recognized. It has even been suggested that the rise in popularity of the interior decorator is in some degree linked to people's inability to make these decisions for themselves, since they're not sure what their "self" really is. The phenomenon of people, particularly women, rearranging the furniture in their house at times of psychic turmoil or changes-in-self is a further suggestion that the house is very intimately entwined with the psyche.

An interesting contemporary development in this regard is the interior decoration of the urban commune. In a number of examples in the Berkeley-Oakland area, it is noticeable that the bedrooms, the only private spaces of the residents, are decorated in an attractive and highly personal way symbolic of the "self" whose space it is. The living rooms, the communal territory of six or eight different personalities, however, are only sparsely decorated, since, presumably, the problem of getting agreement on taste from a number of disparate and highly individual "selves" is too great to overcome. Interestingly, the more normal family house may display an opposite arrangement, with bedrooms functionally but uninterestingly decorated, and the living room, where guests and relatives are entertained, containing the best furniture, family mementos, art purchases and photos and representing the collective family "self." Often the only exception to this may be the bedroom of a teenager or young adult in the family, whose desire to establish his own personality apart from the family is reflected in the very distinctive decoration of his or her bedroom.

In an as yet unpublished study of living rooms, social status, and attitudes, Edward Laumann and James House of the University of Michigan Department of Sociology have found that the decoration, arrangement and furnishings of the living room are good if not perfect clues to status and attitudes. In a random sample of 41 home-owners in Detroit who had annual incomes over $15,000, they found that those with a traditional decor—French or Early American furniture, wall mirrors, small potted

7. L. Rainwater, "Fear and the House-as-Haven," *Journal of the American Institute of Planners*, Vol. XXXIX, No. 1, January 1966, pp. 23-31.

The urban commune often displays a sparsely decorated, shared living room but a highly personalized and private bedroom. (Photos by Mitchell Payne and Linda Montano)

Self-made businessmen and extroverts, concerned about their financial status, often choose ostentatious houses. (Photo by Mitchell Payne and Linda Montano)

plants and/or artifical flowers, paintings of people or still-lifes, clocks—tended to be the white Anglo-Saxon Establishment, occupying job and status positions similar to their fathers. Those with a more modern decor, characterized by modern furniture, wood walls, abstract paintings, solid carpets and abstract-design curtains, tended to be upwardly mobile, non-Anglo-Saxon Catholics whose families had migrated to the United States from southern and eastern Europe after 1900. This group seemed to be responding more to the newly emerging decorative norms decreed by the "taste-makers" rather than the norms set by the established upper classes. [8]

The findings of this study of decorative styles of living rooms seem to tie in well with the results of Werthman's study of choices of house styles, for in both cases there

8. Notes on an interview with Professor Edward Laumann on "Living Rooms, Social Status, and Attitudes," by Christopher Carey, University of Michigan News Service, Ann Arbor, Michigan (mimeo, no date).

appears to be a strong correlation between the style selected and the self-image of the consumer. Both the house facade and the interior design are chosen to reflect how the person views himself in relation to society and the outside world, and how he wishes to present his "self" to family and friends.

These are just a few examples of how the house-as-self linkage becomes manifest in individual and societal behavior and attitudes. No doubt the reader can add many more instances from his personal experience. The thesis is not a new one. But it is important for designers to consider it more deeply as they build more and more homes for clients who they may never directly consult—the poor, the elderly, the suburban tract-house family.

Discussion Questions

1. What is the meaning of the phrase "The House as Symbol"?

2. The author contends that the house has two very important and different components. Name and discuss these two components.

3. A recent study in California suggests that extroverted, self-made businessmen choose quite different house styles than people in the helping professions. Do you agree or disagree with this study and with the illustrations depicting the extroverted, self-made businessmen and the introverted intellectuals? Give reasons for your answers.

4. What is the image of a "home" in the U.S.?

5. In what ways is the house likely to become more of a symbol of self or less of a symbol of self?

6. Do you believe that a major reason why American families do not accept multi-dwellings as a valid image of "home" is because they are a threat to their self-image? Support your answer.

7. René Dubos in the first article of this book states that society is a larger determinant of our needs than our biological requirements. How does this statement relate to this article and do you agree? Support your answer.

16. Planning for Ourselves: Interior Design to Meet Social Needs

by L. Gertrude Nygren

But different persons also require different conditions for their spiritual development; and can no more exist healthily in the same moral, than all the variety of plants can in the same physical atmosphere and climate.[1]

John Stuart Mill

If it is true that people require uniquely personalized conditions for spiritual growth then the dwelling must serve that purpose, for it is the only space where an individual can be granted any assurance of control. Today there is mounting evidence to support Mill's assertion that the personally supportive environment contributes to the fullness of life by bringing human beings closer to the best they can be. It is for these reasons that this paper emphasizes the careful conscious planning of the private spaces in the daily environment of people even though reliance has to be placed on the under-developed insights in social-environmental interactions. In order to design fully healthy social environments it is necessary to begin by (1) recognizing what we are because of our heritage, (2) understanding the socio-cultural milieu of which we are a part, and (3) knowing how to accurately assess our present but ever-changing selves.

To Plan for Ourselves: Recognize Our Roots

No one is ever totally the product of his own time. Man is linked to a chain of values, attitudes, and behaviors forged by those who preceded him. René Dubos expresses this concept in these words, "Normal development is thus a self-directing process in which form and function emerge and evolve together, to a large extent along patterns derived from the past."[2]

Americans have been described as aggressive by nature, a trait inherited from their strong-minded and restless forebears. The extent to which this is true indicates that drastic reductions in spatial dimensions would disrupt the established means by which Americans cope with their strongest emotions. Severely diminished interior-exterior space and increased density would require other compensations, or serious consequences in interactive behaviors could be anticipated. The activities considered to demand privacy are to a large extent a deeply rooted, accepted social form. Bathing in some cultures is a family affair while in others it is regarded as open to only marriage partners, young children, and the ill. A portion of a dwelling is sometimes designated by tradition as men's quarters or women's quarters while in many cultures no such

1. Marshall Cohen, *Philosophy of John Stuart Mill, Ethical, Political and Religious* (New York: Modern Library, 1972), p. 263.
2. René Dubos, *A God Within* (New York: Charles Scribner's Sons, 1972), p. 9.

separations are made on the basis of sex. Manners of lodging and entertaining guests are subject to variations highly related to customs set before the time of the practicing generation.

When such values and their attendant accommodations are ignored, various forms of adaptive action will be attempted unless the people themselves are convinced a change is beneficial and unless they feel secure enough to vary from the norm. When satisfactory resolutions in design of interior space are impossible to achieve, as is most frequently the case for persons with limited financial resources, results will be injurious to the inhabitant in varying ways and degrees. Members of the dominant culture fare better because certain values are rather automatically implemented into the components of their housing. We make errors in shelter decisions for low income families and members of subcultures because we apply the historically developed prevailing assumptions unquestioningly, and because such values are so unconsciously accepted it doesn't occur to anyone that they have to be mentioned.

To Plan for Ourselves: Understand the Socio-Cultural Milieu

Dwelling design must conform to the prevailing values, attitudes, and aspirations of the culture. Although we are carriers of the past, we are also creators of and respondents to the present. As members of complex societies we are pressured to conform by informal as well as formal measures to preserve the dominant values of society; it is considered socially irresponsible not to do so. While the home offers more range in personal options than do semi-public or public spaces, it too is subject to limitations. For example, a person or family would not be allowed to design to accommodate nudism if the sunbathing area were visible from the street because the majority of society considers the behavior to be a serious threat to its values and beliefs. While pushing a lawn mower may be an unappealing form of exercise, it is the price to be paid to maintain friendly relations with the neighbors who keep their "green spreads" closely clipped. Building standards and housing codes are a reflection of the value we place on human life and these legal measures are especially rigid when fire hazards and sanitary practices are involved. Radical departures from traditional installation of lighting, heating, or sanitary systems are difficult to introduce and sometimes regrettably so; but there is an undeniable need to regulate structural features for the protection of both the occupants of a house and their neighbors.

The design of interior space should make allowances for ethnic and racial differences within a society. The same values may be present within subcultures but they often are assigned different priorities and means of implementation. For instance, the members of one ethnic unit of society might follow a pattern of having large families with most family-centered activities taking place at mealtimes. Another group with the same value and composition might follow a pattern involving the total family in activities associated with making a living or leisure time pursuits. The uses made of housing are different in each case and, if allowed, the arrangement of space as well as furnishings will eventually fall into recognizable patterns by neighborhoods or communities. If the house, the interior contents, and treatments needed to support these established social patterns are not present, the inhabitants experience strains and dissatisfactions which will be expressed in varying intensities and types of reactions.

To Plan for Ourselves: Know Ourselves

Interior designs must accommodate the current and also anticipate the future needs which arise out of individual values, attitudes, and aspirations. It must indeed be recognized that these demands are competitive with those implanted from the past and derived from dominant current cultural values. In the United States, where a high value is placed on individual freedom and creative ability, it becomes a formidable challenge to provide the climate for the ego to flourish and for the democracy to support its divergent life styles and yet retain a unified but multifarious nature.

As stated previously, the interior and immediate exterior of the dwelling usually offer the only opportunity for the individual and the family to fulfill both the most significant and the most whimsical of their needs and desires. While environments that are too specialized, such as the large crystal punchbowl, are suitable for one day, those that are too generalized in purpose are like the sofa bed which makes neither a good bed nor a good sofa. A sensitive analysis of personalities, styles of living, and "images of the ideal" is required along with consideration of the commonly shared needs of people in each stage of the life cycle.

In modern times we have seldom looked to ourselves for a definition of the "good life," but rather have chosen to adapt the perceived symbols of it. As any history of Western architecture and interior design will verify, the members of the court copied the artifacts of the royalty insofar as it was possible to do so. During the Colonial period in this country, the educated and affluent obtained furniture from England and France or purchased catalogues from which to make identical copies. The newly rich followed the example of the established rich and respected leaders and built or purchased items as close to the original models as it was possible to obtain. Those in more modest circumstances attempted to fulfill an image of how people slightly more wealthy constructed and furnished their homes. Magazines and businesses encouraged this emulation by featuring the choices of the more elite members of society and gradually these ideals were communicated to people across the continent. This imitative stance has been unconsciously reinforced by teachers who introduce students to periods and styles in architecture and furniture before they have any understanding of how housing and people are related.

Admittedly, a self-directed analysis of social and emotional needs requires time. The gift of a sterling silver spoon has led more than one newly married couple into a form of housing too demanding and inflexible to fit their casual style of daily living and entertaining. It is wise to make those decisions which greatly limit options in housing and furnishings only after a reasonable amount of confidence based on self-knowledge has been developed.

The following considerations are presented to highlight the dichotomous purposes which housing must serve and to stress the point that it is impossible to successfully accommodate the varied needs of one or several persons without forethought. The

CONTRASTING QUALITIES IN DESIGN

Specific Fitness

personal and individually
    determined specifications
egocentric

Stimulation

activating, risky and
    dangerous

Refreshment and Revitalization

mild surprises and delights
changeable
new and novel

General Fitness

impersonal and group
    determined specifi-
    cations, compromised,
    normative

Relaxation (Haven)

quiet, private, rest granting, safe

Stability and Continuity

known locations of articles
designated activity areas
unchangeable old and remodeled

CONTRASTING QUALITIES IN DESIGN (continued)

Inviting (Expansive)	*Exclusive*
comfortable, open	uncomfortable, restrictive
varied, broad purposes	precise, limited purposes

Humanly Dignifying	*Humanly Freeing*
conformance to accepted social symbols, deliberate, enduring	self-directed, spontaneous extemporaneous, temporary

decision-making process consists of obtaining a desirable balance in design qualities such as these and of deciding where and how they can be incorporated.

This paper has dealt with the social aspects of man-environment interactions as a basis for the design of the interior of human dwellings. There is much more to be learned about this relationship. Some students in classrooms today will study the past for a still greater comprehension of the values of critical importance in the design of housing. Others will prepare themselves to translate the diverse values of society into concepts for housing design; still others will attempt to develop valid design guides on the micro scale and in this way help people to "become the best they can be."

". . . house form is not simply the result of physical forces or any single casual factor, but is the consequence of a whole range of socio-cultural factors seen in their broadest terms." [3]

If, as Rapoport writes, housing is a social artifact, which means shaped by societal forces, then it is our responsibility to insist upon what it must be—a humanly supportive environment.

References

Bell, Gwen, and Tyrwhitt, Jaqueline (eds.). *Human Identity in the Urban Environment.* Hammondsworth, Middlesex, England: Pelican Books Ltd., 1972.

Bronowski, Jacob. *Ascent of Man.* Boston: Little Brown & Co., 1973.

Dubos, René. *A God Within.* New York: Charles Scribner's Sons, 1973.

Gowan, Alan. *Images of American Living.* Philadelphia: J. B. Lippincott Co., 1964.

Perin, Constance. *With Man in Mind.* Cambridge, Mass.: MIT Press, 1972.

Rapoport, Amos. *House, Form and Culture.* Englewood Cliffs, N. J.: Prentice-Hall, 1969.

Rozwenc, Edwin. *The Making of American Society.* Vol. 2. Boston: Allyn and Bacon, 1973.

Taylor, John. *Design and Expression in the Visual Arts.* New York: Dover Publications, 1964.

Discussion Questions

1. Why should people collectively participate in public decisions related to housing, even to some decisions that include interior space?

2. Why should individuals and families prepare themselves to contribute to private decisions related to their own housing including interior design?

3. Amos Rapoport, *House Form and Culture* (Englewood Cliffs, N.J.: Prentice-Hall, 1969), p. 47.

3a. What is a social artifact?

 b. Why is it important to consider housing as a social artifact?

4a. What is meant by the phrase *humanly supportive environments?*

 b. What are some of the qualities of housing that contribute to that goal?

 c. Since most of us will not design or build our own housing, are there any ways to increase:

    1) the supportive qualities in new housing?

    2) the supportive qualities in existing housing?

17. Floor Plan Evaluation

by Carol S. Wedin

There are three major activities that occur in most homes: living, working, and sleeping. A well-designed floor plan allows for these activities with minimal inconvenience to the individuals living in the residence. The basic criteria of zoning for specific activities, circulation patterns, and room relationships apply to all structural types, whether the residence is a mobile home, a single-family detached dwelling, or a multi-family dwelling.

Zoning for Specific Activities

The living zone is the most public area of the residence. Access to the living zone from the entrance should be direct. The sleeping zone is the private area. The floor plan should allow for maximum privacy from both interior and exterior noise and disturbance. The working zone may also be referred to as the activity area. This is where the majority of the household tasks such as cooking and laundry are performed. There should be easy access to the working zone from the service entrance. A house illustrating well-defined zoning is shown in Figures 1a and 1b.

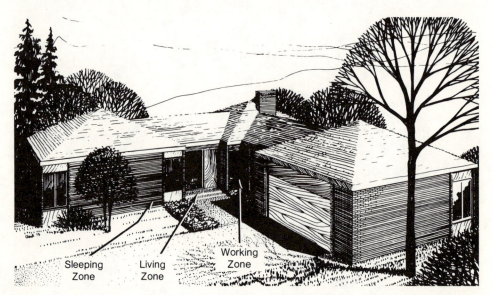

Figure 1a. An exterior view of a residence with well-defined zoning. (Courtesy of John D. Bloodgood, A. I. A.)

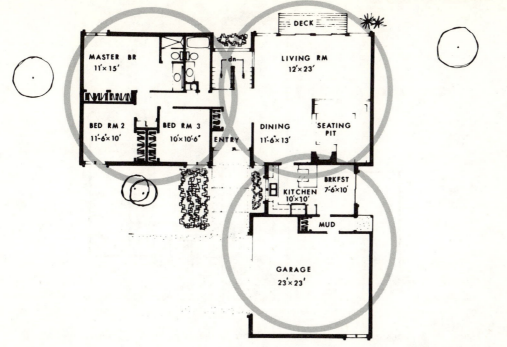

Figure 1b. The floor plan of the residence illustrating the three basic zones. (Courtesy of John D. Bloodgood, A. I. A.)

Living Zone

The living area of the house is where the family relaxes, entertains, enjoys hobbies, and sometimes dines. Frequently it is the only area of the house viewed by visitors. In smaller homes, the living area may consist of just one room as shown in Figure 2.

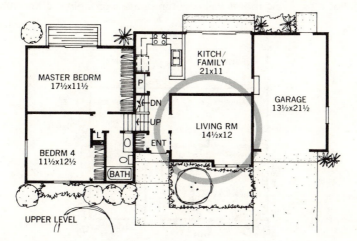

Figure 2. A small residence with only one room in the living area. (Courtesy of John D. Bloodgood, A. I. A.)

More often several rooms are included, such as entrance foyer, library or study, dining room, porch or patio, recreation room, and guest bathroom as illustrated in Figure 3.

Since the living area accommodates numerous activities, the location and size is

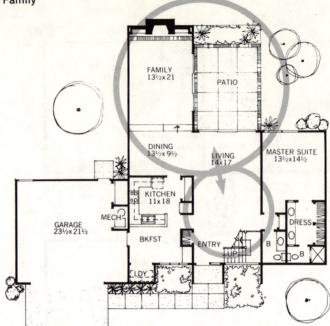

Figure 3. A large residence with several rooms in the living area. (Courtesy of John D. Bloodgood, A. I. A.)

extremely important. The living room should be adjacent to the entrance and be centrally located. A closet for guests' coats should be close to the entry door. With larger homes an entrance foyer is usually included. This is not always possible with the smaller residences. If the entry door is centrally located, cross traffic through the conversation circle can be avoided, as shown in Figure 4. This aspect will be discussed more fully in the section on circulation patterns.

To promote interaction and ease in visiting, a conversation circle should not exceed 10' in diameter. Most living rooms will accommodate a grouping of furniture for one

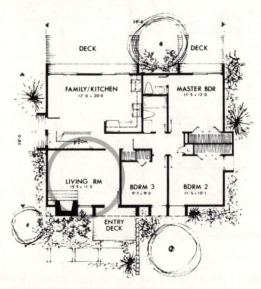

Figure 4. A small residence with entry door leading directly into the living area. (Courtesy of John D. Bloodgood, A. I. A.)

conversation circle. In larger living rooms it is better to group furniture into several circles of conversation or activities. In Figure 5, two conversation groupings are shown for a living room 15'6" x 25' in size.

The living room should be located next to the major dining area in the residence. In contemporary design the dining area is frequently combined with the living room. If the dining area is a separate room one should not have to walk through another room to reach the dining room.

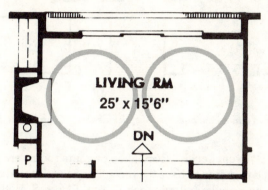

Figure 5. The furniture arranged for two conversational groupings in a larger living room. (Courtesy of John D. Bloodgood, A.I.A.)

Closed and Open Plans A floor plan may be considered as a closed or an open plan. When rooms are separated by walls and doors or other relatively small openings, such as arches, it is called a closed plan. An example of a closed plan is shown in Figure 6. In this plan the living room and dining room are completely separated rooms. The family room is partitioned off from the kitchen with a relatively small opening between the two rooms.

An open plan does not have walls that restrict movement from one room to another in the living zone. Examples of open plans are shown in Figures 1b and 3. In an open plan, furniture placement usually suggests the separation of activities such as dining or television viewing. An advantage of the open plan is flexibility in furniture placement, and, thus, the number of guests that can be accommodated as well. A disadvantage is the lack of privacy. Whether an individual or family selects a closed or an open plan depends on life style and personal needs. An open plan will usually give the appearance of casual, functional living whereas a closed plan can be easily adapted to a more formal living style.

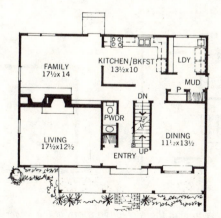

Figure 6. A closed floor plan. (Courtesy of John D. Bloodgood, A. I. A.)

A feeling of spaciousness can be created with an open plan, even in a relatively small residence. This is illustrated in the vacation house shown in Figure 7.

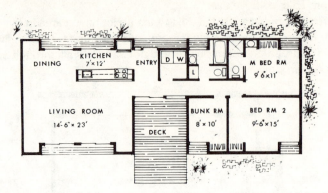

Figure 7. An open plan can create a feeling of spaciousness. (Courtesy of John D. Bloodgood, A. I. A.)

Living Zones on Different Levels   Recreation or game rooms are often used as part of the living zone. It is common to have the recreation room located on a different floor level as shown in the popular, raised-ranch design, Figure 8. With the raised-ranch design the lower level is partially exposed and natural illumination is possible, thus providing maximum space at minimum cost. As shown in Figure 8, the recreation room can be entered from the upstairs living area without passing through the working or sleeping zones.

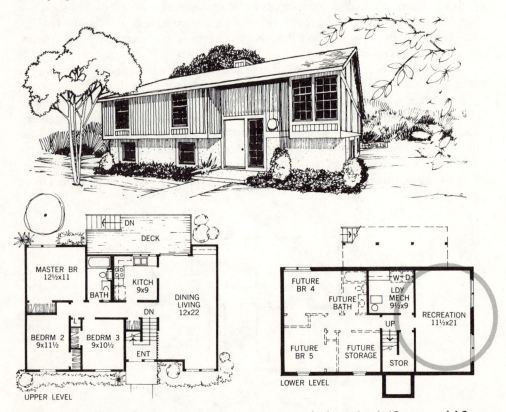

Figure 8. A raised-ranch design with the recreation room at the lower level. (Courtesy of John D. Bloodgood, A. I. A.)

Sleeping Zone

The sleeping zone is the most private area in a residence. Privacy of both sight and sound are desired. Usually bedrooms are grouped in one area of the residence, although with some plans, such as the raised ranch and split level, bedrooms will be located on several levels. A family with pre-school children may want the convenience of having the children's bedrooms close to the master bedroom. When the children are older the parents should have more privacy. Every bedroom should have access to a full bathroom that is not exposed to the living zone of the residence.

In Figure 9, the master bedroom is located on the main floor level with the children's bedrooms located on the second floor. This design has permitted maximum privacy by locating the sleeping zones away from the living zone. With the master bedroom being located in the rear of the house, noise from the street is also reduced. Even if all family members choose to sleep on the second floor of a two-story house it is desirable to have a bedroom on the first floor for ease in caring for the sick or elderly. Often a room used as a den or study can be converted to a bedroom when the need arises.

Two-story and split-level designs provide for easy zoning of the sleeping area. It is more difficult to achieve privacy with a ranch design. With a ranch design attention will need to be given to buffer areas between the sleeping zone and the working and living zones. Closets, storage areas, doors, and hallways can all serve as sound barriers. Properly located shrubbery can reduce exterior sounds.

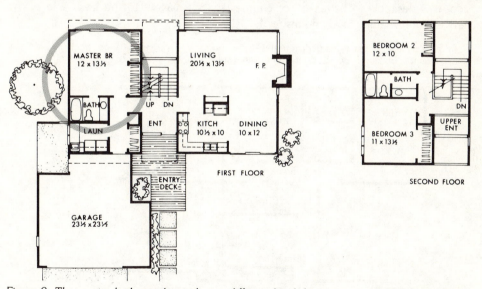

Figure 9. The master bedroom located on a different level than teen-age children's bedrooms and at the rear of the house away from street noise. (Courtesy of John D. Bloodgood, A. I. A.)

Clothing Closets Clothing closets should be located adjacent to the bedroom door. This allows for convenience and ease in caring for the wardrobe as well as changing clothes. Each individual should have a minimum closet space of 24" x 48", with a more desirable space being 24" x 72".

Windows Windows located on two walls to insure good cross ventilation are desirable if the residence is not centrally air-conditioned. All bedrooms should have one window large enough to use as a fire escape. The split-level and raised-ranch designs allow bedrooms to be located at the basement level, while still providing adequate window openings.

Work Zone

The working zone includes the kitchen, laundry, and utility room of the residence. In larger homes, either breakfast or family rooms, and sometimes the garage, may also be located in the working zone.

Kitchen There should be easy access from the kitchen to the service entrance, as well as to the major entrance. The kitchen should also connect with the dining areas. A floor plan illustrating these features is shown in Figure 10.

An inconvenient kitchen is a common complaint of homemakers. Insufficient cabinet storage and too little counter space are frequently problems, especially in smaller residences. Placement of appliances and storage cabinets are important considerations in planning a kitchen which will permit maximum efficiency.

Most kitchens will be divided into four areas: the refrigerator center, the sink center, the mix center, and the range center. Since the surface burners and oven may be two separate appliances, there are kitchens that also have an oven center.

Refrigerator Center The refrigerator is a tall appliance and should be located where it will not block the flow of work from one counter to another. The refrigerator door should open away from the work center. In other words, if the refrigerator door is hinged on the right it should be at the right end of the counter for ease in transferring food to and from the refrigerator. Refrigerators can be purchased with hinges on either side. It is desirable to have 18" of counter space adjacent to the latch side of the refrigerator for setting food and dishes.*

*All measurements given that pertain to the kitchen centers are recommendations made by the Small Homes Council - Building Research Center for medium-sized homes.

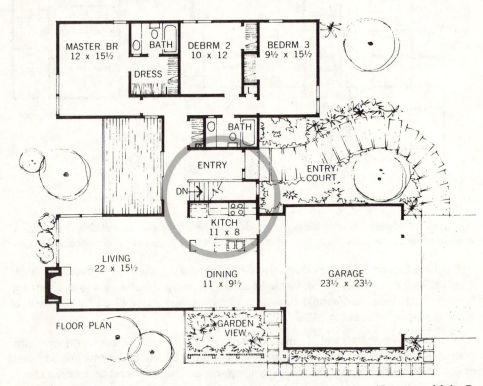

Figure 10. A kitchen with easy access to both service and major entrances. (Courtesy of John D. Bloodgood, A. I. A.)

Sink Center The sink is the major appliance for both food preparation and for cleaning. This center may also include the garbage disposal and dishwasher. Adequate storage for brushes, cleaning supplies, and towels is needed. If the kitchen is arranged for a right-to-left flow of work then it is desirable to have 36" on the right of the sink for stacking dirty dishes and 30" on the left for stacking clean dishes. The number of inches recommended for one center may be combined with the adjacent center. For example, part of the 36" recommended for the sink center may be part of the mix center.

Mix Center The mix center will include cabinets for storage of utensils and supplies used in cooking and baking. It will also include adequate counter area for working. At least 36" of counter space should be allowed. A convenient location for the mix center is between the refrigerator and sink; however, some kitchens will have the mix center between the sink and the range. If the mix center is located between the sink and range, usually more energy is exerted because of the increase in distance from the mix center and the refrigerator.

Range Center The range center should include counter space for serving dishes and storage space for cooking utensils and supplies. Counter space of 24" on each side of the range is recommended for safety and ease in handling and serving hot food. If the oven is a separate appliance, adjacent counter space will be needed for setting out hot dishes. The range should not be located under a window where curtains could catch fire or where operating the windows could be a safety problem.

Work Triangle The sequence of work in preparing a meal is centered around the three major appliances—refrigerator, sink, and range—forming a work triangle. The Small Homes Council - Building Research Center suggests that the work triangle, measuring from the center of each appliance, should not total less than 16' and not more than 26' for the most efficient kitchen arrangement.

Basic Shapes The arrangement of counters and appliances usually takes one of four basic shapes: one-wall, two-wall (also known as corridor), L-shape, and U-shape.

One-Wall Kitchen An example of a one-wall kitchen is shown in Figure 11. A disadvantage of a one-wall kitchen is the number of steps taken to get from the refrigerator to the range. This is a popular kitchen in small apartments and vacation homes.

Figure 11. A one-wall kitchen. (Courtesy of John D. Bloodgood, A.I.A.)

Two-Wall Kitchen A two-wall kitchen can be a very efficient arrangement if the circulation of traffic does not cross through the work triangle. From the standpoint of both efficiency and safety this should be avoided. Notice that in Figure 12 the corridor kitchen is a dead-end room, thereby eliminating the possibility of heavy traffic crossing through the work triange.

L-Shaped Kitchen This arrangement allows for family dining and other family activities within the kitchen. The L-shaped kitchen design usually avoids traffic within the work triangle. Figure 13 illustrates an L-shaped kitchen that provides for a spacious dining/family area adjacent to the food preparation area.

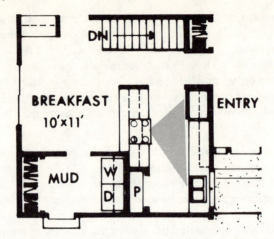

Figure 12. A two-wall kitchen. (Courtesy of John D. Bloogood, A. I. A.)

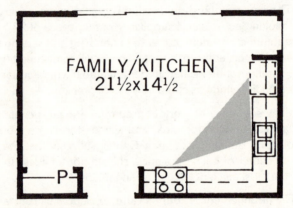

Figure 13. An L-shaped kitchen. (Courtesy of John D. Bloodgood, A. I. A.)

U-Shaped Kitchen A U-shaped kitchen is considered the most efficient kitchen plan if it is not excessively large. A convenient U-shaped kitchen is shown in Figure 14. Notice that the range is located next to the dining area to make the serving of food easy and direct.

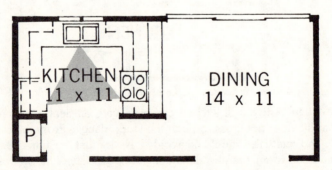

Figure 14. A U-shaped kitchen. (Courtesy of John D. Bloodgood, A.I.A.)

Laundry The laundry area is usually considered to be part of the working zone. In larger residences, the laundry area is commonly located close to the kitchen and service entrance as shown in Figure 15. This makes it possible for the laundry room to serve more than one function, such as both a mud room and clean-up area.

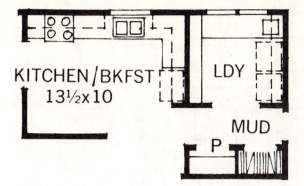

Figure 15. Laundry and mud area located between service entry and kitchen. (Courtesy of John D. Bloodgood, A. I. A.)

An advantage of having the laundry area adjacent to the kitchen is that food preparation or other kitchen activities may take place with relative ease as the laundry is being done. It is most desirable to have a separate space for the laundry equipment and clothes-sorting area rather than forcing these activities into the kitchen. Soiled clothes can easily contaminate food preparation centers.

Other areas in the residence where laundry equipment may be located are the sleeping zone or the basement. A disadvantage of locating the laundry in the sleeping zone is the amount of noise made by laundry equipment. The advantage of this location is that most of the clothing and linens are stored in this area. A basement location necessitates stair climbing, but it also has advantages. There is less demand for basement space, the laundry equipment can be located close to the water heater, and clothes sorting, drip-drying garments, mending, etc. are out of sight from other activities. The laundry area should be easily accessible to the working zone if it is located in another area of the residence. Locating the laundry area adjacent to or below (if in the basement) the kitchen or bathroom will save on plumbing costs.

An efficient laundry area will accommodate for related activities involved in clothing care. Space should be provided for hand washing, sorting, folding, pressing, mending, and hanging of garments for drip-drying as well as hanging of pressed garments. In addition, storage cabinets are required for soaps, detergents, bleach, and other supplies.

Circulation Pattern

An essential consideration in floor plan evaluation is the circulation pattern. A well-designed traffic pattern will greatly add to the overall livability of a residence. Traffic should be able to flow into the three zones of the residence without the necessity of passing through a second zone. A central hall, as shown in Figure 16, will provide for direct and logical traffic flow to the various zones of the residence.

As shown in Figure 17, the size of a room does not necessarily determine the amount of usable space. The traffic flow cuts directly through the dining room and living room, thus making furniture arrangement a problem. Indirect traffic patterns also cause additional housework. Floor coverings will be easily soiled and worn unevenly where cross traffic flows.

Room Relationship

The section describing the three zones within a residence briefly discussed room relationships. In summary, rooms with like activities should be located together. In examining the floor plan illustration of a poor traffic pattern it is evident that if the

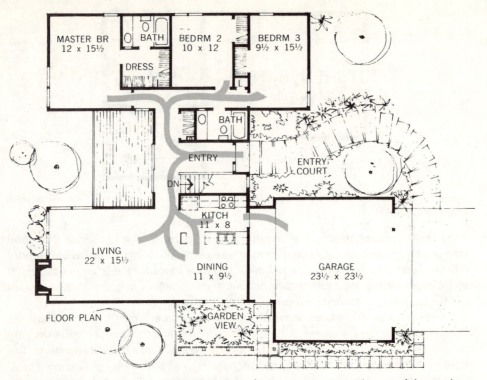

Figure 16. A well-designed central hall provides for easy access to each area of the residence (Courtesy of John D. Bloodgood, A. I. A.)

rooms were arranged in a more logical design much of the traffic flow could be eliminated. The dining room should be located adjacent to the kitchen, but also close to the living room. Closets in a small bedroom should not be separated on two different walls.

In Figure 17 the front bedroom opens into the living room rather than a central hall. There should not be a direct view from the living room into a bedroom or bathroom.

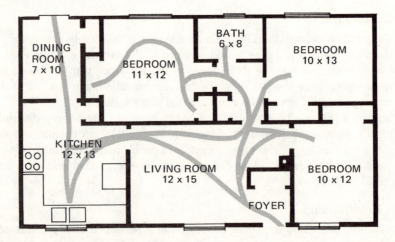

Figure 17. A poorly-designed circulation pattern interferes with furniture arrangement and the useability of space within a residence.

There have been many floor plan illustrations in this chapter that show good room relationship. A review of these illustrations will assist the reader in selecting a convenient, functional, and comfortable residence.

References

Design. Chicago: United States Savings and Loan League, 1963.

Family Housing Handbook. Midwest Plan Service, 1971.

Hepler, D. and Wallach, P. *Architecture Drafting and Design.* New York: McGraw-Hill, 1965.

"Kitchen Planning Standards." Small Homes Council-Building Research Council, Bulletin C5.32, Urbana: University of Illinois, 1964.

Discussion Questions

1. What are the three zones of activity provided in most American dwellings? Which is most public? A service entrance should provide easy access to which zone?

2. Describe what comprises a conversation circle, where it is located, and what is its optimum size.

3. What is a work triangle? What is its optimum size?

4. Explain the difference between an open and a closed floor plan.

5. What are the centers within the American kitchen and what functions are performed at each?

6. Counters and appliances in kitchens are usually arranged in one of four basic designs. Name the basic design shapes and describe the advantages and disadvantages of each.

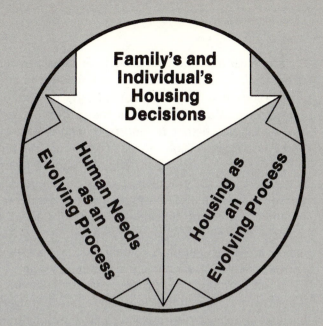

Family's and Individual's Housing Decisions

Human Needs as an Evolving Process

Housing as an Evolving Process

Part Five
Legal and
Financial

18. How to Read a Lease, Consumers Union of United States, Inc.

19. Some Legal Aspects of House Buying, by Neil E. Harl

20. Financing the Home, Small Homes Council-Building Research Council, University of Illinois

21. Home Warranties, by Carol S. Wedin

The legal and financial aspects of housing cause bewilderment for many people. Whether the individual or family rents or purchases a residence, the terminology is often unfamiliar and the documents appear to be extremely complicated. Many people lack the understanding to enable them to objectively analyze whether renting or buying is best for their particular situation. Part Five supplies insights to assist consumers in making rational decisions.

Although most Americans aspire to home ownership, at the present time nearly 40% of the population rents dwellings. The article "How to Read a Lease" will alert the reader to the protections offered by a written lease and to potential sources of difficulties for both the lessor and the lessee. It will also indicate that any differences need to be negotiated or questions clarified before a lease is signed. A valuable tool for prospective renters is the checklist to use as a reference when considering a dwelling.

People purchase housing for a variety of reasons other than as an economic investment. Research indicates that a family frequently purchases a residence because it believes the dwelling and the neighborhood will provide a more desirable environment in which to raise children. Often a family will purchase a residence because it has no alternative due to the lack of adequate rental dwellings. Renters frequently express the desire for home ownership to gain a measure of freedom and privacy. And the pride of home ownership and a "place of our own" is still a dominating factor for people choosing home ownership over renting.

Since purchasing a home is the largest investment many people make in a lifetime, it is important that they know the commitment of their purchase. The buyers should always employ an attorney who will represent their interest and provide guidance and counsel on legal procedure. Examples of the most commonly used documents are included in the article "Some Legal Aspects of House Buying."

The steps a home buyer goes through in financing a home are clearly explained along with illustrations of a transaction for an average-priced house and interest tables in Article 20. The reader will be assisted in understanding financing of a home by the clear and precise definitions of legal and financial terminology.

The article "Home Warranties" will familiarize the reader with recent federal legislation that affects warranties on new houses. Although various forms of warranties have been used by some builders for many years, the average consumer has been perplexed and ill informed about their protection. The Magnuson-Moss Warranty Act of 1975 established strict standards for warranties on consumer products. The article compares three home warranty plans. These will illustrate how home warranties are used for consumer protection with both new and existing houses.

18. How to Read a Lease

Before you move into an apartment, two actions are in order if you want to protect your own interests. One is a careful reading of the lease. The other is a methodical inspection of the apartment. Both actions are discouraged by the nature of the housing marketplace.

With living units scarce in most places, the landlord is in the driver's seat. You're likely to find yourself presented with a form lease—take it or leave it. If you won't sign on the dotted line, there are often others on a waiting list who will. And your tour of the apartment, as often as not, will be hurried and casual, giving little opportunity for systematic examination.

If you're aware of the problems in advance, you can combat them, at least to some degree. This report will give you some hints on how to read a lease and provide you with a checklist of things to note when you're examining an apartment. With knowledge and an organized approach, you may be able to redress, at least in part, the balance of power now stacked against those who rent.

You can use the checklist on pages 206-207 before you move in and save it as a guide for logging any complaints that may come up later in your tenancy. The remainder of this report is designed to translate some of the fine print in a lease into plain English, to help you defend yourself against the more obnoxious provisions commonly found in leases.

Danger Signs in a Lease

Although it's difficult for a tenant to negotiate changes in the lease offered, it's worth a try. Even after you move in, changes in lease terms can sometimes be won from a landlord by an active tenants' association.

The clauses described below are major danger spots on which to concentrate. In quite a few states, many of these clauses have been made illegal by statute or have been ruled unconscionable (and therefore made void) by state courts. However, the official-sounding language of the form lease discourages many tenants from exercising —or even finding out about—their rights. Besides, laws and court precedents vary from state to state. This makes it harder for tenants to become aware of what protections they have.

By all means inform yourself as much as possible about the laws in your own state. Tenants' groups, private attorneys, Legal Services bureaus, or the state Attorney General's office are some possible sources of information.

RESIDENCE OR APARTMENT LEASE

IT IS AGREED this_____day of_____, A.D. 19___, by and between_____

_____

Landlord, and _____

_____

Tenants:

That the Landlord hereby leases to the Tenants, and the Tenants hereby lease from the Landlord, the following described premises, situated in _____ County, Iowa, to-wit:

in consideration of the mutual promises of the parties herein and upon the terms, provisions and conditions following:

1. **LEASE PERIOD.** The duration of this Lease shall be from_____day of_____ 19_____, to and including the_____day of_____ 19_____.

2. **RENT.** Tenants agree to pay to Landlord as rental for said term as follows: $_____ per month, in advance the first rent payment becoming due upon

(Strike   (a) the execution of this lease; or

One)   (b) the _____ day of _____, 19_____

and the same amount per month, in advance on the _____ day of each month thereafter during the term of this lease, with interest on all delinquent rental at 9_____% per annum

In addition to the above monthly $_____ rental, Tenants shall also pay:

All sums above shall be paid to the Landlord at _____

_____, or at such other place as the Landlord may, from time to time, direct.

3. **USE.** Tenants shall use said premises only for residential purposes for Tenants and their children (_____in number) except

_____
(other persons?)   (pets?)

Tenants shall comply with all lawful regulations, restrictions, ordinances and laws applicable to the purpose, use and occupancy of said premises; shall not permit said premises to be occupied for any purpose or permit any act which shall invalidate any policy of insurance on said premises. or increase the fire hazard, and shall pay promptly to Landlord any increase in rate of insurance on the premises resulting from Tenants' occupancy or act; shall bring into or remove from the building by way of the rear entrance, if there be one, all household furniture, machinery and heavy appliances and fixtures; shall locate safes, washing machines, clothes dryers, dishwashers or other heavy equipment as prescribed by the Landlord, and shall not print or affix any sign except with the written consent of the Landlord.

4. **CARE OF PREMISES.** Tenants shall not permit or allow the premises to be damaged by any act or negligence of the Tenants or of any member of their family or of any person on the premises by the permission of Tenants; shall, as a matter of maintenance, keep the property in good order and in a clean, sanitary and safe condition. Without limiting the generality of the foregoing, Tenants shall not permit or allow any damage by pets; shall prevent pipes from freezing; shall promptly repair or replace any part of the fixtures, appliances or premises broken, damaged or destroyed or clogged or frozen (other than by reasonable wear and tear or by situations not caused by Tenants' negligence); shall maintain floors in as good condition as at the beginning of this lease, or as same may hereafter be improved; shall remove snow and all other obstructions from sidewalk; and shall surrender possession of said premises to the Landlord in as good repair and condition as the same are now, or may hereafter be placed (ordinary wear and tear, non-negligent damage by fire or the elements excepted), at the expiration of this lease without notice to quit. Tenants shall not do, or cause to be done, any interior decorating or remodeling unless Landlord consents in writing.

5. **ASSIGNMENT.** Tenants shall not assign this lease nor sub-let said premises or any portion thereof without the written consent of Landlord.

6. **ENCUMBRANCES.** Tenants' property as and when moved on said premises shall not be removed therefrom during the term of this lease except temporarily for uses reasonably and incidentally appropriate to its ownership. There are no encumbrances on said property except as follows:

7. **FIXTURES AND IMPROVEMENTS.** Tenants shall leave upon and surrender to the Landlord with the premises at the termination of the Lease all locks, brackets for curtains, and other fixtures attached to doors, windows or woodwork, and all alterations, additions or improvements made by Tenants.

8. **UTILITIES.** Except as otherwise expressly provided, Tenants shall furnish their own heat and all public utilities. These include gas, water, electricity and city sewage disposal service, if any.

9. **TEMPORARY SUSPENSION.** If, by the express terms of this lease, Landlord is to furnish heat, hot water or other utility, he shall not be held responsible in any way for temporary suspension in supply of same and such temporary suspension shall not be deemed grounds sufficient to terminate this lease or any part thereof.

10. **INDEMNITY.** Tenants shall hold the Landlord harmless for damage or injury which may be sustained by the Tenants from damage caused by breakage, leakage, or obstruction of pipes, and from latent defects not known to Landlord.

11. **RIGHT TO ENTER.** Tenants shall allow the Landlord, his agents or workmen at reasonable times at his discretion, to enter the premises to inspect the same, make repairs or improvements, or show the property to persons desirous of leasing or purchasing. Landlord shall have the right to enter upon and into said premises, if in good faith he does so, in the absence or apparent absence of Tenants to meet an apparent emergency.

12. SALE—CHANGES—TERMINATION. This lease may be terminated by giving Tenants 30 _____ days written notice to quit in event of sale, or if possession is required for removing the building or buildings or materially altering or improving them. Time of termination and yielding of possession by Tenants shall be at the end of such period so designated in the notice.

13. Select either (a) or (b) below by marking "x" in the applicable box. If no such selection is made then (a) shall be the governing and operative provision for this lease.

☐ **(a) RENEWAL.** This written lease is renewed from term to term for the same length of time and upon the same terms, including this paragraph, if Tenants hold possession for three (3) days after the expiration of this lease, provided that either party may terminate such lease during the first thirty (30) days after said three (3) days by giving thirty (30) days notice and the lease shall terminate thirty (30) days after said notice is given.

☐ **(b) HOLDING OVER.** Continued possession, beyond the expiration date of the term of this lease, by the Tenants, coupled with the receipt of the specified rental by the Landlord (and absent a written agreement by both parties for an extension of this lease, or for a new lease) shall constitute a month to month extension of this lease.

14. NO ORAL CHANGES. No statement, representation or promise with reference to this lease or the premises leased, or any repairs, alterations or improvements or the change in the term of this lease shall be binding upon either of the parties unless in writing and signed by both Landlord and Tenants.

ALL AGREEMENTS OF THESE PARTIES TO DATE HEREOF ARE EXPRESSED IN THIS WRITTEN LEASE

15. LIEN. Landlord shall have, in addition to the landlord's lien provided by statute, a lien upon all personal property of Tenants kept or used in said premises during the term of this lease and belonging to Tenants, whether such property is exempt from execution or not, and upon improvements, if any, placed or erected by Tenants on said premises, and upon the unexpired term of this lease, to secure the payments of rent due or to become due, and all expenses including attorneys' fees incurred by Landlord in litigation to collect rent hereunder, or possession, or to procure injunction to prevent removal of personal property, and to secure payment of damages to the premises caused or permitted by Tenants. The lien shall follow the property to whatever location removed, until all secured amounts are paid.

16. OTHER REMEDIES. If Tenants shall fail to comply with any of the terms or conditions of this lease the Landlord in addition to any other remedies may exercise, at his discretion, any one or more of the following remedies, to-wit: (1) declare the rent for said entire term due and proceed to collect the same; (2) elect to declare a forfeiture of this lease and all Tenants' rights hereunder, an ordinary 3 day notice to quit being sufficient for this purpose as well as being the basis for suit for possession. The partial payment or rent due shall not constitute a waiver of right of action for balance due aided by attachment or of action for forcible entry and detainer on account of the unpaid balance of rent for the month upon which part payment was made. In all provisions under this lease time is of the essence and the performance of all other obligations is material.

17. ATTORNEYS' FEES. In case of any action, or in any proceedings in any court, to collect any sums payable or secured by this lease, or to protect the lien herein given, or in any other case permitted by law in which attorneys' fees may be collected from Tenants, or charged upon the property in paragraphs 6 and 15, above, they agree to pay reasonable attorneys' fees.

18. NOTICE. Any notice for which provision is made in this lease unless herein otherwise provided may be given by either party, to the other in any of the following ways: (1) by delivery of written notice; or (2) by service of written notice in the manner provided by law for the service of original notice; or, (3) by sending written notice addressed to the last known address by certified mail with a return receipt demanded; or, (4) by any other method of giving written notice if such notice is actually received; or, (5) if the Tenants are to be given the notice and if the premises be abandoned or vacant, by affixing written notice to any outside door of the dwelling or other building or in some conspicuous position on the premises.

19. REMOVAL BY TENANTS—KEYS—SIGNS. Upon removal from the premises by Tenants prior to the expiration of this lease, or Tenants' nonpayment of rent, Landlord's acceptance from Tenants of the keys to the premises or Landlord's advertising for rent or re-renting of the premises shall not constitute an acceptance by Landlord of a surrender of the lease by Tenants, nor shall it release the Tenants, but any rentals received shall be applied by Landlord on Tenants' rent less expenses incurred by Landlord in re-renting. At the time of the expiration of this lease, or any renewal thereof, or upon forfeiture thereof Tenants shall promptly deliver all keys for said premises to the Landlord at the place designated above for the payment of rent. Landlord shall have the right to place, keep and display in a visible location a "For Rent" or "For Sale" sign on said premises for a period of thirty days prior to the expiration of this lease.

20. DELAY OF POSSESSION. If Landlord is unable to give Tenants possession at the beginning of the term, the rent shall be rebated on a pro rata basis until possession can be given, which rebated rent shall be accepted by Tenants as full settlement of all damages occasioned by said delay, and if possession cannot be delivered within fifteen days of the beginning of said term either party may thereupon terminate this lease by giving the other party notice of such termination.

21. FIRE. If during the term of this lease the building or premises shall be destroyed by fire, the elements or other casualty, or taken by eminent domain, or condemned under police regulations, or partially destroyed, so as to render the premises wholly unfit for occupancy, and if they shall be so badly damaged that they cannot be repaired within 60 _____ days from the date of the damages, or if the Landlord elects not to repair them, this lease shall cease and become null and void from the date of such damage. Tenants shall immediately surrender said premises and rent shall be adjusted to the time of such surrender. If said premises shall be repairable within 60 _____ days from the happening of said damage and the Landlord elects to repair them, the rent shall not accrue while the repairs are being made but shall recommence immediately after said repairs have been completed. In case of termination of the lease under this numbered paragraph the Landlord may re-enter and re-possess said premises discharged of the lease and may remove all parties therefrom. If, however, said premises shall be so slightly damaged by fire or the elements as not to be rendered unfit for occupancy then the Landlord shall repair the same with reasonable promptitude and the rent accrued or accruing shall not cease or be terminated by reason of said damage.

22. MULTIPLE DWELLING. If the property leased is other than a separate private residence, Tenants shall not obstruct the halls or stairways, shall only use the same for passage to and from premises, shall not cover or obstruct any of the skylights or windows that admit light into courts, halls or passageways, shall not make or permit any disturbing noises in the building by themselves, their family, friends or servants or pets, nor do or permit anything by such persons or pets that will interfere with the rights, comforts or convenience of other lessees; shall not play on musical instruments after ten o'clock P.M.; shall not obstruct fire escapes, and shall obey such reasonable multiple apartment rules as the Landlord shall from time to time establish.

23. ANTENNA. Tenants shall have the right to install and shall remove television antenna on said premises and shall be liable for any

and all damages occasioned thereby. They shall deposit $_____ with Landlord before any installation of television antenna upon said premises as security for damages to the premises resulting from such installation or removal.

24. DEPOSIT SECURITY. At the time of execution of this lease Tenants shall pay the Landlord in trust in addition to the rent for

first month hereunder the sum of $_____. If Tenants fully comply with the terms of this lease said amount shall be applied upon the last month's rental under this lease or renewal or extension thereof. If Tenants fail to comply with the terms of this lease, said sum shall be applied by Landlord toward the payment of damages sustained by him by reason of Tenants' failure to comply with the terms of this lease including the non-payment of any rent. The amount of said deposit not so used shall be returned to the Tenants.

If a deposit is made under this paragraph, for additional effective provisions, see Senate File 1004, 65th General Assembly.

25. AS TO PRESENT AND CONTINUING HABITABILITY AND RENTAL VALUE, TENANTS HAVE INSPECTED THE PROPERTY AND FIXTURES AND ACKNOWLEDGE THAT THEY ARE IN A REASONABLE AND ACCEPTABLE CONDITION OF HABITABILITY OR FOR THEIR INTENDED USE, AND THAT THE RENT AGREED UPON IS FAIR AND REASONABLE IN THIS COMMUNITY FOR PREMISES IN THEIR CONDITION. IN THE EVENT THAT CONDITION CHANGES SO THAT, IN TENANTS' OPINION, THE HABITABILITY AND THE RENTAL VALUE OF THE PREMISES IS AFFECTED, THEN TENANTS SHALL PROMPTLY GIVE A REASONABLE WRITTEN NOTICE TO THE LANDLORD. (See *Mease vs. Fox*, 200 N.W. 2d 791.)

26. **CONSTRUCTION.** Words and phrases herein, including acknowledgment hereof, shall be construed as in the singular or plural number, and as masculine, feminine or neuter gender, according to the context.

27.

_____   _____

_____   _____

Landlord   **Tenants**

STATE OF IOWA, _____ COUNTY, ss:

On this _____ day of _____ , A. D. 19_____, before me, the undersigned, a Notary Public in and for the State of

Iowa, personally appeared _____

_____

_____

to me known to be the identical persons named in and who executed the within and foregoing instrument, and acknowledged that they executed the same as their voluntary act and deed.

_____
Notary Public in and for the State of Iowa

P-122—Copyright 1960 by The Iowa State Bar Association*

Even if you think the law is on your side, it's best to keep a troublesome clause out of the lease altogether. The lower courts, which deal with landlord-tenant disputes, often regard leases as holy writ, to be followed literally. Appeals to higher courts are time-consuming and expensive. And even if you win in court—at whatever level— litigation is at best a nuisance that most people would rather avoid. If a lease is so bad that you'd sign it only because you don't think it would stand up in court, then you'd be much better off trying to have the lease modified in the first place.

To strike a clause, the relevant words should be crossed out, and _both_ you and the landlord (or the landlord's authorized agent) should put your initials next to the change. This should be done on _every_ copy of the lease that you sign. If you can't accomplish any such changes, the danger-sign list beginning on the next page will at least give you an idea of what you're getting into. (To see whether these danger-sign clauses are included—and most of them usually are—you must read the _entire_ document. Lease clauses are typically printed in no logical order, and the most important items are often buried deep within a paragraph.)

We present first the meaning of the dangerous clause in plain English, then the way the clause might typically read in a lease's legalese, printed here in italics.

1. _You agree that the landlord isn't liable for repairs._ There are a variety of ways in which leases state that the tenant must pay rent whether or not heat, hot water, and other essential services (such as refrigeration, or elevator service in a high-rise) are supplied and maintained. One formulation: _"This lease and the obligation of_

*As indicated, these complicated forms are trade marked and/or copyrighted by The Iowa State Bar Association and may not be reproduced by any means, without permission from them.

Further, these forms undergo changes from time to time to meet new ideas, new laws, state and federal, and judicial decisions. For that reason and others, sales of these forms are strictly limited to members of The Iowa State Bar Association, who are qualified to explain their meaning and use to the general public. For the legal effect of the use of this form, consult your lawyer.

tenant to pay rent hereunder. . .shall in nowise be affected, impaired or excused because landlord is unable to supply or is delayed in supplying any service or repairs, additions, alterations or decorations."

This clause sets forth the doctrine of "independent covenants," a hoary legalism still applicable to many aspects of landlord-tenant relations, though not applicable to normal business contracts. The doctrine states that the tenant's obligation ("covenant") to pay rent is separate from the landlord's obligation to provide a habitable dwelling. If the landlord doesn't fulfill his part of the bargain, the lease doesn't permit tenants to withhold their rent, as buyers would normally withhold payment for goods or services not delivered. Instead, tenants must sue or pursue some other cumbersome legal remedy.

To counteract this type of clause, several states have established mechanisms under which tenants can withhold rent under certain conditions.

2. *You pay the landlord's attorney's fees.* A typical clause reads: *"The tenant further agrees to pay all costs, including legal fees and other charges that may accrue in the event distraint proceedings are instituted against the tenant, or in the event suit for rent or dispossess proceedings are necessary in order to obtain possession of the premises, or to collect the rent."*

A "distraint" is a seizure of your property to collect a debt; it has been made illegal or ruled unconstitutional in many states. A "dispossess proceeding" is an eviction. Thus, in this common clause you pledge to pay your landlord's legal costs if he tries to seize your property or if he evicts you.

3. *You waive your right to a jury trial.* Typical wording: *"It is mutually agreed by and between Landlord and Tenant that the respective parties hereto shall and they hereby do waive trial by jury in any action, proceeding or counterclaim brought by either of the parties hereto against the other on any matters whatsoever arising out of or in any way connected with this lease, the Tenant's use of occupancy of said premises, and/or any claim of injury or damage."*

This clause has the appearance of fairness, since the landlord also waives his right to a jury trial. But juries are generally more favorable to tenants than judges are, in the unanimous opinion of tenant leaders interviewed by CU (Consumers Union).

4. *You agree to obey rules that may not even have been written yet.* A typical formulation: *"The lessee covenants and agrees that all rules and regulations printed upon the back hereof, or hereafter adopted by the lessor and made known to lessee, shall have the same force and effect as covenants of said lease, and the lessee covenants that he, his family and guests will observe all such rules and regulations."*

Rules often include prohibitions against owning pets, practicing musical instruments, playing TV sets at certain hours, washing cars, storing baby carriages or bicycles in certain areas, or driving nails into the walls.

Such items as the last are constantly violated by almost all tenants. Who, after all, wants to live in rooms barren of all pictures or decorations? But such picky regulations can be used, subsequently, as a pretext for a landlord to keep tenants' security deposits. Or they can provide a pretext for a landlord to evict tenants if he takes a dislike to them or wants their quarters for some other purpose (such as rental at a higher rate to a new tenant). Persons active in tenant-organizing sometimes find themselves suddenly in violation of a rule previously ignored.

Insist on reading the current rules and regulations before you move into any apartment. In some places they're quite reasonable; in others, not. If you have any bargaining power, try to see that particularly objectionable ones are stricken. As for agreeing to follow any rules promulgated in the future, it's best if you don't; second best if the lease provides some arbitration procedure for tenants who disagree with the future rules, or if the lease limits the tenant's obligation to follow "reasonable" regulations.

5. *You agree to pay possible extra rent.* This clause allows the landlord to raise the rent if his operating expenses go up, particularly in the areas of water or sewer assessments, real-estate taxes, pollution-control equipment, or other capital improvements. Typical wording: *"Tenant agrees, during the term of this lease or any renewal thereof that in the event there shall be an increase in real-estate taxes, sewer or water charges above the amount of said taxes, sewer or water charges during the year —, or an assessment charged by the municipality on the demised premises for any period following the date of commencement of this lease, tenant shall pay his proportionate share of said tax increase, charge or municipal assessment."*

Some leases that run more than one year may include an automatic increase in the rent for each year after the first, with only the first year's rent prominently indicated at the top of the lease. The increase from year to year may be a specified dollar amount or a fixed percentage, or it may even be geared to the change in the cost of living.

6. *You give the landlord free rein to enter your apartment.* Leases vary substantially in the degree to which landlords can barge in unannounced and uninvited. A sample of one of the worst "access-to-premises" clauses: *"Landlord or Landlord's agents shall have the right to enter the demised premises during reasonable hours, to examine the same, and to show them to prospective purchasers, lessees, mortgagees or insurance carriers of the building, and to make such repairs, alterations, improvements or additions as Landlord may deem necessary or desirable. If Tenant shall not be personally present to open and permit an entry into said premises, at any time, when for any reason an entry therein shall be necessary or permissible hereunder, Landlord or Landlord's agents may enter the same by a master key, or may forcibly enter the same, without rendering Landlord or Landlord's agents liable therefor."*

Taken literally, that clause means that your landlord can kick your door down to show your apartment to a prospective future tenant while you're not home. In practice, courts have usually ruled in such a way as to restrict a landlord's right of entry to normal business hours, and to require that 24 hours' notice of the entry be given the tenant unless there is a genuine emergency. Courts have also made it clear that the right of access can't be used to harass a tenant. The problem is that you might have to sue to prove that the lease doesn't really mean what it says.

7. *The landlord isn't liable if you're injured, or if your property is damaged.* Most leases have a list of hazards for which the landlord is not to be held responsible. Typically, the list includes *"falling plaster, steam, gas, electricity, water, rain or snow which may leak from any part of said building,"* and several others.

But form leases differ in a key regard. With some, the landlord is not responsible for injury from the listed hazards *unless* he or his agents have been negligent. For the tenant, that's the better situation.

The worse situation is that the landlord is not liable even if the damage was caused by his negligence—and many leases say just that. In some, for example, you agree *"that the lessor shall not be liable for any damage or injury of the lessee."* Or you might agree *"to indemnify and save the lessor harmless from all claims of every kind and nature."*

Such a sweeping excuse from any kind of liability will almost never hold up in court. But if the landlord damages some of your property, you'll probably have to drag him into court to recover damages. Were it not for the standard form lease, landlords might be more willing to make reasonable out-of-court settlements. And, of course, the lease can be used to cow tenants who don't know their rights.

8. *You agree no one else will live with you.* Most leases prohibit anyone not named on the lease from occupying the apartment. For example: *"Tenant will not use nor permit to be used the said premises nor any part thereof for any purpose other than that of a private dwelling apartment for himself and his immediate family."*

It makes no difference whether the visitor helps you with the rent or not. If, two months after moving into your apartment, you want your widowed aunt to move in with you—too bad. You don't control who lives in your apartment.

Of course, few leases prohibit your having guests overnight. It's long-term stays that may present a problem. If a landlord tries to evict a tenant for having a "sub-tenant" (unauthorized occupant), one issue a court would look at is how long the guest had stayed. Whether the guest moved in furniture and whether he or she maintained a separate residence would also have some bearing on the case.

Subletting your apartment—that is, letting someone else live there while you're away and collecting rent from that person while you continue to pay the landlord—is also flatly prohibited under some leases. Under most leases it can be done, but only if the landlord gives written consent. This restriction has some merit, since it gives landlords some reasonable control over who lives in their buildings. But it's an inconvenience and an added problem for tenants, especially those who travel a great deal. About the best you can hope for here is a phrase in the lease saying the landlord agrees not to withhold consent unreasonably.

9. *Any improvements you build in belong to the landlord.* Even though most leases require you to get the landlord's consent before making any alterations, landlords get to have their cake and eat it too. Any improvements the landlord allows you to install become part of his property, enhancing its value for rental to the next tenant. The clause will read something like this: *"The lessee agrees that no alterations, additions or improvements shall be made in or to the premises without the consent of the lessor in writing, under penalty of damages and forfeiture, and all additions and improvements made by the Tenant shall belong to the lessor."*

This clause is intended to refer to such things as built-in shelves, window seats, wallpaper, and towel racks. The logic is that removal of these items might damage the apartment. However, even if the tenant could accomplish their removal without damage, the landlord has the right to keep them under the lease.

10. *You agree the premises are fine as they are.* The windows may be cracked; the refrigerator may be broken; there may be hidden defects in the apartment you won't notice until you've lived there for a short time. But the lease you've signed is likely to say something like, *"The lessee accepts said premises in their present condition."* To buttress this, another clause of the lease will probably say, *"Neither party has made any representation or promises, except as contained herein,* *or in some further writing signed by the party.''* So if the landlord tells you he'll sand and refinish the floors for you, be sure to get it in writing—before you sign the lease. The Checklist for Renters may give you some ideas on what commitments you should seek.

A Checklist for Renters

You can use the list of questions below to check an apartment before you move in. With some exceptions, you can also use it to log complaints about apartment conditions stemming from a landlord's failure to perform proper service or maintenance. Some questions cannot be answered by simple observation and may require interviewing tenants of other apartments in the building or asking the opinion of an expert knowledgeable in building problems (an architect or engineer).

1. What is the rent per month?

2. Is a security deposit required? If so, how much is it and under what conditions is it held?

3. Does the lease say rent can be increased if real-estate taxes are raised, sewer or water assessments are hiked, or for any other reason?

4. Do you pay extra (and how much) for such things as utilities, storage space, air-conditioning, parking space, master TV antenna connection, use of recreation areas (such as pool or tennis courts), installation of special appliances, late payment of rent, etc.?

5. Read the lease carefully. Mark any provisions that seem especially objectionable to you and try to have them removed from your lease. List also the provisions (not included) that you would like, such as a sublet clause. Try to have these added.

6. Assess the maintenance services: Is there a resident superintendent? Are maintenance hours (for usual services) restricted? How is emergency service handled?

7. How is refuse disposal handled? Are facilities easily accessible? Are they well kept and clean?

8. Laundry facilities: How many washers and dryers are available? Are they in good working order? (A washer and dryer for every 10 apartments is a good ratio.)

9. Building lobby: Is it clean and well-lighted? Does it have a lock or other security provisions? Is there a doorman? If so, for how many hours a day? How are deliveries handled?

10. Entrance and exit: Is an elevator provided? If so, is it in good working condition? Are the stairs well lit and in sound condition? Are fire exits provided? Is there a fire alarm or other warning system?

11. Hallways: Are they clean and adequately lit? Are they otherwise in good condition?

12. Are there signs of insects present? Of mice or rats?

13. Bathroom(s): Are the plumbing fixtures in good working order and reasonably clean? Does the hot water supply seem adequate? Are the tiles (if room is tiled) sound?

14. Kitchen: Is the sink in good working order, reasonably clean, and provided with drain stoppers? Does the stove seem to be in good working order and reasonably clean? Is the refrigerator in good working order? Does it have a separate-door freezing compartment? If there is a dishwasher, is it in good working order?

15. Air-conditioning: Is the entire building air-conditioned? If not, are there separate units and are they functioning properly (if it's summer)?

16. Wiring: Are there enough electrical outlets? (Two or three to a room is the minimum.) Do all the switches and outlets work? Are there enough circuits in the fuse

box (or circuit-breaker panel) to handle the electrical equipment you expect to install? (If there is a serious question, get an expert opinion.)

17. Does the heating system seem to be in good working order? Is it providing adequate heat (if it's winter)?

18. Is there a fireplace? If so, are there any signs (such as smoke stains) that it has not worked properly?

19. Windows: Are any broken? Can they be opened and closed easily? Are screens provided? Are there drafts around the window frame? Does the landlord arrange for the outside of the windows (in high-rise buildings) to be cleaned? And if so, how often?

20. Floors: Are they clean? Are they marred or gouged? Do they have any water stains indicating previous leaks?

21. Ceilings: Are they clean? Is the plaster cracked? Is the paint peeling? Do they have any water stains indicating previous leaks?

22. Walls: Are they clean? Is the plaster cracked? Is the paint peeling? Does the paint run or smear when rubbed with a damp cloth?

23. Telephone: Are phone jacks already installed? Are they in convenient locations?

24. Television: Is TV (or hi-fi) playing forbidden at certain hours? Is an outside antenna connection provided? Is there a cable-TV connection?

25. Is ventilation adequate? Is there an exhaust fan in the kitchen?

26. Lighting: Are there enough fixtures for adequate light? Are the fixtures in good working order? Does the apartment get reasonably adequate natural light from the windows?

27. Storage space: Is there adequate closet space? Are there enough kitchen and bathroom cabinets? Is there long-term storage space available in the building for your use?

28. Security: Does the entry door have a dead-bolt lock? A security chain? A through-the-door viewer?

29. Soundproofing: Do the walls seem hollow (when thumped) or solid? Can you hear neighbors upstairs, downstairs, or on either side of you?

30. Outdoor play space: Is it provided? If so, are facilities well maintained?

Discussion Questions

1. Define the terms "lessor" and "lessee."

2. What two important actions should the renter take before he or she moves into an apartment?

3. Is it possible to negotiate with the landlord and change terms that are written into a standard lease?

4. Name possible agencies or offices within your state that you may go to for information about tenant-landlord laws.

5. Discuss the "access-to-premises" clause.

19. Some Legal Aspects of House Buying

by Neil E. Harl

A house is one of the largest purchases a family makes in a lifetime. Every step in the transaction has legal implications—from the signing of a contract to purchase (or offer to buy) to the final closing of the transaction and receipt of a deed to the property. State law has a substantial influence on house-buying transactions and each state tends to be somewhat unique. The following points generalize to a considerable degree and should always be checked against applicable local law.

Should you consult a lawyer before signing the contract?

Yes. The contract binds the buyer and seller and determines their rights and responsibilities in the transaction. To illustrate, the contract should specify who bears the risk of loss to the property by fire, wind, or other casualty from the date the contract is signed until the deal is completed. The contract should also specify how much insurance is to be carried during that period, who pays the insurance premiums, and who receives the proceeds if a loss occurs.

The question of who is to pay the real estate taxes and unpaid assessments (such as for street paving, sewer, street lights) is normally answered in the contract. Real estate taxes are paid some time after they are levied, and the seller generally agrees in the contract to pay the real property taxes up to the date of possession or closing of the transaction.

If you are acquiring a used house, the mortgage holder (mortgagee) may have required that insurance premiums and taxes be paid out of an escrow account. In that event, transfer of the escrow balance may be covered by the contract.

Of course, the contract specifies the date the transaction is to be "closed" and the deed given as well as the possession date. If the transaction covers items of personal property—such as furniture, portable shelves, drapes, etc.—the contract should describe the property.

The contract also specifies how the property is to be owned — husband's name, wife's name; or both names. And the contract contains the legal description for the property — its unique "address." Urban homes are usually described in terms of a plat of the area dividing the tract into lots and blocks. But some residences, especially those outside urban areas, may be described using courses and distances (based on a surveyor's information), metes and bounds (referring to identifiable features like trees or

Neil E. Harl is Charles F. Curtiss Distinguished Professor in Agriculture and Professor of Economics, Iowa State University, and a member of the Iowa Bar. This article was written specially for this book.

boulders to mark boundaries), or the congressional survey that divided much of the country into six-mile-square townships and mile-square sections.

In short, the contract is one of the most important documents involved. Your attorney should review the contract before it is signed.

What if you sign a contract and later change your mind?

If the buyer defaults, the seller generally has several options. The seller may bring a lawsuit for the amount unpaid on the contract or the seller can foreclose by having the property sold under court order. If authorized by state law (and some states require that it be spelled out in the contract as well), the seller may forfeit the buyer's rights, which permits the seller to recover the property and keep all of the payments made by the buyer. Typically, forfeiture requires notice to the defaulting buyer, often as little as thirty days, before the seller can recover the property.

How do you know that you're getting good title?

Since land is permanent, the matter of getting good title is very important. A buyer wouldn't want to lose the property to someone who had a prior claim to it. And the buyer wants the assurance that he or she will be able to sell the property without questions being raised about the quality of title at the time.

In many states, the buyer's attorney examines the title and gives a title opinion stating what defects, if any, have been found in the title. The opinion is based upon a careful review of recorded documents (in a few states) or the abstract of title for the property which is provided by the seller. The abstract of title contains a brief summary of recorded documents affecting title to the land and is widely used. Although the abstract is not absolutely necessary to pass title to the buyer, it is an important and valuable document. When the transaction has been completed, the abstract is given to the buyer and should be stored in a safe place.

The abstract may help the buyer's attorney spot such title problems as defective estate settlement procedures carried out after the property owner died, discrepancies in names (for example, property purchased by G.F. Smith but sold by George Smith), failure of a spouse to sign the deed giving up the spouse's interest in the property, court judgments entered against the property owner, unpaid property taxes, and unreleased mortgages.

Some defects in title may not show up on the abstract. Boundary disputes and unrecorded rights in the property that have built up over the years (such as the right to cross over the property) would not appear on the abstract. Also, liens for materials supplied within a specified period of time (often ninety days) need not appear in the abstract to be valid against the purchaser.

Some title defects are not considered serious. In many states, defects in title that arose years ago may be rendered unimportant by special "curative acts." Most title problems that are serious can be remedied by action of the seller in obtaining explanatory affidavits or quit claim deeds from individuals who have some claim to the property. But it may be necessary to bring a "suit to quiet title" to take care of the title problems that cannot be cleared up otherwise.

In some states title insurance is available to protect the buyer and may be a substitute for a title opinion. With title insurance, the property owner is indemnified for loss if title problems arise. In states authorizing title registration, court action may be taken to assure good title to the property.

The contract normally specifies the quality of title that the seller agrees to give. Typically, the contract specifies "good and merchantable title."

What about mortgages?

If you are buying a new house or one that does not have a mortgage, you may wish to finance the purchase by signing a note and mortgage. The note establishes the promise to repay the loan, and the mortgage gives the mortgagee a security interest in the property. If you default in making payments, the mortgagee could start foreclosure proceedings with the property sold under court order. Once the buyer signs a note, he or she remains liable to pay the amount specified until the obligation is satisfied even though the property may be sold. If a default occurs and the property does not bring enough at the foreclosure sale to repay the mortgage, any deficiency can sometimes be sought from the person who had signed the note.

In the purchase of a used mortgaged house, the buyer may choose to take over the seller's mortgage and pay the seller only his or her equity in the house. The seller's continuing responsibility under the mortgage depends on state law. If the buyer buys the house "subject to" the old mortgage, he or she continues to make the mortgage payments. Upon default, the property could be taken by the mortgagee. But any deficiency would be sought from the one who had signed the note. A buyer "assuming" a mortgage typically pays the seller the difference between the amount of the mortgage and the selling price, and also agrees to be liable for the mortgage debt personally. For a seller who signed the original note and mortgage, potential later liability on the mortgage may be avoided if the seller insists that the mortgage be paid off with the buyer arranging new financing. There may be a penalty, however, for early payment of the mortgage. And if the rate of interest on the mortgage loan is less than the going rate at the time of sale, the home may sell at a premium. For these reasons, and to avoid the additional costs associated with refinancing, the seller often permits his or her mortgage to be taken over by the buyer.

Mortgages are usually recorded by the lender (the mortgagee) to assure a priority claim against the property in the event of default. Thus, a mortgagee agreeing to loan funds on the strength of a first mortgage must record the mortgage in order for the mortgage to take priority over the mortgagor's other creditors. Once recorded, the mortgage remains a part of the title until released. A mortgage release is usually filed routinely upon completion of payments as required by the note.

Can you buy on installment land contract?

Some houses are sold on installment land contract with the payments covering a period of a few months to several years. The seller, rather than a mortgagee, finances the purchase. Typically, down payments are low (usually 30% of the selling price or less). The 30% is the maximum that can be received by the seller in the year of sale and still reported as a gain on the installment method for income tax purposes. The seller usually retains title to the property and gives the buyer a deed when all or a specified portion of the payments have been made. Upon default of the buyer, the seller can bring a lawsuit for the amount due, or may foreclose. Also, the buyer's rights may be forfeited with the seller receiving back the property and retaining all payments and improvements made if requirements for forfeiture under state law are met.

An installment contract usually contains most of the provisions found in a short-term contract for the sale of land of the type used to bind the parties until the date of the closing of the transaction and exchange of deed for the purchase price. An installment contract may also contain provisions for prepayment of principal amounts due. Without such a right to make prepayments, in most states buyers may not depart from the payment schedule. If a right to make prepayments exists, the buyer may also find it helpful to request a clause permitting prepayments to be used later as current payments to avoid default. Otherwise, a prepayment is generally considered to be part of the last payment due and the buyer could be in default despite prepayments previously made.

Installment contracts also specify the method of payment to be followed. For homes, the most common payment method involves a fixed amount of principal and interest each year. The size of each annual payment is constant over the life of the contract with a greater proportion of each successive payment representing principal. Some contracts, however, call for a fixed amount of principal each year with interest figured on the unpaid balance. With such a provision, the total annual payment decreases each year.

What kind of deed should you receive?

A deed is the formal document that passes the title from seller to buyer. Most deeds contain promises to the buyer.

The highest quality deed, and the one preferred by buyers, is the general warranty deed. The seller promises that he and his predecessors all had good title to the property. A special warranty deed usually contains fewer promises and limits the seller's responsibility to defects arising during the seller's period of ownership. A quit claim deed contains the fewest promises and may not be satisfactory alone to transfer the title to land. A seller giving a quit claim deed simply agrees to give the buyer all of his or her interest in the property without promising how extensive that interest might be.

Should the deed be recorded?

Usually, the deed is recorded by the buyer soon after the closing of the transaction in which the buyer makes the final payment and receives the deed. The deed is recorded in a county office, typically the county recorder's office or the office of register of deeds. A small filing fee is imposed, and many states require payment of a special tax (in some states it is known as a stamp tax, documentary stamp tax, or transfer tax) before the deed may be recorded. If it is not clear from local practice who pays the tax, liability for payment should be clearly specified in the contract.

The deed is recorded to establish the buyer's right to the property as against the seller's creditors and as against subsequent purchasers from the seller. An unscrupulous seller might sell the same property more than once. Operation of the land title system varies from state to state but generally protects a subsequent purchaser who is not aware of the earlier purchase.

Should the names of both husband and wife appear on the title?

There are several choices as to the way a house may be owned. The title may be in the husband's name alone, the wife's name alone, or in both their names. The choice may not only have important gift tax and death tax implications, but can also affect the disposition of the property at death.

If the house is owned in the husband's name alone, at his death the property would pass under his will or to his heirs under state law. The value of the house would be subject to tax (federal estate and state inheritance taxes) if the estate is large enough.

For houses owned in joint tenancy between husband and wife (known as tenancy by the entirety in some states), the property passes to the survivor on death of one spouse. A will has no effect on joint tenancy property on the death of the first to die. This right of survivorship assures that the surviving joint tenant will own the property.

For federal estate tax purposes, residences owned in joint tenancy are taxed under one of two rules. A third rule, the "credit for services" rule, is available for *business* property for deaths after 1978. A spouse who participated materially in the business (as defined for social security purposes) is credited with 2% per year of the value of the jointly owned property over the amount of original consideration furnished (plus 6% simple interest).

In general, a personal residence owned in joint tenancy would be subject to either the "consideration furnished" or "fractional interest" rules for federal estate tax purposes. The results may be quite different depending upon which rule applies. For joint tenancies created after 1976 between a husband and wife, one-half the property value is taxed at the death of the first joint tenant if the *joint tenancy transaction was subject to federal gift tax.* This is the "fractional interest" rule. As a general rule, acquisitions of property in joint tenancy are subject to federal gift tax. However, land acquired by a husband and wife in joint tenancy since 1954 is an exception. Such acquisitions are not subject to federal gift tax (a gift from the one providing more than a proportionate part of the funds to the one providing less than a proportionate part) unless reported on a federal gift tax return filed on time. Thus, to take advantage of the "new" federal estate tax rule for a residence owned in joint tenancy, it is necessary for the acquisition of the residence to be reported as a gift. Otherwise, the "old" federal estate tax rule applies.

Under the old "consideration furnished" rule, the full value of joint tenancy (or tenancy by the entirety) property is subject to federal estate tax except to the extent the survivor can prove that he or she provided part of the funds when the property was acquired or the mortgage paid off. The burden is on the survivor to prove that he or she was a source of funds. If the wife survives, she might be able to prove that she had received income from employment outside the home, a gift from an outsider or an inheritance, and that these funds had made their way into the property in question. The "consideration furnished" rule applies wherever the "fractional interest" rule is not applicable.

State inheritance tax treatment of joint tenancy property varies from state to state with some paralleling the federal rule and others taxing half or less of the value at the death of the first joint tenant.

Joint tenancy may be acceptable for couples with small estates who do not have a will. Death taxes are not a matter of great concern. Moreover, in many states joint tenancy ownership of property permits simplified estate settlement at the death of the first joint tenant. Also, the survivorship feature assures passage of the property to the surviving joint tenant rather than the children. However, joint tenancy is generally less advisable as estates increase in size because of additional death taxes and costs as compared to tenancy in common.

Houses may be owned by a husband and wife as tenants in common. Upon the death of one tenant in common — the husband, for example — his interest (usually one-half) passes under his will or to his heirs. The death taxes are imposed only on his interest in the property.

Income tax aspects of house transfer

Sale of an old residence or sale and purchase of a new residence may have important income tax implications. Although the residence is a personal asset and is not depreciable (except to the extent used for business purposes), gains on sale are taxable. There are, however, various ways to defer or postpone the payment of income tax on the gain. Losses on sale of a house used as the principal residence are personal losses and are not deductible for income tax purposes.

If the old residence is sold and within eighteen months before or after the date of sale a new residence is acquired at the same or greater cost, the gain on the old residence carries over into the new one and is not immediately taxable. However, if the new residence costs less than the amount received for the old one, part of the gain is taxable for income tax purposes. If a new residence is constructed, it must be occupied within two years after sale of the old residence to be eligible for income tax deferral.

In general, the last principal residence purchased and used during the replacement period has constituted the new residence for tax postponement purposes. However, starting with sales or exchanges of residences after July 26, 1978, more than one residence may qualify for tax postponement during a replacement period if the owner relocates for employment purposes. To qualify, a sale must be in connection with commencement of work at a new principal place of work, and the taxpayer must satisfy both the geographic and length of employment requirements for deductibility of moving expenses.

For sale of the principal residence after age fifty-five, up to $100,000 of gain may be excluded from income ($50,000 for a separate return by a married individual). To be eligible, the property must have been owned and used as the taxpayer's principal residence for three or more of the last five years before sale. The election to exclude the gain from income may be made only once in a person's lifetime.

The rule permitting up to $100,000 of gain to be excluded from income was enacted in 1978. Previously, the gain on up to $35,000 of adjusted sales price for a residence could be excluded after age sixty-five on a once-in-a-lifetime basis if the residence had been used as the principal residence for five of the last eight years before sale.

If a residence is sold with installment payments spread over at least two taxable years and with payments in the year of sale no more than 30% of the sale price, gain on sale may be reported for income tax purposes as payments are received. The seller, in computing gain each year, must calculate "gross profit" and "total contract price." Gross profit is defined as the selling price less the adjusted basis (see discussion in the next paragraph). Total contract price means the amount to be paid by the buyer. To compute the amount of gain reportable as income, the principal payments received by the seller are multiplied by a percentage computed by dividing the gross profit by the total contract price.

> Example: A residence with an adjusted basis of $24,000 and a mortgage of $20,000 is sold for $60,000. Gross profit is $60,000 - 24,000 = $36,000. Total contract price is $60,000 - 20,000 = $40,000.
>
> $$\frac{\text{Gross profit}}{\text{Total contract price}} = \frac{36,000}{40,000} = 90\%$$

If payments in the year of sale total $10,000, 90% or $9,000 would be capital gain and $1,000 would be return of capital which is not taxable. The interest received would, of course, be ordinary income. Each payment received would be subject to the same treatment with 90% reported as capital gain and 10% as return of capital.

The amount of the selling price of a residence that is subject to income tax depends upon the income tax *basis* of the residence. The portion of the selling price representing the residence is not subject to income tax. If the residence was purchased, the income tax basis is the purchase price plus capital improvements made (such as a room addition) and minus depreciation claimed (if any). For residences received by gift, the income tax basis is the giver's (donor's) basis plus capital improvements made since the date of the gift and minus depreciation claimed. If a residence is inherited, the rules for determining the recipient's income tax basis are more complex. For deaths before 1980, all property owned at death, including the residence, receives a new income tax basis at death equal to the value used for federal estate tax purposes. For deaths after 1979, only the gain representing the part of the deceased's holding period before 1977 is eliminated at death. The gain for the period after 1976 carries over to the recipient with three additional adjustments.

It is important to maintain good records of improvements to the residence. That information is generally needed for figuring the income tax liability on sale of the residence.

Any taxable gain on sale of a residence is generally reported as long-term capital gain if the residence was owned for more than one year. Although recognition of gain on sale of a residence is relatively rare, in light of the special income tax opportunities applicable to a residence, 60% of any long-term capital gain would be excluded from income (except, possibly, for the alternative minimum tax that is rarely applicable) with 40% of the long-term capital gain taxable as ordinary income.

Office in the home

An income tax deduction may be claimed for a portion of the home expenses, plus a depreciation allowance. But that's possible only if an area of the home is used regularly and on an exclusive basis as the taxpayer's principal place of business or as a place of business used by patients, clients or customers in the normal course of the taxpayer's trade or business; or if a structure detached from the dwelling is used in connection with the taxpayer's trade or business.

There are two exceptions to the "exclusive use" requirement: (1) where the dwelling is the sole, fixed location of a trade or business involving sale of products at retail or wholesale and a specific part of the residence is used for inventory storage, and (2) where the residence is used to provide day care services to children, handicapped individuals, and the elderly under certain circumstances.

Vacation homes

For vacation homes rented out for less than fifteen days each year, both income and expenses are to be disregarded. Beyond that, the income tax treatment depends upon the amount of personal use.

If personal use exceeds the greater of fourteen days or 10% of the days actually rented, an income tax deduction may be claimed within limits. Deductions aren't permitted to exceed rental income less such deductions as interest, property taxes; and casualty losses that would be deductible anyway. And the deductions attributable to rental are limited to the proportion of total days use the facility was rented at a fair rental. Again, that deduction does not include those expenses that are deductible anyway.

Property tax

Homes are generally subject to a local (and in some instances a state) property tax. Although property taxes are deductible for income tax purposes, the annual property tax bill is a major expense of home ownership.

Homes are revalued periodically (usually every two to four years) for property tax purposes. It is important to review carefully the revaluation figures for the lot and the structure or structures on the lot. Typically, a period of time is specified for objections to be raised to the new values. If the figures are out of line with comparable residences in the same taxing district, consideration should be given to appealing the new values during the prescribed period.

In some states, owner-occupied homes are eligible for a homestead deduction or credit against the property tax. And many states permit a deduction for veterans of military service. These should be checked carefully for eligibility requirements. Some property tax deductions and credits require action each year to maintain eligibility.

CAVEAT: If this is a transaction governed by the Iowa Consumer Credit Code [Senate File 1405, Sixty-fifth General Assembly (See part.c-ularly at page 12 of the Act, Section 1.301, 15, 15a(1) ("regularly engages") to a (5)] DO NOT USE THIS FORM.

NOTE: Use this form only when a 12-month period of redemption is desired. Use Form 13.1 for the six-month period and 60-day period.

★

REAL ESTATE MORTGAGE—IOWA

This Indenture made this_____day of_____, A. D. 19_____

between _____

_____ **Mortgagors**

of the County of _____, and State of Iowa, and _____

_____

_____ **Mortagee,**

of the County of _____, and State of _____.

WITNESSETH: That the said Mortgagors in consideration of _____

_____ **DOLLARS**

($_____) loaned by Mortgagee, received by Mortgagors and evidenced by the promissory note here-inafter referred to, do, by these presents **SELL, CONVEY AND MORTGAGE,** unto the said Mortgagee _____

_____

_____

the following described Real Estate situated in the County of_____, State of Iowa, to-wit:

together with all personal property that may integrally belong to, or be or hereafter become an integral part of said real estate, and whether attached or detached (that is, light fixtures, shades, rods, blinds, venetian blinds, awnings, storm windows, storm doors, screens, linoleum, water heater, water softener, automatic heating equipment and other attached fixtures), and hereby granting, conveying and mortgaging also all of the easements, servient estates appurtenant thereto, rents, issues, uses, profits and right to possession of said real estate, and all crops raised thereon from now until the debt secured thereby shall be paid in full. As to any such personal property, or fixtures, or both, a **Security interest hereby attaches thereto,** as provided by the Uniform Commercial Code.

Said Mortgagors hereby covenant with Mortgagee, or successor in interest, that said Mortgagors hold said real estate by title in fee simple; that they have good and lawful authority to sell, convey and mortgage the same; that said premises are Free and Clear of all Liens and Encumbrances Whatsoever except as may be above stated; and said Mortgagors Covenant to Warrant and Defend the said prem-ises against the lawful claims of all persons whomsoever, except as may be above stated.

Each of the undersigned hereby relinquishes all rights of dower, homestead and distributive share in and to the above described prem-ises, and waives any rights of exemption, as to any of said property.

CONDITIONED HOWEVER, That if said Mortgagors shall pay or cause to be paid to said Mortgagee, or his successor in interest, said sum of money which shall be legal tender in payment of all debts and dues, public and private, at time of payment, all at the time, place, and upon the terms provided by one[1] promissory note of Mortgagors to Mortgagee, of even date herewith, and shall perform the other provisions hereof, then these presents will be void, otherwise to remain in full force and effect.

1. **TAXES.** Mortgagors shall pay each installment of all taxes and special assessments of every kind, now or hereafter levied against said property, or any part thereof, before same become delinquent, without notice or demand; and shall procure and deliver to said Mort-gagee, on or before the fifteenth day of October of each year, duplicate receipts of the proper officers for the payment of all such taxes and assessments then due.

2. **INSURANCE.** Mortgagors shall keep in force insurance, premiums therefor to be prepaid without notice or demand, against loss by fire, tornado and other hazards, casualties and contingencies as Mortgagee may require on personal property, as herein referred to, and on all buildings and improvements on said premises, in companies to be approved by Mortgagee in an amount not less than the full insurable value of such personal property and improvements, or not less than the unpaid balance herein, whichever amount is smaller, with such in-surance payable to Mortgagors and Mortgagee, as their interests may appear. Mortgagors shall promptly deposit such policies with proper riders with the Mortgagee.

3. **REPAIRS TO PROPERTY.** Mortgagors shall keep the buildings and other improvements on said premises in as good repair and condition, as same may now be, or are hereafter placed, ordinary wear and tear only excepted; and shall not suffer or commit waste on or to said security.

4. **ATTORNEY'S FEES.** In case of any action, or in any proceedings in any court, to collect any sums payable or secured by this mortgage, to protect the lien of title herein of the Mortgagee, or in any other case permitted by law in which attorney fees may be col-lected from the Mortgagors, or charged upon the above described property, they agree to pay reasonable attorney fees.

5. **CONTINUATION OF ABSTRACT.** In event of any default herein by Mortgagors, Mortgagee may, at the expense of Mortgagors, procure an abstract of title, or continuation thereof, for said premises, and charge and add to the mortgage debt the cost of such abstract or continuation with interest upon such expense at the highest legal rate applicable to a natural person; or if the Mortgagor is a corporation, then at the default rate provided in the note secured hereby.

6. **ADVANCES OPTIONAL WITH MORTGAGEE.** It is expressly understood and agreed that if the insurance above provided for is not promptly effected, or if the taxes or special assessments assessed against said property shall become delinquent, Mortgagee (whether electing to declare the whole mortgage due and collectible or not), may (but need not) effect the insurance above provided for, and need not, but may and is hereby authorized to pay said taxes and special assessments (irregularities in the levy or assessment of said taxes being expressly waived), and all such payments with interest thereon at the highest legal rate applicable to a natural person (or, if the Mort-gagor is a corporation, then at the default rate provided in the note secured hereby) from time of payment shall be a lien against said premises.

7. ACCELERATION OF MATURITY AND RECEIVERSHIP. And it is agreed that if default shall be made in the payment of said note, or any part of the interest thereon, or any other advance or obligation which may be secured hereby or any agreed protective disbursement, such as taxes, special assessments, insurance and repairs, or if Mortgagors shall suffer or commit waste on or to said security, or if there shall be a failure to comply with any and every condition of this mortgage, then, at the option of the Mortgagee, said note and the whole of the indebtedness secured by this mortgage, including all payments for taxes, assessments or insurance premiums, shall become due and shall become collectible at once by foreclosure or otherwise after such default and, without notice of broken conditions; and at any time after the commencement of an action in foreclosure, or during the period of redemption, the court having jurisdiction of the case shall, at the request of the Mortgagee appoint a receiver to take immediate possession of said property, and of the rents and profits accruing therefrom, and to rent or cultivate the same as he may deem best for the interest of all parties concerned, and shall be liable to account to said Mortgagors only for the net profits, after application of rents, issues and profits upon the costs and expenses of the receivership and foreclosure and the indebtedness, charges and expenses hereby secured and herein mentioned. And it is hereby agreed, that after any default in the payment of either principal or interest such sums in default secured by this mortgage shall draw interest at the highest legal rate applicable to a natural person; or if the Mortgagor is a corporation then at the default rate provided in the note secured hereby.

8. DEFINITION OF TERMS. Unless otherwise expressly stated, the word "Mortgagors", as used herein, includes successors in interest of such "Mortgagors"; the word Mortgagee", as used herein, unless otherwise expressly stated includes the successors in interest of such "Mortgagee". All words referring to "Mortgagors" or "Mortgagee" shall be construed to be of the appropriate gender and number, according to the context. This construction shall include the acknowledgment hereof.

9. The address of the Mortgagee is_____
(Street and Number)

_____
| (City) | (State) | (Zip Code) | (See last sentence of Section 447.9 Code of Iowa.) |

10. ADDITIONAL PROVISIONS. The following additional provisions are hereby incorporated herein: **(Insert due date or due dates if desired)**[2] The principal obligation herein, the one promissory note above referred to is payable $_____ on _____ and $_____ on _____.

IN WITNESS WHEREOF, said Mortgagors have hereunto set their hands the day and year first above written.

_____

_____
Mortgagors

STATE OF IOWA, _____ COUNTY, ss:

On this_____day of_____, A. D. 19____, before me, the undersigned, a Notary Public in and for the State of Iowa, personally appeared_____

_____

to me known to be the identical persons named in and who executed the foregoing instrument, and acknowledged that they executed the same as their voluntary act and deed.

_____, Notary Public in and for the State of Iowa

[1]Only one original promissory note is contemplated with the use of this mortgage form.

[2]CONSIDER THE STATUTE OF LIMITATIONS. If this loan constitutes a long term transaction (over ten years), consider the advisability of making the maturity date or dates in the original note a matter of public record by insertion in this mortgage. See Iowa Land Title Examination Standards. Problems 10.4 and 10.5.

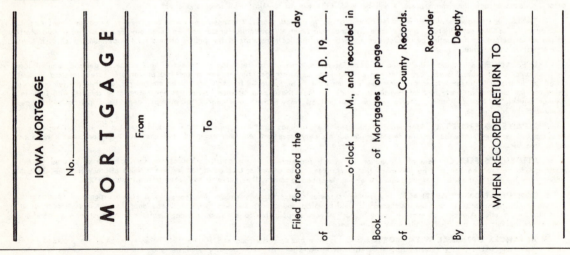

WARRANTY DEED

Know All Men by These Presents: That _____

_____

_____, in consideration✱

of the sum of _____

in hand paid do hereby **Convey** unto _____

_____

Grantees' Address: _____

the following described real estate, situated in _____ County, Iowa, to-wit:

And the grantors do **Hereby Covenant** with the said grantees, and successors in interest, that said grantors hold said real estate by title in fee simple; that they have good and lawful authority to sell and convey the same; that said premises are **Free and Clear of all Liens and Encumbrances Whatsoever** except as may be above stated; and said grantors Covenant to **Warrant and Defend** the said premises against the lawful claims of all persons whomsoever, except as may be above stated.

Each of the undersigned hereby relinquishes all rights of dower, homestead and distributive share in and to the described premises.

Words and phrases herein including acknowledgment hereof shall be construed as in the singular or plural number, and as masculine or feminine gender, according to the context.

Signed this_____day of_____, 19_____.

• Real Estate Transfer Tax: See (The Code, 1973, Chapter 428A)

STATE OF **IOWA**,

COUNTY OF _____ } ss.

On this_____day of_____, 19_____ before me, the undersigned, a Notary Public in and for the **State of Iowa**, personally appeared _____

_____

_____

(Grantors' address)

to me known to be the identical persons named in and who executed the foregoing instrument, and acknowledged that they executed the same as their voluntary act and deed.

_____

....Notary Public in and for the **State of Iowa**

Please type or print names under signatures as per Sec. 335.2 Code of Iowa

STATE OF_____, _____COUNTY, ss:

On this_____day of_____, 19____, before me, the undersigned, a Notary Public in and for said County and said State, personally appeared _____

_____

_____

to me known to be the identical persons named in and who executed the foregoing instrument, and acknowledged that they executed the same as their voluntary act and deed.

_____, Notary Public in and for said County and said State

STATE OF_____, _____COUNTY, ss:

On this_____day of_____, 19____, before me, the undersigned, a Notary Public in and for said County and said State, personally appeared _____

_____

_____

to me known to be the identical persons named in and who executed the foregoing instrument, and acknowledged that they executed the same as their voluntary act and deed.

_____, Notary Public in and for said County and said State

Warranty Deed

TO

Entered upon transfer books and for taxation this_____day of_____, 19___. _____Auditor By_____Deputy

Filed for record, indexed and delivered to County Auditor this_____day of_____, 19___. at_____o'clock_____M., and recorded in Book_____of_____, on page_____of_____County Records Recorder's and Auditor's Fee $_____PAID. _____Recorder By_____Deputy

WHEN RECORDED RETURN TO

Discussion Questions

1. What comprises a contract to purchase? Is it negotiable?

2. Mr. Citizen is having a new house built for him. Before the house is completed it is damaged by a tornado. Who is liable for the damages?

3. What is involved in getting a title for the land? What is a title abstract?

4. Discuss the advantages and disadvantages of joint tenancy and tenants in common.

5. Discuss the differences between a general warranty deed, a special warranty deed, and a quit claim deed.

6. What happens if the buyer defaults on a contract?

20. Financing the Home

Home Ownership

For most families, building or buying a house is the biggest investment of their lifetime; therefore, if you are thinking about home ownership and are typical of most prospective home owners, you should give consideration to the many economic factors involved.

Since home ownership is a savings investment which entails some costs, you should know something about these costs. You should know how much you can spend for housing and whether you can afford to invest in a home. You should also know the business procedures involved in home financing. Unless you have some knowledge of these matters before you develop your plans to build or buy, you may encounter disappointments.

This [article] presents general principles for financing a home. State laws and conditions vary so that some modification of the practices described on the following pages may be necessary in certain areas.

Financing Plan

Very few families have enough savings to pay for a home in a lump sum. Most of them have to borrow money to finance a home since the builder or the seller usually must be paid in full at the outset. They generally make a down payment from their savings and borrow the remainder.

The amount of down payment must be related 1) to the amount which can be borrowed, and 2) to the price of the house. The total amount available for a home, stated as a formula, is therefore:

Down payment + Amount you can borrow = Total amount
(Savings available *(Based on your ability* you can spend
for housing) *to repay)* for a home.

In setting up your financing plan, you must:

- Determine how much money you can pay as a down payment. This will be your initial **equity** (share) in the property.

    The down payment usually will take most of your savings earmarked for housing. Certain preliminary and other costs involved in arranging the loan and securing the property will also have to be covered by this portion of your

Issued by the Small Homes Council-Building Research Council, University of Illinois. Revised by the SHC-BRC staff from University of Illinois Bulletin Vol. 68, No. 24, September 30, 1970. Earlier editions by Russell M. Nolen. Used by permission. Update January, 1978 specially for this book.

savings. (Be sure you retain enough savings to meet family emergencies, such as sickness and unemployment.)

• Find someone who, on your promise to repay, will lend you the balance of the money needed. To secure the loan, you will give the lender a **mortgage** on your property (conditional title to the property as a pledge of repayment).

• Set up a plan to repay the money which you borrow. This repayment must include not only the amount of money borrowed **(principal),** but also **interest** on the money—rent, so to speak, for the use of the money.

Your repayment plan will be based on your budget allowance for housing—or the share of your monthly income set aside for housing. This allowance will probably be used for regular monthly payments to pay the interest and to repay the loan. Taxes and hazard insurance are sometimes included in the monthly payments. Your housing budget should also include provisions for maintenance and improvement.

Some loans are now being made with a **variable interest rate.** This encourages lending institutions to make long-term loans because their return on the loan is governed by changes in the money market rather than being fixed at the original rate. A common proposal is to relate the interest rate charged on the loan to the Federal Reserve discount rate, which is the rate at which banks can borrow money from the Federal Reserve System. For the protection of the consumer, several safeguards should be included in the variable interest rate mortgage contract. These include a maximum increase in the interest rate over the life of the loan (perhaps 2%), and a maximum rate of increase in the interest rate (perhaps limited to ½ of 1% in each 6-month period). Also, the borrower should have the option of refinancing the loan at any time of interest rate increase without penalty. Similarly, if the Federal Reserve discount rate decreases, the decrease must be reflected in the variable interest rate within similar limits.

Necessary Outlay for Home Ownership

Expenses involved in home ownership and financing vary greatly. They depend on the rate of repayment of the loan, and on interest rate, taxes, insurance, and the cost of maintenance and improvement. These expenses must be met when due.

Loan and Interest

Every cent of interest which you pay on borrowed money is an expense, although it may be an income tax deduction if deductions are itemized. The less you pay in interest, the better is your home ownership investment. You can reduce interest costs through:

• *A low interest rate.* Obtain the lowest rate possible on the basis of your record as a credit risk.

• *A large down payment.* The greater the down payment, the greater is your equity in the property and the less you will have to borrow. As a result, your total interest costs are less. Sometimes a large down payment also permits the lender to set a lower interest rate since the risk is reduced.

• *A short payment period.* The more you pay each month, the shorter period of time you will have to pay and, hence, the less total interest you will pay.

• *A loan which permits prepayment* (payment in advance of the due date).

Example		
Amount of loan: $40,000		Interest rate: 9%
	20-year loan	30-year loan
Monthly payment	$359.90	$321.88
Total payment	$86,380.80	$115,876.80
Difference in monthly payments	=	$38.04
Difference in total payments (due to interest charges)	=	$29,496.00

Because a long-term loan requires smaller monthly payments than a short-term one, it is usually best to secure a relatively long-term loan which permits prepayment without penalty. This assures moderate monthly payments and allows you to pay faster if your earnings permit. If you pay off the loan as quickly as possible, you will save interest costs; you will also build up your equity in the property faster.

Property Taxes

Tax rates on real property vary widely in different localities. Find out your rates from your local officials or a lending agency. Assessments for civic improvements may be added to your tax bill. Taxes tend to increase over the years.

Hazard Insurance

To protect their mortgage loan on the investment, lending agencies require you to carry fire, wind, and other insurance on your property. Your policy should also provide enough insurance to protect your equity. See your insurance agent for detailed information.

Mortgage Insurance

Mortgage insurance protects the lender against loss on the loan. Borrowers under FHA programs pay ½ of 1% of the amount outstanding on the loan as a mortgage insurance premium. In addition to the federal program, there are a number of private companies offering mortgage insurance. On a mortgage where a down payment of less than 25 or 30% is made, the lender may require the borrower to carry mortgage insurance in addition to or instead of FHA insurance until the outstanding amount of the loan is reduced to a specific percentage of the value of the property. Private mortgage insurance premiums may vary from ½ of 1% to 1% on the outstanding loan.

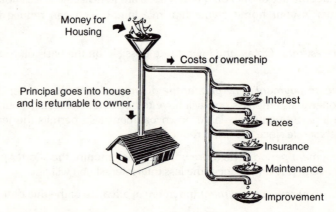

Maintenance and Improvement

On new homes, maintenance costs will be low for the first few years, but they will become greater as the house grows older. It is much easier to save for major maintenance items such as painting, roofing, furnace replacement, and other such major items than to be confronted with a large bill in one year, or to obtain secondary financing for these maintenance items.

Some people can reduce maintenance costs by doing much of the work themselves. Their costs being less, they can finance a larger loan. Neglecting maintenance in order to stay within an over-optimistic budget is not wise, since neglect usually results in greater maintenance costs later.

Other Expenses—Preliminary, Extra

Preliminary Costs

Certain expenses which are "preliminary" to the loan must be budgeted before the size of the down payment can be determined. These expenses vary, depending on whether you are buying or building a home. Some of them may be included in the loan; others must be paid in cash at the time the loan is made. Occasionally some of these expenses are paid by the seller of the property.

When buying a home, preliminary costs usually include:

Appraisal fees.

Loan fees, if any, of your lending agency.

Revenue stamps, notary fees.

Fees for recording the mortgage and the deed to the property.

Legal charges for examining and transferring the title to the property (to show clear ownership).

Pro rata insurance and property taxes (that portion of the taxes and insurance already paid by the seller for which you must reimburse him).

Engineer's survey of property, if needed to establish property lines.

When building a home, preliminary costs include most of those for buying a house, plus such costs as:

Cost of plans or architectural services.

Interest on the loan advances ("pay-outs") to contractors.

Premiums for insurance (fire, theft, hazard and liability, depending on your agreement with your contractor).

Inspection fees.

Typical Transaction

Total funds available for purchase of house		$59,500
Cost distribution		
Closing costs	$ 2,250	
Cost of lot	10,000	
Actual cost of house	47,250	
Total		$59,500
Fund requirements:		
Closing costs	$2,250	
Down payment	5,725	
Required cash on hand		$ 7,975
Face amount of mortgage		51,525
Total		$59,500

In "FHA loans," there are usually certain additional preliminary expenses, such as: 1) the first month's mortgage insurance premium; 2) an advance payment for a pro rata share of the first year's taxes; 3) the first year's premium on hazard insurance; 4) fees for photographs of the house; and 5) FHA loan examination fee. The examination fee is paid when the application for the loan is made; the other items must be paid when the loan is closed.

Extra Costs

In building or buying a home, you may find it necessary to incur certain other expenses, such as landscaping, laundry and kitchen equipment (or repair or modernization if an existing house has been purchased). These expenses must be paid for from your savings unless they are included in the loan.

For Satisfactory Home Financing

- Borrow as little as necessary, instead of as much as you can.

- Do not overbuild or overbuy. If you spend more for housing than your budget will support, you may have to forego necessities as well as comforts. You may even be obliged to sell your property at a loss—or you may lose it. It may be desirable to have a lending agency check your estimate of the amount you can spend for housing, and also advise you on financing the home before you sign any agreement or contract.

- Remember a loan on a home is a serious obligation. It is up to you to tailor your expenditures so that they are in line with the financing charges which you assume. You should expect some changes in income over the years.

- Seek legal advice if you have any doubts about any phase of home financing or ownership—i.e., legality of the title, conditions of the loan, the terms of the general contract, the agreement on occupancy.

Obtaining the Loan

A mortgage loan on a house entails a risk to both the lending agency which advances the money, and to the prospective home owner who promises a large part of his income for a period of years in payment for the house.

In return for its risk, the lending agency has a legal claim to the house for security until the loan is repaid; the home owner, on the other hand, has the use of the house and the promise of eventually owning it free of debt. Both the lending agency and the home owner therefore are interested in the house until the loan is paid in full.

Because of the long-time investment involved, the house, to be a good risk for both the home owner and the lending agency, must be so located, designed, and constructed that it will retain a value well in excess of the loan balance for not only the period of the loan, but longer. The risk of depreciation (or depression in the value) of the property must be assumed by the home owner.

Home financing is a mutual program as far as the home owner and the lender are concerned. To avoid loss to either or both, the home must be financed on a sound basis. A sound mortgage is one in which 1) the prospective home owner's credit record indicates that he will be able to make the loan payments; and 2) if unforeseen events occur which prevent the home owner from making his payments, the value of the house at that time will be sufficient to satisfy the unpaid balance of the loan (the mortgage debt).

A foreclosure is not desired by either the lending agency or the home owner.

The Lending Agency

The lending agency's "stock in trade" is money—not property. Its funds usually represent savings of individuals for which the lending agency is acting as a trustee. These savings must be protected. The lending agency, therefore, does not want to take over property any more than the home owner wants to lose it. The agency wants only to receive interest on its money while it is being used and to have the money returned.

The Home Owner

To obtain a loan, the prospective home owner must establish himself as an approved credit risk. He must assure the lending agency that his income (earning capacity) and his reputation for paying debts warrant a loan being made to him. His credit record also is an important consideration in determining the amount of the loan which can be made.

In obtaining any loan, the home owner should make a point of understanding thoroughly every detail—i.e., how much he must pay, when he must pay it, and exactly what property he is pledging as security. He must recognize as a serious responsibility his obligation to pay back the cash he is borrowing.

Types of Mortgage Loans

Mortgage loans are classified by the plan for repaying the loan. There are several types, but the one most commonly used today is the **constant payment plan** (the regular amortized mortgage loan).

Under this systematic loan reduction plan, the home owner at regular intervals (usually each month) pays a fixed amount which includes both interest and payment on the loan principal. The monthly payment is the same during the life of the loan. That part of the monthly payment which is used to repay the loan principal increases each month since the amount paid for interest decreases. (Interest payments become less as the loan principal becomes less.)

For example: A home owner borrows $35,000 at 8½% interest on a 25-year loan. His monthly payments are $281.84 for a period of 25 years. The interest the first month on the $35,000 will be $247.92. The payment on the principal will thus be $33.92 making the unpaid balance $34,966.08. The interest in the second month will be 1/12 of 8½% on the $34,966.08 or $247.68. This leaves $34.16 to be paid on the loan principal, making the unpaid balance $34,931.92. In this manner, payments continue to reduce the loan so that at the end of 25 years the loan is repaid.

Taxes and property insurance premiums may be included in the regular monthly payment. These are in addition to the interest and loan payments. If taxes should increase, these monthly payments would increase.

A variation of the regular amortized mortgage plan is the open-end plan. A clause in the mortgage gives the borrower the privilege of obtaining additional funds (for purposes such as remodeling) after the loan has been reduced without going through the formality of rewriting the mortgage. The total loan outstanding at any time is usually restricted to the amount of the original loan.

Other amortized mortgage plans permit increasing payments or decreasing payments each month. These are not in common use.

Another type of mortgage is the straight mortgage. It is used less today than formerly. This plan requires that the loan be paid in full on a specified date (usually one to five years). Interest is paid at stated periods. (The terms of the loan may permit prepayment.)

FHA and VA Loans

Frequent reference is made to "FHA loans" and "GI or VA loans." These are not mortgage plans, but are government insurance or guarantees on loans. The government does not provide the money for the loans; the funds come from the lending agencies through which home owners obtain loans. The government merely sets up credit and building standards which, if met, permit the loan to be insured by the FHA (Federal Housing Administration) or guaranteed in part by the VA (Veterans Administration).

FHA borrowers underwrite the insurance since each pays 1/2 of 1% of the amount outstanding on his loan into a common insurance pool each year. This pool covers any loss and may pay dividends to the borrowers if losses are small. This FHA insurance premium is included in the borrower's monthly payments. GI borrowers pay no insurance fee on VA guaranteed loans.

The insurance and guarantee features of FHA and VA loans liberalize home financing since they protect lenders against loss, thereby reducing the large margins of security which lending agencies set up to protect themselves. Lenders thus are induced to make larger loans in relation to the value of a house than they could without the guarantee. Since most lenders are trustees for other people's savings, either a safe margin of security or government assurance against loss is necessary.

Package Loans

Often when a family buys a newly completed house from a contractor or enters into a contract for the building of a home, the financing has been previously arranged by the contractor who offers a "package" loan. Under it, the buyer pays a regular amount monthly over a period of years. This includes payment on the loan principal, interest, taxes, insurance. If you should assume a "package" loan, make sure you understand its terms.

Where to Go for a Loan

Every mortgage transaction involves individual problems of financing. Seek advice about loans from reliable lending agencies before you obligate yourself in any way. Established sources of loans (listed alphabetically) include:

- Banks (commercial and savings).
- Mortgage bankers who represent individuals, banks, insurance companies or other institutional investors.
- Savings and loan associations (or building and loan associations).
- Title and trust companies who may loan their own funds.

Having decided on home ownership and a specific piece of property (either an existing house, or land on which to build a house), you should consult one or more reliable lending agencies in your community about a possible loan. Explain your problem, investigate their terms, ask questions, and talk the matter through in detail. Remember that lending agencies are in competition with each other just as any other business firm. Try to find the agency that will give you the type of loan that best meets your requirements.

Information Needed

To evaluate the loan plans offered by various lending agencies you must have certain information. Ask the agencies questions such as:

- *How soon can I get the loan?* (FHA and VA loans may take longer than others.)

- *What are the terms of the loan?* What are the interest rates? How many years will the loan run? Can this period be extended at a later date? Approximately what will be the total amount of interest? What is the amount of monthly payments? Is there a period of grace? Is there a penalty for failure to pay on time?

- *What method of paying taxes do you require?* Do I pay my own taxes? Can tax money be included in the monthly payments?

- *Is a monthly deposit of funds required to pay insurance?* What kind of insurance must I carry? How much?

- *Are there prepayment privileges?* If so, on what basis can I make payments in advance of the amount due as stated in the loan contract? Is there any penalty for advance payments? Can I pay off the loan in full prior to its maturity? Will prepayments be credited as regular payments at a future time if I wish this? In case of prepayments, will I pay interest only on the balance due?

- *When are the payments due?* Do I receive notification of due date?

- *What "preliminary" costs will I have?* What will they amount to? When do they have to be paid? Can they be included in the loan?

- *Can my "extra" costs be included in the loan?*

Construction Loans

If you are going to build a house, you will probably need money to pay your builder as construction progresses. If so, ask lending agencies whether you can get money for these advance pay-outs to your builder. Find out the charges for such a construction loan. Ask:

- *At what stages of the construction can I get the money?* Can I arrange these construction loan advances and my final mortgage as one contract? Who will handle the entire payments to the builder (my funds as well as those loaned to me)?

- *What inspection, if any, is provided as a check that my house will be built according to specifications?* Or, is it my responsibility to have inspections made by an architect or other qualified person?

Consult a lending agency on the *possibility* of obtaining a loan before you incur large expenses for plans, working drawings and specifications. Later, when the possibility of getting a loan is assured, you will need plans and specifications so that the amount of the loan can be determined.

Applying for a Loan

Having found a loan plan which meets your needs, you are now ready to make application for a loan. This is your formal request for the loan from the lending agency which you have selected.

Application

Information generally asked for in application forms includes:

- The amount of loan you want.

- The terms and conditions of the loan requested (including whether a GI or FHA loan is desired).

- Personal data so that the lending agency may judge your credit responsibility. This information will include credit references, current income, current obligations, possible future expenses.

• Identification and description of the property on which you want the loan and which you will pledge as security.

Investigation

On the basis of the application form, the lending agency will verify: 1) the personal information submitted, 2) the fact that you have—or will have—the property described, and 3) your right to pledge the property as security.

Property Appraisal

The lending agency before granting the loan must form an opinion as to the value of the property described. This is a point which can present misunderstandings since the borrower's appraisal and the appraisal of the lending agency may not agree. For this reason, the latter's valuation is generally not revealed to the borrower.

The lending agency's appraisal is not on a man's house as property on the current market, but as security. It represents the market value of the property during the life of the loan if the house should ever be sold. It does not recognize the high prices of homes in inflationary periods, nor does it recognize special usefulness to a particular homeowner. The property might cost a great deal and be very desirable to one family, but it might not have an appeal to other people should it be offered for sale. (In a GI loan transaction, the price of the property cannot exceed the VA appraisal.)

Factors which determine the desirability of the property over a period of time and, as a result, the lending agency's appraisal are:

• The location as regards community and neighborhood. (Before buying a lot, check the location with respect to resale value.)

• Size of property (both lot and house).

• Physical soundness of the structure.
• Desirability of the architectural design of the house.

If a construction loan is desired, these points are judged by plans, working drawings and specifications.

Decision as to the Amount of the Loan

After investigating your credit rating and appraising the property to be financed, the lending agency tells you how much it can lend.

If you cannot obtain the amount of the loan you need from the first lending agency you interview, try another reliable agency. If this application does not result in the desired loan, re-examine your proposal to see what is wrong with it. It may be that your house is too individual in its design, or that it may not retain its value because of its location, or that your earning capacity is not great enough to carry the amount of the loan you need.

In an FHA loan, the appraisal of the Federal Housing Administration determines the amount of the loan which it will insure.

Letter of Commitment

Usually, before the loan is formally granted, the lending agency will issue a letter of commitment in which the terms of the mortgage are outlined. This enables you to make contracts with an architect and contractors, and also to proceed with arrangements to purchase property. Be careful about making any payments until your lending agency has definitely committed itself to granting the loan.

Closing the Loan

After the loan has been approved, title records of the property must be examined. Certain papers must be signed in order to "close the loan." At that time: 1) you are usually required to make your down payment (or to pay the rest of it if you have already paid part) and to pay the preliminary costs; and 2) funds are turned over to you by the lending agency so that you can complete your purchase. Documents you will sign are:

- *The note or bond*—The promise to repay the money borrowed.

- *The mortgage*—The pledge of property to secure your promise that you will repay the principal and also pay the interest.

- *Affidavits and receipts* relating to the above two documents.

In these papers, you will be referred to as the mortgagor; the lending agency as the mortgagee. Before signing any of these documents, you should read them carefully, making sure that you understand them thoroughly. If you do not, ask questions or consult your attorney. Documents usually involved in the closing of a loan are described in the chart below.

Documents	Purpose	Provisions	Holder	Remarks
Note or Bond	The promise to repay the money borrowed.	Sets forth: •Amount of loan. •Conditions of the promise to repay.	Lending agency until loan is repaid.	You should have a copy.
Mortgage	Pledge of property to secure the promise to repay.	•Sets forth conditions under which you pledge the property as security. •Gives lender the power to acquire the property if you fail to repay the loan as agreed.	Lending agency until loan is repaid in full. That the loan has been discharged is then entered on the public records.	You should have a copy.
Deed* (to the property)	Evidence of ownership.	Presents evidence that you own the property.	In some states, the deed with revenue stamps on it is recorded and given to you; in others, it may be held in trust by a third party (in escrow) until the loan is repaid.	•Deed should be recorded by county register-of-deeds. •You should have either the deed or a copy of it.
Certificate of Title* (or Opinion of Title)†	Assurance that title to property is unmistakably in your name.	Declares that the title to the property is "clear" or "marketable"—that is, no one else has claim to the property except you. (It is derived from the abstract.)	You, the home owner. (This is usually given you with the deed.)	•Be sure the title is investigated. •Title search is usually arranged for by lending agency. Certificate is prepared by an attorney or by a title company.
Abstract†	Legal description of property and history of previous ownerships.	Describes property and all transactions back to grant from United States government. (It is prepared by an abstract company and checked by an attorney.)	Lending agency until loan is paid in full.	•If you have a certificate of title, you probably will not get the abstract. •The abstract should have the deed and mortgage recorded on it.
Fire Insurance Policy	For protection of loan on property and your equity.	Is written in your name with a mortgage clause attached.	Lending agency.	•You should have a copy. •Be sure amount of insurance is sufficient to protect your equity.

* Where the Torrens system is used, deed and title procedures differ.
† Title insurance may be advisable. For one premium, your claim to ownership is protected as long as you own the property.

Assuming an Existing Mortgage

If you are considering the purchase of a house with an existing mortgage, be certain that you understand the terms of the loan as previously made, as well as the terms of the purchase contract. Weigh these terms against your budget allowance for housing to make sure that you are financially able to handle the obligations.

In assuming such existing indebtedness, have the papers examined by someone who is qualified to advise you. Be particularly cautious on the matter of when actual ownership is conveyed to you. As evidence that you have paid your money and own the property, you should possess the deed and the opinion of clear title.

Discount Rate or "Points"

The limit for interest rates permitted on mortgages is controlled by law in most states. When this limit is lower than prevailing mortgage rates, the loan may be discounted in order to achieve the desired effective interest rate. That is, the lender pays out less than the face amount of the loan to the seller of the house. The amount of the reduction, or discount rate, may vary from zero to 15%.

At times when interest rates are high, legal limits on mortgage interest rates may penalize home buyers. It is sometimes better for the borrower if the interest rate is higher and the loan is made without a discount. Discounts, unlike interest costs, are not tax deductible and can never be reduced through prepayment or refinancing. Since the discount is payable when the loan is made, the true cost of borrowing is significantly higher than the basic interest rate. For instance, if the discount rate is 5% or "5 points," the amount of money given to the seller will be 95% of the face amount of the mortgage, or $950 per $1,000 of mortgage. If a 8%, 20-year loan, which was discounted 5% is held to maturity, the true annual interest cost will be 9.2%. If, however, the mortgage is paid off at the end of 5 years, the true annual interest increases to 9.6%.

The discount should not be confused with the lender's commission or loan fee, which is included in the closing costs (page 223).

What Can You Pay for Housing?

Housing is one of the largest items in the family budget. For most families, it will take 20-35% of their net income, either in rent or in ownership.

No formula can be established for determining exactly how much a family can afford to spend for a home. Low-income groups must spend a large part of their budget for housing, food, and clothing. As the annual income increases, the family has greater freedom to choose the amounts to be spent for such things as housing, cars, and recreation, or to be kept as savings.

Modifying Factors

Your budget allowance may be modified by certain factors:

Two families having the same income may allot entirely different amounts for a home. Factors such as stable employment or a large savings for a down payment might enable a family with an annual income of $18,000 to spend up to $54,000 for a home. Another family having the same income might spend more for a car, or for vacations and entertainment, leaving less income for home ownership.

- A family with a number of children has greater requirements for food, clothing, and medical care, and often less income remains for home ownership than in a smaller family. Sometimes, however, large families make greater use of the home for recreation, and therefore can budget more for housing than can a small family which is "never at home."

There are three alternative methods of determining a budget for housing:

- The first, easiest, and least accurate is the "rule of thumb" often used, which is "you can afford a home costing an amount equal to 2½ times your gross annual income." This would require a 20-35% of the take home pay for housing, including taxes, insurance, maintenance, improvement, and utilities.

- The second, and somewhat more accurate, method is to determine how much you are paying now for housing. This figure can then be adjusted up or down, depending upon how your present expenses are fitting into your budget.

- The third, and most accurate, method is to analyze your expenses and income, and determine on the basis of a budget how much of your income is available for housing. A general family budget can be figured by filling in the blanks below. The amounts can be either on a monthly or a yearly basis.

    If you want to put more income into your home, you probably can do so by cutting down on some other items in the family budget, such as recreational expenses. Do not, however, consider making major changes in your living patterns.

Food and Clothing	$ _____	**Total Net Income** $ _____
Medical Care	$ _____	(Take-home Pay)
Life Insurance		Minus Total Living Ex-
and Savings	$ _____	penses Other Than Housing $ _____
Recreation	$ _____	
Transportation (including		**Income Available**
Cars)	$ _____	**for Housing** $ _____
Installment Payments	$ _____	Minus Estimated Utilities
Other Family Expenses	$ _____	for the New House $ _____
Total Living Expenses		BUDGET FOR HOME
Other Than Housing	$ _____	OWNERSHIP $ _____

    The table on page 232 shows the major expenditures in financing a home after the down payment and preliminary or closing costs are paid.

    The payments on the loan and the interest charges are fixed according to the interest rate and the period of payment. They are based on a systematic loan reduction plan (constant monthly payment plan).

    For the purpose of the table, the expenses per year for every $1,000 loaned on the house are assumed to be $25 for taxes and assessments, $5 for insurance, and $25 for maintenance and improvement.

    Insurance costs per $1,000 of current replacement cost will probably be about the same over the years, but will change as replacement costs change. Taxes and cost of maintenance and improvement will vary in different sections of the country. They have been estimated at a reasonable average here because experience has shown that many people do not allow enough for these items. The figures should be adjusted where modifications are known.

PAYMENT PERIOD	8% INTEREST			9% INTEREST			10% INTEREST		
	20 Years	25 Years	30 Years	20 Years	25 Years	30 Years	20 Years	25 Years	30 Years
Interest and Payment on Each $1,000 of Loan per Year (based on a systematic loan reduction plan)	$ 100	$ 93	$ 88	$ 108	$ 101	$ 97	$ 116	$ 109	$ 105
Taxes and Assessments	25	25	25	25	25	25	25	25	25
Insurance	5	5	5	5	5	5	5	5	5
Maintenance and Improvement	25	25	25	25	25	25	25	25	25
Total Annual Outlay on Each $1,000 Borrowed*	$ 155	$ 148	$ 143	$163	$ 156	$ 152	$ 171	$ 164	$ 160
Total Interest to Maturity on Each $1,000 Borrowed	$1007	$1315	$1642	$1160	$1520	$1898	$1318	$1727	$2138

*To determine the total annual outlay for home ownership, multiply this figure by the loan in thousands of dollars, and add $55 per year for each $1,000 down payment, since taxes, assessments, maintenance, and improvement apply to the total value of the house, not just the amount borrowed.

How Expensive a Home Can You Afford?

Having determined your budget for home ownership, and the annual cost of home ownership for each $1,000 of the loan, you can now estimate the total amount which you can spend for a home. The chart on page 233 shows the total price of the house that your monthly budget allowance for housing will finance (principal, interest, taxes, insurance, maintenance, and improvement) at the different interest rates and the different terms of payments. It is based on the previous table which showed the major expenditures in financing a home.

You must pay taxes and insurance and set aside money for maintenance and improvement on the total value of the house, including both the mortgage amount and your down payment. The table includes the taxes, insurance, maintenance, and improvement on the mortgage amount only. For each $1,000 down payment, you will have deducted approximately $4.50 per month or $54 per year for taxes, insurance, maintenance, and improvement from your budget for home ownership to find your "budget allowance for mortgage." The taxes and insurance are sometimes added to your monthly payments, and the lending agency pays your insurance and taxes for you, in order to be sure these items are paid. The maintenance and improvement expenses are not a part of the mortgage payment, but should be set aside for major projects.

To use the table, find your "budget allowance for mortgage," in either the monthly or annual column on page 233. Then read across to the rate of interest which you can obtain and the number of years the loan will run. This figure will give you the amount of the mortgage loan which your budget can finance. Add the amount of the down payment which you can make, and you will have an estimate of the total cost of the home you can afford. (The amount of the loan which you can obtain may be much less.)

BUDGET ALLOWANCE FOR MORTGAGE		AMOUNT OF MORTGAGE WHICH BUDGET WILL FINANCE									DOWN PAYMENT (after closing costs)	TOTAL AMOUNT YOU CAN SPEND FOR A HOME
		8% Interest			9% Interest			10% Interest				
Monthly	Annual	20 Years	25 Years	30 Years	20 Years	25 Years	30 Years	20 Years	25 Years	30 Years		
$100	$1,200	$7,740	$8,110	$8,390	$7,360	$7,690	$7,890	$7,020	$7,320	$7,500		
120	1,500	9,680	10,140	10,490	9,200	9,620	9,870	8,770	9,150	9,380		
150	1,800	11,610	12,160	12,590	11,040	11,540	11,840	10,530	10,980	11,250		
175	2,100	13,550	14,190	14,685	12,880	13,460	13,820	12,280	12,800	13,125		
200	2,400	15,480	16,220	16,780	14,720	15,380	15,790	14,040	14,630	15,000		
225	2,700	17,420	18,240	18,880	16,560	17,310	17,760	15,780	16,460	16,880		
250	3,000	19,350	20,270	20,980	18,400	19,230	19,740	17,540	18,290	18,750		
300	3,600	23,230	24,320	25,170	22,090	23,080	23,680	21,050	21,950	22,500		
350	4,200	27,100	28,380	29,370	25,770	26,920	27,630	24,560	25,610	26,250		
400	4,800	30,970	32,430	33,570	29,450	30,770	31,580	28,070	29,270	30,000		
450	5,400	34,840	36,490	37,760	33,130	34,620	35,530	31,580	32,930	33,750		
500	6,000	38,710	40,540	41,960	36,810	38,460	39,470	35,090	36,590	37,500		

Examples

1. Mr. W's budget shows $390 per month "allowance for home ownership." He has $8,000 for a down payment after allowing for preliminary costs. He can get a 8% loan for 25 years. How much can he spend for a home?

First, he must allow $4.58 a month per $1,000 down payment for taxes, insurance, maintenance, and improvement, a total of about $40 per month. This leaves $350 as his budget allowance for mortgage. Read down the column, "Budget Allowance for Mortgage" to $350 a month, and across to the column "8% interest — 25 years" to find $28,380. This is the amount of mortgage his budget will finance. Add $8,000 (down payment) to $28,380. This makes the total cost of the property which he can pay for and maintain $36,380.

2. Mr. H. wants to buy property selling for $38,000. He has $10,000 down payment after closing costs, and will borrow the remainder at 9% for 30 years. How much of his income must be set aside to cover the cost of ownership?

From $38,000, subtract $10,000. This leaves $28,000, the amount of loan required. According to the table under "9% interest — 30 years," a $28,000 loan requires about $350 per month or $4,200 per year as the budget allowance for mortgage. To determine the total cost of home ownership, he must remember to set aside approximately $50 per month for taxes, insurance, maintenance, and improvement on that portion of the property represented by his $10,000 down payment, since these items are not included elsewhere. His total for home ownership will then be $400 per month. Adding the estimated utilities will give the total monthly budget for housing.

Addendum Defining the Alternative Mortgage Instruments

by Carol S. Wedin

There has been a growing concern over the past several years that the standard mortgage with a fixed term is not flexible enough to meet the needs of home owners during successive phases of their financial life cycles. The Federal Home Loan Bank Board (FHLBB) proposed major changes as far back as 1972. The initial proposals for new mortgage designs were met with opposition from some congressional committees as well as labor unions and consumer groups. The resistance weakened as the cost of housing continued to spiral upwards and the cost and availability of mortgage credit made it more difficult for young families to purchase a home.

In 1978, after several years of experimentation with alternative mortgage instuments (AMIs), the FHLBB authorized these new types of mortgage instruments for use by federal savings and loan associations: the variable-rate mortgage, rollover mortgage, graduated-payment mortgage, and reverse-annuity mortgage.

Although the standard fixed-rate, level-payment mortgage is expected to continue to remain the most common, many borrowers want and need a choice of home finance arrangements. The availability of AMIs will allow greater flexibility for home owners to meet their financial needs with appropriate mortgage instruments.

To alert readers to the various options now available to home owners, definitions of AMIs are presented in the following paragraphs.

Variable-rate mortgage. The interest rate of this instrument is tied to a reference index which reflects changes in market interest rates; thus, actual future payments are not known at the time of loan origination. (The variable interest rate mortgage contract is briefly discussed on page 221.)

Rollover mortgage. This instrument is a long-term loan which is refinanced at regularly scheduled times. Any adjustments of interest rate or other terms of the loan at refinancing would be without administrative fees to the borrower.

Graduated-payment mortgage. This instrument's scheduled payments begin at a level lower than that of a comparable standard mortgage instrument. Payments gradually rise until a predetermined point is reached, after which they remain constant. The graduation period and rate of increase and the interest rate are fixed at loan origination. This design is particularly attractive to young families buying their first homes. *Reverse-annuity mortgage.* This instrument provides periodic payments to home owners based on accumulated equity; the payments are made directly by the lender or through purchase of an annuity from an insurance company. The loan becomes due either upon a specific date or when a specified event occurs, such as the sale of the property or death of the borrower. The reversed-annuity mortgage can enable retired couples to use the equity in their homes and live in them at the same time.

It is cautioned, however, that the availability of AMIs will depend on the lending institution (i.e., a federally chartered association or a state chartered association). Besides the federally chartered savings and loan associations there are some state chartered savings and loan associations as well as mutual savings banks that use AMIs.

References

Federal Home Loan Bank Board. *Regulations Authorizing Alternative Mortgage Instruments for Federally Chartered Associations.* Washington, D.C.: December 1978.

Kaplan, Donald M. "Alternative Mortgage Instruments: A Summary of AMIRS Findings, Conclusions." *The MGIC Newsletter,* Milwaukee Mortgage Guaranty Insurance Corporation, May 1978.

Discussion Questions

1. Discuss the difference between variable interest rate and fixed interest rate.

2. Define the following terms: equity, mortgage, principal, open-end mortgage plan, prepayment mortgage plan, and package loans.

3. What lending agencies loan money for residential buildings?

4. Who provides the money for FHA and VA loans?

5. What is meant by "preliminary costs"? Give specific examples.

6. Discuss the purposes of the following documents: note, mortgage, deed, certificate of title, and abstract.

7. Why is it impossible to use a specific formula to determine how much a family should spend on housing?

8. Define the ways you can reduce interest cost and explain how this works.

21. Home Warranties

by Carol S. Wedin

For most people, purchasing a home is serious business and can be a frightening experience. The legal and financial implications are confusing and bewildering. The new home owner frequently discovers that there is greater consumer protection with the purchase of a new $25 radio than with the purchase of a $50,000 house. Historically, the principle of *caveat emptor* has applied to the purchase of real property. *Caveat emptor* means "let the buyer beware." In other words, it is up to the buyer to know exactly what he or she is getting and what the warranty covers.

New Warranty Legislation

By definition, we would expect a warranty to be a "guarantee of the integrity of a product and of the maker's responsibility for the repair or replacement of defective parts."[1] While the consumer has been receiving more assurance of protection on many products, this has not held true on houses. The Magnuson-Moss Warranty Act passed by Congress on January 3, 1975, establishes federal standards for "consumer product" warranties. The act was written primarily to curb alleged abuses in automobile and appliance warranties. Although the act was not specifically written for new housing, it does affect warranties on new homes.

The act sets strict standards for all warranties covering consumer products. It defines consumer products as follows:

> The term "consumer product" means any tangible personal property which is distributed in commerce and which is normally used for personal, family, or household purposes (including any such property intended to be attached to or installed in any real property without regard to whether it is so attached or installed).[2]

The Federal Trade Commission (FTC) has been granted the power to make rules to enforce the terms. In the case of housing there is a frequent question as to what is real property and what is personal property. Real property has been defined as the land and, generally, whatever is erected, growing upon, or affixed to the land.[3] Personal property has been defined as everything that is subject to ownership and not coming under the domination of real estate.[4] The Magnuson-Moss Warranty Act redefines for

1. Henry B. Woolf, ed., *Webster's New Collegiate Dictionary* (Springfield, Mass.: G&C Merriam Company, 1974), p. 1320.
2. Kenneth C. Peters, "How the Magnuson-Moss Warranty Act Affects the Builder/Sellers of New Housing," *Real Estate Law Journal* 5 (1977), pp. 338-363.
3. Maurice A. Unger, *Real Estate Principles and Practices* (Cincinnati: South-Western Publishing Company, Inc., 1969), p. 17.
4. *Ibid.*, p. 52.

warranty purposes what has been the distinction between real estate and personal property by the courts for years. Because a new house comprises some 5,000 components, it becomes extremely difficult to sort out consumer and nonconsumer products. Some items which are attached or built into a home are regarded as consumer products under the FTC interpretation of the act. For example, a thermostat is considered a consumer product while a radiator is not a consumer product. Listed in Table 1 are some of the consumer products and nonconsumer products found in a new house. This listing of products is only a partial list to give the reader an understanding of the complexity of home warranties. Moreover, the FTC can change the rules from time to time.

The Magnuson-Moss Warranty Act does not require home builders or anyone else to provide warranties. It does, however, set standards that must be met if warranties on consumer products are offered. Also, builders who choose to make no consumer product warranties must comply with the requirement that manufacturer's warranties

Table 1. Typical consumer products and products not considered as such when sold as part of a new home covered by the Magnuson-Moss Warranty Act

Items considered as consumer products

Heating and Ventilation	**Mechanical/Electrical**	**Appliances**
Boiler	Central vacuum system	Refrigerator
Heat pump	Smoke detector	Freezer
Electronic air cleaner	Fire alarm	Trash compactor
Exhaust fan	Fire extinguisher	Range
Thermostat	Garage door opener	Oven
Space heater	Chimes	Kitchen center
Furnace	Water pump	Dishwasher
Air conditioning system	Intercom	Oven hood
Humidifier	Burglar alarm	Clothes washer
	Electric meter	Clothes dryer
Plumbing	Water meter	Ice maker
Whirlpool bath	Gas meter	
Garbage disposal	Gas or electric barbecue grill	
Water heater		
Water softener		
Sump pump		

Items not considered as consumer products

Heating and Ventilation	**Plumbing**	**Miscellaneous Items**
Radiator	Sprinkler head	Cabinet
Convector	Water closet	Door
Register	Bidet	Shelving
Duct	Lavatory	Window
	Bathtub	Floor covering (includes
Mechanical/Electrical	Laundry tray	carpeting, linoleum, etc.)
Garage door	Sink	Wall or wall covering
Electrical switch and outlet	Shower stall	Ceiling
Light fixture	Plumbing fittings (shower	Vanity
Electric panel box	head, faucet, trap,	Gutter
Fuse	escutcheon, and drain)	Shingle
Circuit breaker	Medicine cabinet	Chimney and fireplace
Wiring		Fencing

Source: Adapted from Garen Bresnic, "Consumer Comes Home: A Look at the New Federal Warranty Act." In *Bay State Builder,* April 1977, pp. 12, 13.

must be made readily available to the home buyer. For example, the manufacturer's warranty for the furnace must be readily available to the prospective buyer. Home builders are in the position of a retailer when passing on the manufacturer's warranties to purchasers, and they are in the position of a manufacturer with respect to any warranties which they themselves give. It should be noted that although the Magnuson-Moss Warranty Act does not require home builders to give a warranty, there are some states that now require this protection for new-home buyers.

Variations in Warranties

In the past some builders have offered their own warranties, but due to the variations in these warranties, confusion for the consumer resulted. In 1972, only 38% of new-home owners received any type of a warranty.[5]

New homes purchased with mortgages guaranteed by the federal government are required to carry a one-year warranty. This requirement was established with the Housing Act of 1954. In spite of the Federal Housing Administration (FHA) standard warranty, research shows that 24% of new construction under the Section 235 program was seriously defective. It is estimated that defective housing is costing U.S. home owners $200 million a year.[6]

Although warranties and insurance programs have been used, the housing industry has been lax in promoting education about the differences in home warranties. The Magnuson-Moss Warranty Act will, hopefully, both increase consumer confidence and serve as a marketing tool for the housing industry. To illustrate the differences among the warranty plans, this article includes a comparison of three warranties in Table 2 which are adapted from information prepared by the Office of Consumer Affairs for the *HUD Challenge* magazine. The three plans are: the National Association of Home Builders' Home Owners Warranty (HOW) Program, the National Association of Realtors' (NAR) Home Protection Program and the FHA standard warranty.

In the *HUD Challenge* article, "Home Warranty Plans: How They Stack Up," we read:

> While the HOW warranty operates for a ten-year period, the NAR warranty runs for one or two years, depending upon the plan, the FHA is for one year. HOW's warranty is designed to cover operating failures within a new home in several stages; during the first year, the builder must make good on any failures to meet approved construction standards — such as faulty insulation, improper construction, plumbing and electrical defects — at no cost to the home buyer; during the second year, the builder continues to be responsible for certain defects in the heating, cooling, electrical and plumbing systems as well as structural defects; after the second year, a national insurance plan directly insures the consumer against certain major structural defects for the next eight years. Like the HOW warranty, NAR covers operating failures including structural problems and heating, plumbing, electrical and other systems within the house but operates for a much shorter time and covers resale homes, not new ones. FHA's warranty also covers faulty workmanship or materials in new homes but is limited to defects arising from construction practices where there is nonconformity with established building specifications or plans.
>
> Beyond these differences in length and scope of coverage, the plans also vary in exclusions from the warranty, deductibles, and cost. Under HOW and FHA, exclusions from coverage involve loss due to fire, flood or other "acts of God," normal shrinkage and buyer neglect. In comparison, NAR's program limits coverage to inspected and approved items. With HOW and FHA, there are no deductibles from the warranty while

5. Richard J. Canavan, "Home Building Industry's Warranty Program, A Real Comer," *Realtor* (April 1977), p. 18.
6. National Association of Home Builders, *NAHB Journal-Scope* (March 7, 1977), p. 37.

with NAR, there is a deductible of $100 per element per occurrence. Concerning cost of the program, FHA is free to the home owner along with HOW, which costs the builder $2 per thousand of the cost of the house to enter it in the program (with a minimum of $50). In contrast, under NAR's plan, the cost may be paid by either the buyer or seller and usually runs about $200. [7]

7. Virginia H. Knauer, "Home Warranty Plans: How They Stack Up," *HUD Challenge* (November 1976), pp. 8-11.

Table 2. Comparison of three home warranty plans available to consumers

Key Criteria	HOW	NAR	FHA
1. Plan coverage	Covers only operating failures. 1st yr.—faulty workmanship or materials. 2nd yr.—heating, plumbing, electrical and A/C systems; structural soundness. 3rd—10th year—major structural defects. Plan covers new homes.	Covers only operating failures. Heating, plumbing, electrical, and A/C systems; structural soundness of exterior and interior walls, including floors and ceilings. Plan covers resale homes.	Covers faulty workmanship or materials. Plan covers new homes.
2. Length of coverage	10-year plan	Not less than one year. Two current plans are for one year, and one plan for two years.	One year
3. Warranty exclusions	Loss due to fire, floor or other acts of God, normal shrinkage, buyer neglect.	Coverage limited to inspected and approved items. Exterior structures (garage, etc.).	Loss due to fire, flood or other acts of God, normal shrinkage, buyer neglect.
4. Policy transferable	Yes, within the 10-year period.	Yes, within the period of contract.	Yes, within the one-year period.
5. Deductible	None	$100 per element per occurrence.	None
6. Cost	$2 per thousand with a minimum of $50.	Premium left exclusively to participating companies; usually runs about $200.	No Cost
7. Covers condominiums	Yes, with some provisions.	Not required. One plan does; two do not.	Yes
8. Includes termite inspection	No	No	No
9. Insulation requirements	House must meet either FHA or Local Council standards.	Not included in inspection.	House must meet FHA requirements.
10. Program includes uniform complaint resolution mechanism	Yes	No	No

11. If applicable, cost of mechanism to buy	In case of unresolved dispute between buyer and builder, buyer may request conciliation. Arbitration is the next step if problem is not resolved.	N.A.	N.A.
12. Sponsor commitment or involvement	Administered by the Home Owners Warranty Corp. which is advised by a 15-member advisory board. Builder participants must be approved by Local Warranty Council. Rejections can be appealed to the National Council. Approvals must be renewed annually. Builder's plans for each new house must be approved by Local Warranty Council prior to construction.	NAR developed specifications for program and approves individual companies participating in program. A 10-member Home Protection Committee is responsible for all policy considerations and monitoring the Home Protection Plans. Boards of Realtors are not required to make any commitment to review complaints, or liability for conduct of approved program.	FHA has powers under 518a to either force builder to live up to provisions of warranty or it can make repairs itself and bill builder for cost of repair.
13. Underwriter of program	In an underwriters insurance company.	All three plans currently in operation are backed by insurance policies.	Individual builders cover cost of repairs.
14. Inspection arrangements	Where adequate building codes and acceptable inspections by FHA, VA, or the local municipality exist, Local Councils' inspections are not necessary. Otherwise, the Local Warranty Council is responsible for inspection.	NAR does not select inspectors, only approved companies engage professional engineers to perform the necessary inspections.	FHA's field staff conducts inspections.
15. Consumer monitoring	Advisory Board is made up of representatives from consumer and public interest groups, government, national publications, architects, manufacturers, lenders and attorneys.	None	None

Source: Adapted from Virginia H. Knauer, "Home Warranty Plans: How They Stack Up." *HUD Challenge,* November 1976, pp. 8-11.

Conclusion

Consumers should be aware that home warranties do exist and that many builders offer warranties. It is important that consumers understand there are many differences among the warranty plans. A warranty offers the buyer some protection on his or her house purchase and, therefore, increased consumer satisfaction. Since warranties serve as a marketing tool for the seller they can be advantageous to both buyer and seller. Home warranties have the potential to stimulate housing purchases and increase consumer satisfaction.

References

Bresnic, Garen. "Consumer Comes Home: A Look at the New Federal Warranty Act." *Bay State Builder,* April 1977, pp. 12-13.

Canavan, Richard J. "Home Building Industry's Warranty Program, A Real Comer." *Realtor* April 1977, pp. 16-18.

Knauer, Virginia H. "Home Warranty Plans: How They Stack Up." *HUD Challenge,* November 1976, pp. 8-11.

National Association of Home Builders. *NAHB Journal-Scope,* November 22, 1976, pp. 3-5.

_____ . *NAHB Journal-Scope,* March 7, 1977, p. 37.

Peters, Kenneth C. "How the Magnuson-Moss Warranty Act Affects the Builder/Sellers of New Housing." *Real Estate Law Journal* 5 (1977): 338-363.

Unger, Maurice A. *Real Estate Principles and Practices.* Cincinnati: South-Western Publishing Company, Inc., 1969.

Discussion Questions

1. Does the Magnuson-Moss Warranty Act guarantee the buyer of a new home a warranty on the purchase?

2. Why are there problems in identifying "consumer products" and "nonconsumer products" in housing?

3. Define the terms "real property" and "personal property."

4. How can a home builder be in a position as both a retailer and manufacturer at the same time?

5. Under what conditions are home warranties required?

6. Briefly discuss major differences in these three warranty programs: HOW, NAR, and FHA.

7. Is there any warranty program that covers both new and existing housing?

8. How can warranty programs serve as an advantage to both the consumer and the housing industry?

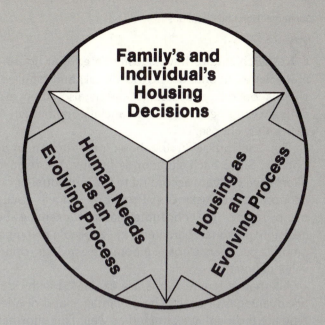

Family's and
Individual's
Housing
Decisions

Human Needs
as an
Evolving Process

Housing as
an
Evolving Process

Part Six
Consumer
Housing
Decisions

22. Housing Alternatives, by William J. Angell

Research studies have substantiated that housing decisions are frequently made on emotional bases. Individuals and families are often unaware of the various options available to them; also, they are not fully aware of the differences in personal and financial commitment depending upon the alternative they choose.

The final article in the book provides an in-depth analysis of housing options. Since each situation is unique, the relative advantages of a specific alternative will vary according to the individual or family's personal, social, and economic circumstances. Professor Angell discusses the following seven micro factors the consumer should examine before making a housing decision: personal characteristics, available resources, initial occupancy costs, monthly occupancy costs, income tax savings, opportunity costs, and net sale value of house.

Alternative tenure forms are explained with discussion of advantages and disadvantages of each. The advantages and disadvantages of each structural type are thoroughly examined as well. This information will not only be useful in making personal housing decisions, but will help a variety of professionals who give advice and counsel to individuals and families for housing-related decisions.

Current census and trade data on the total housing stock in the United States are given to show the level of present production. After studying Parts One through Five, it should be possible to understand that the impact of the macro forces and the collective demands of the micro units serve to determine the nation's present housing inventory.

22. Housing Alternatives

by William J. Angell

Introduction

American families[1] annually invest or reinvest over a trillion dollars[2] to improve and maintain their housing situations. On the average, these families spend and borrow more for housing than any other budget item. Several facts underscore the financial magnitude of the consumer's housing decision:[3]

— the average sales price of a new house has been in excess of $61,000 since mid-1978 [59, 14].

— the purchase price of previously occupied houses has averaged more than $52,000 since the summer of 1978 [14].

— in the twelve-year period between 1967 and 1978, the average home buyer's monthly mortgage interest payment increased 230%, double the rate of inflation [73, 72].

— by 1978, 44% of the average urban consumer's expenditures went for housing whereas 19% was spend for food and 6% for clothing [13].

— by the mid-1970s, American housing consumers carried a mortgage debt in excess of $763,000,000,000, a debt substantially greater than that owed by the federal government [77, 70].

In addition to the financial magnitude of housing decisions, a housing change may have significant positive or negative social and psychological impact upon the family [40]. Gross suggests [18], "The emotional effects of buying a home may well be one of the most profound experiences a young couple will ever have . . ."

Despite the financial and socio-psychological importance of housing decisions,

William J. Angell is Associate Professor and Extension Housing Specialist at the University of Minnesota. This article was prepared specially for this book.

1. In this chapter, the term "family" refers to any group of individuals who make collective housing decisions or to single-person households.

2. This amount includes the down payments and cash purchases paid annually as well as the mortgage debt outstanding for all nonfarm residential property. The investment action is active on the part of the consumer — e.g., prepaying a mortgage, making a down payment, assuming a mortgage obligation. The reinvestment action is, on the other hand, passive on the part of the consumer — e.g., continuing to pay monthly mortgage and property tax charges. The actual annual cash flow of what consumers spend for housing is around $250 billion plus $50 billion in debt originated.

3. Dwellings referred to are those financed with conventional mortgages. Conventional financing represents approximately 65 to 90% of all mortgages for new houses and 79% of all mortgages held against residential property (1970-1978) [14].

many consumers invest their money and time carelessly and arbitrarily. The result is frequently frustration, confusion, and disillusionment [38, 20].

The American consumer encounters a series of competing values and constraints when attempting to make a housing change. On the one hand, the consumer is subjected to unparalled financial, legal, political, and technological complexities and competing interests [52]. On the other hand, the consumer finds few sources of information which are both helpful and accurate [19]. Given this situation, the consumer must be sensitive to one's housing desires and, more importantly, the alternatives available to satisfy these desires. With this understanding, the consumer will be equipped to make decisions that contribute the most to his or her quality of life.

The first step in wise decision-making includes evaluating housing alternatives. Since each house or dwelling unit is unique in factors such as design, style, location, size, and price, each represents an alternative. To further effective decision-making, however, classification of alternatives according to basic characteristics is desirable. Next, it is desirable to establish the interrelationship between the major sets or combinations of alternatives. The first task is relatively simple — defining individual alternatives and, thus, sets of similar alternatives. A casual review of literature reveals the following major housing alternatives or questions:

1. Move or not to move?
   —move to another dwelling
   —not move and remodel present dwelling
   —not move and adapt family to present housing
2. If remodeling . . .
   — to rehabilitate or to restore?
   — to add?
3. If moving . . .
   — to build?
   — to buy?
   — to rent or to lease?
4. If building or remodeling . . .
   — to do-it-yourself (owner building) or to contract (custom building)?
   — to use stick-building, pre-cut, panelized, or modular construction?
5. If buying, type of occupancy or tenure . . .
   — fee simple ownership? [4]
   — condominium ownership?
   — cooperative ownership?
6. If buying or renting . . .
   — new or existing dwelling?
   — detached single-family house, mobile home, townhouse, or apartment?

This list delineates a broad range of important consumer housing alternatives although it is not by any means exhaustive.[5] It should be emphasized that when a family changes its housing situation, it inevitably combines several individual alternatives. For instance, two of the most prevalent types of housing changes are: to move and to rent an existing apartment; or to move and to buy in fee simple an existing detached, single-family house. To rationally approach housing decisions, however, a person must understand and assess comparable alternatives rather than the complex

4. Definitions follow.
5. Additional questions may include: source and type of financing; number of rooms; style; materials; location; and so on.

set of all housing alternatives. The consumer, in this way, may make rational trade-offs and compromises that best fulfill his or her unique situation. Utilizing this approach, the the consumer evaluates no more than 4 alternatives at one time rather than attempting to comprehend more than 100 possible combinations simultaneously, many of which may be irrelevant. Finally, this approach encourages the consumer to understand the basic interrelationship of the major combinations or sets of individual alternatives. Such an interrelationship was suggested (by the modifier "if") and is illustrated in Figure 1.

Figure 1 reflects a model of consumer housing alternatives. The linkages (interconnecting lines) represent the basic combinations of consumer housing decisions. As will be noted later, major sets of alternatives are composed of individual elements which are generally mutually exclusive with a few notable exceptions (e.g., leasehold condominium apartment or a mobile home owned in fee simple but placed in a mobile home park on a leasehold basis). There are not linkages where interrelationships are either irrelevant or extremely rare (e.g., owner building of a mobile home or apartment). A dashed line between "build" and "fee simple" indicates that fee simple ownership is the assumed form of tenure if the consumer decides to build a house.

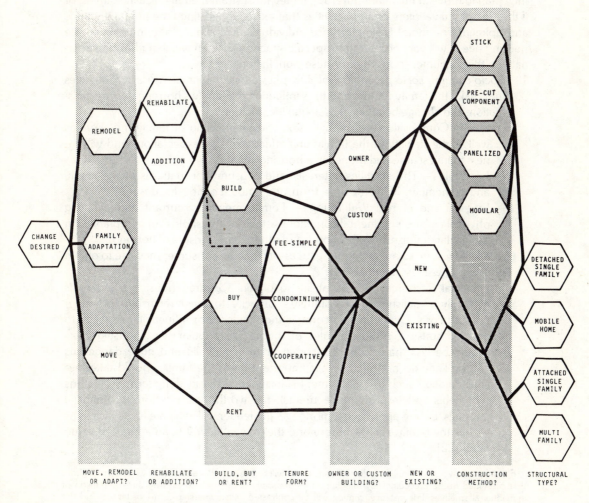

Figure 1. Decision-making model for consumer housing alternatives

Although the model represents a flow diagram or a sequence of consumer decisions,[6] housing research has not provided conclusive evidence that the consumer attaches greater importance to tenure considerations (i.e., rent or buy in fee simple, condominium, or cooperative forms) than to structural types. What would the consumer trade off first, for example, if forced to compromise his or her tenure and structural preferences (e.g., for fee simple ownership of a detached single-family house)? Recent trends toward mobile homes, townhouses, and apartments sold on a fee simple, condominium, or cooperative basis, however, suggest that ". . . structure norms are compromised first"[17].

Housing Need Modifiers

Each family is unique, and thus the relative advantages and effective availability of a specific alternative will vary according to the family's personal, social, and economic circumstances. Owning a detached single-family house in fee simple is an American norm that is embedded in tradition and folklore and encouraged by popular magazines, federal and state income tax policies, and community regulations. Buying a home, however, may be extremely unwise or unrealistic for many families especially if they plan to move in the near future[51], if they must strain their financial resources, or if they simply have interests and activities that exclude investing time in maintenance and upkeep. The moral is simple: since individuals are unique, they must recognize housing needs will vary according to specific situations. When weighing housing alternatives, the consumer should assess these eight factors:

1. *Socio-cultural, socio-psychological and physiological characteristics* are qualities that make the family unique and thus influence the family's housing desires, satisfaction, and change behavior. These qualities include:
    — Family Composition — The age, sex, and relationship of family members as well as the stability of the family unit affects housing expectations and willingness to invest time and money in a housing change.
    — Life-Style — The activities, interests, and consumption patterns of the family and its members affect the type, form, and amount of housing desired.
    — Physical and Mental Well-Being — Family members' current and evolving physical abilities and mental conditions establish "thresholds" of acceptability in design, layout, size, neighborhood, and other characteristics of housing.
2. *Available resources* are a unique set of assets that the consumer may use to obtain housing. These resources include:
    — Financial Resources — The ability to obtain a desired housing standard is generally established by the family's capacity to meet recurring (monthly) housing costs. Dependable income is the major factor influencing capacity to pay for housing. Although rules of thumb are popular (e.g., housing costs should be less than 25% of income), they are invalid and quite dangerous [78,4]. They do not reflect other important items the family should take into consideration such as employment stability and security, long-term obligations (i.e., debts and installment payments), net worth, and nonhousing financial priorities. Before approving a mortgage, the lender will evaluate these factors as well as the family's credit history and the loan collateral (loan-appraised value ratio) [22].

---

6. In the following examination, selected alternatives will be presented in a sequence which departs from that presented in the preceding flow diagram. This departure is desirable to simplify the comparison of individual alternatives. For instance, renting will be contrasted with ownership forms of tenure and the question of buying or building will be examined following discussion of new-existing alternatives.

— Property Assets or Net Worth — The consumer's assets may either be liquidated for initial costs or down payment or be pledged as collateral for a loan when a housing change occurs. Assets frequently liquidated by housing consumers include: excessive cash in checking accounts, savings accounts, stocks, bonds, cash value of whole-life life insurance policies, and net sale value of presently owned housing (sales price minus selling costs and mortgage balance). Assets frequently pledged for a loan (or assessed by a lender in terms of their value off-setting outstanding debts) by housing consumers include: appraised market value of the housing to be purchased, built, or remodeled as well as other real property and personal property such as automobiles, furniture, and equipment.

— Human Resources — Individuals may decide to use their own carpentry, painting, wiring, or plumbing skills as well as their time and energy to reduce labor costs for new construction, remodeling, and maintenance. Approximately 20% of the new houses built each year involves the owner working as the general contractor or furnishing some labor or doing both [9]. When an individual considers contributing his or her time and skills, however, it is important to guard against overestimating one's ability while underestimating the time required to complete the task.

3. *Initial occupancy costs* are first encountered when moving and buying or renting another housing unit. The amount of these expenses may vary widely according to the specific housing change: if buying — required down payment, utility deposits, prepayment expenses, and settlement costs; and if renting — required deposit and prepayment of rent. While a renter's initial costs may be very small, a home buyer using or obtaining mortgage financing will face initial costs that average 2% of the purchase price in addition to the down payment [5].

4. *Monthly occupancy costs* are recurring expenses the consumer must be willing to bear to provide a satisfactory home. When renting, these expenses may be included in a single monthly rent payment. When owning, however, these expenses may involve separate payments for:[7]

— Mortgage Principal and Interest — Influenced by the amount borrowed as well as by the demand for loans by business, industry, and units of government.

— Property Taxes — Established by the dwelling's taxable value and local mill-levies.

— Property Insurance — Influenced by the dwelling's replacement or market value as well as the quality of local services, especially fire protection.

— Maintenance and Repair — Influenced by the dwelling's age and equipment.

— Utilities — Influenced by the dwelling's location and thermal characteristics as well as local utility rates.

— Other costs such as premiums for credit life or decreasing term insurance if required by the mortgage lender, park rent for a mobile home, and association or management fee for condominiums, cooperatives, and neighborhood associations.

5. *Federal and state income tax savings* disproportionately favor the upper-income owner, but not the renter or lower-income owner, by allowing deduction of mortgage interest and property tax payments from taxable income. When prorated monthly, these deductions reduce the owner's housing costs, especially for upper-income owners.

7. See Appendix E for a detailed dollar breakdown.

Several states recently have extended income tax advantage to lower-income owners and to renters.

6. *Opportunity costs.* The individual who invests his or her money expects to receive interest or dividends as from a savings account or time certificate. However, home owners who make an initial down payment and increase their equity through monthly loan payments as well as renters who pay an initial deposit forego receiving interest on their investments. This foregone interest is an opportunity cost. The exact amount of opportunity cost varies according to the amount invested (down payment, equity, or deposit), the period or term of the investment, and the after-tax interest rate the individual could realize in alternative forms of investment.

7. *Net sale value of house.* Home owners generally expect the value of their homes to increase as inflation and construction costs rise [21]. Recent trends have indicated that existing houses have increased in value at a rate similar to new houses. For example, between 1974 and 1978, the sale prices for new homes increased 54% while prices for older houses increased 50% [14]. There is no guarantee, however, that a particular house will increase in value. To approximate the expected net sale value of a house, estimate the expected sale value at the end of occupancy and then subtract selling costs. Depending on appreciation of the house and the amount of selling costs (generally 4 to 10% of the selling price), the home owner may encounter a profit on his or her housing investment. This profit may be subject to capital gains taxes and is worth less because inflation has increased the cost of the consumer's subsequent housing [30, 51]. Thus, the average home owner generally finds housing is a hedge against inflation rather than a capital growth investment.

8. *Community demographic and economic conditions* are factors shaping the supply and effective availability of housing. These factors include:
   — Age and Employment of Population — The age and employment-income situation of the community's population influence the demand for specific housing alternatives and, thus, the cost and availability of housing in general.
   — Existing Dwelling: Vacancy Ratio — The proportion of dwellings for sale or rent directly influences the availability and price of specific housing alternatives.
   — Net Additions to Housing Stock — The rate at which new dwellings are added to the housing stock through new construction as opposed to the rate at which dwellings are lost from the stock (demolition, disaster, condemnation, conversion, etc.) stimulates modest short-term changes in the overall vacancy ratio. New construction is dependent upon a host of factors including available developable land, skilled labor, materials, and, in turn, building and zoning codes, public services, union trade and apprenticeship rules, etc.

Since these eight factors relate differently to each family, they influence the relative advantage and effective availability of each housing alternative. Consequently, when weighing alternatives, a family constantly should consider its unique situation.

Residence Change

During the past several decades social scientists have studied the family's unique relationship to its housing and the methods by which the family adjusts its housing to changing circumstances and preferences. Morris and Winter have noted that family housing adjustments may take these forms [36, 37]:

1. Family adaptation where the family alters its composition and, thus, housing preferences by postponing childbearing or by encouraging a decline in family size (e.g.,

suggesting an aging parent move to a nursing home or an older child move to an apartment).
2. Residential mobility where the family moves from one housing environment to another that more closely fulfills preferences.
3. Residential adaptation when the family adjusts its present housing to fulfill preferences by remodeling (additions or alterations).

Family Adaptation

While the family adaptation process of housing adjustment is an alternative the consumer may wish to consider, it is difficult to determine from research either its frequency or importance. One of the few insights into the frequency of family adaptation is an observation by Abu-Lughod and Foley which indicates that only about half of the households wishing to move actually do [1]. Presumably, a large portion of the nonmovers must employ family adaptation to some degree.

Whatever the case, family adaptation may be the most desirable alternative for the family that cannot afford or does not desire to move or remodel. This situation is generally more relevant for owners since renters usually find it easier and less expensive to move. Some of the more common forms of family adaptation include postponing childbearing, encouraging household members to move, and taking in boarders to share expenses. While research is inconclusive, it appears that many forms of family adaptation cause social and psychological stress substantially greater than encountered when moving or remodeling. Changing one's housing by moving or remodeling is socially accepted as an indicator of individual success and upper mobility while family adaptation often is perceived as a stopgap compromise.

Move (Residential Mobility)

The most prevalent and visible form of housing adjustment is residential mobility. Each year, about 20% of the nation's households move, and, according to a study conducted by the Bureau of the Census, nearly half of these moves are motivated by the desire to find more satisfactory housing [68]. The popularity of moving varies substantially between owners and renters. According to the 1976 Annual Survey of Housing there were 40% of all renters, but only 10% of owners, that began either renting or owning in 1976 [65]. Comparatively, renters occupy a dwelling an average of slightly more than three years while owners average over twelve years (see Appendix A).[8] These trends reflect some of the relative advantages of moving when compared to remodeling. Remodeling is generally not a viable alternative for renters since they frequently are prohibited from altering or adding to these dwellings. Even if this were not the case, the renter has little legal assurance that his or her rent will not increase or that he or she will not be evicted with the expiration of the lease. With this insecurity, moving is more desirable for the vast majority of renters.

Second, owners and renters alike may be dissatisfied with their housing in ways that cannot be remedied by remodeling. For instance, a consumer may be dissatisfied with the social or physical characteristics of the neighborhood [66], local zoning regulations

8. Two important distinctions should be noted between the 14.6 million households that moved in 1976 [65]. First, 3.8 million households were "new" with a different head. This group was proportionately most likely to move to a rental situation (83%) while leaving the former household. On the other hand, the 10.7 million households with the same head moved from one dwelling to another — thus, establishing the mobility rate. (See Appendix A: 7,102 of the 22,914 same-head, renter households moved = 31%; 3,547 of the 47,251 same-head, owner households moved = 7½%.) The majority of the same-head households moved to the same tenure situation (76% of renters moved to a rental unit; 63% of owners moved to an owned unit; 35% more renters moved to ownership than owners moving to renting).

may prohibit adding space to the dwelling, or the financial cost of correcting a poor design, correcting structural defects, or improving mechanical systems may be excessive.

On the other hand, the disadvantages of moving should be considered. First, the substantial cost of initial occupancy and selling tend to restrict owners' mobility [5]. As noted earlier, the renter's moving costs tend to be minimal while owners may encounter costs totaling several thousand dollars. Furthermore, owners are more likely to have children than renters [55, 68]. The family with children may view moving as undesirable since neighborhood and school associations would be disrupted. Nonhousing pressures such as employment changes tend to be less significant for middle-aged families with children than the younger or lower-income individual with changing career aspirations or income situations [47].

Remodel (Residential Adaptation)

The third form of family housing adaptation, remodeling, involves altering or adding to the existing dwelling. Remodeling may range in scope from simply finishing a basement or attic to complete renovation and is primarily an alternative relevant to the owner rather than the renter.

According to a survey reported in *Building Supply News,* over 10,000,000 remodeling projects were initiated in 1974 including [35]:[9]
— 2,800,000 kitchens
— 850,000 exterior room additions
— 3,150,000 interior room additions within dwellings (e.g., kitchens and bathrooms)
— 2,500,000 bathrooms
— 803,000 garages or carports

This survey is similar to, although higher than 1974 projections made by another trade journal, *Professional Builder* [42]. It is impossible to determine from either source to what extent multiple remodeling projects were carried out in the same dwelling or what number were completed in owner-occupied dwellings. The *1976 Annual Survey of Housing* offers some limited insight: 6,693,000 owners (14%) reported making alterations while 2,145,000 owners (4%) reported making additions costing $100 or more in the previous twelve months. Despite the lack of comparatively valid data, it appears clear that (1) remodeling is an alternative available almost exclusively to owners, not renters; (2) remodeling projects and expenditures are dominated by interior alterations (2/3 to 3/4) rather than additions; (3) remodeling expenditures tend to be concentrated in units occupied seven years or less (55% in 1976). Therefore, remodeling appears to be a form of housing adjustment employed to supplement rather than replace moving [61, 60, 64].

Furthermore, when both remodeling (improvement) and maintenance expenditures are compared, significant differences may be observed according to the age of the household head (male with wife present):
— less than forty-five years old: 67% of expenditures for remodeling, 33% for maintenance [60].
— sixty-five years old or older: 33% of expenditures for remodeling, 67% for maintenance [60].

9. There is a lack of data which accurately describes the scope and prevalence of remodeling. However, three sources of information which offer some insight into remodeling are: annual Bureau of Census reports indicating remodeling expenditures for owner-occupied dwellings [61, 64]; housing industry projections and surveys of remodeling for all residential property; and building permit data. Since much remodeling takes place outside of permit-issuing jurisdictions or simply escapes recording, building permits are one of the poorest indicators. While census and industry sources are also incomplete, they offer somewhat more reliable reflections of remodeling activity.

Thus, younger home owners, especially recent buyers, are more likely to invest in additions or alterations to their homes while elderly owners are more prone to invest in maintenance (upkeep) and the replacement of major items (e.g., furnace, water heater, wiring, piping, roofing, etc.). These figures tend to indicate that the desirability of remodeling varies for different types of housing consumers.

Since 20 to 25% of general remodeling expenditures is for work done entirely by the owner [60, 61], it may be assumed that younger owners stretch their housing dollar by doing the work themselves. The potential savings of do-it-yourself remodeling averages about half for additions and up to two-thirds for interior alterations [7]. Other significant but intangible advantages of do-it-yourself remodeling are that (1) work may proceed at the owner's pace, convenience, and ability to pay; (2) the do-it-yourselfer knows exactly what he or she has upon beginning and finishing remodeling; and (3) the individual may gain a sense of self achievement.

On the other hand, inherent in remodeling are problems that may restrict its desirability as an alternative: (1) home improvement financing generally carries a higher interest rate than a home mortgage; (2) family living is disrupted by the dust, dirt, noise, and inconvenience associated with remodeling; (3) completion often takes longer and is more expensive than anticipated as unexpected problems arise; and (4) there is a tendency to overimprove from a financial (resale) standpoint. The exact financial (resale) wisdom of remodeling a specific dwelling depends on location, condition, and the nature of the improvements. To obtain specific information, a consumer should contact an appraiser who is familiar with the local housing market.

Tenure

During the past thirty years, federal and state regulations have improved and now broaden consumer housing alternatives. Today, housing consumers may choose the form of tenure or occupancy that best serves their needs, preferences, and circumstances. The four major forms of tenure or occupancy alternatives available are: leasehold (rent) and ownership in fee simple, condominium, and cooperative.

Before considering the relative advantages and disadvantages of tenure alternatives, it is important to recognize several variables. First, state statutes are the single most important definition of tenure since they shape the consumer's basic legal rights and responsibilities relative to obtaining, occupying, and transferring property. These statutes vary substantially across the United States. Secondly, during recent years, state statutes generally have clarified and strengthened housing consumers' rights and responsibilities, especially renters and condominium and cooperative owners. Finally, individual consumers may occupy their homes in combinations of tenure or occupancy. For example, a mobile home consumer may own his or her home in fee simple and occupy a lot in a mobile home park on a leasehold basis. For this reason, the consumer should recognize the importance of legal advice when making a housing change.

Rent (Leasehold)

In this form of tenure the consumer is a tenant who receives the exclusive possession and use of property such as a dwelling unit, usually in exchange for payment of a specific rent. The terms of leasehold tenancy are defined by state statutes (and therefore vary substantially) and a lease which may be written, verbal, or implied.

The traditional concept of renting is based upon the economic and common-law relationship between a tenant farmer and a wealthy landowner or lord. During the past decade, this agrarian relationship has been substantially modified through statutory

changes in many states. Yet, these changes have been neither uniform nor adequate to neutralize the powerful position of an unethical landlord in a "tight" market (i.e., high demand, restricted supply). In many states, for example, landlords continue to [8, 64]:
— rent dwellings that are grossly substandard
— be relieved of all responsibilities to maintain or repair their units
— evict tenants for purely subjective or personal reasons
— retain tenants' security deposits without just cause

Despite these inequities, renting is a housing alternative selected by 35% of the households in the United States [65]. Renting is more prevalent among certain types of housing consumers which generally include nonhusband or nonwife households (single, widowed, divorced), lower-income households, more geographically mobile individuals, urban residents, and younger people [70, 8, 65]. Several trends reflect some of the relative advantages and disadvantages of renting rather than buying.

First, renting permits greater flexibility to adjust one's housing situation as income or family units change and employment opportunities arise. It is usually much easier and less costly to terminate leasehold occupancy than to sell fee simple, condominium, or cooperative property. Financially, a consumer generally would be wiser to rent rather than buy if he or she does not anticipate living in a dwelling for at least 3½ years during average inflationary periods (i.e., less than 5%) [51].

Second, the initial costs of renting are minimal since the renter does not encounter down-payment and settlement costs. Generally, the renter must make only a deposit and prepay a month's rent while the average buyer faces initial expenses ranging from 2 to 5% of the purchase price and down payments averaging 25 to 30% of the purchase price [14, 5]. Since the renter has a very small financial investment in housing, he or she has greater investment flexibility and does not encounter "opportunity costs" as does the buyer.

Furthermore, monthly costs are usually much easier to predict since costly maintenance and repair are generally the landlord's responsibility. Likewise, the time necessary to maintain the dwelling is usually less for the tenant than the owner.

Renting obviously does not build up equity, provide a hedge against inflation, or provide income tax savings to the degree that owning does. This latter fact is especially relevant for consumers in higher tax brackets. In addition, the renter has no assurance that the landlord will not raise the rent when the lease expires, while the home owner with a "fixed term" mortgage generally has a better idea what his or her future housing costs will be for twenty to thirty years, especially for principal and interest. Also, the tenant usually has less control over his or her housing since activities and improvements generally are restricted by the lease.

When considering leasehold occupancy, remember that tenancy may be created by an oral or implied (from conduct of the parties) agreement as well as a written lease. This form of occupancy is known as "tenancy at will." The major problems associated with "tenancy at will" are: the likelihood of misunderstanding, the difficulty of substantiating the terms (rights and responsibilities) of occupancy and thus enjoying the basic discretionary power of the courts for enforcement, and, finally, the insecurity created by the fact that occupancy may be abruptly terminated or rent increased at the will of the landlord. For these reasons, a written lease is generally desirable.

Another important fact to recognize is that leasehold occupancy also may be involved in situations where the consumer holds property in fee simple, condominium, or •cooperative ownership. Examples of these situations include "ground leases" where mobile home owners lease lots in a mobile home park or leasehold condominiums where the condominium association leases from a developer or third party the right to enjoy exclusive use of improvements (i.e., individual dwelling units, common areas, recreational facilities, etc.) for a specific amount of time, usually fifty to ninety-nine years, in exchange for rent. As land costs escalate, ground leases are becoming more popular for mobile homes, single-family houses, townhouses, and apartments. Today, approximately two-thirds of mobile home owners rent the ground their units sit upon [65].

Fee Simple Ownership

A second traditional tenure alternative is fee simple ownership in which the property owner is entitled to all of the rights and privileges to use the property as he or she desires. These rights and privileges, however, are not absolute. They have been restricted through local zoning, subdivision, building codes, and, since the late nineteenth century, housing codes as well as state statutes establishing eminent domain, adverse possession, devise by will, the conveyance or transfer of ownership by deed (i.e., upon sale), and lien interests (i.e., judgment, tax, and mortgage) [33]. Despite these restrictions, fee simple ownership grants the owner the most substantial interests and rights in property. It remains the most popular form of tenure in the United States with over 63% of the dwelling units held in fee simple [64]. To a major degree, this popularity is based upon several advantages.

First, fee simple or exclusive ownership has been the safest financial investment and hedge against inflation that many consumers could make. With the exception of the years during the Great Depression, the value of residential property held in fee simple generally has increased at a rate greater than inflation while the costs of the original mortgages have remained constant [14, 77, 70]. For example, between 1967 and 1978, the sale prices for older (preoccupied) houses increased 102% [14] while inflation as measured by the consumer price index rose 90% [72].

Second, through mortgage financing, the owner has a form of forced savings and "financial leverage" (see Appendix D) whereby equity is built up at a rate greater than inflation. This equity may be liquidated upon sale or used as collateral for a loan if desired. The costs (interest) of home mortgages also have been substantially less than other forms of credit available to the consumer. The owner also generally enjoys greater income tax savings than the renter since he or she may deduct property tax and interest payments from his or her taxable income. This savings amounted to $5.1 billion from federal taxes alone in 1972 [74], approximately $130 for each home owner.

Finally, fee simple ownership gives the individual the greatest freedom to use, maintain, and improve the property. There is no need to wait for someone (i.e., landlord or caretaker) to do this work nor will the owner be forced to move because of an unsympathetic landlord or board of directors.

Fee simple ownership, however, involves some disadvantages as noted previously: transfer (selling costs) and initial costs are quite substantial; down payment and increasing equity are not without financial risk; investment flexibility is limited; some monthly costs such as maintenance and repair are less predictable; greater amounts of time, energy, and managerial skills are usually demanded; and it is generally more difficult and time consuming for an owner to terminate occupancy than for a renter.

Cooperative Ownership

A third and relatively new form of tenure in the United States is cooperative ownership in which the individual becomes a stockholder or member in a nonprofit corporation and thereby receives the exclusive right to occupy a dwelling unit and to partici-pate in the corporation as a tenant-stockholder. Cooperative ownership became an obtainable tenure alternative in 1950 when Congress authorized the Federal Housing Administration (FHA) to insure loans made to nonprofit corporations representing cooperative owners (stockholders).

Cooperative tenure offers several advantages similar to other types of ownership tenure [39]: a form of forced savings, a hedge against inflation, income tax savings, and, in comparison to leasehold occupancy, little or no expense for vacancies or land-lord profit. All of these advantages are related to the individual's percentage of stock ownership. Another advantage unique to cooperative ownership is that the individual tenant-stockholder jointly maintains the greatest control over both his or her own dwelling and the immediate environment. This form of joint management may have important social benefits for people desiring interpersonal contact.

The fact that cooperative housing is financed by a single loan to a corporation rather than directly to individual owners is the most unique characteristic distinguishing cooperatives from other forms of tenure [75]. This fact is also the basis for most of the cooperative's disadvantages.

First, the individual tenant-shareholder may find it more difficult, time consuming, and costly to sell his or her interest (stock) in the cooperative since the buyer must raise an adequate down payment to finance the purchase under the original mortgage (i.e., cannot pay cash or refinance with a new mortgage). This limitation may be especi-ally severe if the seller has enjoyed substantial appreciation or if a sizable equity has been built. In many cases the buyer also must be approved by the board of directors before the sale can be completed.

Each tenant-stockholder in a cooperative is jointly liable and, thus, each usually can be assessed a proportion of another stockholder's pro rata share of mortgage, tax, insurance, utility, management, and maintenance charges if that stockholder defaults on payments. Because there is only a single mortgage made to the corporation repre-senting the group of owners, most financial institutions will not accept an individual's equity in cooperative stock as security for a loan.

Finally, the individual tenant-stockholder's freedom to use (including renting to a nonmember), maintain, and improve the dwelling unit may be restricted according to the cooperative's bylaws and declarations and be controlled by the cooperative's board of directors. The desirability of a cooperative is dependent largely upon the ability of individual tenant-stockholders to make wise decisions collectively and, perhaps, to contract for a professional management and maintenance service.

In the thirty years since FHA-insured financing became available for cooperatives, this form of tenure has been most popular in New York, Florida, Hawaii, and other metropolitan areas where land costs have been high. Generally, cooperative housing has been an alternative most favored by higher income buyers and, to a lesser extent in recent years, college students and young professionals [64]. Cooperatives have been increasing in popularity in recent years; in the seven years between 1970 and 1976, occupied cooperative units increased 60% to 405,000 units [64]. As previously noted, cooperatives may be sold on a leasehold basis in many states, where a ground lease is extended to the corporation.

Condominium Ownership

Condominium ownership is another new, increasingly popular and changing form of tenure in the United States. The individual has fee simple ownership of his or her dwelling unit as well as shared undivided interest (ownership) of additional property and facilities held jointly with other owners. Condominium ownership became popular following the National Housing Act of 1961 (Section 234) which authorized the FHA to insure financing to individual condominium buyers. Subsequent legislation in 1968, creating a model statutory plan for state adoption, stimulated the first generation of condominium laws in the United States. Currently, all states have condominium statutes, many of them under revision. Although state statutes vary substantially, condominium tenure is generally possible for owners of all types of structures whether mobile homes, townhouses, single-family houses, or apartments [23].

Condominium ownership, as any form of tenure, is created and defined by certain legal documents. The legal instruments necessary to establish a condominum include: the master deed which creates condominium ownership for the property; the record plot which graphically describes individual units and common areas; and the bylaws which create the association's administration and regulations. Because of the complexity of the instruments and state statutes, it is imperative to have competent legal advice when purchasing a condominium.

According to estimates from the National Association of Home Builders (NAHB) [46], the construction of condominiums accounted for approximately 10% of the housing built during the early 1970s. Bureau of the Census data indicate that condominium ownership increased 60% between 1970 and 1976 to 630,000 occupied units [74]. This trend is continuing in new construction (20% of the multifamily units started in 1976 were intended for condominium sale) [57] as well as the conversion of rental units to condominium ownership.

Marketing surveys have indicated that condominium buyers are primarily previous renters, married couples with young children, if any, and the professionally employed individual [2]. It appears that condominium tenure is a more attractive alternative to young families who may lack the financial resources to purchase a house (fee simple) or do not have the desire to invest substantial amounts of time in maintenance activities. Several trends reflect the relative advantages of condominium occupancy.

Since individual owners are responsible for their financing, condominium owners generally find it easier to pruchase and sell their property than do cooperative tenant-stockholders. The condominium owner also enjoys greater freedom to use (including renting) or improve the dwelling than either the renter or cooperative owner [49].

Second, the condominium owner's financial risk (liability) is not intermingled with other owners to the degree found in cooperatives [44]. Usually, only maintenance and management costs are shared in condominium developments while cooperative owners share all costs.

As with leasehold and cooperative tenure, exterior maintenance and the upkeep of common areas and facilities generally are not the responsibility of individual condominium owners although the owner indirectly pays for these services through association fees. To many consumers, the condominium approach is a desirable balance combining fee simple ownership of a dwelling unit and joint control of common areas without direct maintenance responsibility.

Finally, the condominium owner enjoys advantages similar to other forms of ownership. These are a form of forced savings, a hedge against inflation, and income tax savings. Past Internal Review Service rulings, however, have challenged the income tax advantage by disallowing property taxes on common areas to be deducted from the individual condominium owner's taxable income.

The disadvantages of condominium ownership are related to the undivided shared interest in common areas and facilities. While this arrangement permits each owner to have input into the maintenance and management of the development, the individual's interest may not be reflected in collective decisions such as exterior paint colors, level of upkeep, operation budgets, and assessments [24].

Condominiums may be sold on the leasehold basis (ground or recreation leases) in many states. Although the leasehold approach may reduce the initial purchase price of a condominium dwelling as much as 30%, this savings generally is negated by monthly lease payments. Furthermore, the leasehold does not offer the income tax advantages that standard association ownership provides. Leasehold condominiums also have been a major source of consumer complaint in recent years and thus should be approached only after careful evaluation and competent legal counsel.

New or Existing

Once the consumer decides to move, this change may be to either a new or existing (previously occupied) dwelling. Again the desirability of each alternative depends largely on the consumer's own needs, desires, resources, and circumstances as well as the nature of the community's housing market.

Census data allow a comparison between construction and subsequent sale or leasing of new housing units and the sale or leasing of existing units. While analysis is seriously limited by incomplete data, it appears that approximately eight to ten times as many housing consumers move to an existing dwelling (preoccupied) than to a new dwelling (see Appendix A). This trend appears especially strong for renters of multifamily dwellings and least strong for mobile home and condominium and cooperative apartment buyers. This indicates that the relative advantages and disadvantages of moving to new and existing housing may be related to tenure and/or structural type. For instance, it may be hypothesized that because renters of multifamily dwellings can easily terminate their tenancy, they exert this privilege more frequently when dissatisfied with their housing. For this group of consumers, the alternative of new versus existing housing may be less relevant than for mobile home and condominium and cooperative apartment owners who experience greater difficulty and expense selling and moving to a new home. Furthermore, the high ratio of new to existing units lessens the relative availability of previously occupied mobile homes, condominiums, and cooperative units.

Whatever the situation, consumers find that new and existing housing have unique advantages and disadvantages. These factors generally affect owners directly and renters indirectly.

Utility costs, especially for heating and cooling, are usually less than comparative costs for older (existing) housing since insulation and weather stripping tend to be better and the heating-cooling plant more efficient.

New dwellings are generally better planned for contemporary living patterns and equipment than older dwellings. New developments and communities are also usually better planned than older areas. For example, in new developments such features as curved streets, cul de sacs, open spaces, and rear-yard pedestrian walkways frequently are included while older areas may be laid out on a sterile grid pattern.

Buyers generally receive more favorable mortgage terms (lower down payment, lower interest rate, longer term) on new, rather than on existing dwellings [14].

Also, when moving into a new dwelling, the consumer frequently has the option of making some decisions about interior finishing details (e.g., wall coverings, paint colors, floor coverings, plumbing fixtures, equipment, millwork, and trim) as well as exterior materials and landscaping. The individual may be able to do some of the finishing work and thus save initial costs.

Finally, when moving into a new dwelling, the consumer is not purchasing or renting someone else's mistakes and problems. It is also much easier to obtain the original specifications to determine the quality of the materials and equipment in new dwellings.

There are several major advantages of existing dwellings as compared to new dwellings.

The purchase price of previously occupied houses averages less than the price of newly built houses. For example, by mid-1978 the average sales price of a new single-family house was in excess of $61,000 while previously occupied houses averaged $52,000 [14]. Unlike new dwellings, existing houses have also established a "track record" of tax, utility, and insurance expenses. Consequently, it is easier to accurately predict and budget for all occupancy costs.

Craftsmanship and finishing details, natural materials, and a wide range of floor plans, designs, and styles may be found to a greater extent in older dwellings than in new ones. Older neighborhoods also are established with mature landscaping whereas the final character (land use, traffic patterns, landscaping) of new areas is difficult to predict.

During periods of rising interest rates and tight mortgage money, buyers of existing dwellings may be able to assume the seller's mortgage at a more favorable interest rate than is available for new dwellings. Approximately 12% of the owner-occupied dwellings in the United States have been financed by assuming the seller's mortgage [71, 53].

Finally, problems associated with new construction (settling, "nail pop," and shrinkage) and certain other defects (absence of vapor barrier, poor quality windows, and wet basements) are easier to observe in order to determine what corrective measures may be necessary. The consumer may find it possible to purchase and rehabilitate an older (existing) dwelling at less cost than buying a new dwelling especially if the buyer is willing to do much of the work.

Buy or Build

The majority of consumers who move select a dwelling unit which has been pre-occupied (existing) or for which construction has been completed. This situation is reflected by the vast number of buyers and renters (i.e., 97%) moving to existing single-family houses as well as to new and existing mobile homes, townhouses, and apartments [65]. For these consumers the alternative of building a new home is irrelevant. Consumers wishing to own (fee simple) a new single-family house, however, find the question of building or buying a new house becomes extremely important. Thus, the following consideration will focus upon the buy-build alternative from the perspective of this type of consumer.

During recent years, about 80% of the residential construction in the United States has been on a speculative basis where the final consumer was unknown when construction began. Only about 20% of new construction — about 40% of nonmobile home, single-family construction — has been built for a specific consumer. This situation is reflected in this data summarizing residential construction for 1970-1976 (see Appendices B and C):

Multifamily (townhouses and apartments)	3%
Mobile Homes	19%
Detached single-family	50%
• Speculatively-built	(3/5 = 31%)
• Custom-built	(1/5 = 11%)
• Owner-built	(1/5 = 11%)

Further examination of single-family construction data indicates substantial differences between metropolitan and rural areas. In rural areas, owner-built housing comprises over 30% of the privately owned single-family houses started, but it accounts for only 10% of metropolitan starts [58]. Custom-building is also proportionately twice as common in rural areas as in metropolitan areas (33% compared to 14%). Speculative building dominates in metropolitan communities (about 76% compared to 36% in rural areas) [58]. Thus, the relevancy of building as opposed to buying a new house may depend upon the urban-rural character of the community where the consumer wishes to live.

The overwhelming frequency of buying, as opposed to building, is reflected by census and construction data. For example, as noted in Appendices A, B, and C:

— approximately 5.4 million households moved to owner-occupied dwellings in 1976 (65);

— only 1,026,000 new detached single-family housing units were completed in 1976 of which only 406,000 were custom- or owner-built [58].

Thus, less than 10% of the households moving to an owner-occupied dwelling in 1976 chose to build a new house. This predominant trend toward buying as opposed to building reflects some of the basic advantages of buying.

It is easier to buy rather than to build. Fewer complications and decisions arise when buying. Contracts do not need to be negotiated. Building permits, zoning, and subdivision regulations do not impose constraints. Difficult-to-obtain construction financing is not a relevant factor. Increasing labor and material costs are not a concern. Material shortages, poor weather, and sloppy craftsmanship do not cause problems. Furthermore, the buyer encounters no problems visualizing what the dwelling will look like or how it will function when completed. The completed dwelling rather than sketches, plans, or complicated specifications is evaluated. Less time is required to buy a house than to build one. It is possible to purchase a house in a matter of days while building usually involves months of preparation and work: to develop or select plans and specifications, to bid and negotiate, to prepare land, to obtain financing, and to supervise and complete construction.

The vast number of existing and speculative-built units offers the consumer a wide range of choices when buying. Prices may range from a low of several thousand dollars for a used (preoccupied) mobile home to about $52,000 (1978 average) for an existing single-family dwelling [14]. The least expensive custom-built house, however, is generally substantially more expensive than the average price of speculative-built and existing dwellings in most communities. The cost savings of buying a speculative-built unit is greatest when the builder has developed an entire subdivision.

Despite the significant advantages of buying a dwelling, building a home specifically for one's own family is a strongly embedded American ideal reinforced through popular magazines, newspaper articles, and the advertising of material suppliers. Against this backdrop, approximately 40% of the households moving to a new detached single-family house choose to build rather than buy [57]. This trend is stronger in rural areas where little speculative construction takes place and in situations where buying is not generally feasible (e.g., for farm families) [57]. Despite the major disadvantages of higher costs, greater time requirements, and so on, building a house offers some unique advantages.

The consumer can develop the site and plan the house exactly as he or she wishes within the constraints of budget and local regulations rather than purchasing a speculative house built for a hypothetical family. It may be possible to incorporate features not generally found in speculative-built houses which reduce long-term costs, maintenance responsibilities, or are otherwise desirable (e.g., double-glazed glass, additional insulation, and efficient fireplaces).

Finally, it may be possible for consumers to reduce the costs of building by doing some of the work themselves and, at the same time, to gauge the progression and cost of building according to the family's needs, interests, and budget.

The degree to which the consumer will realize these advantages depends largely upon the type of construction selected as well as the amount of work and supervision he or she provides. These two factors represent a need to further examine alternatives available to the consumer choosing to build his or her own house.

Owner Built/Custom-Built

The 310,000 to 410,000 households who build new houses each year are evenly divided between owner-builders (doing some or all of the work themselves) and individuals hiring a custom builder. In a study of owner-built housing, Angell and Olson [9] noted that owner-builders are generally younger and have lower incomes than individuals building through a custom-builder. Thus, it appears that owner-building allows the consumer an opportunity to build a new house according to his or her own needs and within the constraints of income, time, and skills. In addition to the substantial time and skill requirements of owner-building, the do-it-yourselfer faces the often difficult challenge of arranging construction financing. The severity of this problem is reflected by the fact that more than 40% of owner-builders pay cash rather than obtain mortgage financing [57]. Owner-builders face other significant challenges including: obtaining adequate discounts from material suppliers; receiving prompt service from subcontractors (e.g., electricians, plumbers, heating-cooling installers, etc.); efficiently scheduling material delivery and construction; and gaining the support and approval of building code officials. Depending on the individual's ability to work within these constraints, owner-building may reduce the initial costs of building by a maximum of 45% although the savings is frequently much less.

Form of Construction

Major technological advances have been widely implemented in construction practices during the past thirty-five years. For the consumer planning to build a house, a general understanding of the various forms of construction is important. The four major forms of construction are: stick-built (on-site), precut and component fabrication, panelized, and modular. Although it is very difficult to determine where one segment ends and another begins, each construction form has certain characteristics and advantages.

Stick-Built

Stick-built construction is the traditional and most common form of building where most elements of the dwelling are prepared piece-by-piece and assembled on the construction site. Approximately three-fifths of the residential construction in the United States is of the stick-built type.[10] The major advantages of stick-built construction include maximum flexibility in design and construction, and the greatest opportunity for owner involvement (i.e., do-it-yourself) during construction. Stick-building is, however, extremely susceptible to delays and problems caused by weather. In some communities, materials, designs, and other features may be restricted by the experience, whims, and wishes of local builders, subcontractors, and tradespeople.

10. In 1972, for example, approximately 440,000 housing units built were factory-built (18%) in addition to 576,000 mobile homes (24%). The balance, 1,363,000 units or 58%, were stick-built [50, 56].

Precut and Component Fabrication

Precut and component fabrication is one step removed from on-site stick-building. This form of construction relies upon off-site preparation (i.e., cutting) of structural and finishing material and, perhaps, fabrication of certain components (e.g., roof and floor trusses, pre-hung doors, stairways, plumbing trees, bath and kitchen cores, etc.), which are then delivered to the building site for final assembly. In a recent examination of component manufacturers, Lythe estimates that 90% of all light construction employs one or more manufactured components [28]. The popularity of off-site preparation and component fabrication is related to several distinct advantages: on-site construction time is reduced; shortage of local labor is minimized; it is easier to control quality; material waste may be reduced; and delays due to weather are less likely. The combined results of these factors is that construction costs may be reduced. Currently, many lumberyards as well as specialized component manufacturers market their products to owner-, custom-, and speculative-builders. Many owner-builders are attracted to pre-cut "packages" since suppliers often arrange construction financing.

Panelized

Panelized construction is the most common and basic form of manufactured housing. During the 1970s, panelized construction appears to have accounted for 15 to 20% of the new housing built.[11] Panelized construction by definition involves the assembly of precut elements and fabricated components into flat wall, floor, and ceiling panels. Depending on the degree of completion, panelized construction may be of two types: open-panel, in which one or both sides are left unfinished and open, and closed-panel, in which both sides of the panel are enclosed by interior and exterior finished materials. Closed-panels normally include wiring, plumbing, windows, doors, and insulation. The advantages of panelized construction are essentially the same as precut and component fabrication although such things as cost savings and reduced time requirements are potentially greater. Design and construction flexibility may be reduced, however, if the consumer is purchasing a "packaged home" through a franchised dealer.

Modular

Modular construction represents the most substantial form of factory-built housing. According to estimates by Reidelback, approximately ninety thousand housing units or about 6% of all residential construction annually is of the modular form [46].[12] The primary difference between this and other forms of construction is the degree to which fabrication takes place off-site in the manufacturer's plant.[13] Before delivery to the building site, the manufacturer combines all the home's components into room or sectional modules complete with plumbing, heating, wiring, doors, windows, trim, and so on. The dwelling is essentially complete and needs only be placed on the consumer's foundation and connected to utility services. Modular construction maximizes the advantages of precut and component fabrication and panelized con-

11. According to estimates by Schulin [50] about 80% of the factory-built housing in 1973 (excluding mobile homes) was panelized. This number represents about 300,000 to 350,000 housing units or about 15% of all residential construction and about 20% of non-mobile home construction.

12. In 1973, 2,058,000 housing units were started of which Reidelback estimates 90,000 are modular units [47]. This sum represents about 5% of all housing starts and 6% of the 1,478,000 non-mobile home starts.

13. While mobile homes are essentially a form of modular construction, they are excluded from this analysis since they are built to a separate building code and are sold, taxed, and financed differently than relatively more permanent modular housing.

struction, but the disadvantages of reduced design and construction flexibility are generally intensified.

It is clear that the consumer choosing to build a new house faces important additional decisions about the amount of work to do himself or herself and the type of construction which best suits his or her needs and resources as well as the nature of the community's housing market.

Structural Type

The consumer choosing to move will find four basic types of residential structures: detached single-family houses, mobile homes, townhouses, and apartments. Each type of structure, depending on state statutes, may be occupied on a fee simple, condominium, cooperative, or leasehold basis. In addition to the comparative advantages of each form of tenure, structural type offers the consumer another opportunity to select a housing alternative which best fulfills his or her own needs.

According to 1970 and 1976 census data, the nation's occupied housing stock was proportionately composed of these structural types [55, 64]:

	1970	**1976**
Detached single-family houses	42.1 million (66%)	47.7 million (64%)
Attached single-family homes (including townhouses)	1.9 million (3%)	2.9 million (4%)
Mobile homes	2.1 million (3%)	3.6 million (5%)
Multifamily dwellings	17.3 million (27%)	19.8 million (27%)

The tenure of occupied housing units in 1970 was: fee simple — 83% of the detached single-family houses, 85% of the mobile homes, 56% of attached single-family units, and 17% of the multifamily dwellings; and leasehold — 17% of the detached single-family houses, 15% of the mobile homes, 40% of the detached single-family units, and 81% of the multifamily dwellings [55]. Small proportions of each type also were occupied in condominium or cooperative tenure although these units have been concentrated in the multifamily stock.

Since 1970, significant changes have occurred in the rate of construction for each structural type. Substantial increases have been observed in the rate of mobile home and townhouse construction. With these increases, the character of the nation's housing stock is becoming more varied. Thus, the consumer, especially the buyer or renter desiring to move to a new (i.e., not existing) dwelling, will discover a greater choice of structural types. There is, however, a lack of research available to aid the consumer in forming decisions about structural types. While several studies have compared single-family dwellings with another type of residential structure, no study has produced a comprehensive comparative analysis of all four structural types.

Detached Single-Family House

Without question, the single-family house is traditionally the most popular and predominant form of American housing. In a survey of 1,003 consumers who seriously intend to purchase a new home in the near future, the home-building trade journal *Professional Builder* reported that nearly 93% preferred a single-family house [45]. In comparison to consumers who prefer to purchase an attached house (townhouse or apartment), the prospective buyers of single-family houses attached greater importance to the perceived advantages of a good investment, a good place to raise children, and privacy [32]. Similar advantages probably are perceived by renters, too, but this fact was not reported.

In a more recent marketing survey (1977), another trade journal, *House and Home,* reported that attached single-family shoppers were younger, had fewer children, and higher incomes than detached single-family shoppers [10, 11]. These findings tend to reflect those reported several years earlier in *Professional Builder* and to reflect the advantages of this structural type.

The resale value of the single-family dwelling (if purchased) is usually better than for other structural types with similar features (e.g., location, age, condition, size, etc.). This situation may be related to the recent trend of selling townhouses and apartments conflicting with the traditional slow growth of consumer acceptance of innovations in housing. There is, however, no reason to believe that owner-occupied townhouses and apartments will not enjoy appreciation at a rate similar to detached houses in the immediate future.

Visual and acoustical privacy is less likely to be a problem in detached houses than in townhouses or apartments. It should be noted, however, that it is possible to build effective sound partitions using existing construction technology. Thus, this problem may be reduced in well-designed attached-dwelling developments.

Exterior open space for children's play areas, gardening, and pets is usually in close proximity to the single-family dwelling and use is seldom restricted. This often is not the case in mobile home parks, townhouse developments, and apartment complexes. Furthermore, the occupant (especially owner) of a single-family house generally has more opportunities to alter the dwelling through remodeling (especially addition) than the mobile home, townhouse, or apartment occupant.

The detached single-family house has several substantial disadvantages which the consumer should also weigh before selecting a structural type. One of the most important disadvantages relates to costs. Land, labor, and material costs associated with construction are greater than for other types of structures [39]. Consequently, the

Single-family detached dwellings in a Maryland subdivision. (United States Department of Agriculture-Soil Conservation Service)

purchase price (and therefore, to a degree, rent) is usually more expensive. Utility costs and the time and energy necessary for repair and maintenance usually are more than in similar townhouses and apartments. Finally, a recent study conducted for the Department of Housing and Urban Development found that construction of single-family houses is a major factor causing undesirable environmental impact: land sprawl, traffic congestion, and air and water pollution [76].

Despite these disadvantages, the detached single-family house remains an American norm strongest among families with children. In a study of new dwelling units in the seventeen largest metropolitan areas of the United States, Lansing et al. observed significant differences in the characteristics of families who moved to new apartments and single family homes [26].

| | *Percent Moving to New* | |
Mover's Life-Cycle Stage	*Apartments*	*Single-Family Homes*
Young, Single	84	6
Young-Married, No Children	73	27
Married, Youngest Child under 5	30	70
Married, Youngest Child 5 to 18	16	84
Married, Over 45, No Children under 18	62	38
Not Now Married, Over 45	85	15
All Families	49	51

Lansing also noted a relationship between higher income and moving to new single-family homes. This analysis tends to indicate that families with children prefer to move to (new) single-family homes rather than (new) apartments, especially when income and financial assets are adequate for such a move.

From this analysis, it appears that the relevant question is: Will family income remain adequate and does the family have sufficient assets (for down payment) to effectively participate in the single-family housing market? For consumers without sufficient financial resources and the desire to make a substantial financial investment, the detached house may be an inappropriate alternative. This situation is reflected in the growing rate of townhouse and mobile home construction.

Mobile Home [14]

The mobile home is a rapidly emerging form of American housing. Growth began with the post-World War II housing shortage when mobile homes were used primarily as stopgap housing. Since 1965, mobile homes have comprised 13 to 22% of the housing starts in the United States. During this period, the number of mobile homes has increased fourfold while single-family houses and apartments have increased only about 30% [31]. Much of this growth is a result of two interrelated trends: increased formation of households created by young people marrying and the inability of the nation's housing industry to produce dwellings affordable by young families and others with incomes below the national average. These facts were reflected in the 1970 census [55]:

— Mobile home residents were more likely to be married than the average American household (83 versus 70%).
— Mobile home buyers were generally younger (thirty-three versus thirty-seven

---

14. Although mobile homes are essentially single-family detached dwellings, they are constructed to different building codes and marketed quite differently than conventional single-family houses.

median years) or over fifty-five (20 versus 11% of buyers) with median incomes 30% below buyers of new conventional detached housing.

— Mobile home residents were more likely to be members of smaller households than the average American household (2.3 versus 3.2 average size).

Also relevant is the fact that about 10% of mobile home buyers in 1970 were farmers [67], many of whom found other housing alternatives impractical because of cost (e.g., building) or nonavailability (e.g., preowned dwellings, townhouses or apartments). Some mobile home residents may view their dwellings as interim (stop-gap) housing until they can purchase a single-family house. This fact was indicated by a 1966 census survey which reported that two-thirds of the nation's mobile home owners hope eventually to move to a conventional detached house [71].

It appears, therefore, that mobile homes represent a compromise for many consumers, especially younger families who wish to minimize cost, acquire equity, and still occupy a detached dwelling. Whether mobile homes actually offer the consumer the best alternative is related to the consumer's personal and financial situation as well as to several advantages and disadvantages.

The major advantage of the mobile home is that the purchase price and initial costs are substantially less than for similar dwellings. For example a 860-square-foot, 14-foot-by-70-foot mobile home usually was sold for $14,500 in 1976 with an average down payment of 10%, while the average conventionally financed (new) housing was priced at $48,000 and required an average down payment of approximately 25% [31, 14]. Thus the mobile home buyer encounters lower initial costs and less foregone interest than most conventional home buyers.

Mobile home financing is usually much easier to arrange than mortgages for other types of structures. It is also extremely convenient to purchase and finance a mobile home, especially for younger families, since the purchase price and loan can include appliances and furnishings.

Mobile house in a midwest mobile home park. (Photo: Iowa State University Photo Service)

Finally, the mobile home resident generally finds acoustical privacy is less likely to be a problem than in townhouses or apartments.

Despite these advantages, a great deal of controversy surrounds mobile homes, reflecting important disadvantages the consumer should examine. Foremost are claims that mobile homes are more susceptible to wind and fire threats. Although evidence is not conclusive because of lack of national data, the author's examination of unpublished American Red Cross disaster statistics revealed that the incidence of mobile home wind destruction was over 500% greater than that for detached single-family dwellings between 1970 and 1977 [3, 6]. Furthermore, while the average mobile home is only about five years old compared to more than twenty years for one- and two-family dwellings, the incidence of fire is only slightly less in mobile homes (1:120 annually compared to 1:95) [15, 12]. The severity of fire is, however, generally worse in mobile homes, whether measured by dollar damage (30 to 40% of mobile home fires result in total destruction) or loss of life (fatalities are reportedly four to ten times more likely in mobile home fires) [29]. While there is evidence that proper tie-downs, more stringent building codes, and fire detection alarms may reduce these problems [12], there is no indication that safety improvements will limit fire and wind threats to the degree enjoyed by occupants of other types of residential structures. Reflecting wind and fire threats, premiums for mobile home insurance are generally two to four times greater than premiums for single-family houses [12].

Other financial disadvantages of mobile homes are also significant. Higher interest rates are usually charged for mobile homes (12% average for new units, higher for older units) and the method by which interest is calculated ("Rule of 78s") penalizes borrowers who prepay their loans [49]. Since most mobile homes are financed on installment contracts, there is substantially less protection against foreclosure and repossession than conventional home owners enjoy [12]. Mobile homes have historically depreciated in value at a rate of 20 to 25% the first year and 5 to 10% each year thereafter [34]. During years of rampant inflation, mobile home owners have generally continued to realize less appreciation in their investments in comparison to other owners. This situation is largely the result of the practice of treating land separately from the dwelling. The home usually is sold on a fee simple basis while the land is often leased from a park owner. This arrangement also gives rise to serious landlord-tenant conflict.

While these financial disadvantages have an impact directly upon mobile home buyers, they also influence the costs of renting a mobile home. Weighing these advantages and disadvantages, the rationale of buying a mobile home to develop equity must be questioned seriously, especially when the purchase is dependent upon installment financing. Perhaps the financial and safety deficiencies of mobile homes will improve with better building code enforcement, continuation of the trend toward double-wide homes, placing mobile homes on permanent foundations, improved state landlord-tenant statutes, and more favorable mortgage financing.

Townhouse

During the 1970s, townhouses have been the fastest growing segment of the nation's housing market. Although attached single-family dwellings (townhouses) accounted for only 3% of the dwelling units in 1970 [55], *Professional Builder* estimated that 40% of the new home buyers in 1975 would purchase an attached house [45] — mostly townhouses.[15] A townhouse is by definition a dwelling unit

---

15. Excluding mobile homes.

which shares one or more common (party) walls with adjoining units. The number of units connected in a cluster may range from the duplex to twelve or more units. As with other structural types, townhouses may be occupied on a fee simple, condominium, cooperative, or leasehold basis [25].

Despite the increasing rate of construction, there is a lack of research to assist the consumer in evaluating townhouses. One of the few studies on townhouses, done for the Urban Land Institute (ULI), reported that major attractions to townhouse buyers were the opportunity to build equity and freedom from maintenance responsibilities [42]. These perceived advantages also were substantiated by a study conducted for *Professional Builder* [45]. The ULI study reported, however, that 75% of the townhouse residents said they would probably not move to another townhouse [41]. This trend tends to indicate that many townhouse residents compromise the desire for a detached single-family house, perhaps because of financial and location considerations. The wisdom of selecting a townhouse will, however, depend on the consumer's personal characteristics as well as the relative advantages and disadvantages of townhouses.

The major advantage of a townhouse is that construction cost and therefore purchase price are potentially lower than similar detached houses. This cost savings is possible through more intense land use, shorter utility connections, use of party walls, and greater scales of economy associated with building a number of units on the same site. This advantage may be diluted when builders include expensive common facilities such as parks, playgrounds, and clubhouses that substantially boost purchase prices.

When properly planned, efficient and appealing land development may occur. This type of land use, including park-like and wooded natural spaces, is most likely to be found in townhouse developments which use innovative site planning.

Southern Hills townhouse condominium development in Des Moines, Iowa. (Photo: Hedrick-Blessing, John D. Bloodgood, Architect)

Maintenance and utility expenses are usually less than in similar detached dwellings since party walls reduce exposed exterior surfaces as much as 70% For this reason, the time and energy necessary for exterior maintenance and upkeep are less than that for detached dwellings.

As the ULI study notes, townhouses are not without problems. Unless properly planned and built, visual and acoustical privacy may be adversely affected. This problem appears to be most severe in townhouse complexes with higher densities (over eight units/acre), little open spaces, thin party walls, poorly planned parking areas, and complexes with a high child and pet population [41]. Individual townhouse owners also may find their use of exterior areas limited (e.g., paint color, landscaping, gardening, additions, etc.) by the home owner's association. Former owners of detached houses also may find it difficult to adjust because of their independent psychological attachment to yard and other exterior work.

It should be emphasized that the relative advantages of a specific townhouse may vary substantially according to tenure, organization of owners' association, and quality of planning and construction.

Apartment

According to the 1976 Annual Survey of Housing, over 25% of the nation's housing was composed of multifamily units [64]. During the past forty years, little significant change has been observed in the proportion of multifamily units even though construction frequently has fluctuated from year to year. This situation suggests that apartments fulfill a vital role in the nation's housing stock.

As previously noted, Lansing et al. found that young single people and young married families without children as well as older individuals and older married couples without children were more likely to move into a (new) apartment than a (new) detached single-family house [26]. Families with lower incomes also tend to move to an apartment rather than a single-family house. Although at face value these factors tend to indicate that apartments are a preferred alternative for certain types of consumers, there is evidence which suggests many apartment dwellers base their selection on necessity (e.g., low income or inability to maintain) rather than preference. Lansing noted that only about 15% of the families[16] moving to a (new) apartment formerly occupied a single-family house and most of this group were either older couples or individuals [26]. This reflects the process of aging rather than a general shift in preferences to apartments. Apartments do, however, offer significant advantages which the consumer should examine within the context of his or her own situation.

The costs of building an apartment are generally less than comparable single-family dwellings [39]. Consequently, the purchase price or monthly rent may be less as well. This savings is possible through more intense land development, shorter utility connections, use of common partitions, and greater scales of economy associated with multi-unit construction. As with some townhouse developments, however, this savings potential often is reduced when builders include many common amenities such as pools and party rooms.

The time required for maintenance as well as for the expense of maintenance and utilities are usually less than that required for similar detached and attached single-family houses and mobile homes. This savings is the result of reduced exterior surfaces — up to a 90% reduction. Reduced exterior exposure, however, also limits natural lighting and ventilation.

16. Excluding single-family dwellings that continued to be occupied by parents, other relatives, or roommates of the movers.

Harbor Point condominium high-rise in Chicago. (Courtesy of Harbor Point, Inc.)

Walk-up rental apartment dwelliings in Washington, D.C. (United States Department of Agriculture; photo by Murray Lemmon)

Finally, apartments are frequently the only type of housing available in many desirable locations: central cities, college campuses, scenic areas, and so on. It should be noted, however, that many older apartments and older single-family houses which have been converted into apartments have been zoned into noisy areas deficient in aesthetic values.

Many of the disadvantages of townhouses also may be associated with apartments: lack of visual and acoustical privacy, restricted use of exterior areas, and bans on pets and children. Furthermore, apartments usually are smaller than other types of dwellings, with the possible exception of a mobile home.

Summary

The purpose of this examination has been to promote effective consumer decision-making by examining factors that modify an individual's housing needs and by delineating major housing alternatives within a sequence or structure of inter-dependent choices. Examination of census data, industry statistics, and research has offered insights into the nature, prevalence, and advantages of each type of alternative. Data have also given insights into the types of consumers attracted to different types of housing and their experiences. Based upon these perspectives, the consumer is better prepared to make decisions which will complement his or her quality of life.

To housing students, educators, and researchers, the model of consumer decision-making also provides a structure to interpret and order a complex variety of literature and public policy. Such a framework is absolutely essential if meaningful learning, teaching and research are to be realized and if professionals are to play a more significant role in ameliorating societal housing problems through public policy and other forms of collective action.

Appendix A

Quantitative Profile of Occupied Housing Stock (1000s) 1970-1976

	1976 [64, 65, 58]	1970-1976 Change [55]
Number of Households (Occupied Housing Units)	74,005	+17%
— Renting	26,101 (35%)	+11%
• Moving to Renting in 1976	9,924 (38%)	--
New Household (Different Head)	3,187 (32%)	--
Same Household (Same Head)	6,737 (68%)	--
From Owner Occupancy	1,321 (20%)	--
From Renter Occupancy	5,416 (80%)	--
• Detached Single-Family Dwelling Occupancy	7,242 (28%)	-6%
Completed in 1976 for Occupancy	10 (0%)	--
• Attached Single-Family Dwelling Occupancy*	1,235 (5%)	+56%
• Mobile Home Occupancy	640 (2%)	+99%
Shipped in 1976 for Occupancy**	25 (4%)	--
• Multifamily Dwelling Occupancy*	16,984 (65%)	+15%
Completed in 1976 for Occupancy*	263 (1%)	--
— Owning	47,904 (65%)	+20%
• Condominium	634 (1%)	+62%
• Cooperative	405 (1%)	+62%
• Fee-Simple	46,865 (98%)	+19%
• Moving to Owning in 1976	4,665 (10%)	--
New Household (Different Head)	653 (14%)	--
Same Household (Same Head)	4,012 (86%)	--
From Owner Occupancy	2,226 (55%)	--
From Renter Occupancy	1,786 (45%)	--
• Detached Single-Family Dwelling Occupancy	40,476 (84%)	+18%
Complete in 1976 for Occupancy	1,016 (3%)	--
Speculatively-Built (For Sale)	610 (60%)	--
Custom-Built	210 (21%)	--
Owner-Built	196 (19%)	--
• Attached Single-Family Dwelling Occupancy*	1,660 (3%)	+49%
• Mobile Home Occupancy	2,987 (6%)	+49%
Shipped in 1976 for Occupancy**	246 (8%)	--
Site Rented (adjusted for not reported)	1,749 (68%)	--
• Multifamily Dwelling Occupancy	2,781 (6%)	+6%
Completed in 1976 for Occupancy*	74 (2%)	--

*Data from 1976 does not separate units completed between multifamily and attached single-family units. Therefore, the occupied stock of both structural types was combined to calculate the proportion completed in 1976.

**Mobile home shipment data did not separate units intended for sale as opposed for rent. Ten percent of the units shipped were allocated to the rental stock based upon the experience of recent years [67].

Appendix B

Privately Owned Housing Units Completed (1000s) 1972-1976 [57, 62]

Year	Total (100%)	Single-Family		Mobile Homes		Multifamily	
1972	2547	1143	(44%)	576	(23%)	828	(33%)
1973	2581	1174	(45%)	567	(22%)	840	(33%)
1974	2021	932	(46%)	329	(16%)	760	(38%)
1975	1509	866	(58%)	213	(14%)	430	(28%)
1976	1608	1026	(64%)	246	(15%)	336	(21%)
Average	2053	1028	(50%)	386	(19%)	639	(31%)

Appendix C

Privately Owned Single-Family Houses Completed (1000s) 1972-1976 Total [57]

	Total		SMSA*		Non-SMSA	
Built for sale (speculatively-built)	3084	(61%)	2395	(76%)	690	(36%)
For owner occupancy (custom-built)	1068	(21%)	433	(14%)	634	(33%)
For owner occupancy (owner-built**)	914	(18%)	331	(10%)	582	(31%)
Total	5066	(100%)	3159	(100%)	1906	(100%)

*SMSA (Standard Metropolitan Statistical Area): A county or group of counties which contains at least one city of 40,000 or more and which is socially and economically integrated with the central city.
**Owner-built: Owner functioning as a general contractor and/or furnishing some or all of the labor him or herself.

Appendix D

Privately Owned Single-Family Houses (1000s) Started 1973-1973 and Completed 1974-1976 [55, 56]*

Year	Built for Sale (Speculative)		For Owner Occupancy (Custom)		For Owner Occupancy (Owner-Built**)	
1963	603	(60%)	191	(19%)	217	(21%)
1964	568	(59%)	184	(19%)	213	(22%)
1965	592	(62%)	180	(19%)	186	(19%)
1966	441	(57%)	174	(23%)	157	(20%)
1967	502	(60%)	168	(20%)	162	(20%)
1968	536	(60%)	178	(20%)	172	(19%)
1969	483	(60%)	170	(21%)	148	(18%)
1970	496	(62%)	166	(21%)	142	(18%)
1971	741	(66%)	223	(20%)	161	(14%)
1972	846	(66%)	252	(20%)	177	(14%)
1973	673	(62%)	238	(22%)	178	(16%)
1974	538	(59%)	211	(23%)	169	(18%)
1975	494	(58%)	174	(20%)	187	(22%)
1976	610	(60%)	210	(21%)	196	(19%)

*Since 1973, the Bureau of the Census has not reported detailed owner-building housing starts. Therefore, completion data present the best possible relative picture of owner-building. This change, however, biases the picture slightly.
**Owner-built housing involves the owner functioning as a general contractor and/or furnishing some or all of the labor him or herself.

Appendix E

Typical Owner-Occupancy Costs of a Single-Family House

As illustrated in *Housing Costs in the Late Seventies*, the consumer generally encounters four basic types of housing expenses: initial development and construction, initial occupancy, monthly occupancy, and selling costs. Of greatest direct concern are the expenses paid or budgeted on a month-to-month basis such as mortgage payments, property taxes, property insurance, utility bills, and maintenance costs. Angell examines these expenses and presents the following example of a typical $55,000 house purchased in 1979 [4, 63, 14]:

$55,000 purchase price (also market value [MV]) with 5% appreciation per year
  1,100 initial costs (2% of MV)
 11,000 down payment (20% down)
 44,000 mortgage at 10% for 30 years

Item	Average Monthly Expenses				30-Year Total
	First Year		30-Year Period		
● Principal (30-year average)	$122.22	17%	$ 122.22	11%	$ 44,000.
● Interest (30-year average)	263.92	38	263.92	24	95,010.
● Taxes (at 2% of MV per year)	91.76	13	198.08	18	71.310.
● Insurance (at ½% of MV per year)	22.94	3	49.52	5	17,827.
● Utilities (at 3% of MV per year)	137.50	19	297.12	28	106,965.
● Repair-Maintenance (at 1½% of MV per year)	68.75	10	148.56	14	53,482.
Total	$707.09	100%	$1079.41	100%	$388,594.

This example reflects an assumption that inflation will average 5% per year for all occupancy costs except principal and interest (i.e., a fixed, not variable, rate mortgage). An analysis of the effect of the 5% appreciation or inflation rate reveals:

— $237,699 gross resale value in the thirtieth year.

— $225,599 net gain for a return of approximately 10¼% interest compounded annually before taxes with an initial (20% down payment plus cost) investment of $12,100. If the initial investment was reduced to $3,850 (5% down plus costs), a $233,849 net gain for a return of approximately 15¾% interest compounded annually would be realized before taxes.

This analysis reflects the principle of "financial leverage" where an individual enjoys the full benefit of property appreciation with limited capital investment [79]. The analysis, however, does not establish the relative investment wisdom of buying since it does not establish the following: (1) the after-tax cost of interest and property taxes; (2) the opportunity cost associated with the owner's increasing equity; (3) the variation between present and future price and cost between different areas; and (4) the occupancy cost of alternative mortgage financing tenure and structure forms.

While considering monthly occupancy costs, it may be surprising to realize that all monthly housing costs, except for principal, do nothing to pay for the lot or house itself. The other expenses are the operating costs paid by the home owner for the money borrowed (interest), for public services (taxes), for insurance protection, for heat, light, water, sewer, and telephone service (utilities), and finally, for maintenance and repair.

Literature Cited

1. Ahu-Lughod, Janet and Foley, Mary M. "The Consumer Votes by Moving." In *Urban Housing,* edited by William L. C. Wheaton, pp. 175-90. New York: Free Press, 1966.

2. Aist, Herbert T. "The Marketing Scene." *House and Home,* October 1972, p. 74.

3. American Red Cross. "Statistics on Mobile Homes Destroyed and Damaged by Type of Disaster: Fiscal Years 70 through 78." Unpublished statistical summary. Washington, D.C.: 1978.

4. Angell, William J. *Buying a Minnesota Home* (Bulletin 414). St. Paul: Agricultural Extension Service, University of Minnesota, 1978.

5. Angell, William J. *Housing Costs in the Late-Seventies* (Folder 315). St. Paul: Agricultural Extension Service, University of Minnesota, forthcoming.

6. Angell, William J. "Incidence of Fire and Wind Damage and Destruction of Mobile Homes and Single-Family Dwellings." Unpublished Report. St. Paul: Agricultural Extension Service, University of Minnesota, September 1, 1978.

7. Angell, William J. *Remodeling Older Minnesota Homes* (Bulletin 417). St. Paul: Agricultural Extension Service, University of Minnesota, 1978.

8. Angell, William J.; Mowry, Betty; and Patrick, Abigail. "A Forgotten Consumer: The Renter." *Proceedings of 8th Annual Meeting,* American Association of Housing Educators. Madison: University of Wisconsin, 1974.

9. Angell, William J., and Olson, Phillip S. *Owner-Built Housing* (Bulletin 429). St. Paul: Agricultural Extension Service, University of Minnesota, 1977.

10 Cahm, Joel G. "What Attached-Home Shopper Want." *House and Home,* September 1977, pp. 78-81.

11. Cahm, Joel G. "What Single-Family Buyers are Looking For." *House and Home,* July 1977, pp. 75-79.

12. The Center for Auto Safety. *Mobile Homes: The Low-Cost Housing Hoax.* New York: Grossman Publishers, 1975.

13. The Conference Board. "The Two-Way 'Squeeze', 1978." *Economic Road Maps,* April 1978, pp. 2-3.

14. Federal Home Loan Bank Board. "Mortgage Markets . . ." (Tables S.5.1, S.5.3, and S.6.1). *FHLBB Journal,* July 1978.

15. "Fires and Fire Losses Classified, 1973." *Fire Journal,* September 1974, pp. 33-35.

16. Foote, Nelson N., et al. *Housing Choices and Housing Constraints.* New York: McGraw-Hill, 1960.

17. Gladhart, Peter M. "Family Housing Adjustment and the Theory of Residential Mobility: A Temporal Analysis of Family Residential Histories." Ph.D. dissertation, Cornell University, 1973.

18. Gross, Jackson W. "Buying a Home Aids Marriage." *FHLBB Journal,* July 1972, pp. 14-17.

19. Hempel, Donald J. *A Comparative Study of the Home Buying Process in Two Connecticut Housing Markets* (Real Estate Report 10). Storrs: Center for Real Estate and Urban Economics Studies, University of Connecticut, 1970.

20. Hempel, Donald J. "Family Buying Decisions: A Cross-Cultural Perspective." *Journal of Marketing Research,* August 1974, pp. 295-302.

21. "Home Resale Price Studies Boost Loan Underwriting." *Savings and Loan News,* May 1973, pp. 80-84.

22. "How Do You Rate Loans and Why?" *Savings and Loan News,* May 1974, pp. 60-66.

23. Johnakin, Stephen G. "A Second Generation of Condominium Statutes." *Urban Land,* December 1974, pp. 10-13.

24. Karr, James N. *The Condominium Buyer's Guide.* New York: Frederick Fell Publishers, 1973.

25. Krasnowiecki, Jan Z. "Townhouse Condominium Compared to Conventional Subdivision with Homes Association." *Real Estate Law Journal,* Spring 1973, pp. 323-367.

26. Lansing, John B.; Clifton, Charles Wade; and Morgan, James N. *New Homes and Poor People: A Study of Chains of Moves.* Ann Arbor: Institute for Social Research, University of Michigan, 1969.

27. Lansing, John B., et al. *Residential Location and Urban Mobility.* Ann Arbor: Institute for Social Research, University of Michigan, 1964.

28. Lythe, Robert J. "The Component Manufacturer." *Automation in Housing,* December/January 1973/74, pp. 67-78.

29. Maier, Peter L. "Petition Requesting the Adoption of Three Mobile Home Construction Standards in Order to Achieve Greater Fire Safety." Submitted to U. S. Department of Housing and Urban Development, March 18. Washington D.C.: Center for Auto Safety, 1975.

30. Main, Jeremy. "A Man's Home Is His Capital." *Money,* December 1972, pp. 28-33.

31. Manufactured Housing Institute. *Quick Facts About the Manufactured Housing Industry*, Arlington, Va.: May 1977.

32. Michelson, William; Belgue, David; and Stewart, John. "Intentions and Expectations in Differential Residential Selection." *Journal of Marriage and the Family*, May 1973, pp. 189-96.

33. Minnesota Department of Commerce. *Minnesota Real Estate Manual*. St. Paul: Minnesota Documents Section, 1974.

34. "The Mobile Home Market." *Appraisal Journal*, July 1972, pp. 391-411.

35. "Modernization: Coming On Strong." *Building Supply News*, November 1975, pp. 40-46.

36. Morris, Earl W., and Winter, Mary. *Housing, Family, and Society*. New York: John Wiley and Sons, 1978.

37. Morris, Earl W., and Winter, Mary. "A Theory of Family Housing Adjustment." *Journal of Marriage and the Family*, February 1975, pp. 79-88.

38. Munsinger, Gary M. et al. "Joint Purchase Decisions by Husbands and Wives." *Journal of Consumer Research*, March 1975, pp. 60-66.

39. National Commission on Urban Problems. *Building the American City*. Washington, D.C.: U. S. Government Printing Office, 1969.

40. Newman, Sandra. *The Residential Environment and the Desire to Move*. Ann Arbor: Institute for Social Research, University of Michigan, 1974.

41. Norcross, Carl. *Townhouses and Condominiums*. Washington, D.C.: Urban Land Institute, 1973.

42. "Outlook 1974: A Special PB Report on the Housing Market." *Professional Builder*, December 1973, pp. 22-25.

43. Pfeiler, Thomas. "Condominium Financing: Some Legal Basics." *Legal Bulletin*, September 1972, pp. 249-64.

44. Piper, John B. "Condominium Economics." *Appraisal Journal*, April 1973, pp. 260-63.

45. "Professional Builder's National Consumer Builder Survey on Housing." *Professional Builder*, January 1975, pp. 81-97.

46. Reidelback, J. A. "The Modular Manufacturer." *Automation in Housing*, December/January 1973/74, pp. 57-66.

47. Rossi, Peter. *Why Families Move*. Glencoe, Ill.: Free Press, 1955.

48. Rothenberg, Henry H. *What You Should Know About Condominiums*. Radnor, Pa.: Chilton Book Company, 1974.

49. Salm, L. Joseph. "A Discussion of Yields on Loans." Unpublished report. Chicago: United States Savings and Loan League, 1970.

50. Schulin, Robert. "The Home Manufacturer." *Automation in Housing*, December/January 1973/74, pp. 27-35.

51. Shelton, John P. "The Cost of Renting versus Owning a Home." *Land Economics*, February 1968, pp. 59-72.

52. Smith, Wallace J. *Housing: The Social and Economic Elements*. Berkeley: University of California Press, 1971.

53. Struck, Ronald. "The Average Life of a Single-Family Mortgage." *FHLBB Journal*, June 1974, pp. 15-20.

54. Swain, Craig. "The Affordability of Unaffordable Housing." Unpublished paper. Minneapolis: University of Minnesota, November, 1977.

55. U. S. Bureau of the Census. *Census of Housing: 1970 Detailed Housing Characteristics*. HC(1)-B1 United States Summary. Washington, D.C.: U. S. Government Printing Office, 1972.

56. U. S. Bureau of the Census. *Construction Reports — Characteristics of New One-Family Houses, 1973* (C-25 Series). Washington, D.C.: U. S. Government Printing Office, 1974.

57. U. S. Bureau of the Census. *Construction Reports — Characteristics of New Housing, 1976* (C-25 Series). Washington, D.C.: U.S. Government Printing Office, 1977.

58. U. S. Bureau of the Census. *Construction Reports — Housing Starts* (C-20 Series). Washington, D.C.: U. S. Government Printing Office, 1978.

59. U. S. Bureau of the Census. *Construction Reports — Price Index of New One-Family*

Houses Sold (C-27 Series). Washington, D.C.: U. S. Government Printing Office, 1978 (second quarter).

60. U. S. Bureau of the Census. *Construction Reports — Residential Alterations and Repairs, 1972 Annual Report* (C50-72A). Washington, D.C.: U. S. Government Printing Office, 1973.

61. U. S. Bureau of the Census. *Construction Reports — Residential Alterations and Repairs: Annual 1976* (C50-76A). Washington, D.C.: U. S. Government Printing Office, 1977.

62. U. S. Bureau of the Census. *Construction Review*. Washington, D.C.: U. S. Government Printing Office, April 1978.

63. U. S. Bureau of the Census. *Current Housing Reports — Financial Characteristics for the United States and Regions: 1976, Part C*. Washington, D.C.: U. S. Government Printing Office, 1978.

64. U. S. Bureau of the Census. *Current Housing Reports — General Housing Characteristics for the United States and Regions: 1976, Part A*. Washington, D.C.: U. S. Government Printing Office, 1978.

65. U. S. Bureau of the Census. *Current Housing Reports — Housing Characteristics of Recent Movers for the United States and Regions: 1976, Part D*. Washington, D.C.: U. S. Government Printing Office, 1978.

66. U. S. Bureau of the Census. *Current Housing Reports — Indicators of Housing and Neighborhood Quality for the United States and Regions: 1976, Part B*. Washington, D.C.: U. S. Government Printing Office, 1978.

67. U. S. Bureau of the Census. *Mobile Homes: Current Housing Subject Reports (HC(7)-6)*. Washington, D.C.: U. S. Government Printing Office, 1972.

68. U. S. Bureau of the Census. *Population of the United States — Trends and Prospects: 1950-1990 (Series P-23)*. Washington, D.C.: U. S. Government Printing Office.

69. U. S. Bureau of the Census. "Public Use Samples of the 1970 Census — 5 Percent SMSA and County Group Samples." Unpublished tabulation by Minnesota Analysis and Planning System, University of Minnesota, St. Paul.) Washington, D.C.: 1972.

70. U. S. Bureau of the Census. *Statistical Abstracts of the United States* 98th ed. Washington, D.C.: U.S. Government Printing Office, 1977.

71. U. S. Bureau of the Census. "Survey of the Owners of New Mobile Homes." Unpublished report for the Department of Housing and Urban Development. Washington, D.C.: 1967.

72. U. S. Bureau of Labor Statistics. *Monthly Labor Review*. August, 1978.

73. U. S. Bureau of Labor Statistics. *Relative Importance of Components in the Consumer Price Index*. Washington, D.C.: U.S. Government Printing Office, 1977.

74. U.S. Department of Housing and Urban Development. *Final Report of the Task Force on Housing Costs*. Washington, D.C.: U.S. Department of Housing and Urban Development, May 1978.

75. U.S. Department of Housing and Urban Development. *HUD-FHA Comparison of Cooperative and Condominium Housing* (HUD-321-F). Washington, D.C.: U.S. Government Printing Office, 1972.

76. U.S. Department of Housing and Urban Development, and Environmental Protection Agency. *The Cost of Sprawl: Detailed Cost Analysis* (prepared by the Real Estate Research Corporation for the Council on Environmental Quality). Washington, D.C.: U.S. Government Printing Office, 1974.

77. U.S. League of Savings Associations. *Fact Book, 1976*. Chicago: 1976.

78. U.S. League of Savings Associations. *Homeownership: Realizing the American Dream*. Chicago: 1978.

79. Zerbst, Robert H. et. al. "Evaluation of Financial Leverage for Real Estate Investments." *The Real Estate Appraiser*, July-August 1977, pp. 7-11.

Discussion Questions

1. What are the alternative tenure forms? Discuss the advantages and disadvantages of each tenure form.

2. Give an example of how a family may be living in a dwelling with both fee simple and leasehold tenure.

3. What are the alternative structural types? Discuss the advantages and disadvantages of each structural type.

4. What are the major advantages of buying a ready built house rather than contracting to have one built for you? There are also disadvantages to building your own house; discuss these advantages.

5. In the study conducted by Lansing et al. they observed significant differences in the characteristics of families who moved to apartments and families who moved to single-family houses. Discuss the differences in the characteristics of these families.

6. What are the two interrelated trends that have contributed to the growth of mobile homes?

7. Using the flow chart on page 247, follow through the decision-making steps an individual or family would encounter in purchasing a conventional, detached, single-family dwelling.

8. The author describes seven factors he refers to as "Housing Need Modifiers." Identify these factors and give a specific example for each.

9. Define the terms "speculatively built" and "custom built." Explain why more homes are speculatively built.

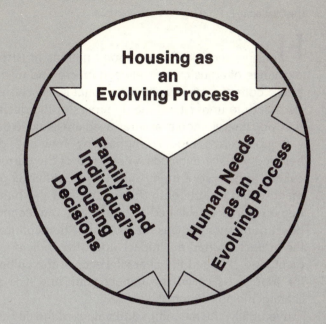

Housing as
an
Evolving Process

Family's and
Individual's
Housing
Decisions

Human Needs
as an
Evolving Process

Summary—
The Challenge
in Housing

Housing decisions in developed nations must be made during a ceaseless exchange of adjustments between macro and micro forces. This explains why public consensus and lasting personal satisfactions are difficult to attain. It is necessary to understand the dynamics of the decision-making process, otherwise any intervention measures used are likely to be inappropriate.

Opposite is a model emphasizing how the decision-making process is believed to have evolved. A construct of the current process would show the culture to consist of many subcultures within all of *society*, and the *environment* would include both the natural and the human-built. In the beginning, human beings established a culture, and the *technology* which evolved was a direct outgrowth, as was the artifact of that culture. Both the technology and the artifact exerted an impact upon the individual and the natural environment, and changed the characteristics of the culture. This cycle, indicated by the triangle, is called the impact path, and it is a never-ending process of change and adjustment.

Eventually, the meanings and values of the culture became institutionalized, and gradually the production and regulatory institutions gained sufficient power to determine what technologies would be developed into what artifacts. This power, shown by the loop, allowed these institutions to bypass the culture, with the result that many decisions were not fully weighed. The decision-making loop also indicates that the artifacts which developed did not make full use of the technology available.

Human beings evolved meanings and values and organized themselves into groups to insure the preservation of those values. Any innovative ideas were evaluated according to how well they appeared to serve the common good and it was on this basis that they were promoted or suppressed. Changes in agricultural practices especially were proposed with great care because an error could mean the elimination of a people.

Insight into how house forms evolved out of technical decisions has not been a highly investigated area of study, but Amos Rapoport believes technology is a response to social forces. According to Rapoport, the average member of the primitive group was capable of building his own house by the prescribed methods and forms which were very culturally embedded. When the dwelling models were fully adjusted, they fulfilled most of the social unit's cultural, physical, and maintenance needs. The preindustrial vernacular housing which followed differed from primitive housing in that a building tradesman was employed in the construction of dwellings. Every member of the society, however, knew how to build and participated in the choice of housing type and other design processes. It was the use of tradesmen which initiated building by technicians and professionals. "Tradition as a regulator disappeared," says Rapaport, who explains how the loss of a commonly shared value and image of the world led to diversity of house form which supported technical specialization. Gradually, "experts" were the only members of society capable of constructing housing as building became

Impact Path and the Technology Development Decision Making Loop

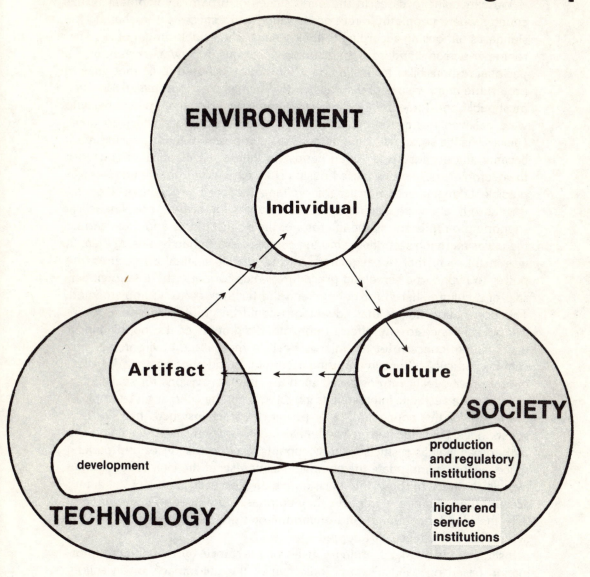

SOCIAL INSTITUTIONS

PRODUCTION — Finances, Labor, Building and Manufacturing Industries

REGULATORY — Governments

HIGHER — Family, Education, Law, Religion

SERVICE — Voluntary, Special Interest

increasingly complex to fulfill a new cultural value — originality. In this way Rapaport explains how we came to accept the values of strangers. [1]

We can point to cases in the early stages of urban development in this country where people by direct participation were successful in shaping the standards of housing according to their values. The establishment of the one-room-per-person standard is an example of citizens in New York assuming a personal responsibility for instituting what they considered to be measures to protect the moral values of the newly arrived emigrants. Eventually, however, most public and some private decisions were assigned to hired personnel who were believed to have superior knowledge and skills from which to make choices. As the society which emerged was composed of many subcultures, it became efficient for these "hired hands" to ignore the essential character of their "employers," and because housing is an expensive durable good, it was possible to maintain a practice of omitting feedback procedures. Governmental officials were often neither adequately informed nor financially supported to represent all the interests of their constituents and they learned there was more job security in ignoring complex issues than by raising them. It was in this way that the regulatory and producing institutions secured the power to bypass the screening procedure which formerly the total membership of a culture shared for determining the technology to be implemented. This domination meant that advantages could be granted to one segment without reference to any effects upon other segments of the population or even without concern for the injuries dealt to the natural environment. The common practice of locating housing according to the price of land regardless of any other qualities it possessed such as safety, provisions for social interaction, or the aesthetic interest of its inhabitants can be cited as an example of the results of this concentration of power. In other instances heavily used streets have been located in residential areas, defacing and devaluing the property as well as restricting the occupants' access to services and parking space, all to accommodate the commercial interests of the city. These are but two illustrations of how the decision-making process may not take into account the full range of impacts; they emphasize the need to consider carefully the long-term human and environmental effects of technical changes before they are extensively adopted.

Institutions of higher learning can be of assistance by contributing information based on valid research indicative of the full impacts of an action. Because individuals have little power, there is a need to help them organize service units to study people in relation to housing and to serve as knowledgeable participants in procedures leading to public decisions. Since there is a tendency for residents to consider only personal and immediate ends, competent professionals will always be required to make certain all relevant factors are adequately presented and objectively evaluated before the final resolution of an issue is made.

The Environmental Impact Statement is a formalized procedure designed to

---

1. Amos Rapoport, *House Form and Culture* (Englewood Cliffs, N.J.: Prentice-Hall, 1969), p. 6.

predict all important effects of an action. This instrument, when well-conducted, contributes greatly to the resolution of complex issues, but it is costly to conduct demanding refinements to eliminate unnecessary steps.

In conclusion, villages, cities, communities, regions and nations will have many decisions to make which will affect people within the context of an ever-changing world. Housing can either become a major objective worthy of prime attention because of the role it plays in determining the social and physical welfare of people or, as has happened so often in the past, it can be regarded as merely a means to other ends.

Informed, concerned citizens can stimulate officials and professionals to take the aggressive action necessary to develop housing strategies supportive of healthy living environments for the most poorly housed as well as for the many more whose housing falls short of meeting all basic needs. Holistic approaches and newly discovered insights are tools which have never before been available to apply to the reordering of values and social institutions. The reduction of housing problems is a possibility if committed people, working together, are willing to explore ways to make use of these tools.

The technology used to support and maintain housing as well as the artifact itself generates continuous impacts upon human beings. The impacts are transferred to the individual and the family by way of the physical and cultural environment. Because there is such diversity of needs and contributions within these primary elements, all major housing decisions need to be examined from many points of view. These points of view constitute the nature of housing perspectives.

Glossary of Acronyms

AMIs — alternative mortgage instruments
BMIR — below market interest rate
BRAB — Builders Research Advisory Board
CBD — central business district
CDBG — Community Development Block Grant
CU — Consumers Union
FEA — Federal Energy Administration
FHLBB — Federal Home Loan Bank Board
FHA — Federal Housing Administration
FmHA — Farmer's Home Administration
FNMA — Federal National Mortgage Association
FSLIC — Federal Savings and Loan Insurance Corporation
FTC — Federal Trade Commission
GI — government issue
GNP — gross national product
HAP — Housing Assistance Plan
HFAs — Housing Finance Agencies
HHFA — Housing and Home Finance Agency
HOLC — Home Owners Loan Corporation
HOW — home owners warranty
HUD — Department of Housing and Urban Development
MIT — Massachusetts Institute of Technology
MV — market value
NAHB — National Association of Home Builders
NAR — National Association of Realtors
OPEC — Organization of Petroleum Exporting Countries
PHAs — Public Housing Authorities
REM — rapid eye movement
RPA — Resources Program Assessment
SMSA — Standard Metropolitan Statistical Area
ULI — Urban Land Institute
VA — Veteran's Administration

Index

Abstract of Title, 229

Acoustics, 42. See Noise

Adobe Houses, 20, 21

Aesthetics, 24, 31-33, 40, 44, 64, 114, 120, 122, 144. See Art and Beauty

Affidavits, 209, 229

Agreement to Purchase. See Contract to buy

Air Conditioning, 48, 49, 52, 161-62, 163, 189, 206

Alternatives, 245-78

Alternative Mortgage Instruments, 79, 233-34

Amortized Mortgage. See Mortgage

Angell, William, 245-78

Apartment, 14, 120, 146, 191, 199-207, 246, 248. See Flats and Multi-family units

Appliances, 37, 45, 49, 52, 81, 161-65, 190, 191, 206, 236, 266. See Furnishings

Appraisal, 228, 249

Appraisal Fees, 223. See Closing costs and Preliminary costs

Architect, 147, 149, 227, 228

Architecture, 149, 150, 181

Area for Eating. See Kitchen

Area for Food Preparation. See Kitchen

Area for Relaxation. See Bedroom and Recreation areas

Area for Rest. See Bedroom

Area for Socialization. See Living room and Recreation areas

Arrangement of Furniture, 175. See Appliances

Art, 155-56, 160

Art Deco, 35

Artifact, 2, 113, 181-82, 281-83

Art Nouveau, 35

Attached House. See Multi-family units and Townhouse

Attorney Fees, 203

Balloon Payment, 83

Bathroom, 158, 160, 184-95, 206, 252. See Toilets

Bauhaus School, 39

Barlowe, Raleigh, 56-77

Beauty, 36, 39, 43, 149, 166. See Aesthetics

Bedroom, 132, 158, 161, 175, 184-95

Below Market Interest Rates, 86

Boulding, Kenneth E., 100, 107-16

Brick, 20

Build, 246, 247
  custom-built, 247, 261, 262
  owner-built, 247, 261, 262
  speculatively-built, 247, 261, 262

Building Codes, 44, 54, 81, 83, 250, 255, 261, 267. See Codes

Builders. See Developers

Buyer, 97, 198, 208-35, 241, 246-49. See Ownership

Cape Cod Colonial, 18, 19

Capital Gain, 214

Case, Duncan, 126-37

Central Business District, 118, 120

Churchill, Winston, 10

Circulation within the House, 144, 184-95

Cities, 4, 9, 14, 56-77, 95, 100, 102, 107-37, 140, 149, 150-53, 155

Closed System, 37, 45, 262. See Industrialized housing

Closing Costs, 223. See Preliminary costs

Clustered Housing, 65, 76, 268. See Multi-family units and Townhouse

Codes, 73, 89, 93-98, 122, 180. See Building codes, Housing codes, and Zoning

Colonial Houses, 17-27, 181

Color, 162, 165

Comfort, 5, 13, 22, 49, 52, 113, 144, 149, 161, 163, 182

Commercial Banks. See Lending institutions

Community, 42, 96, 97, 100-06, 114, 118, 122, 147, 180, 228. See Neighborhoods and Economic base of communities. balanced community 126-37
Community Development Block Grant, 89, 100, 123
Components, 37, 44, 45, 81, 261. See Pre-cut components
Condominiums, 65, 239, 245-78
Constant Payment Plan, 225, 231
Construction Loans, 227, 228
Consumer, 44, 51, 58, 59, 79, 97, 178, 198-207, 236-41, 245-78
Consumers Union of United States, 199-207
Contemporary, 26
Continuity of Life, 139
Contract to Buy, 208, 209
Contractors. See Developers
Convenience, 22, 23, 147, 184, 190
Cooper, Clare, 170-78
Cooperative Ownership, 245-78
Cost of Housing, 30, 31, 66-70, 78-82, 93, 105, 129, 130, 152, 220-35, 248, 249. See Occupancy costs, Opportunity costs, and Preliminary costs
Creativity, 149
Crowding, 6, 8, 156-59, 161, 166. See Density
Cultural, 110, 112, 138-42, 150, 155, 156, 162, 170, 179, 180, 281-83

Deed, 209, 211, 217, 218, 229, 230, 257
general warranty deed, 211
quit claim deed, 209, 211
special warranty deed, 211
Demand, 56-61, 78
Density, 35, 42, 52, 58, 62, 96, 111, 113, 179. See Crowding
Department of Housing and Urban Development, 32, 38, 54, 59, 86, 93, 134, 265
Depreciation, 74, 76, 114, 213, 214, 224
Desegregation, 75
Detached House. See Single-family units
Developers, 68, 69, 97, 118, 119, 122
Dining, 184-95
Discount Rate, 230
Discrimination, 126-37. See Segregation
Disease, 5, 145-69
Down Payment, 130, 220-35, 249, 255, 256
Dubos, Renē, 2, 3-16, 179
Dutch Colonial, 19-21
Dwelling Types. See Alternatives

Eating. See Dining and Kitchen
Eclectic, 24, 25
Economic Base of Communities, 102
Emotional Factors. See Crowding, Needs, Noise, Privacy, and Values

Energy, 30, 47-55, 73, 103, 104
Environment, 5, 10, 100-42, 158, 159, 170, 172, 181, 281. See Community and Neighborhoods
Equity, 129, 210, 220-35, 250, 255-66
Escrow, 208

Factory Components. See Components, Pre-cut components, and Technology
Family Room. See Recreation areas
Family Values. See Values
Farmers' Home Administration, 47, 54, 85, 89
Federal Energy Administration, 51
Federal Housing Administration, 66, 84, 226, 238, 256. See FHA insured mortgages
Federal Reserve System, 221
Federal Style, 23
Federal Trade Commission, 236
Fee Simple, 246-78
FHA Insured Mortgages, 66, 222-27
FHA Standard Warranty, 238-41
Financing, 36, 78, 79, 114, 198, 200-36
Flats, 153-55. See Apartment
Floors, 20, 159, 193, 207
Floor Plans, 184-95
Food Preparation. See Kitchen
Foreclose, 84, 89, 209, 210, 224, 267
Forfeiture, 209, 210
Foyer. See Floor plans
French House, 20, 21
Fuel. See Energy
Function, 36, 40, 49, 144
Furnishings, 37, 160, 171, 175, 180, 181, 186, 187, 193, 208, 266. See Appliances

Gable Roof, 45
Gambrel Roof, 20
Gans, Herbert, 126
Garbage Disposal, 154, 162, 163, 191
General Panel System, 35, 36
Geographic Space, 101, 170
Georgian Colonial 22, 23
Ghetto, 126-37, 175
Government, 30, 83-92. See Department of Housing and Urban Development, Farmers' Home Administration, Federal Housing Administration, and Veterans' Administration
Graduated Payment Morgage, 233-35
Greek Revival, 24, 25
Gropius, Walter, 35, 39

Habitat, 41, 42
Half-Timber Medieval, 17
Hallway, 206. See Floor plans
Harl, Neil, 208-19
Health, 5, 31, 32, 54, 93, 94, 96, 97, 104, 114, 128, 144-69, 179, 248. See Safety

Heating, 48, 49, 65, 158, 159, 161, 165, 180
High-rise, 11, 41, 51, 117-25, 153-55, 166, 173. See Apartment
Historic Preservation, 103, 122
History, 17-27, 110, 122, 150, 180, 181
Home Ownership, 90. See Ownership
Home Warranties, 198, 236-41
Housing Codes, 94
Housing Finance Agencies, 83
Human Needs, 5, 9, 27. See Needs
Humidity, 161, 162

Impact Path, 281-83
Improvements, 132, 222, 223, 252. See Maintenance
Individuality, 32
Industrialized Housing, 31-46, 94. See Pre-cut components, Panel system, Modular housing, and Technology
Industrial Revolution, 25, 27, 31
Inflation, 30, 44, 78, 79, 152, 228, 245, 250, 255, 256, 267
Inspection Fees, 223
Installment Land Contract, 210, 213, 267
Insulation, 238
Insurance, 208, 220-33, 256
Interest, 69, 114, 211, 220-35
Interest Rate, 79, 221, 267
Italian Renaissance, 22
Interior, 45, 94, 171, 175, 178, 180, 184. See Interior design
Interior Design, 179-83

Joint Tenancy, 211, 212
Judgments, 209, 255

Kibbutz, 10
Kitchen, 22, 158, 187, 190-93, 206, 252
Koch, Carl, 35, 36

Labor, 78, 80, 81, 104, 264
Labor Unions, 44, 80
Land, 30, 35, 44, 51, 56-79, 96, 104, 118, 152, 260, 264
Landlord, 75, 89, 114, 118, 120, 130, 199-207, 254, 255, 268, 269
Landscaping, 52, 170, 224
Laundry, 49, 154, 159, 184, 193, 206, 224. See Floor plans
Le Corbusier, 40
Lease, 89, 199-207, 246, 247. See Renting
Leasehold, 247-78. See Renting
Legal, 198, 208-19
Legislation. See Government
Lemkau, Paul, 32, 145-69
Lending Institutions, 117-25, 134, 220-35
Lien, 95, 209, 255
Life Style, 26, 43, 120, 127, 128, 152, 156, 181, 187, 248

Lighting, 49, 163, 180, 207
Living room, 175, 177, 184-95. See Floor plans
Loans, 104, 223-28, 249. See Lending institutions and Mortgage
Location, 108, 155, 253
Log Cabin, 18, 22, 27, 33, 54, 148
Loos, Adolf, 39
Lots, 65-69, 78, 96, 131, 132, 214, 228
Lustron Homes, 35, 36

Maintenance, 37, 146, 206, 221-33, 252, 255, 265, 269. See Improvements
Manufactured Homes, 93. See Industrialized housing, Modular housing, Panel system, Pre-cut components, and Technology
Marketing, 81, 82
Market Value, 273, 274
Materials, 78, 82, 93, 264
Mead, Margaret, 100, 138-42
Mid-rise, 51. See Apartment and Flats
Minimum Property Standards, 54
Mortgage Insurance, 83
Minorities. See Discrimination and Segregation
Mix Center, 190-93. See Kitchen
Mobile Homes, 32, 37, 49, 51, 52, 65, 88, 90, 93, 131, 174, 184, 245-78
Mobility, 6, 63, 70, 120, 251
Model Cities Program, 86
Modular Housing, 32, 44, 246, 261, 262. See Industrialized housing
Mortgage, 114, 122, 210, 215, 216, 220-35, 256
Move, 165, 171, 245-49, 250-52
Muessig, Paul, 31-46
Mullin, John R., 117-25
Multi-family Units, 65, 172, 184, 257, 259, 269. See Apartment and Flats
Mumford, Lewis, 11

National Association of Home Builders, 79, 238-41, 257
National Association of Realtors, 238-41
Needs, 8, 9, 31, 40, 54, 100, 102, 104, 138-42, 144-69, 173, 181, 187. See Human needs, Physiological needs, and Psychological needs
Neighborhoods, 75, 76, 86, 100, 113, 117-42, 165, 228, 251
New Towns, 114, 150-53. See Planned communities
Noise, 146-48, 153, 154, 160, 163, 165, 166, 184, 189, 193. See Acoustics and Health
Notary Fees, 223
Note, 210, 229

Occupancy Costs, 244, 249

Odors, 160, 162
Open End Mortgage, 225
Open Floor Plan, 188
Open System, 37, 41, 262
Operation Breakthrough, 38, 39, 43, 81, 93
Opportunity Costs, 250, 254
Orientation, 52
Ornament, 36, 39, 40
Ownership, 114, 130, 150, 230. See Home ownership

Package Loan, 226
Panel System, 33, 44, 45, 246, 247, 261, 262. See Technology
Personal Property, 236
Physiological Needs, 5, 138. See Health and Needs
Planned Communities. See New towns
Planned Unit Development, 76, 77
Planners, 6, 117-25, 147, 152
Points. See Discount rate
Population, 58, 102, 103, 107-18, 150-56
Powers, Ronald C., 100-06
Pre-cut Components, 44, 246, 247, 261, 262. See Industrialized housing
Prepayment Expenses, 249
Preliminary Costs, 223, 227, 229, 231, 249.
Prepayment Privileges, 210, 221, 222, 227
Price of Housing. See Cost of housing
Principal, 220-35, 249
Privacy, 8, 22, 23, 42, 95, 113, 115, 120, 138, 158, 160, 163, 172, 173, 175, 179, 184, 187, 189, 198, 263, 267
Production, 78, 80, 83
Proposition, 13, 109
Property Values. See Values
Psychological Needs, 5. See Needs
Public Housing, 84-87, 149, 153
Public Housing Authorities, 85

Quality of Life, 100, 120, 122, 246

Raised-ranch Style, 188, 189
Ranch Style, 67
Range Center, 190-93. See Kitchen
Rapoport, Amos, 170, 182, 282
Real Property, 236
Recreation, 7, 73, 97, 103, 104, 158, 185, 206, 231
Recreation areas, 188. See Floor plans
Redlining, 75, 122, 131-35
Refrigerator Center, 190-93. See Kitchen
Regulatory Action, 78, 79
Rehabilitation, 75, 85, 87, 95, 117-25
Remodeling, 71, 75, 76, 225, 246, 247, 251-53, 264
Renting, 75, 79, 86, 95, 114, 122, 130, 131, 150, 198, 199-207, 230, 245-78

Rent Supplement Program, 86
Resources, 104, 105, 126, 128
Rest, 138, 163. See Bedroom
Revenue Sharing, 133
Revenue Stamps, 223
Reverse Annuity Mortgage, 233-35
Rogg, Nathaniel H., 78-82
Rollover Mortgage, 233-35
Room Relationship, 144, 158, 161, 184-95
Row House, 22, 23, 24. See Townhouse
Rural, 56-77, 95, 100-06, 111, 112, 260

Safdie, Moshe, 41
Safety, 13, 93-97, 140, 191. See Health
Sales Agreement. See Contract to buy
Saltbox Colonial, 19
Savings and Loan Associations. See Lending institutions
Scatteration, 56-77
Sears, Roebuck and Company, 33
Section 8, 89
Section 23, 89
Section 235, 87, 88, 238
Section 236, 87, 88, 90
Sectional Housing, 45. See Industrialized housing
Security Deposit, 203, 206
Segregation, 100, 126-37.
Self-image, 104, 170-78
Seller, 208-35, 241
Services (goods and services), 100-06, 109, 149, 152, 155, 157, 281-83
Single-family Units, 35, 42, 51, 90, 120, 129, 172, 184, 245-78
Sink Center, 190-93. See Kitchen
Sleeping Area, 158, 162. See Bedroom and Floor plans
Slums, 85, 90, 153, 157. See Ghetto
Social Change, 101-06
Social Support, 100. See Services
Society. See Cultural
Solar Energy, 52-54
Space, 147, 150, 160, 170, 179, 180. See Density, Floor plans, and Health
Spanish House, 20, 21
Split-level Style, 189
Sprawl. See Land and Suburbia
Stairs, 154, 158
Standard Metropolitan Statistical Area, 118
Stick Construction, 261
Stimulation, 5, 11, 140, 145, 162
Storage, 52, 159, 160, 189-91, 206, 207
Straight Mortgage, 225
Strandlund, Carl, 35
Subdivision Controls, 51, 73, 83, 96, 225, 260
Subsidies, 50, 72, 79, 81, 83, 87-91, 114, 133, 134, 152, 172

Suburbia, 4, 7, 9, 42, 51, 56-78, 111, 114, 118, 127-37, 150, 151, 172, 173
Symbol, 111, 144, 170-78, 181, 182. See Symbolism
Symbolism, 8, 9, 13, 32, 33, 119, 150
Systems Building. See Closed system, Industrialized housing, and Open system

Tax Benefits. See Taxes (income)
Taxes (income), 50, 72, 90, 212-14, 221, 244
Taxes (property) 37, 54, 69, 75, 105, 109, 128, 204, 206, 208, 214, 221-33, 256
Techbuilt Housing System, 36
Technology, 4, 30, 31-46, 81, 100-6, 162, 281-83
Tenant, 75, 86, 87, 89, 114, 158, 199-207, 254
Tenants in Common, 211, 212
Tenure, 244-78
Terratecture, 54
Title, 211, 212, 229
Title Insurance, 209
Toilets, 148, 154, 158, 164. See Bathroom
Townhouse, 50, 52, 246-48
Trailers. See Mobile homes
Transportation, 63, 70, 101, 113, 129, 151

United States Forest Service, 58, 65
Urban, 7, 11
Urbanism. See Cities

Urban Renewal, 85, 86, 118
Utilities, 63, 64, 72, 206, 249, 256
Utility Deposits, 249
Utility Room, 190. See Floor plans

Vacation Homes, 37, 58, 188, 191, 214
Values (human), 30, 111, 126, 174, 179, 180
Values (property), 123, 224, 228
VA Guaranteed Mortgages, 226, 227
Variable Interest Rate, 221, 233-35
Ventilation, 52, 189, 207
Veterans' Administration, 84. See VA guaranteed mortgages
Victorian, 24-26, 118-22

Wachsman, Konrad, 35
Warranties. See Home warranties
Water Heater, 49
Windows, 9, 22, 45, 52, 54, 189, 191, 207
Wood, 20
Work Triangle, 191-93. See Floor plans and Kitchen
Wright, Frank L., 26

Yearns, Mary H., 83-92

Zoning, 51, 73, 77, 78, 83, 96, 113, 123, 131-35
Zoning (within the house), 144, 184-95, 250, 251, 255, 260. See Floor plans

Date Due

SEP 1 7 1982		
SEP 1 2 1983		
Renew Until		
OCT 5 1983		
APR 1 1 1990		
APR 0 3 1996		